Socioeconomic Transformation in the Sasanian Empire

EDINBURGH STUDIES IN ANCIENT PERSIA

Visit the Edinburgh Studies in Ancient Persia website at
edinburghuniversitypress.com/series/esap

Socioeconomic Transformation in the Sasanian Empire

Late Antique Central Zagros

Hossein Habibi

EDINBURGH
University Press

Edinburgh University Press is one of the leading university presses in the UK. We publish academic books and journals in our selected subject areas across the humanities and social sciences, combining cutting-edge scholarship with high editorial and production values to produce academic works of lasting importance. For more information visit our website: edinburghuniversitypress.com

Grateful acknowledgement is made to the sources listed in the List of Illustrations for permission to reproduce material previously published elsewhere. Every effort has been made to trace the copyright holders, but if any have been inadvertently overlooked, the publisher will be pleased to make the necessary arrangements at the first opportunity.

Edinburgh University Press Ltd
The Tun – Holyrood Road
12(2f) Jackson's Entry
Edinburgh EH8 8PJ

Typeset in 11/13pt Sabon by
Cheshire Typesetting Ltd, Cuddington, Cheshire, and printed and bound in Great Britain

A CIP record for this book is available from the British Library

ISBN 978 1 4744 7556 3 (hardback)
ISBN 978 1 4744 7558 7 (webready PDF)
ISBN 978 1 4744 7559 4 (epub)

Contents

Illustrations

MAPS

FIGURES

GRAPHS

LIST OF TABLES

Preface and Acknowledgements

Seeing that Truth may in no wise be reached,
We may not waste this life thus ignorant.
Then see you do not take your hand from the cup!
Unknowing's our state, or drunk or vigilant.

Omar Khayyám

Omar Khayyám advises that absolute truth is not accessible. Nonetheless, as one of the greatest minds of his era, and perhaps of all time, he dedicated his life to the progress of different branches of knowledge and science, alongside writing some insightful and winning quatrains in his spare time, for which he is more celebrated in the Iranian World. So, my quoting him serves not as an excuse, but rather as an already-formed response to prospective criticism of this book – in fact, if the *book* were not to provide enough material for critics, involvement in classical Persian literature and the above translation by me of one of Khayyám's well-known quatrains would for sure. On the contrary: it is a reason for daring to do what is difficult in a time of hardship. The present book is an example of such written by an early-career scholar during a period of unemployment and confronting the apocalyptic situation caused by the outbreak of the Covid-19 pandemic. Therefore, it deals with problematic subjects such as Sasanian settlement patterns and built environment in the Iranian highlands, Sasanian ceramics, pastoralism and historical nomadism, and historical and political geography.

Passing by a pottery studio, the wise polymath of Nishapur also spoke about a vase that, sitting among its two thousand quiet but articulate fellow pieces of ceramic, yelled suddenly: 'Where are the potters? Where are the buyers? Where are the sellers?' Like the pot questioning the transitory nature of existence and of history, I have a passion for knowledge concerning the life of those who one day made, and perhaps bought and sold, the vases and all the other kinds of cultural materials whose shards are dispersed over archaeological sites. In particular, recent developments in Sasanian scholarship occurring roughly during the past couple of decades have deepened this interest of mine. Projects carried out in several territories of the Sasanian Empire, but also in other parts of the late antique world in the Byzantine realm, have indicated the diverse dynamics and distinct nature of the transformations that occurred in different areas in this period, in many cases featuring various sorts of infrastructural developments and demographic rise. However, in the Sasanian areas, only a few works have yet been carried out on the regional scale. Notwithstanding its strategic location and its economic, political and military significance for the Sasanian state, in particular the Central Zagros region in central western Iran is far less explored than the neighbouring lowlands in south-western Iran and southern Mesopotamia.

Socioeconomic Transformation in the Sasanian Empire is an interdisciplinary study of the cultural landscape of the *Late Antique Central Zagros*. It aims at examining the socioeconomic structures of the societies living in these spatiotemporal horizons and situating them within the wider context of the late antique Near East. Spatial organisation of sites and settlement systems are studied in relation to different environmental variables. However, the sociopolitical milieu and historical processes that might to some extent account for these patterns and structures are also considered, avoiding environmental determinism. Examination of geographical conditions and environmental settings of microenvironments in a diverse region, either naturally or socially, along with archaeological and ethnographic sets of evidence, historical records and epigraphic and sigillographic data about administrative and historical geography, and palaeoecological data, constitute a useful, complex and fairly firm foundation for this research. The book, therefore, recognises diversity in a single geographical zone and questions false generalisations and dichotomies, both in ancient foreign Mesopotamian and Greco-Roman literary traditions and modern literature. The varied and complex arrangement of socioeconomic transformations in the different intermontane plains and valleys of the Central Zagros is also identified according to a diachronic approach exploring the long-term cultural processes, since, in the interpretation of data and sources, inferences deriving from evidence about pre-Sasanian times are quite constructive. Moreover, this book does not overlook the roles played by groups with distinct ways of life practising different subsistence strategies, in a spectrum from mobile pastoralism to more sedentary economies such as irrigation agriculture, which are to a degree traceable in cultural materials and historical documents. Hence, local distinctions are taken into account while considering the impacts made by the hegemonic presence of the centralist power of one of the last world empires of pre-medieval times. Consequently, benefiting from the most recent developments in the field, *Socioeconomic Transformation in the Sasanian Empire* is an up-to-date examination which presents the social and economic history of the late antique Central Zagros in the context of the Sasanian Empire by building on archaeological research carried out in other territories and engaging in recent debates regarding the economy and function of the Sasanian state. The systemic approach adopted here sets an example for future regional studies in other areas of the Sasanian realm facing the challenges still to be tackled in the scholarship.

In light of the vast extent of the region and the current state of knowledge, however, drawing on a variety of case studies of discrete regions as sample areas seems inevitable. The archaeological landscapes of these areas, then, are compared to other cases on the basis of parallel data. Furthermore, models for the explanation of historical, cultural formation processes and human niche construction that also had impacts on and repercussions for the late antique transformations in each of the sample areas are provided. It is also noteworthy that although some of the historical events of the period are considered in the systemic analyses and discussions provided for the Central Zagros region, particularly in the chapter conclusions but also in Chapter 2 generally, the political history of the Sasanian era and subjects such as the fall of the Sasanian dynasty and the consequent fate of different territories are beyond the scope of this book.

Among the challenges this research faced are the difficult conditions of conducting intensive total-coverage surveys in mountainous areas. The geomorphic features of these zones render ineffective the application of remote sensing techniques for aerial reconnaissance of the traces of human activities that have altered landscapes. Also, the Sasanian ceramic repertoire of the Central Zagros is poorly studied, chiefly due to limited publication of the securely-dated collections acquired from systematic excavations in the Sasanian deposits in this region. Moreover, compared to permanent settlements, the identification of transhumant and nomadic campsites and recognition of their attributes can be an issue in archaeological surveys given the usually poor surface materials, and site location, morphology and form. These challenges may be substantially addressed by designing projects seeking particularly to address each of the above-mentioned issues, and by the subsequent publication of the complete results of the fieldwork projects.

The transliteration of place names, geographical features, archaeological sites and persons in Persian, Arabic, Kurdish, and Turkish follows local usage. In an attempt to represent the languages and the respective dialects in the closest way, diacritics are used and long vowels are marked, such as Jōneqān, Zāyandeh-rōd, Sirwān, Tappeʰ Bardnakōn, Qal'e Seyrom-shāh and Jahāngir Yāsi. This is the case throughout the book, except in cases where the normal English spelling of a common name is widely used in the academic literature internationally, such as Tal-i Malyan, Pasargadae, Tepe Yahya, Tell Mahuz, Lorestan, Damghan, Abdanan.

Over the past decade, I have had the opportunity to join several fieldwork projects all across the Zagros region in Iran. From the northern areas of the mountains in Ahar County of East Azerbaijan Province to the Central Zagros in Kāmyiārān of Kermanshah, Abdanan of Ilam, and Ardal of Chaharmahal va Bakhtiyari and to the Southern Zagros in Baft County of Kerman, each of the excavations and surveys has been a unique experience for its own sake that has influenced my approach to the archaeology of the Zagros Mountains. Hence, I should wish to thank everyone with whom I have had the chance of collaborating on these projects. The archaeological data examined in Chapter 4 were acquired via the survey and excavations in Farsan County led by my good colleague, Dr Alireza Khosrowzadeh. I am thankful to him for granting me access to the reports and for his suggestions in the course of my examination of the materials.

The earliest stages of preparation of the present book took place when I held a postdoctoral fellowship at the Institute for Advanced Studies in the Humanities (IASH) at the University of Edinburgh in 2018 and 2019. My research project at this institute was in fact the forerunner of *Socioeconomic Transformation in the Sasanian Empire*, and I would therefore like to thank the Director, Prof. Steve Yearly, all the staff and my colleagues at IASH for supporting my research project, both intellectually and financially, and for developing such an astonishing scholarly environment for the exchange of ideas, and a hub for the progress of knowledge.

I wish to appreciate Prof. Eberhard Wolfram Sauer, of the Classics department at Edinburgh University, who was very supportive when I first told him about the idea for this book in Edinburgh. He has maintained this encouraging attitude by sharing books and papers, which have been of constant use and interest to me, and by generously taking time to read the first draft of this work and suggest revisions that eventually led me to later develop the material. My deepest gratitude goes to Prof. Josef Wiesehöfer, who for years has played the role of mentor to me, not only in academic matters but also in life. Regular scholarly discussions and instructive comments on my PhD dissertation during my stay at the Christian-Albrecht University of Kiel, proofreading, helpful suggestions regarding research works of mine including this book, and sending me his published and unpublished works, which have always been sources of inspiration to me, are only some examples of the kind and open support he has offered me at different stages of my academic career, for which I am so humbled and honoured. Prof. Rika Gyselen and Prof. Yaqub Mohammadifar also have my most sincere appreciation. Rika has made a substantial contribution to the section dealing with the political and administrative geography of the Central Zagros in the Sasanian era in Chapter 2, generously forwarding me her trail-blazing research, indisputably one of the most monumental works in the field, and commenting on the first draft of the section. Yaqub, my PhD supervisor, has also improved Chapter 3 with his constant support and insightful suggestions. Many thanks also go to Dr Silvia Balatti for her valuable remarks and suggestions, in our discussions at the Christian-Albrecht University of Kiel, based on our common interest in mountains and mountain people, and for generously sharing her publications with me.

I wish to take this opportunity to express my appreciation to Edinburgh University Press for admitting of this book for publication when it was only in the form of a raw proposal and some sample materials. I am thankful to all the staff at EUP, particularly Prof. Lloyd Llewellyn-Jones, the Series Editor of Edinburgh Studies in Ancient Persia; Grace Balfour-Harle, the desk editor in charge of this book; Carol MacDonald and Sarah Foyle, respectively former Senior Commissioning Editor and Assistant Editor of Classics and Ancient History; and Rachel Bridgewater and Isobel Birks, respectively Senior Commissioning Editor and Assistant Editor in the subject area. Thanks also to Michael Ayton, the copy editor. Furthermore, I should like to express my appreciation to the anonymous readers and reviewers whose helpful recommendations and advice were considered in the peer-review process connected with the proposal and first draft of the book and surely enriched the final result.

Last but not least, special thanks go to my friends, whose friendship has delayed the preparation of this book to some extent, yet whose virtues seem even more genuine to me in these strange days of quarantine and seclusion.

This book is dedicated as a token of my love to my mom, Mahēn, and to the memory of my late father, Farāmarz, for their devotion to the happiness and well-being of me and my brothers in their best years. Although this book is so inadequate in contrast to their unconditional love, it is all I have.

Hossein Habibi
Shahrekord, Nowruz 1401/March 2022

Series Editor's Preface

Edinburgh Studies in Ancient Persia focuses on the world of ancient Persia (pre-Islamic Iran) and its reception. Academic interest with and fascination in ancient Persia have burgeoned in recent decades and research on Persian history and culture is now routinely filtered into studies of the Greek and Roman worlds; Biblical scholarship too is now more keenly aware of Persian-period history than ever before; while, most importantly, the study of the history, cultures, languages and societies of ancient Iran is now a well-established discipline in its own right.

Persia was, after all, at the centre of ancient world civilizations. This series explores that centrality throughout several successive 'Persian empires': the Achaemenid dynasty (founded c. 550 BCE) saw Persia rise to its highest level of political and cultural influence, as the Great Kings of Iran fought for, and maintained, an empire which stretched from India to Libya and from Macedonia to Ethiopia. The art and architecture of the period both reflect the diversity of the empire and proclaim a single centrally constructed theme: a harmonious world-order brought about by a benevolent and beneficent king. Following the conquests of Alexander the Great, the Persian Empire fragmented but maintained some of its infrastructures and ideologies in the new kingdoms established by Alexander's successors, in particular the Seleucid dynasts who occupied the territories of western Iran, Mesopotamia, the Levant and Asia Minor. But even as Greek influence extended into the former territories of the Achaemenid realm, at the heart of Iran a family of nobles, the Parthian dynasty, rose to threaten the growing imperial power of Rome. Finally, the mighty Sasanian dynasty ruled Iran and much of the Middle East from the third century CE onwards, proving to be a powerful foe to Late Imperial Rome and Byzantium. The rise of Islam, a new religion in Arabia, brought a sudden end to the Sasanian dynasty in the mid-600s CE.

These successive Persian dynasties left their record in the historical, linguistic and archaeological materials of the ancient world, and Edinburgh Studies in Ancient Persia has been conceived to give scholars working in these fields the opportunity to publish original research and explore new methodologies in interpreting the antique past of Iran. This series will see scholars working with bona fide Persian and other Near Eastern materials, giving access to Iranian self-perceptions and the internal workings of Persian society, placed alongside scholars assessing the perceptions of the Persianate world from the outside (predominantly through Greek and Roman authors and artefacts). The series will also explore the reception of ancient Persia (in historiography, the arts and politics) in subsequent periods, both within and outwith Iran itself.

Edinburgh Studies in Ancient Persia represents something of a watershed in better appreciation and understanding not only of the rich and complex cultural heritage of Persia, but also of the lasting significance of the Achaemenids, Parthians and Sasanians and the impact that their remarkable civilisations have had on wider Persian, Middle Eastern and world history. Written by established and up-and-coming specialists in the field, this series provides an important synergy of the latest scholarly ideas about this formative ancient world civilisation.

Lloyd Llewellyn-Jones

List of abbreviations

ARAB = Ancient Records of Assyria and Babylonia
AwKL = Awan King List
BAMI = Belgian Archaeological Mission in Iran
BIN = Babylonian Inscriptions in the Collection of James B. Nies
CAS = complex adaptive systems
CMT = Choga Mami Transitional
DB = Darius I's Bisotun inscription
DEM = Digital Elevation Model
DP = Documents présargoniques: deuxième partie
ED = environmental determinism
ICAR = Iranian Center for Archaeological Research
KKZ = Kirdīr's Ka'be-ye Zartosht inscription
MHD = Mādyān-ī Hazār Dādestān
Mid. Pers. = Middle Persian
New Pers. = New Persian
NPi = Narseh's Paikuli inscription
Old Pers. = Old Persian
PDT = Puzriš-Dagān tablet
PFA = Persepolis Fortification archive
RICHT = Research Institute for Cultural Heritage and Tourism
RIMA = Royal Inscriptions of Mesopotamia Assyrian Periods
RINAP = The Royal Inscriptions of the Neo-Assyrian Period
RTC = Recueil de tablettes chaldéennes
SAA = State archives of Assyria
SKL = Sumerian King List
ShKL = Šimaški King List
ŠKZ = Šābuhr I's Ka'be-ye Zartosht inscription

THIS BOOK IS DEDICATED TO MY MOTHER, MAHĒN,
AND TO THE MEMORY OF MY FATHER, FARĀMARZ.

1 *Introduction. A Regional Examination of the Central Zagros during Late Antiquity*

1.1 PAST AND PRESENT CENTRAL ZAGROS: NATURAL AND HUMAN GEOGRAPHY

1.1.1 *Natural Geography of the Central Zagros*

The Central Zagros region equates to the mid-west area of Iran, which, running from north-west to south-east, may (with a rough approximation for the sake of simplicity) correspond to the modern provinces of Kurdistan, Kermanshah, Hamadan, Ilam, Lorestan and Chaharmahal va Bakhtiyari (Map 1.1). Central western Iran is bordered to the north by the Northern Zagros, to the east by the Central Iranian Plateau, and to the south and south-west by the alluvial lowlands of Khuzestan and Mesopotamia. Thus, the Central Zagros is located on the boundary of three major climatic zones (Matthews et al. 2013: 26–7), making it, geographically, an interesting case as regards the examination of rapid but frequent changes of climate (Melville 1984; Kehl 2009: 2–4). The region is a mountainous area with environmental features considerably under the influence of the climate setting caused by the Zagros Mountain chains. The complexities in topography and moisture sources make this a complicated interplay (Taylor 1996; Ranhao et al. 2008; Saeidababdi et al. 2016). The orographic effect is reflected in the variations of temperature and precipitation (Wright 1961), and 'the general inclination of the mountains which are exposed to westerly disturbances causes large amounts of precipitation and snowfall' (Azizi et al. 2013: 96; see also Zaitchick et al. 2007). In the Central Zagros, regional precipitation has positive effects on tree growth. While the mean annual precipitation for the region is around

469mm, the average elevation of the region is around 2,000m a.s.l. The elevation ranges from 28m a.s.l. close to the Iran–Iraq border to 4,221m a.s.l., Zardkooh Mountain (Azizi et al. 2013: 97–9; Saeidababdi et al. 2016: 440), and the major vegetation formations in the region are savannah/steppe-forest of the Zagros foothills and oak woodland of the Zagros Mountains. Around 3 million ha of forest in the Central Zagros Mountain range is covered by various oak species, mainly dominated by Quercus persica, Quercus infectoria, Olive and Quercus libani Lindl (Azizi et al. 2013: 96; Fatahi 1995). Nonetheless, the rate of the Zagros woodlands in different parts of this region also depends on the density and size of villages and the movement of nomads utilising them (Wright et al. 1967: 419–20, 442). The natural landscape of the Central Zagros Mountains, however, is varied across the intermontane plains and valleys of its different areas on the leeward or windward sides in terms of different climatic factors and environmental resources (Alijani et al. 2008; Azizi et al. 2010; Safarrad et al. 2013). The folded zone holds cooler parts of the region than the warmer low-lands of the Zagros thrust zone (Heydari 2007). Different elevation ranges and topographic features play key roles in determining the varied climate conditions of this region on a local scale (Zohary 1973; Kehl 2009). These factors are influential on climatic variables such as temperature, air pressure, precipitation, humidity and the distribution of floral and faunal species. Consequently, across the Central Zagros, various human groups have evolved different modes of subsistence, adopted according to the natural landscape and its accessible resources. The Central Zagros highlands hold the Seymareh landslide, which is 'recognized as the largest rock ava-lanche in the world and one of the largest sub-aerial landslides of any type' (Roberts and Evans 2008). Several important permanent rivers originating from these mountains support rich agriculture-based urban cultures far from the Central Zagros, in the alluvial lowlands of south-western Iran (Azizi et al. 2013: 96; Saeidababdi et al. 2016: 438; Marrieta-Flures 2014). Moreover, the Zagros Mountains as an elevated heat source exert the main impact in the formation of a thermally driven circulation over the Middle East (Zarrin et al. 2011).

Concerning our focus period, the notable point is that there is no evidence available in terms of climatic change in the Zagros areas in the Sasanian period. In fact, apart from some small-scale variations of climate that occurred continually during historical times, no overall change has occurred in the climate of the region

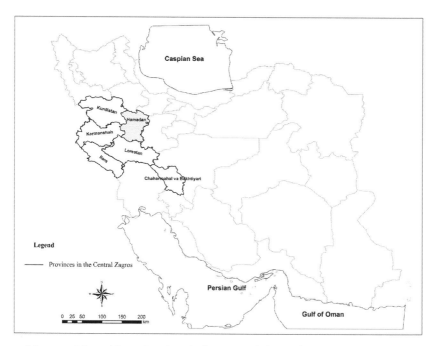

Map 1.1. Map of Iran showing the location of the modern provinces that are roughly part of the Central Zagros region. (Source: Author)

within the last 2,500 years. While admitting issues in the study of the palaeoclimate and palaeoenvironment of the Central Zagros (Matthews et al. 2013), scholars have specified that after about 5500 BP the climate may have shown minor fluctuations but no major changes (Van Zeist and Wright 1963; Van Zeist 1967; Van Zeist et al. 1968; Wright et al. 1967: 442; Kuniholm 1990). Modern vegetation patterns in the Near East have been fairly stable for about 4,000 years (Miller 2004: 136). Moreover, before 300 BCE, the modern sea level in the depression in front of the folded and uplifted outer Zagros became fixed and the Persian Gulf formed (Wright and Neely 2010: 2). According to Gasche's studies (Gasche 2005; 2007), we know that the south of the Khuzestan plain was not populated until the later half of the first millennium BCE. It was not until then that the Persian Gulf shoreline moved backward to the current location. It is noteworthy that recent research on the Karkheh River (Heyvaert et al. 2012) has clearly indicated human influences on the Late Holocene shifts of this river. Also, it has been demonstrated that the modern irrigation measures utilise old drainage patterns. Scholars, however, have not exclusively studied the small-scale climatic variations of historical times. Nonetheless, in light of the data regarding the Sasanian imperial investment in the irrigation system and construction of water canals in the alluvial plains of south-western Iran (Wenke 1987; Heyvaert et al. 2012) and Nippur (Altaweel et al. 2019: 15, 19; Campopiano 2017), the Lower (Adams 1981; Jacobsen 1982) and Middle Diyāla/Sirwān valleys (Glatz 2018; Panahipour 2018; 2019) and Hamrin (Kim 1991) in Mesopotamia, on some rivers, such as the Karun, Karkheh, Jarahi, Diyāla/Sirwān, Tigris and Euphrates, we may consider that the probable small-scale climatic variation occurred in these regions during the Sasanian period. But, as such research projects have not yet been undertaken in the Central Zagros, it is not possible to confidently infer such a conclusion about this region. That said, it is indicated that a series of large volcanic eruptions between the second quarter of the sixth century and around the first quarter of the seventh century, and changes in the axis of the Earth, resulted in a cold and dry period between 536 and 660, called the Late Antique Little Ice Age (Alizadeh et al. 2021: 316–17). Parallel palaeoecological and archaeological data, as well as historical accounts, specify the broad climate fluctuations of the Late Antique Little Ice Age from the early sixth century that led to significant impacts on the economic infrastructures and brought about societal repercussions in the late antique Near East (Alizadeh et al. 2021 with references).

1.1.2 *Human Geography of the Central Zagros*

Besides its position between different climatic zones, this region is also situated between different cultural zones. Hence its location, strategically and geopolitically, has been an important factor for different populations and states through history. Its rich natural resources were also important traits, rendering it an attractive target for Mesopotamians for expansion, or even colonisation/trade, since the sixth millennium BCE (Stolper 1984; Schacht 1987; Altaweel et al. 2019: 18; Glatz and Casana 2016; also, for chronological correlations between the Chalcolithic Central Zagros and lowland Mesopotamia see Henrickson 1985: 95–102).

Ethnic categorisation in Iran merely based on a linguistic or religious criterion is problematic, as figures provided in different reports differ significantly (Elling 2013: 18–21; Yaghoubian 2014; Yesiltas 2016: 55). As regards our focus area, while in one report the figures for the Lori-speaking population are 2 per cent of the total population of Iran and for Kurds 7 per cent, another organisation states a different number of 6 per cent for the former (Elling 2013: 18). In this case, the difference arises from the fact that there is as yet no consensus on whether the Bakhtiyaris, Mamasanis and Boyer-Ahmadis should be grouped together with the Lors or Persians (Elling 2013: 21).

Regarding ethnoreligious diversity in the Central Zagros region, here I briefly point to some of the statistically major groups on the basis of available figures.[1] As each of these ethnic groups has inhabited certain territories, the factor of region of residence is a good predictor of ethnicity. Nonetheless, the borders of these regions are more fluid and mixed due to the long-standing socioeconomic interdependence between different populations (Majbouri and Fesharaki 2019). The Shi'a Persian population lives in Hamadan Province and the eastern intermontane plains of the province of Chaharmahal va Bakhtiyari, Chaharmahal area, while Iranian Kurds mainly inhabit the provinces of Kurdistan, Kermanshah and Ilam (Rezaei and Bahrami 2019: 81), alongside minor Kurdish populations residing in Hamadan and Lorestan Provinces. Whereas 75 per cent of Kurds, except for those living in Kurdistan Province (Ezzatyar 2016: 10–11), follow Shāfiʿī Sunnite Islam, influenced by Sufism, the rest of the Kurdish population of the Central Zagros is primarily Shi'ite Muslim. Shi'a Lors dwell in Lorestan, Ilam, the western areas of Chaharmahal va Bakhtiyari and southern counties of Hamadan (Crane et al. 2008: 40, Table 3.1). Laks make up another Shi'a group settled solely in the Central Zagros, in Kermanshah, Ilam and Hamadan Provinces (Aliakbari et al. 2015). Worthy of mention is the fact that Turkic-speaking Qashqai groups, also traditionally Shi'a Muslim, settle in Hamadan, Chaharmahal va Bakhtiyari and Kermanshah – particularly in its Sonqor County. Among religious minorities living in the Central Zagros are Jews (mainly in Hamadan city), Yārsānis, Zoroastrians, and Oriental Orthodox and Protestant Christians. Therefore, the Central Zagros can be regarded as both ethnically and religiously heterogeneous.

1.2 TOWARDS AN INTERDISCIPLINARY LANDSCAPE ARCHAEOLOGY OF THE CENTRAL ZAGROS

1.2.1 *Regional Settlement Pattern Studies in the Landscape Archaeology Setting*

Study of landscape goes back to German geography of the nineteenth century and its discussions about landschaft.[2] This geography was limited to physical geography, in which human behaviour was mostly understood as a phenomenon extensively influenced by natural landscape (Kluiving et al. 2012: 1). In the *Dictionary for Geography* it is mentioned that landscape archaeology was formed through the works of P. Vidal de la Blache in France and developed as part of the regional approach to the examination of landscape (Monkhouse 1970: 204). Also, it was in this period that the Berkley school of cultural geography introduced the concept of cultural landscape. This idea implies that most of the characteristics of a landscape are shaped by human interference. The intellectual foundations of the new perspectives on landscape in archaeology go back to the 1920s (Anschuetz et al. 2001: 157). In this century, landscape archaeology, which in its initial stage was in debt to the environmental approach, incorporated some of the principles of this point of view in landscape research, among which one may mention the extensive interdisciplinary approach towards investigation of human–environment interactions. Given their hybrid perspective regarding the biology of human societies, environmental archaeologists study human actions in their natural settings. Through collaboration with scholars from various disciplines, they have used diverse techniques and interpretations of biological and earth sciences and geophysics to study the relationship between individuals and their environment (Denham 2008: 468; Reitz et al. 2013: 3–10). In the same way, archaeological research with a landscape perspective incorporates the work of researchers with different kinds of expertise in the three categories biological, physical and cultural (Burger et al. 2008.). This is one of the special potentialities of this paradigm, gained through importing concepts and models from a vast range of fields (not all of them equally scientific) and combining them into a single framework to study human societies (Zedeño 2008: 210–11; Kowalewski 2008: 251).[3] Furthermore, the hybrid tendency of this approach has led it to embrace different schools of thought. Different understandings of landscape archaeology arose out of the unbridged gaps in the theoretical basis of the social sciences in the last two centuries.[4] On the one hand, the geographer Friederich Ratzel claimed that the distinction between different human groups is the outcome of the impacts of environment received by each population. On the other, in the opinion of Emile Durkheim, who assumed society to be the collective conscious outcome of structures of common law, human interaction with the natural environment does not earn such a significant role (Anschuetz et al. 2001: 158).

The processualist viewpoint of the new archaeologists is influenced by the positivistic ideas of 1960s–1970s geography (Anschuetz et al. 2001: 164). The 1980s cultural geography focused on visual aspects and landscapes as its observation mode. This perspective played an important role in the formation of post-processual archaeology (Widgren 2012: 121). According to this view, landscape is constructed through social experience that is impacted more by politics than by environmental conditions. Therefore, these types of research, by borrowing some concepts from human philosophies, adopt a methodology for exploring social values and beliefs rather than the process of human adaptation to the ecosystem (Anschuetz et al. 2001: 165; Kluiving et al. 2012: 1–2). Apart from phenomenalism (Magnusson Staaf 2000: 135–6) and the ideas of Kant and Heidegger about space (Dobrez 2009: 5), the creative geography[5] of the early twentieth century was a source for the human-based phenomenological approach (Tilley 2008; Johnson 2007: 122; McFadyn 2008: 307; see also Hassan 2004: 318) in landscape archaeology.[6]

Since the 1960s, when archaeologists started to study landscape, two main movements have been shaped in this domain, each of which, according to their epistemologies, has developed a range of methods to fulfil specific purposes. The processualists maintain an ecological-functionalist viewpoint and regard environment and economy as the main causes behind human actions. They try to perform measurable research and make predictions on this basis, and this usually involves studies of settlement patterns, settlement models, and regional-scale insights using methodological advances in spatial analyses, Geographic Information Systems (GIS) and non-site-based applications. The other movement, as discussed above, with post-processual archaeologists such as Christopher Tilley among its proponents (Duke 2008: 279; Clark and Scheiber 2008: 6), considers landscape as a culturally constructed structure that creates cognition and memory. Therefore, an interesting feature of landscape archaeology is that it includes both positivistic processual archaeology and post-modern ideas of post-processualism, and has provided a setting in which researchers with different intellectual backgrounds may work together (Wilkinson 2004: 334–5; Anschuetz et al. 2001: 176). Notably, there is still no consensus on how landscape archaeology should be defined. For example, different authors place different emphases on the natural – that is, ecological, geomorphological and hydrological – features and the cultural aspects – for example, technological, organisational and ideological structures – of the human environment (Anschuetz et al. 2001: 158).

According to different definitions of the notion of space, different scholars provide a variety of standpoints on spatial analysis (Dobrez 2009: 5; Anschuetz 2001: 189; Conolly and Lake 2006: 3–4). When it comes to the meaning of landscape one sees a similar situation in the social sciences, and the only notable agreement has been on the interaction between the human and its ecosystem (Conolly and Lake 2006: 3–4). However, Wilkinson's (2004: 334) definition of landscape and its archaeology seems to be comprehensive and firm; despite its emphasis on cultural factors, it basically supposes landscape to be the compound product of natural environment and sociocultural structures. In this approach, although the purpose of landscape archaeology is considered to be the study of the formation and management of landscape through economic, social, religious, symbolic, or cultural processes, the role of natural landscape is also acknowledged in the construction of myths and history and the formation of human behaviour.

Landscape archaeology does not have a long history. The term was probably first used in the mid-1970s, but it did not become common until the mid-1980s (David and Thomas 2008a: 27). Nonetheless, the development of landscape archaeology in the second half of the twentieth century was one of the most exciting and dynamic progressions in the history of the discipline.[7] Nowadays, landscape history plays a focal role in politics and research on environmental settings and their anthropogenic impacts at the global level (Widgren 2012: 117–18). For decades, landscape archaeology provided a framework with which archaeologists could examine the different non-site and site-based kinds of relationship between contemporary populations. Furthermore, this paradigm has the potential to enable research projects studying the cultural transitions of societies on temporally and spatially large scales. Landscape can be understood as a repertoire of resources that bring either capabilities or limits to the human groups in which they reside. Spatial interrelations between individuals, soil, water and raw material resources can be considered in the same vein (David and Thomas 2008a: 25). The landscape perspective is capable of answering some of the questions that archaeology faces today.[8] A relatively long time has elapsed since archaeologists noticed the task of shifting focus from a single site to the scale of questions addressing cultural transformation and regional variation. Since the 1960s, various distributional approaches (non-site, off-site and siteless) in landscape archaeology have appeared in which it is supposed that human behaviour takes place throughout the landscape and that archaeological materials are distributed in a more or less continuous way, but with various structures and intensity (Richards 2008: 551–2; Gaffeny and van Leusen 1995).[9] On the basis of these considerations, it becomes possible to investigate activities that lie beyond the scale of limited site-based activities. Among such research focuses, one may mention regional socioeconomic processes, agro-pastoral subsistence strategies concentrated in rural areas, and evolutionarily cultural procedures. The landscape approach provides cultural-historical frameworks with which to evaluate and interpret the spatial and temporal aspects of the organisational structure of material culture. Offering the promise of empirical observation and objective evaluation, this standpoint also proposes an action plan for designing research according to which different researchers with various academic backgrounds may contribute collectively in order to construct a more comprehensive understanding of patterns of adaptation and cultural change (Anschuetz 2001: 161–2).

'Settlement patterns broadly are the regularities formed by the distributions of multiple places where people lived or carried out activities' (Kowalewski 2008: 226–7). The earlier definition of settlement patterns comes from studies of the 1930s cultural ecology of Britain. The introduction of regional settlement pattern studies in archaeology in the late 1940s and early 1950s was the outcome of these, mainly spatial, studies, that resulted in wide-scale reception of the notion of the ecosystem and the insights of systems theory, welcomed by cultural anthropologists, geographers and ecologists, in archaeological literature (Anschuetz 2001: 168–74). Settlement patterns are distinct from settlement systems. Regional patterns are the static environmental arrays of archaeological evidence that are experimentally recognisable, but settlement systems are the dynamic settlement processes behind the patterns relating to human behaviour and cultural interactions (Kowalewski 2008: 226; Banning 2002: 156; Duffy 2015: 85). Moreover, spatial analysis is either the pattern through which settlements, buildings or artefacts are distributed through space, or the ways in which they are connected together on the basis of formation processes, historical associations, and the movement of people, materials and information between them (Banning 2002: 155). In spatial analysis of landscape archaeology, carried out usually by means of the Geographic Information System (GIS) program, an attempt is made to recognise the special spatial structure of regional settlement patterns. GIS is a computer-based program capable of collecting, managing, integrating, visualising and analysing geographically referenced information (Conolly 2008: 583). This technology, in particular, has opened up new avenues for understanding and interpreting land and resource utilisation on estimated scales (Zedeño 2008: 211). It offers a host of analytical possibilities for examining the spatial organisation of material culture and the interaction between the human and the environment (Conolly and Lake 2006: 31). The use of GIS in archaeology began in the 1980s, when its capacity for recording and analysing the types of spatial information generated by archaeologists was indicated (Winterbottom and Long 2006: 1,356–7). Through the 1990s and subsequently, archaeological GIS has entered a more self-reflective and critical phase that has addressed many concerns raised about its contribution to knowledge (Conolly 2008: 584). In recent years, archaeology has progressed impressively by using remote sensing methodology and tools. Satellite images have been analysed to map settlement systems within their environment (Wilkinson 2000: 221). Through the widespread adoption of the techniques of dynamic modelling, such as GIS systems, we may witness the greater integration of methodologies, so that archaeologists will be able to work within a more uniform framework of analysis (Wilkinson 2004: 352). Geographical model-based paradigms within GIS packages provide archaeologists with a new set of quantitative tools for the exploration of spatial patterns at macro and micro scales (Anschuetz et al. 2001: 168–70). Spatial technology gives us the ability to employ landscape-based approaches to archaeological study and allows sites and artefacts to be contextualised more widely. It also provides an opportunity to study the interactions between different populations on regional and inter-regional levels. The use of GIS in landscape archaeology research, then, has led to some interesting insights into culture–nature interaction (Winterbottom and Long 2006: 1356). The main types of questions that may be addressed using this program are diverse and are related to various aspects of location, condition, trend, routing, pattern and modelling (Conolly and Lake 2006: 2, Table 1.1). It is notable that, in recent years, criticisms have been raised concerning the problem of environmental determinism (ED) in the model-based approaches of the studies using new technologies. Nonetheless, the methodology has been revised and such concerns properly addressed (Gaffeny and van Leusen 1995; Banning 2002: 10).

1.2.2 *Regional Study of the Central Zagros*

The Central Zagros and its neighbouring alluvial plains of southern Mesopotamia and south-western Iran experienced an intense population increase along with pressure on environmental resources in the Sasanian period, due to the specific socioeconomic conditions applying in this period. Besides historical documents ranging from Sasanian to early Islamic times, several archaeological surveys testify to this. The number of archaeological sites, in both overall quantity and individual categories, reached a level that was in many areas (in contrast to in preceding eras) unparalleled. Scholarship on Sasanian history and archaeology has noted that this empire underwent transitions in different fields. Little work, however, has been done on the phenomenon on a regional scale. Without a comprehensive study of the associated data on such a scale, we cannot recognise the phenomenon and analyse the factors that caused it, ultimately leading us to overlook its important impact on the late antique world. This book, hence, uses landscape archaeology as an interdisciplinary scientific approach, based on which diverse techniques and interpretations drawing on different forms of expertise can be incorporated into one single framework. Using this perspective in a regional spatial analysis can lead us to detect the hidden reasons behind settlement systems, sociopolitical transformations and historical processes. In addition to this, source criticism of historical documents is of high importance in the present work. However, given the considerable extent of the Central Zagros, tackling the huge task of studying the whole region evenly seems virtually impossible. Then, we draw on a variety of case studies of discrete regions as sample areas so as to compare their archaeological landscapes and contextualise them within the broader geographical zone of the Central Zagros. Archaeological data are acquired from the recently conducted archaeological surveys in two provinces and the excavation of a site in each of them. The spatial distribution of material culture is analysed against the parallel historical and ethnographic evidence in order to achieve synergic results considering diverse cultural and natural factors. The present book studies the nature of the socioeconomic transformation that took place in the Central Zagros, exploring different sample areas within the region. Nonetheless, this monograph does not cover the accounts of the historical events that happened in this region during Late Antiquity, but considers them and offers new insights concerning the socioeconomic policies of the Sasanian central state. This task is undertaken on the basis of examining different data sets relating to the Central Zagros and comparing them with the evidence about infrastructural development and state-level investment and planning in other territories of the empire delivered by (chiefly recent) regional research projects.

Thus, this book offers an original and novel contribution to the archaeology of the Sasanian period. By developing an interdisciplinary analysis of the spatial distribution of material culture, based on newly-discovered archaeological data and in accordance with historical and ethnographic evidence, it bridges the gap of the hitherto largely overlooked cultural landscape of the late antique Central Zagros as one of the most important areas of the Sasanian realm. Thematically, the book provides a systemic examination of the socioeconomic transition that occurred in the region during Sasanian times. It thereby extends and critically complements a number of recent works on the infrastructural developments in different territories of the Sasanian Empire.

1.3 THE ECONOMY OF THE SASANIAN EMPIRE

Here, we do not aim at presenting a comprehensive view of different aspects of the economy of the Sasanian state. However, it is necessary to provide a succinct account of the main modes of production and profit in the empire, so far as this is relevant to the focus of the present book. Therefore, the inferences regarding the socioeconomic conditions of the late antique Central Zagros may be framed according to this context and construed more clearly.

Like all pre-industrial empires, the Sasanian state is known as an agrarian empire. Where the environmental factors were promising and the security of the (probably excess) food production and the settled population was guaranteed, local clients, or the central Sasanian authorities, would invest in developing agricultural and arboricultural infrastructures.[10] These activities could range from planning large-scale irrigation distribution systems involving different types of water canal to constructing other structures aimed at the control and management of water such as diversions, aqueducts, dams and weirs. Besides historical documents,[11] archaeological data from different regions testify to such projects.[12] Apart from the economic and strategic intentions of the political power, the policy was also ideologically backed by the version of Zoroastrianism followed by the Sasanians, according to which practising cultivation was considered a religious tenet and a pious deed (Tafazzoli 1354 [1975]: 18). Evidence of such infrastructural developments and demographic growth is especially studied in different territories of the late Sasanian Empire (see below and n. 12). These transformations rather overlapped with the administrative, political and economic reforms of the Sasanian state in the sixth century (see Chapter 2,

s. 2.3). Also noteworthy is that the above-mentioned regional, environmental phenomenon, related to climate fluctuations that occurred across the late antique world, has recently been underscored, and has been regarded as accounting for sociopolitical changes in this era, at least as triggering factors, more than in previous studies (Alizadeh et al. 2021 with references).

Another aspect of the Sasanian socioeconomic system that was closely linked to agriculture is urbanism (e.g. Alizadeh et al. 2015: 142; Alizadeh et al. 2021: 317–18). The Sasanian Empire was one of the most important actors in the late antique world. Due to the interwoven economic networks and complicated military interactions operating on an inter-regional scale, it had to face the challenges, alongside the opportunities, offered by the zeitgeist of Late Antiquity. Development of urbanism was one of the key features of such a sociopolitical milieu. The late Sasanian-early Islamic historical sources refer to the Sasanian Kings' interest in founding new cities and the flourishing urban culture of this period (Farnbagh Dadagi, 16.206–9; Ibn Balxī, 60.15–21; Khayyam, *Nowrōznāme* 3.1; de Menasce 1966; Brunner 1983; Daryaee 2002; Pigulevskaya 2008: 159–64, 223; for archaeological attestations, see Mousavi and Daryaee 2012: 1,077–85; cf. Puschnigg 2006: 19). These population centres, however, were multifaceted phenomena. While these cities could become hubs for newly-founded industries, they might reflect the political ideology of the Sasanians. As is clear in some cases, such as the imperial cities of Ardašīr-Xwarrah and Bīšābuhr (Chegini and Nikitin 1996: 40–2, 56; Huff 2008; 2014; Habibi, in press), these centres, according to features such as name, planning and distinct monuments, could form part of the propaganda of the Sasanian state. Either founded from scratch or developed from an earlier settlement, these urban foundations could host the population of dispersed villages. Such transformation is studied in different regions, from the alluvial plains of Mesopotamia and south-western Iran (Adams 1962; 1965; 1981; 2006; Adams and Hansen 1968; Wenke 1975–6; 1981; 1987; Neely 1974; 2011; 2016; Potts and Roustaei 2009; Alizadeh et al. 2015: 126, Fig. 14, Tab. 3: the highest pre-medieval demographic growth and settlement density of the Rāmhormoz region in Parthian and Sasanian times) to eastern Syria (Lawrence and Wilkinson 2017: 6–7, 15) and north-western Iran and the southern Caucasus (Alizadeh and Ur 2007; Alizadeh 2014; Ur and Alizadeh 2013; Lawrence and Wilkinson 2017; Wordsworth and Wencel 2018). The concentrated population and its products and yields could be more easily monitored, controlled and protected in these cities. Given the fact that long-distance trade played a main role in the Sasanian economy (Ammianus Marcellinus, *Rerum gestarum libri qui supersunt* xxiii: 6, 11; Procopius, *Wars* i: 20; Daryaee 2009: 136–40; Schippmann 1990: 91–2; see below), these centres were closely related to roads and trade networks too. Therefore, they were a crucial part of the economic system of the empire, and by extension of the late antique world (Morony 1994: 227).

Late antique inter-regional networks formed around interests in high-quality agricultural products, for whose production different regions were famous (Daryaee 2010a: 402). This point leads us to the other basis of the Sasanian economy: trade. Although long-distance trade was a main source of revenue for the Sasanian state, it was not, in all its guises, totally state-based. Activity was mostly undertaken by independent individuals or companies, even though, according to their profession as involving commerce, *wāzargānīh*, the social rank of Zoroastrian merchants, were inferior to other classes (Daryaee 2010a: 403–4). Nonetheless, as an important source of income, the central state would try to regulate the transit trade. To do so, the Sasanians employed various means, including construction and maintenance of the associated infrastructures of fortresses, forts, roads and ports, and levying taxes on them and on commodities. An example of such could be the late Sasanian fort of Fulayj facing onto the Indian Ocean (Priestman et al. 2022; al-Jahwari et al. 2018; Dabrowski et al. 2021). Hamza Eṣfahāni (1844–8: 46–9) points to eight ports founded by Ardašīr I on the Persian Gulf or the rivers leading to it. The central state would even engage in military operations when required. Among such activities were the campaigns of Ardašīr I to the regions on the southern shore of the Persian Gulf (Dinawarī 1985: 45), and those of Šābuhr II deep into the Arabian Peninsula, and of Xusrow I to Ethiopia and his conquest of Yemen in the 570s (Whitehouse and Williamson 1973: 32–44, with more bibliography; Morony 2004: 185; Daryaee 2010a: 406–7).

Networks of Iranian merchants formed well beyond Sasanian territories. Iranian trade diaspora developed in the Indian subcontinent, south-east Asia, and western, southern and south-eastern China from the fourth century onwards (Morony 2004: 184–5; Ritter 2009: 150). Sasanian outposts emerged at the northern and southern shores of the Persian Gulf, Banbhore in Sind and Kilwa on the east coast of Africa (Daryaee 2010a: 404–7). Therefore, the Sasanians controlled the overland international trade hosting the roads between China and the Mediterranean Region (Bivar 1970), and, particularly during the late Sasanian period, Persian shipping dominated Indian Ocean commerce (Whitehouse and Williamson 1973; Whitehouse 1991: 217; Morony 2004: 185). The Sasanian *drahm* is found as far afield as Sweden and China (Gyselen 1997: 106; Daryaee 2010a: 405–8). Moreover, seals, bullae and other artefacts made according to typical Sasanian artistic conventions are discovered from West to Central Asia and even beyond, from Europe to Southeast Asia (Ritter 2017: 277). The monetary expansion and spread of the currency and administrative materials are associated with the scale and success of Iranian trade in this era.

We mentioned the official support for the settled mode of subsistence during Sasanian times. However, Sasanian territories held nomadic and transhumant[13] populations as well.[14] In fact, agropastoralist and transhumant communities incorporated both modes of animal husbandry and agriculture on different scales into their multi-resource economy for millennia, particularly in the area that forms the focus of this book. Pastoralism has been a key feature of the economic system of the Central Zagros through history. Various environmental and cultural variables brought about the transition of pastoralism in different periods. In other words, different conditions led to adaptations favouring one side of a spectrum with sedentism and mobility at its poles. According to this approach, the false dichotomy of sedentary agriculture–nomadic pastoralism is prevented. Therefore, the development of each of the subsistence strategies (and by extension the groups practising them) is not considered to be oppositional, as assumed by some scholars (e.g. Adams 1965; 1981; Glatz and Casana 2016; Glatz 2018), but complementary.

The deposits of different sites in the Zagros highlands and northern Susiana plain hold sets of evidence about the presence of domestic goat and sheep and pastoralism from around 8000 BCE onwards (e.g. Clutton-Brock 1978; 1981: 56–7, 60–1; Zeder 1999; Zeder and Hesse 2000; Hole 1978: 137; 1979: 195; 1984: 54; Potts 2014: 41). The documented data regarding the development of pastoralism in Fars (Sumner 1986; 1994; Alizadeh 1988a; 1988b; 2003; 2004a; 2004b; 2009; 2010; Alden 2013), the alluvial lands of Mesopotamia and Khuzestan, and the highlands of Zagros (Mortensen 1972; 1974; Hole, 1979; 1980; 1996; 2004; Gilbert 1983; Zarins 1990; Bernbeck, 1992; Abdi 2002, 2003; Mashkour and Abdi 2002; Mashkour 2003; Mashkour et al. 2005; Alizadeh et al. 2005; Greco 2003; Paulette 2013) during prehistoric times are well-researched. Nonetheless, as these data are almost wholly archaeological,[15] archaeologists have interpreted them differently on the basis of distinct methodologies emphasising ethnographic analogies, archaeological sciences, or written historical sources (Potts 2014; Khazanov 2009: 122; Rosen 1992; Watson 1980).

There is, however, consensus as to the close interrelations of pastoralists with agrarian and urban societies in the Central Zagros and the neighbouring alluvial plains to its south and south-west, although the nature and rate of this interdependence vary for different kinds of herdsman husbandry – that is transhumance, agro-pastoralism, semi-nomadic pastoralism and pastoral nomadism – in different periods, as argued by Khazanov (2009; see also Khazanov 1984: 19–24). The heterogeneity of natural resources in the Central Zagros region provides different types of land resources. Enough precipitation and the proper soil of some of the intermontane valleys of the highlands make dry farming possible. Numerous permanent rivers offer copious seafood resources which, alongside forests of acorns and fruits, could form part of the economy of the groups living in the region. Strategic passageways and paths across the arduous Zagros Mountains also allow for control and management of communication and trade not only inside the region but on an inter-regional scale (see Chapter 2). Moreover, rich pasturelands in peripheral areas are seasonally available to pastoralists of the highlands, but out of reach of bounded agriculturists settled in the alluvial plains. Therefore, particular conditions offered by hinterlands provided opportunities for the formation of a multi-resource economic system (Salzman 2004; see also Cribb 1993: 16–17; Balatti 2017: 37–8). This economic foundation was flexible enough to permit adaptation to environmental conditions in the less predictable and dry climate of the highlands and adjustment to the political circumstances of different periods. In this sense, vertical pastoral nomadic groups of the Central Zagros, in a later development (Sahlins 1968: 33; Spooner 1971: 201; 1973: 6; Hole 1979: 207; Krader 1981: 499; Khazanov 1984: 89–90), emerged in close accordance with the transformative processes that occurred in their associated settled agriculturalist and urban societies (Smith and Young 1972: 41; Rowton 1973a; 1973b; 1974; Lees and Bates 1974; Adams 1981). Dynamic interactions between agriculturalists and pastoralists brought about selective pressures for specialised pastoralism (see Lees and Bates 1974) as a result of the expansion of irrigation agriculture and industries and an increase of population density in urban areas. Development of urban areas, intensification of irrigation agriculture and surplus product were among the key reasons behind the development of pastoral nomadism (Lees and Bates 1974; Bernbeck 1992: 84; Kradin 2002: 383; Greco 2003: 66–8; Palumbi 2010). The developed mode of pastoralism used mounted animals, such as horses, for long-range and long-term seasonal migrations (see Binford 1982; 1983) and marauding raids and brigandage. Therefore, mobile pastoralists could exploit environmental resources more efficiently than transhumant and agro-pastoralist groups and be more independent of sedentary populations.[16] This eventually led the populations dependent mainly on pastoralism to exploit the varied land resources in peripheral areas, which were not available to settled agriculturalists, more efficiently. On the other hand, specialised herders were never economically self-sufficient, as they essentially needed the agricultural and industrial products of sedentary zones to survive (Khazanov 2009: 120–5; Lees and Bates, 1974: 191; Baharvand 1367 [1988]: 86; Glatzer and Casimir 1983: 308; Liu 2001; Schuyler 2005: 357; Balatti 2017: 38). In the Central Zagros region, a more mobile way of life for pastoralists resulted in healthier and larger herds (Adriansen, 2005: 208; 2008: 215), a stronger economy, military strength (Lees and Bates 1974: 191), control over inter-regional paths, trade opportunities (Spooner 1971: 201–2; Baharvand 1367 [1988]: 205–6) and planned economic exchanges (Hole 1984: 56; Altaweel and Paulette 2013). The regular economic interaction with settled groups, as a main aspect of the subsistence of pastoral nomads, could result in the foundation of some bazar cities (for the notion, see Myles 1941: 35) in either *sardsīr* (summer quarters) or *garmsīr* (winter quarters). These were places to which settled artisans and farmers could bring their products to trade with nomads during certain seasons.[17] Nonetheless, building up exchange networks with sedentary societies was both economic and social in terms of risk-management strategies (Baharvand 1367 [1988]: 89; Bernbeck 1992: 84; for the notion see Moritz et al. 2001). These relationships could ensure the survival of pastoral mobile populations in the case of biological crises of any kind, natural disaster or intergroup conflict that might jeopardise herds and the very existence of the group. Therefore, both the natural characteristics of the Central Zagros region and the specialised mode of the mobile pastoralist economy would lead to interwoven ties between highlands and lowlands. While population pressure and difficulties of canal irrigation in sedentary zones could bring about adaptation of pastoral nomadism (Lees and Bates 1974), the natural conditions of the highland ecosystem would require seasonal movements towards lowlands and regular encounters with their population centres (Cribb 1993: 8; Moghaddam and Miri 2007: 27; Balatti 2017: 44–8). According to Rowton's model of Zagros's enclosed nomadism (Rowton 1974), such interactions led to a symbiosis between settled agriculturalists and mobile pastoralists. This general economic system, therefore, could prove efficient and lead to population growth.

We discussed the evidence concerning urban development and irrigation agriculture intensification during the Sasanian period. Archaeological and pollen evidence from around the mid-first millennium BCE to the mid-first millennium CE signifies agricultural, arboricultural and horticultural developments in different areas of ancient Iran (Djamali et al. 2009; Djamali et al. 2010; Djamali 2016; Shumilovskikh et al. 2017). These large-scale projects could be carried out under the imperial investments or supported by local landlords for tax-framing, or might represent the continuation of local long-held human niche construction (Wilkinson and Boucharlat et al. 2012). But in any case, they have implications for our understanding of the cultural landscape of the era. These complex stratified urban societies were capable of producing surplus craft products, and irrigation agriculture developed considerably during this time. It is, then, no surprise that late antique written sources inform us of pastoral nomadic populations living in the Sasanian realm. Middle Persian and early Islamic accounts point to the nomads, called kurds (see Potts 2014: 120–1, also Grenet 2003: 32) and Kermanis, in the Sasanian military (Ibn Balxī, 168.8–15; Cereti 1995: 206; see also Jackson Bonner 2011: 85–8 and Sauer et al. 2022: 603, n. 25 for other foreign nomads). Unlike in the case of the Deylamites from the Alborz Mountains, sources do not provide detailed information about the role kurds played in the imperial army. Ibn Balxī (168.8–10) only notes that they were an instrumental and key part of the army of Pārs because of their resilience and possession of armaments and herds, and that the Muslim conquest of the Sasanian Empire had substantial consequences for them demographically. Their co-option into the Sasanian army indicates that the state utilised them (Daryaee 2009: 40–1). There are also historical remarks on the connection of Ardašīr I's ancestors to kurds, *kurdagān* (Farahvashi 1386 [2009]: 4–5; Bosworth 1999: 11), despite their unreliablity. Moreover, Mādyān-ī Hazār Dādestān, Book of a Thousand Judgements, contains an interesting passage referring to nomads (Wahrāmān, 42: 58). As Potts (2014: 122–3) noted, the fact that this text deals with the legal ramifications of pasture usage by nomads testifies to the common occurrence of nomadic migration that prompted their regulation under Sasanian law. Also, this passage in the long chapter of *A Dictum Alongside Others*, *dar i guft abāg guft*, denotes that these migrations took place according to the vertical nomadic model during certain seasons and in established patterns via particular areas. Another significant literary source of the period is the Synod lists published by Chabot (1902), which mention the seats of Bishops and Metropolitans of the Church of the East held by 424 CE. Among these seats is the so-called Mashkena dhe-Kurdu, which was the Bishopric of Kurdish (nomadic, that is) encampments in Pārs (Chabot 1902: 285). Apparently, the area, whose exact whereabouts is not clarified, hosted considerable nomadic populations that gave their name to it. Thus, their population and culture were both noticeable and distinct enough to be acknowledged by the dominant political power of the time and by those settled in cities and villages.[18] Regarding parallel archaeological data about pastoralism, it is, in many cases, challenging to distinguish pastoral nomadic and herdsman husbandry economies merely on the basis of archaeological material (Khazanov 2009: 125; Alden 2015: 997). However, some archaeological sites from Late Antiquity, although in widely separated areas, represent data for the expansion of pastoralism in the form of the architectural remains of courtyard/compound homesteads of different size. These comparable structures are studied in the Hamrin Basin (Valtz 1985), Dehloran plain (Neely 2016), northern Sirwān/Diyāla River valley (Panahipour 2019: 12–17, Fig. 12) and Abdanan plain (see Chapter 3). Neely (2016: 244–5) specified that this architectural type is also attested by ethnographic study of the Central Zagros transhumant and nomadic pastoralists, alongside agro-pastoralist villagers (Digard 1981: Fig. 132; Mortensen 1993: Figs 5.60 and 5.61; Watson 1979: Figs 5.6 and 5.9).

Developing urban centres and their specialised industrial sectors needed satellite sites producing a part of their requirements and facilitating regional communication and inter-site interaction. Transhumant pastoralism could provide for dairy requirements for the main urban centres as benefiting from the opportunities coming from such a relationship (*supra*). Nomadic population, however, could play a more important role in this economic system. Particularly in a region such as the Central Zagros, vertical pastoral nomadism has been a significant factor. This phenomenon is based on the regular long and middle-range migrations (Mortensen 1972; 1976; Henrickson 1985; Abdi 2003) that brought about a firm interwoven socioeconomic interdependence between settled and nomadic populations on an inter-regional scale. This system has been developing since the Middle Chalcolithic period (Abdi 2002; Abdi et al. 2002) and has been perpetuated by social and economic links (Rowton 1974). As mentioned above, written sources point to the fact that nomadic peoples were officially part of the fiscal, military and religious structures of the Sasanian state. Therefore, during this period, an Iranian empire considered the role of nomads in its system, and to some extant controlled their power, although the strategy was not entirely unprecedented (see Chapter 2, n. 15).

The ancient Zoroastrian literature provides evidence for ideological support for pastoralism, as discussed in relation to agriculture in the Sasanian period (for the significant status of herds in the *Avesta*, see Boyce 1377 [1998]: 46–7). In the *Avesta* (Doustkhah 1371 [2005]: 879, 882) and the *Greater Bundahišn* (Farnbagh Dadagi, 8.68, 9.73, 94), *Gew/Gāwo/Gāwoš*, Mid. Pers. *hadayōš/hadayā*, is the holy First/Pure/Sole-created bull, Mid. Pers. *Gāw ī ēw-dād*, from whose descent all beneficial quadrupeds stem. His spirit, *gewš-ōrwana*, is the goddess who protects these animals from human mistreatment (Doustkhah 1371 [2005]: 10).[19] Yet this is cited more frequently in the Young Avestan texts than in the Gāthās and the Yasna Haptaŋhāiti. Moreover, the Pahlavi text *Mēnō-ye Xerad* describes where cattle and sheep flocks rest as the third most delightful land, right after where a fire-temple was constructed and before a cultivated land that had been abandoned (Tafazzoli 1354 [1975]: 18).

1.4 THE FIELDWORK

The Zagros basin covers zones that are distinct geologically and topographically. These features, consequently, have formed different stratigraphic successions, environmental conditions and natural landscapes in each of the zones (Oberlander 1965; Sepehr and Cosgrove 2004). Abdanan and Farsan Counties, the sample areas under examination, are geologically located in the Zagros-Fold-and-Thrust Belt, but in its discrete parts. On the one hand, Abdanan plain is situated on the verge of the Zagros Simply Folded Belt close to the Dezful Embayment. Farsan plain, on the other, is located in the Imbricated Zone of the Zagros Thrust Belt near the Sanandaj–Sirjan Zone in the Central Iranian Micro-Continent (Vergés et al. 2011: Figs 1, 3 and 6).

Therefore, archaeological fieldwork projects are conducted in each of the counties according to their topographic features and natural landscapes. In Abdanan, seven seasons of reconnaissance surveys have been carried out between 2000 and 2010 (Motarjem and Mohammadifar 2000; Mohammadifar and Motarjem 2001; Moradi 2005; Ahmadi 2008; Javanmardzadeh 2010; Abdollahi and

Sadeghi-rad 2010). Each of these studies focused on a particular area of the county. Hence, archaeological sites of different types and periods have been identified and documented in Abdanan. Finally, in January–February 2015, this author led a structural, total-coverage survey focused on 106 Sasanian sites across the county (Habibi and Mohammadifar 2020; see Chapter 3). In terms of excavation, however, no site has been excavated in Abdanan so far. But thanks to the large-scale salvage projects carried out in Dare-shahr County and Seymareh River basin, some important Sasanian sites of the Central Zagros have been excavated in the neighbouring areas to the north and north-east of Abdanan. These projects, then, provide interesting sets of archaeological evidence about the role this region played in Sasanian times. Excavations at the palatial complex of Barz-e Qawāleh/Ramāvand (Hourshid and Mousavi Haji 2015; Karamian and Farrokh 2017), the historical city of Dare-shahr (Lakpour 2010, Niakan 2017; 2019: Figs 13 and 14; Sa'adati and Naseri Somei 2019), the fort of Qal'e Seyrom-shāh (Mohammadifar 2014; Mohammadifar and Tahmasebi 2014), and the monuments unearthed at Qala Gouri (Hasanpour 2014; 2015; Hasanpour et al. 2016), Rouha (Niakan 2019) and Lelar (Motarjem 2015; Niakan 2015a), deliver significant evidence concerning the late Sasanian period. These findings may locate the centre, *šahrestān*, of the Sasanian province Mihragān-Kadag known from sigillographic data and later historical sources (see Chapter 2, s. 2.4).

Farsan County was the subject of an intensive survey in 2007 that led to the discovery of sixty Sasanian sites including a rock-cut tomb, nomadic campsites and permanent settlements of different sizes (Khosrowzadeh and Habibi 2015; Habibi and Heydari 2015; see Chapter 4). Among the large settlements found is the site of Tappe[h] Bardnakōn. Given its interesting surface materials and the clandestine excavations, it was selected for two seasons of excavations, carried out in October–November 2017 and September 2018 (see e.g. Khosrowzadeh et al. 2020a). These campaigns brought to light a hitherto unknown administration centre of the late Sasanian Empire, the canton of Rāwar-kust-ī-rōdbār (see Chapter 4, s. 4.3).

Different types of datasets, hence, have been discovered. As expected, potsherds are the most common kind of archaeological material (see Chapter 5). However, pieces of glassware are also found, particularly among the surface materials of the site of Jōliyān (AS.034) in Abdanan and the excavations at Tappe[h] Bardnakōn (FS. 119) in Farsan. Moreover, samples of glassware relating to the late Sasanian period are acquired from the site Rouha in Dare-shahr

County (Niakan 2019: 142, Fig. 2). Stucco panels, mostly partial, are also found at the above-mentioned sites in the Seymareh River basin (Karamian and Farrokh 2017; Niakan 2019: 142, picture 11; Hasanpour 2014; Hasanpour et al. 2016: 51, Fig. 6; Saʿadati and Naseri 2019, Table 1). These specimens are of high importance not just because of their implications regarding the monumental scale of architecture at these places, but also because they are comparable with other samples of Sasanian collections discovered at sites in different parts of the empire. Apart from these architectural ornaments, some types of buildings examined in the sample areas are informative in the sense that they may offer insights into the sociopolitical milieu of the Sasanian Central Zagros. These structures include a rock-cut funerary structure, fire-temples, forts and manor houses of Abdanan, alongside the explored palatial complexes in the adjacent Seymareh region. In Farsan, we may mention a rock-cut niche, and the spaces related to administrative activities and, probably, a repository for discarded bullae at Tappe[h] Bardnakōn (FS. 119). Excavations at this site led to the discovery of a corpus of 559 clay sealings, a silver coin, a large amount of metallurgical and glass slags, fragments of metal ware, gems, tar pieces, oyster shells and cowries. The drachma coin dates from the first ten years of the reign of Husraw II (590–628), whose acronym for the monetary workshop seems to be AY, that is, Ērān-xwarrah-Šābuhr (Gyselen 1979); however, ŠY, Šīrāz, may also not be ruled out (Khosrowzadeh et al. 2020a: 22). These sets of data, alongside the acquired administrative bullae,[20] shed light on the inter-regional interactions that maintained Tappe[h] Bardnakōn, and Farsan County, in the late Sasanian period.

1.5 STRUCTURE OF THE BOOK: SASANIAN SITES, SETTLEMENT PATTERNS AND MATERIAL CULTURE IN THE CENTRAL ZAGROS

In each of the sample areas, we will analyse regional patterns of spatial distribution of material culture according to the functions of Sasanian sites. As discussed, each of the regions under examination is located in discrete zones of the Central Zagros topographically and environmentally. Settlement systems and their formation processes, therefore, are expected to be distinct. Examination of different types of sites may help us to understand these processes better. Therefore, taking into consideration the natural and political circumstances of the period in the context of settlement patterns informs us of the causes behind the regional spatial distribution. Evaluation of data on such a geographical scale enables us to examine the material manifestations of historical socioeconomic transformations and developments that are still accessible and that otherwise may be hardly recognised. It also provides an opportunity to study different aspects and impacts of these cultural processes.

Nonetheless, conducting this macro-scale research also brings particular challenges. The Central Zagros is a geographical zone with areas that are environmentally distinct and that differ ethnologically. This large and diverse region may have experienced complex cultural processes in Late Antiquity that were of a multifaceted nature and challenging to interpret. To recognise the nature and scale of such developments requires an interdisciplinary approach to data. Analyses based on remote sensing methods employing satellite- or aircraft-based imagery have recently proved to be promising in some domesticated landscapes (for the concept, see Widgren 2012) such as in northern Sasanian frontiers or alluvial plains in southern Mesopotamia. Nonetheless, in the Central Zagros, satellite imaging and aerial photography are generally less efficient. The mountainous topography of this region, which is in many areas covered with hills of different heights, makes it hard to monitor archaeological sites in the common shapes of tappe[h]/tell. Moreover, nomadic campsites are usually as level as their surroundings.

NOTES

1. Nonetheless, to mention just one among several minorities in the region, we may recall that the Iranian Jews, as an ethnoreligious group, have historically been an important community influential in terms of the socioeconomic structures of the major city of Hamadan and, to some extent, in terms of those of Kermanshah (Sanasarian 2004: 44–8).
2. For its definition see Monkhouse 1970: 205; Johnston 1981: 183–4; Olwig 1996.
3. For some examples of multi-disciplinary approaches in this domain, see French 2003; Compana and Piro 2009; Carvalho et al. 2013.
4. When it comes to the quality of interaction between human groups and the environment in which they live.
5. Gestaltende Geographie, derived from the Lanschaftenkunde (landscape sciences) of German geography of the late nineteenth century, which examined ecosystems in terms of the mutual influence of inhabitants or environment on cognition and perception.
6. For problems relating to the phenomenological approach in landscape archaeology see Burger et al. 2008: 206–8; Mohammadifar and Habibi 2018.

7. See Darvill 2008: 68. See also David and Thomas 2008b; Kluiving et al. 2012; Strang 2008a: 51–2; Johnson 2007 for the history, different definitions, and schools of landscape archaeology; Aston 2002 for the English school in landscape archaeology; Kowalewski 2008: 242–3; Barker et al. 2006 for use of regional scale spatial analysis in studying different empires; Anschuetz et al. 2001; Fleming 2006 for landscape archaeology from a post-processual perspective; Baugher and Spencer-Wood 2010 for gender analysis of power in a feminist framework of landscape archaeology.

8. See Wilkinson (2004: 341; 2000: 226) for the exciting capabilities of landscape archaeology in the Near East.

9. See Wilkinson 1982 and 1989 for some cases of successful research based on this approach.

10. Although archaeological surveys in many regions under the rule of the Sasanian Empire have demonstrated that the period coincided with investment in the development of economic and military infrastructures and population growth (see Chapter 3), one nonetheless has to consider that this was not always the case. In areas where the ecosystem was not suitable for an agriculture-based economy, or where geographical location had little or no importance for international trade, or in some frontier zones where the safety of the population and its products were issues, instead of such a phenomenon, patterns of militarised landscape, nucleated population or demographic decline may be discovered (Kennet 2007; Ulrich 2011; Lawrence and Wilkinson 2017). For a study of the deep history of arboriculture, especially concerning plane and walnut planting, as either an economic or a cultural activity in ancient Iran, see Potts 2018.

11. Wahrāmān, 22; Brunner 1983: 760; de Menasce 1966; Elman 2004: 140–9; Campopiano 2017. See also al-Mas'ūdī's *Murūğ*, II. 210, which, quoting Husraw I, considers prosperous agriculture vital for successful and just government.

12. The main relevant publications are Neely 1974; 2011; 2016; Adams 1962; 2006; Adams and Hansen 1968; Wenke 1975–6; 1981; 1987; Jacobsen 1982; Hartnell 2014; Wilkinson et al. 2015; Alizadeh 2014; Alizadeh and Ur 2006; 2007; Ur and Alizadeh 2013; de Gruchy and Jotheri 2019; Altaweel et al. 2019: 15, 19; Carter et al. 2006; Panahipour 2018; 2019.

13. The meaning we consider for transhumance accords with S. Jones' definition (2005; see also Balatti 2017: 40–1). For its different definitions in the anthropological-archaeological literature, see Hole 1978: 155–62; Palumbi 2010: 158; Alden 2013; Potts 2014: 4.

14. The periodic invasions of the Inner Asian nomads were influential enough for this to be one of the important reasons behind the shifts that happened in Sasanian political ideology during later periods of the dynasty (Potts 2014: 124–56; Howard-Johnston 2010: 41–6;

Börm 2016: 624–5; Wiesehöfer 2010: 121–8, 140–2; Habibi, in press). Nonetheless, by 'nomads' here we mean those groups indigenous to Ērānšahr who lived inside the Sasanian realm and integrated in the socioeconomic system of the empire. In the late antique-early medieval sources, these herding peoples are called 'kurds' (Potts 2014: 121–4).

15. The Mari archive is an exception, but is rich in terms of the information it provides about the role and interactions of pastoralists in Bronze Age Mesopotamia (Paulette 2013: 131–2).

16. This does not mean that these pastoralist economies were formed in a linear evolutionary process through time. But different types and forms of pastoralism could be practised by contemporary groups living even in the same region. It is worth mentioning again that these were adaptations which could take place in different conditions and as a community practice (Bernbeck 2008: 65). Therefore, besides ecological crisis and natural conditions, political and socioeconomic factors could be behind such transformative processes in different spatiotemporal horizons. As regards political conditions, conflicts with states and chaotic periods of social disorder and insecurity could encourage highly mobile modes of subsistence, such as those experienced by Yomut Turkmens or the Lors of Lorestan during the Qajar period (Irons 1974; Baharvand 1367 [1988]: 31–6; Balatti 2017: 46 with more references). On the other hand, either forced sedentarisation, as a controlling strategy of centralist states (Salzman 1971; Beck 1980: 347–9; Cronin 2000; 2003; 2005), or peaceful periods may lead to the general trend of sedentarisation (Hole 1978: 134; Johnson 1969: 2–3). The diverse social organisation of each pastoral system can also be effective in this process. Different nomadic groups have developed distinct social risk management strategies. In Iran, Kurd (Barth 1953; Leach 1940) and Baseri (Barth 1961) families probably settle down after losing herds. But in this situation, the Qashqai (Beck 1980), the Yomut (Irons 1994) and the Baluch (Salzman, 2004) may rebuild their livestock, being hired as shepherds via generous herding contracts, while economic dynamics allow Komachi (Bradburd 1989) and Lor (Black-Michaud 1972) households to remain within the pastoral economy only as poor shepherds (Moritz et al. 2011). Various ecological variables also have implications for such socioeconomic adaptations, among which are abundant yearly precipitation, extreme temperature, and industrial exploitation of land resources such as petroleum for sedentarisation (Khazeni 2006: 210–311), while several factors may lead to a more mobile way of life: soil salinisation, anthropogenic degradation and difficulties with irrigation – and, therefore, food crisis, alongside ecological crises such as draughts, floods, pandemics, and plagues and insect pests. Moreover, other sociocultural factors currently favouring sedentarisation are the charms of a modern urban lifestyle, which promises more opportunities for younger

generations using new communication platforms and technological developments.

17. For instance, such socioeconomic relationships between Persian villagers and city-dwellers of the Chaharmahal area – western Iṣfahan and the Bakhtiyari nomads – led to the foundation of villages such as Chelgerd and Farsan in the modern province of Chaharmahal va Bakhtiyari. Up until around half a century ago, these places were primarily economic hubs holding seasonal small bazars in the summer quarters of the Bakhtiyari tribes. Settled artisans could annually set up their temporary workshops or bring their products during summer. A documentary made by the then National Television of Iran during the Pahlavi period shows that these small settlements could host around a hundred shops (Manoto TV, Tunel-e Zaman, Series 14, Episode 2). These sites gradually developed into the cities of Chelgerd and Farsan from the late Qajar period onwards (Khazeni 2006). This process particularly intensified owing to the forced sedentarisation and pacification of the nomads of Iran (*takht-e qāpū*) by Reza Shah between 1928 and 1935 (Cronin 2000; 2003; 2005). In the winter quarters, on the other hand, Dezful was a traditional Lor market town (Potts 2013: 203).

18. Istakhri (17.1–3) testified to this fact concerning the population of nomads in early Islamic Fārs.

19. The Avestan Aẏareratha is a mythical hero and is among the Zoroastrian immortals whose main duty is to safeguard the Pure Cow. In Middle Persian literature he is called Goupat-šāh, which literally means the ox's guardian (Doustkhah 1371 [2005]: 1,047, 1,048). Also, on the first-created bovine in Zoroastrian literature, see Agostini and Shaked 2013: 101, fn. 21; Brunner 1978: 77–8.

20. The author co-authored articles with Rika Gyselen and the excavators of the site, Alireza Khosrowzadeh and Aliasghar Norouzi, examining the iconography of the seal impressions of the Tappe[h] Bardnakōn archive and the content and features of its administrative bullae (Khosrowzadeh et al. 2020a; Khosrowzadeh et al. 2020b; 2020c; see also Chapter 4).

2 *The Historical Geography of the Central Zagros*

2.1 INTRODUCTION

Chapter 2, organised in three main sections, discusses the historical geography of the Central Zagros from around the mid-third millennium BCE to the mid-seventh century. It explores the accounts of residents of this region from their emergence in the literary traditions of their Mesopotamian and Elamite neighbours to their descriptions in the written sources of the Sasanian–early Islamic sources. However, we do not intend here to examine historical texts and material evidence regarding Zagros toponyms, the extent and path of Sumerian, Akkadian and Assyrian kings' campaigns in the region, or the various political entities of the realm of the Central Zagros in different periods. Scholars with different areas of expertise have been trying to reconstruct different aspects of the historical and political geography of the Central Zagros in the Bronze and Iron Ages since the late nineteenth century.[1] To do so, they have studied different sets of data, including the Assyrian and Babylonian Commemorative Texts of Annals, and *kudurru* stones, along with epigraphic or anepigraphic rock reliefs and some archaeological sites. Nonetheless, researchers have not yet reached consensus in many cases, as relevant archaeological and epigraphic evidence is largely lacking and, when available, is not easy to interpret (see e.g. Lanfranchi and Rollinger 2021: 57–9). Such long-discussed arguments are beyond the scope of this book. However, a brief state-of-the-art presentation of the data associated with the diverse peoples inhabiting the intermontane plains and valleys of the Central Zagros long before Late Antiquity helps us to recognise the long-term cultural processes behind the later sociopolitical milieu and historical events.

2.2 THE THIRD AND SECOND MILLENNIA BCE: SOCIOPOLITICAL DIVERSITY AND CONFRONTATION WITH MESOPOTAMIAN-ELAMITE EXPANSIONISM

Sumerians, Babylonians and Assyrians in Mesopotamia and the Elamites of the Khuzestan lowlands and Southern Zagros interacted with the inhabitants of central western Iran under various circumstances and in different eras. These groups documented their interactions using different media such as tablets, rock reliefs, inscriptions, *narû*, and *kudurru* stones. Although they do not represent the point of view of the local peoples of this region, these sets of evidence present the most important sources of information about the Zagros highlanders over a long period of time, roughly from the mid-third to the mid-first millennium BCE.

The presence of several territorial political entities in the Central Zagros is attested in literary sources – predominantly from the Mesopotamian or Elamite perspectives – at least from the mid-third millennium. By this time, at least three main political powers existed in the western Central Zagros and Upper Diyāla basin (see Glatz and Casana 2016; Ahmed 2012; Biglari et al. 2018: 27–8). Recorded by archival sources, these local polities are Lullubum (Maidman 1987: 163; Zaccagnini 1977: 23), Gutium (Eidem 1985: 98; Bryce 2009: 266) and Simurrum (Eidem and Laessøe 2001: nos 1 and 2; Ziegler 2011).

From early in the mid-third millennium to around the mid-first millennium BCE, Gutians were depicted in Babylonian sources as raiders threatening civilisation (Oppenheim 1969: 309; Cooper 1983: ll. 152–7; Lewy 1971: 739; Hecker et al. 1994: 798; Parpola 1970: 138; Reiner 1984: 80; Michalowski and Reiner 1993: 27–8; Balatti 2017: 7–9). They are charged as having overthrown the Akkad dynasty in the second millennium BCE (Jacobsen 1939: 116–21; Kutscher 1989: 62–3, 67–8). Therefore, the *Sumerian King List* (SKL) places the dynasty of Gutium after Akkad, yet shows considerable variations regarding its length (Sallaberger and Schrakamp 2015: 113). Scholars also present different opinions about the geographical extent of the kingdom of Gutium in Mesopotamia and the chronology of the Gutian period, between c. 40 and 150 years (Hallo 1957–71: 713–14; 2005: 156; Boese 1982: 33–5; Dittmann 1994; Glassner 1986: 45–50; 1994; Pomponio 2011; Steinkeller 2015; see Sallaberger and Schrakamp 2015: 127–8, 113–16 for a brief review). The Gutian dynasty was weakened around the last century of the third millennium by the uprising of strong figures in Elam and Babylon – Puzur-Inšušinak, Utu-hegal, Gudea and Ur-Namma. Puzur-Inšušinak launched military operations across the Zagros and occupied northern Babylonia, which probably provided proper circumstances for the final defeat of the last Gutian ruler, Tirigan, by Utu-hegal (Steinkeller 2013a: 297–8).

Gutium, as a geographical name, appears for the first time in an Old Babylonian copy of the Early Dynastic period sources (Hallo 1957–71: 709). The references to the toponym continue, with some variation, in other Old and Middle Babylonian texts (Ahmed 2012: 68–70).[2] As with Lullubum (see below), the same is true for Gutium, in the sense of it having vague cultural implications from a Mesopotamian perspective and the fact that it did not always refer to the same people, but to Zagrosian highlanders in a general sense. Despite its obscure geographical location and frontiers, particularly in earlier times, evidence from the second and first millennia BCE helps us to locate Gutium in the intermontane Zagros lands to the east of Mesopotamia (Van Dijk 1970: 1972; Eidem and Læssøe 2001: 32; Van De Mieroop 2002: 408; Oshima 2012: 242; Edzard and Farber 1974: 71; Edzard et al. 1977: 65–6; cf. Cameron 1969: 41 and Ahmed 2012: 69–73, n. 171).

As for the heartland of Lullubum, there is almost a consensus among scholars as to the identification of the Šahrazūr plain on the Zagros foothills around modern Solaymaniyah, to the east of Kirkuk (Cameron 1969: 40; Westenholz 1997: 142; Frayne 1992: 703; Zadok 2005b; Altaweel et al. 2012: 9; Ahmed 2012: 76–7; Schrakamp 2012: 4166; Steinkeller 2013a: 294; cf. Streck 1900: 294; Álvarez-Mon 2013: 230; Balatti 2017: 6). The city of Lulluban mentioned in Old Akkadian texts from Gasur (near modern Kirkuk) is located by Frayne (1992: 61) in modern Ḥalabja in the south-west of Lake Zirēbār near Marivan. He also identifies Lulluban, attested in a text from Ebla, LGN no. 230 (Ahmed 2012: 75), with Lullubuna of the third-millennium *Early Dynastic List of Geographical Names* from Abū Ṣalābīḫ. The different derivations of the name of the land and its inhabitants are also recorded in the Ur III documents (Thureau-Dangin 1910: I, nos 211 and 828; Pettinatto et al. 1977: no. 249, line 1; for its different forms, see Ahmed 2012: 75, n. 202). Notwithstanding some optimistic suggestions (Astour, quoted by Zadok 2005b; Speiser 1930: 91–4; Álvarez-Mon 2013: 230), it is uncertain whether the Lullubians ever formed a distinct ethnolinguistic group (Klengel 1988: 165; Eidem 1992: 51, 53; Zadok 2005b; 2012; Schrakamp 2012: 4166; cf. Ahmed 2012: 75–6). References to the anthroponomical derivations of the word are recorded in Babylonian and Assyrian sources from the second millennium BCE (Fincke 1993: 190–3; Nashef 1982: 188–9; Parpola 1970: 228–9; Zadok 2012). As Zadok (2005b) points out, 'Old Babylonian sources show the extension of the term Lullu to an international "social" label', implying a barbarous trait for the inhabitants of the mountain areas of the western-central Zagros region.[3] Several simultaneous Lullubian kings recorded in historical documents of this era to the early first millennium BCE (Eidem and Læssøe 2001: 63: 24–5; 64: 22; RIMA 2, A.0.101.1, ii 46; RIMA 2, A.0.101.1, ii 77–8) indicate the low political integration of the region, which reflects the sociopolitical milieu across the Central Zagros during this era. This is also in accord with the situation described by the Neo-Assyrian sources concerning several kings of Zamua, the Neo-Assyrian Lullumē or ancient Lullumu or Lullubum, that is.[4]

Zadok (2005b) also argues that Lullubi was at the periphery of the Akkad kingdom during the late third millennium BCE, yet he concludes that the exact extent of the Lullubian land and its geographical delimitation in the second millennium BCE (Klengel 1965: 166–7) are not clear. The last quarter of the third millennium was an era of frequent conflict between Lullubians and the main political powers of southern Mesopotamia, the Sargonic and Ur III dynasties (Schrakamp 2012; Balatti 2017: 6–7). Although temporarily, Lullubum was under the direct rule of the Third Dynasty of Ur, being incorporated in the north-eastern section of the ma-da belt – a periphery zone as part of Shulgi's system of defensive settlements within the conquered territories (Steinkeller 2013a: 294, 304–12, Figs 1 and 2; 2018: 194–5).[5] To this equation, one has to add the neighbouring kingdom of Simurrum/Šimurrum.[6] The rock relief of ANnubanini, King of Lullubum, on a cliff at Mount Hezār Gereh, possibly ancient Mount Batir (see Al-Rawi quoted by Potts 2020: 61), in Sarpol-e Zohāb in western Kermanshah, known as ANnubanini I (Edzard 1973), is dated by authorities to the Akkadian, end of Ur III, Issin Larsa, and beginning of the Old Babylonian periods (Edzard 1973; Hrouda 1976; Frayne 1990: 704; Mofidi Nasrabadi 2004; Potts 2020: 61). This relief, along with the adjacent inscriptions of the Simurrian king Iddi(n)-Sîn, the so-called ANnubanini II (Walker 1985: 178–90; Frayne 1990: 712; 1992: 634; Kienast and Sommerfeld 1994: 395; Shaffer et al. 2003: 22), reveals a period of rivalry between the powers in the region aimed at dominating Ḥalman, modern Sarpol-e Zohāb (Levine 1973: 24–7; Reade 1978: 140, Fig. 2; Postgate 1979: 592; Ahmed 2012: 249; Parpola and

Porter 2001: 11; Gentili 2012: n. 4; Glatz and Casana 2016: 131; Potts 2017: 346; 2020: 60),[7] and the significant pass it held (Ahmed 2012: 248, 254, 264–5).[8]

Similar to Lullubum's (see above and n. 4), Simurrum had a strategic location (see below). The ancient road linking southern and northern Mesopotamia passed through the Šahrazūr and Rāniya plains.[9] Also it had access to the adjacent Gates of Zagros to its south-east and, therefore, to the significant road passing the Zagros Mountains that was later, in medieval times, known as the Great Khorasan Road (Glatz and Casana 2016: 128). This position was probably the main reason for the Old Akkadian and Ur III involvements in Simurrum, particularly Shulgi's attacks (Frayne 1992: 707; Steinkeller 2013a: 294, 306–7, 310; 2018: 194–5).

Although this toponym is mentioned in Early Dynastic II documents (Gurney and Kramer 1976: 38), the first clear remark of the name of Simurrum is in Old Akkadian archival texts, as an enemy of Sargon and Narâm-Sîn (Gelb and Kienast 1990: 49; Frayne 1993: 8 and 87; Ahmed 2012: 232). This kingdom has to date been attested in textual sources relating to the era between the twenty-fourth and eighteenth centuries BCE (Altaweel et al. 2012: 9; cf. Balatti 2017: n. 28, ch. 1). There are also references to Šimurrian men, among them a smith, *simug* (*RTC* 249: col. i, line 9 and col. ii, line 12; cf. Steinkeller 2013a: 299–301), in the documents of the second dynasty of Lagaš in the late third millennium (George 2011: 29–47). Later, in the early second millennium BCE, an archival document (*BIN* 9 no. 421) not only mentions the city of Simurrum (lines 10 and 16) but also, more importantly, points to the diplomatic relationship between the king of Simurrum and Išbi-Erra of Isin (see also Frayne 1992: 707). This evidence, alongside the above-mentioned Simurrian monuments of Bētwate and Sarpol-e Zohāb, indicates the period when this polity became independent from the Ur III Empire – perhaps around 2000 BCE (Frayne 1992: 707; Shaffer et al. 2003: 39; Mofidi Nasrabadi 2004: 302–3; Altaweel et al. 2012: 1, 10–11; Ahmed 2012: 254).

The position of Simurrum, which lay in the east Transtigridian region (Frayne 1992: 707; Altaweel et al. 2012: 9–10, 11), is located according to the information delivered by the inscriptions and inscribed rock reliefs of Iddi(n)-Sîn, king of Simurrum,[10] that were apparently found in the district of Bētwate around the city of Rāniya in Solaymaniyah Governorate (Shaffer et al. 2003: 26–7). The eponymous centre of this kingdom is identified with the archaeological site of Qal'a Shīrwāna, roughly 200km south-east of Bētwate (Frayne 1997: 265–9; Eidem and Lsessee 2001; Shaffer et al. 2003: n. 100;

cf. Frayne 2011: 511; Ahmed 2012: 302). This site is situated on the bank of the Sirwān River in a location not far from the city of Karḫar, another frequently attacked target of the Ur III state, identified with modern Qaṣr-e Shīrīn to the west of Kermanshah (Frayne 1999: 141; Ahmed 2012: 300). However, the so-called Aɴnubanini II relief in Sarpol-e Zohāb, as mentioned above, indicates the interest of Iddi(n)-Sîn, king of Simmurum, and his heir Aɴzabazuna in extending the Simmurean realm into the adjacent south-eastern region of Ḥalman – around 300km south-east of Bētwate – if not including it in their territory (Shaffer et al. 2003: 28; Altaweel et al. 2012: 11).

Another state that ruled in parts of the Central Zagros in the third millennium BCE is Awan. As a rival political entity of Babylonian city-states, its name appears twice in the Old Sargonic *Sumerian King List* (*SKL*) in the middle of the third millennium BCE (Frayne 1993: 22–4, Sargon 8, Caption 15; 51–8, Rimush 6: 37–42 = Rimush 7: 13–18 = Rimush 8: 12–14; Potts 2016: 81; also for the *SKL*, see Sallaberger and Schrakamp 2015: 13–22; Jacobsen 1939; Marchesi 2010). Here it is stated that Awan brought the kingship of the First Dynasty of Ur to an end (Col. iv 5–6), and, after three kings reigned for 356 years (Jacobson 1939: 94, l. 8–16), it was overthrown by Kiš (Col. iv 17–19). The other important source about the Awan dynasty is the small Old Babylonian tablet discovered at Susa. This king list contains two twelve-named lists of the kings of Awan and Šimaški (Scheil 1931: 2; Gelb and Kienast 1990: 317–20; Sallaberger and Schrakamp 2015: 23–5; Potts 2016: 136, Plate 5.2). Notwithstanding the doubts cast as to the historical and chronological reliability of this text, particularly the Awan section (Gelb and Kienast 1990: 318–19; Glassner 1996: 26; Steinkeller 2007; Sallaberger and Schrakamp 2015: 24–5; De Graef 2006: 52–5, 68; 2012: 524, n. 25), the *AwKL* indicates that this kingship perhaps was an important Iranian political power since the late Early Dynastic period given the seven predecessors it enumerates for Luhhishshan, the contemporary of Sargon (Steinkeller 2018: 181).

As mentioned, Awan appears in sources dating to the middle and late third millennium BCE (Potts 2016: 78). Yet after it was terminated in Sargonic times (Steinkeller 2013a: 296), Awan is only mentioned once by Ibbi-Sîn (2028–2004 BCE), and as a geographical term (Ahmed 2012: 61). Steinkeller (2018: 177–9, 184) correctly regards Awan as the earliest native term recorded for an Iranian territory, but whether it is a native correspondent to the Babylonian Elam, as he suggests, is not clear since currently we cannot specify the geographical extent and delimitation of the third millennium

Awan state with confidence (see below). However, different locations have been proposed for the ancient Awan (see Ahmed 2012: n. 54).

Vallat (1993: 26, 122–3, 125; see also Ahmed 2012: 60) locates Awan in a vast area from the Central Zagros to the east at Tappe[h] Sialk in Kashan in Central Iran with an unspecified northern border. Yet this territory is not aligned with the available evidence, as the more eastern areas of the Central Iranian Plateau of this time held Šimaški (see below). Steinkeller (2013a: 296–7; 2018: 177–9) tentatively recommends that an area to the east of Susa, including southeastern Khuzestan and Anšan/Fars up to the borders of Marḫaši (modern Jiroft: for example, Steinkeller 2013b and 2014a), should be identified as Awan. His identification is based on Michalowski's suggestion (2008: 115) that AdamDUN, Tappe[h] Sorkhegan in the vicinity of Shushtar,[11] in the land of Awan, might be considered. He also refers to a passage in three Old Babylonian copies of one of Rimuš's inscriptions (C6, C8 and C10) that remarks on the capture of Sidga'u, general of Marḫaši, taking place 'between Awan and Susa, on the Qabiltum/Middle River' (Steinkeller 2013a: 296–7; Potts 2016: 82). Dyson (1965: 55–6) and Carter (1971: 229–30) propose Tappe[h] Musiyan in the Dehloran plain as the site of Awan (see also Schacht 1987: 175–6), whereas at present we know that Dehloran held Arawa/Uru'a, another important city of the Elamite federation of this period (Stinkeller 1982: 244–6; 2018: Fig. 10.1; see below). On the other hand, other scholars propose a location in the area around Dezful and Andimeshk (Hinz 1971: 647; Edzard and Farber 1974: 20; Edzard et al. 1977: 21; Schacht 1987: 175).

However, Awan's location is one of the rather uncommon cases in the historical geography of pre-Islamic Iran which archaeology, along with literary sources, has largely corroborated. Accordingly, Potts (2016: 78 and 85) proposes that Godin III: 6 pottery assemblages found in the highlands of Lorestan and the Kangavar valley represent the material correlate of Awan. He claims that although comparable painted and plain ceramics have been discovered in the contemporary archaeological contexts in Dehloran, Susiana, the Hamrin basin and Diyāla region, the material culture collections representing the Godin III: 6 culture and the ceramic and metal weapons datable to the mid-third millennium found in Lorestan and in the Poshtkooh tombs indicate the existence of a relatively coherent cultural zone that was the territory of historical Awan (Potts 2016: 88–90, Table 4.3). Indeed, the links between the materials examined in the Diyāla valley and the lowlands of Mesopotamia, Dehloran and Susiana with Lorestan and the Poshtkooh in the Central Zagros confirm the socioeconomic and political relationships between these regions in the mid-third millennium. Therefore, the assemblages of material culture recovered from the archaeological contexts of this temporal horizon support a more north-western location than the Susiana Plain, a location, that is, in the highlands of the Central Zagros from Lorestan to the west of the Kabirkooh mountain range, which encompassed the Pishkooh, northern and central Abdanan, and the mountainous section of the south-eastern Poshtkooh.

As regards the above-mentioned battlefield of Rimuš and Marḫaši on the Qabiltum/Middle River, Potts identifies the Seymareh River as the river (Potts 2016: 95–6; cf. Steinkeller 2013a: 297, who suggests the Karun). But the Seymareh runs along the Ilam–Lorestan border around Dareh-shahr County of Ilam that is located to the east of the Kabirkooh range and in the Pishkooh area. To consider the Seymareh, then, is to imply a place in the Pishkooh for the battle, as opposed to Potts' own identification, in which case it leaves the Poshtkooh outside the territory of Awan. The Seymareh joins the Kashkān River just before the Gāvmīshān Bridge to create the Karkheh River. The Karkheh enters the Susiana Plain from its north-western edge and thence flows southerly along the Ilam–Khuzestan border and passes west of the archaeological site of Susa. In my opinion, the ancient Qabiltum River is most probably to be identified with the Karkheh, particularly the part of the river which runs along the border of the modern provinces of Ilam and Khuzestan to the west of Susa. According to the inscription of Rimuš of Akkad, this river flows 'between Awan and Susa'. To the west and south-west of this part of the Karkheh River are located the consecutive Kalāt District of Abdanan County and the Dasht-ʿAbbās plain in Mousian District of Dehloran County in Ilam Province. As mentioned above, Arawa/Uruʾa is identified with the neighbouring area to the north-west of Susiana, on the Dehloran plain. Historical documents not only remark on this location to the north-west of Khuzestan (e.g. Gelb and Kienast 1990: 50, D-3 and D-4; Steinkeller 1982: 240, 244–6: called as the 'lock of Elam'; see also Steinkeller 2018: 194), but also on its natural resources. These sources, from the late Early Dynastic to Sargonic periods, recorded the export of a bituminous stone (Frayne 2008: 232–3, En-metena 28) and a particular type of lax grown here (DP: Pl. CII. 371 and 372) to Mesopotamia, which confirms a location in modern Dehloran (see also Steinkeller 2018: 183). Therefore, the most likely area to be suggested as the location of the battle stated in the inscription is the lowland area of Abdanan to the east and south-east of this county in Kalāt District.

This district is a geographically intermediate zone between the highlands of the south-eastern Poshtkooh and the alluvial plains of Khuzestan. In the period under examination, this area bordered on Awan (the Pishkooh and the highland Poshtkooh) from the north and north-west, Arawa (modern Dehloran) from the west and south and Susiana from the east and north-east.

Archaeological assemblages discussed above also provide some insights into this point. The fifteen seasons of survey and excavation of the Belgian Archaeological Mission in Iran (BAMI), from 1965 to 1979, were designed to investigate Bronze and Iron Age cemeteries in the Poshtkooh region (e.g. Vanden Berghe 1968; 1970a; 1970b; 1973a; 1973b; 1979a; 1979b; Vanden Berghe and Haerinck 1984; Vanden Berghe and Tourovets 1992; Haerinck 1986; 2008; 2011; Haerinck and Overlaet 1998; 2002; 2004; 2006a; 2006b; 2008a; 2008b; 2010a; 2010b; Overlaet 2003; 2005). In the south-eastern Poshtkooh, in Abdanan County, these projects led to the examination of ancient cemeteries with tombs and archaeological material relating to the Bronze Age from the early II and III phases to the Late Bronze, including the cemeteries of Posht-e Qal'e-ye Abdanan, Qabr Nahi, Takht-e Khan, Tawarsa, and the only Late Bronze Age tomb found in the Poshtkooh at Sarāb-e Bāgh (Haerinck 1986; Haerinck and Overlaet 2008a: 295; 2010: 39–41; Vanden Berghe 1973: 26; Vanden Berghe et al. 1982: 54–5, Fig. 20; Potts 2016: 87–8, Table 4.3). But it is interesting to note that all these sites are located in the northern and central areas of Abdanan, that is Markazi and Sarāb Bāgh Districts. Apparently, a similar material culture has not yet been found in Kalāt District to the south-east of the county. Kalāt includes Mourmouri and Āb-anār lowlands making up the alluvial area of Abdanan that leads to the Susiana Plain. It is possible that this area was populated by groups with a culture distinct from[12] that adduced previously in Lorestan and the mountainous Poshtkooh, or else it was not part of the same political entity (Awan, that is).

This area is within easy reach of southern Babylonia and Susiana, and actually there is almost no geographical barrier between southern and central Mesopotamia, Dehloran, southern and eastern Abdanan and Susiana. Dehloran and Abdanan are on the ancient route Urusagrig—Dêr—Susa (Steinkeller 2013a: 306–7, Fig. 2; 2018: 194–5, Fig. 2; Potts 2016: 234–44),[13] which was a section of the later Achaemenid route system of Royal Road accounted by Herodotus (see n. 9). The trajectory ran from Dêr in central Mesopotamia to Dehloran. Upon reaching Dehloran, it probably split into two paths. One route headed for the east towards the central and southern plains of Sarāb Bāgh and Kalāt in Abdanan. The other ran in the direction of Dasht-ʿAbbās to the south, in the Mousian District of Dehloran. The two paths re-joined in Dasht-ʿAbbās and went on as a single road, passing the Karkheh River, to the Susiana plain. As discussed above, the similarities of material culture in the highlands and lowlands of Awan, Arawa, Susiana and central and southern Babylonia during this period therefore make sense, since the areas had shaped close and long-term cultural bonds, despite the status of their political relationship in terms of alliance or rivalry.

Šimaški/Simaški was another Elamite state in central western Iran which ruled during the early second millennium BCE (c. 1930–1880 BCE) (De Graef 2008). However, the first remarks on this polity reckon on the existence of this kingdom in the twenty-first century BCE. After his Zagros conquests, Puzur-Inšušinak's victory inscription mentions a Šimaškian 'king' who paid homage to him (Steinkeller 2013a: n. 60). On the basis of chronological considerations and the order of the rulers of Šimaški in the Šimaški King List (*ShKL*; see Sallaberger and Schrakamp 2015: 24–5), Steinkeller (2013a: 302–3; 2014b: 288–9; 2018: 192) identifies this unnamed king as Kirname (*ShKL* no. 1). It is possible that the Old Babylonian Susa tablet, containing two lists of '12 kings of Awan' and '12 kings of Šimaški' (see above), documented two consecutive dynasties (Steinkeller 2018: 184). Therefore, Šimaški probably replaced Awan after the fall of Puzur-Inšušinak at the hands of the allied forces, which perhaps included the army of the Šimaškian ruler Ebarat I (Yabrat, *ShKL* no. 3),[14] who was an ally of the Ur III rulers preceding Ibbi-Sîn (Steinkeller 2007: 227, n. 47; 2018: 194–5; De Graef 2015: 294–6). But Šu-Sîn's royal inscriptions about his retaliatory invasion of Šimaški indicate that some Šimaškian lands, under the leadership of Zabšali, revolted against him and perhaps his ally Ebarat I (De Graef 2015: 296; Steinkeller 2018: 196). According to the geographical information provided by these sources, it is proved that 'the Su' cited in these sources were people of the land of Šimaški – LU2.SU^{ki}, that is (Steinkeller 1988; 2007; see also De Graef 2015: 294–6; cf. Stève et al. 2002: 432–3, who identified it with Susiana). Here sixteen distinct Šimaškian principalities are named, among which are Zabšali, Šigriš, Yabulmat, Alumidatum, Karta and Šatilu (Steinkeller 2014b: 291). There is also a significant passage in these sources that sheds light on the location of the sixteen principalities in a vast area reaching 'from the border of Anšan up to the Upper Sea' (Frayne 1997: 303; cf. Alizadeh et al. 2015: 140–1 with references, which considers Anšan as the most probable centre of Šimaški, with the distribution of Kaftari pottery as its material correlate). This description has led Zadok (1991: 227) to locate these lands in an area stretching from Fars Province to the Caspian Sea (see also Potts 2016: 133). Steinkeller (2007; 2014b: 291–5), on the basis of the same passage and more precisely, seeks them 'within and around the Zagros zone of the modern provinces of Kermanshah, Kurdistan, Hamadan and Lorestan'. Despite various opinions about the location of Šimaški (see Ahmed 2012: 273; De Graef 2015: n. 2), an area in the Central Zagros region seems to be the most probable. Šu-Sîn's campaign in this region led to the incorporation of the Šimaškian land of Karta, apparently situated in a position peripheral to the Ur III core area, into the mada-belt of the Ur III state (Steinkeller 2014b: 291). This also brought about the free access of the victorious Neo-Sumerian king to the eastern highway through the Central Zagros, reflected in the fact that Šimaški is one of the most frequent destinations stated in Ur III texts (Steinkeller 2013a: 306). This locality is also backed by a passage in the Haladiny inscription of Iddi(n)-Sîn (col. ii: lines 90–1, see Ahmed 2012: 257–8) pointing to a conflict between Šimaški and Simurrum. Šigriš, which is probably identical with the Neo-Assyrian Sikris/Sikrisi, according to a Puzriš-Dagān tablet (PDT 473: 1–5), was a neighbour of the other Šimaškian principality of Zidatum (Steinkeller 2014b: 292). It therefore is to be found in the Zagros, to the south of the Great Khorasan Road (Stolper 1982: 45; Medvedskaya 1999: 57–9). As plausibly argued by Steinkeller (2014b: 291–2; 2013a: 311–12), Zidanum, Zidahri, Šigriš and Abullat were located along this significant road, in the general area between Kimaš and Huwurti/Hurti (Steinkeller 2013a: 304–12; see above), that is, between Kermanshah and Hamadan or perhaps even further east on the Hamadan Plain. Therefore, the Šimaškian adversaries of Šu-Sîn were situated in the areas stretching from the Central Zagros to the north-western parts of the Iranian Plateau. This has led Steinkeller (2014b: 293; 2018: 195) to tentatively seek Ebarat's principality (Šimaški proper?) in a locale between Huhnur(i) (Tappe[h] Bormi near Ramhormoz) and Anšan (Tal-i Malyan) or perhaps further to the north-east, somewhere in the general area of Işfahan. In my opinion, on the basis of the geographical extent of Šimaški recorded in the royal inscriptions of Šu-Sîn, a southern area of the Central Zagros in the highlands to the north-east of Susiana and west of Işfahan, the modern province of Chaharmahal va Bakhtiyari, is more probable for this identification. This region is situated along a historical road connecting the Central Iranian Plateau and Khuzestan and was at least part of the late

Middle-Elamite realm, given some recent discoveries (Henkelman 2011: n. 24; Potts 2016: 244; see Chapter 4).[15]

Kassites formed another ethnic group whose homeland was in the Central Zagros region. They, and likewise Awanites and the so-called Šimaškians, founded an imperial power in the Near East. The Kassite state competed with the potent Middle-Elamite and Assyrian powers over gaining hegemony in some areas during the latter half of the second millennium (c. 1600–1150 BCE). For instance, in Assyria's backyard, the area from the strategic Šahrazūr plain to the east towards Kermanshah and the Zagros Gates was under Kassite sovereignty (Altaweel et al. 2012: 11–12; Glatz and Casana 2016: 131–2; Potts 2017).[16] Given the present state of knowledge, however, we are not currently able to locate their homeland, *māt Kuššuhi*, precisely, yet Mesopotamian historical sources from around the mid-second to the first half of the first millennium BCE determine an area in the Central Zagros highlands (Stol 1987: 54; Heinz 1995: 167; Charpin 2004: 339–40; Sessmannshausen 1999: 411–12; 2004: 292; Parpola 1970: 86, 197; Radner 2003: 61; Zadok 2005a; 2005b; Malko 2014: 79–80). Two main Kassite population centres in the Central Zagros were the principalities of Namar and Bīt-Ḫamban (Levine 1973: 22; Brinkman 1968: 247–59; Radner 2003: n. 8; Potts 2020: 60). Namar is attested from Early Dynastic times (Frayne 1992: no. 237) and is identical with Assyrian Namri. It was located to the west of modern Kermanshah (Reade 1978: 138–9; Fuchs 2011: 233; Potts 2016: 234; 2017: 347), around Kerend-e Gharb, that is Kassite Karintaš (Potts 2017 with references), and the site of Choghā Gavāneh, perhaps ancient Palum (Abdi and Beckman 2007: 48, ChG 5, 5).[17] Ḫamban was situated along the Great Khorasan Road towards the east of Kermanshah Province in an area between Kermanshah and Bisotun (Forrer 1920: 90; Herzfeld 1968: 13; Kinnier Wilson 1962: 113; Reade 1976: 139; 1978: 137–9; Medvedskaya 1999: 53). Also, another predominantly Kassite land was Ḫalman, which is identified with the modern Hulwān and the area around Qasr-e Shīrīn and Sarpol-e Zohāb, centred on the latter (Borger 1970: 1; Levine 1973: 24–7; Reade 1978: 140, Fig. 2; Postgate 1979: 592; Zadok 2005a; Parpola and Porter 2001: 11; Gentili 2012: n. 4; Potts 2017: 347; 2020: 60). Nevertheless, it is worth mentioning that Kassite people were present in Mesopotamia not only while ruling there, but also prior to the formation of Karanduniaš, the Kassite kingdom of Babylonia, at least from the Old Babylonian period, and also after the collapse of their dynasty at the hands of the Elamite Šutruk-Nahhunte I (Sessmannshausen 1999: 411–12 and 417–18;

Smet 1990: 11; Brinkman 1976–80: 466b and 470–1; Zadok 2003: 482, n. 6; 2005a with bibliography). Moreover, along with literary evidence (Balatti 2017: 10), the material culture of Early Iron Age Pishkooh and Poshtkooh presents clear associations with Kassite artistic traditions (Overlaet 2003: 8; Haerinck and Overlaet 2006b; Álvarez-Mon 2013: 225) and testifies to the cultural interactions between the groups settling those areas and Kassite people.

2.3 LOCAL DEVELOPMENTS IN THE FIRST MILLENNIUM BCE: THE CENTRAL ZAGROS AS A CORE AREA

The Neo-Assyrian political hegemony largely replaced the earlier Babylonian-Elamite influence in the Central Zagros in the early first millennium BCE. Several petty kingdoms of the region struggled for independence, while Assyrians and Elamites exercised their powers to dominate the highlands in order to exploit their rich natural resources, recriuit troops, and hold over the infrequent passageways through the Zagros ranges so as to secure the flow of commodities and information and access to the lands beyond (Liverani 2003: 1–12; Radner 2003: 37–46; Balatti 2017: 137–43). This rivalry is reflected in the account of the political turmoil made in the important Zagrosian kingdom of Ellipi as the Elamite and Assyrian states backed different successors to King Daltâ in 708 BCE (ARAB 2: 23–4). This was also the reason for the rather frequent alliance of the Neo-Elamites with the Neo-Babylonian kings against Assyria. Moreover, Ellipi was part of the anti-Assyrian coalition that fought alongside the forces from Elam, Parsuaš, Anšan and Pašeru, against the Neo-Assyrian state in the battle of Ḫalula (RINAP 3, Sn. 23: 35; see also Henkelman 2003a: 198, n. 56). Although, initially, this clash was mainly disastrous for Elam and its allies – though from a Zagrosian point of view it ended by either power being dominated by Media – Elam was perhaps under Median rule during Astyages' reign (Dandamaev and Lukonin 1989: 61; Zawadzki 1988: 143; cf. Rollinger 2021: 342–3), while Assyria had already been subjugated by a Median–Babylonian coalition in 612 BCE (Potts 2016: 289, 304).

After the irregular Middle-Assyrian raids of the late second millennium, the more systemised exploitations of the Neo-Assyrian Empire defined politics in the Central Zagros up until the latter part of the seventh century BCE.[18] Namri's struggle against the expansionist strategies of different Assyrian kings at this time led to periods of military campaigns and rebellion in this area from the late tenth to the early eighth century BCE (Kessler 1998: 92; Potts 2017: 349). The same holds true for Lullumī (Levine 1972: 6; 1974: 20; 1989), which by this time Assyrians interchangeably named Zamua/Mazamua.[19] Thus, both of the polities of Namri and Zamua, for instance, were turned into Assyrian vassals to solve the issue in the Zagros (Levine 1989; Radner 2003: 3,940). To do this, therefore, Assyrian kings established new Assyrian provinces in the Central Zagros: Zamua was established by Shalmaneser III in 842 BCE,[20] Parsua and Bīt-Ḥamban by Tiglath-pileser III in 744 BCE, and Ḫarḫar/Kār-Šarrukīn and Kišesim/Kār-Nergal by Sargon II in 716 BCE (Lanfranchi and Rollinger 2021: 65 with references). Direct control over the region and resettlement and deportation of populations were hence among the political and economic strategies executed by the Assyrians in the Zagros highlands.[21]

Despite the recent discoveries regarding the economic and political organisation of the Middle-Elamite Kingdom at least in some parts of the Southern Zagros highlands (see n. 15), political diversity was a key feature of the cultural milieu of the Central Zagros, and north-western Iran (Lanfranchi and Rollinger 2021: 5961), during the third and second millennia. This fragmented political landscape persisted roughly during the early four centuries of the following millennium. Various territorial, political entities still held control over different parts of central western Iran in this period, and the intermontane valleys and plains were not unified until the Median state expansion dating from the late seventh century BCE. The diverse petty king-doms of the Central Zagros were on the path of developing unity under the leading force of the Medes, while the Neo-Elamite state experienced a period of multicentricity (Henkelman 2003a: 184; 2003b: 258; Salaris and Basello 2019: 812, n. 23).

As mentioned, one of the main Zagrosian kingdoms during the early half of the first millennium was Ellipi, Middle Babylonian Ullipi (Sessmannshausen 2001: 151), which is attested in Assyrian and Babylonian sources. Its location is identified, primarily on the basis of the Neo-Assyrian Annals and the Queries to the Sun God, Šamaš (Starr 1990), to the south of the Great Khorasan Road, north of Elam,[22] south-west of the Median land of Ba'it-ili (ARAB II: 10, ii 23; 99; 183), part of which was called Bīt-Barrû, to the south of Ḫarḫar (RINAP 1: 84, § i 5'–11'a; RINAP 3/1: 63, § 2830). Hence, its extent is specified in the Pishkooh area from modern Boroujerd in the east to around the Iran–Iraq border in the west (Levine 1974: 1046; Reade 1978: 141; Vera Chamaza 1994: 103; Medvedskaya 1999: 63; Dandamaev and Medvedskaya 2006; Álvarez-Mon 2010: 1956;

Potts 2016: 258; Mollazadeh and Goudarzi 1395 [2016]; Balatti 2017: ch. 3: n. 37; Saeedyan 1397 [2018]: 106–7).

Archaeological manifestations of Ellipi may be sought in Lorestan Province in the sites of Tappe[h] Baba Jan on the southern edge of the Delfan plain and Sorkhdom-e Lori in Koohdasht County.[23] The culture of Baba Jan Level III (c. ninth–eighth century BCE) associated with the so-called *genre Luristan* ceramic tradition, or Baba Jan III Painted and Plain Baba Jan Common Wares, as Goff prefers (Goff 1978: 29; see also Goff 1968: 105–34; 1969: 115–30), may correlate with this important buffer state located between the Assyrian and Elamite territories. The monumental structures of Manors on the Central Mound and the Fort and Painted Chamber on the East Mound (Goff-Meade 1968: 112–15; Goff 1969: Figs 2, 3 and 4, 117–22, 126–7; 1970: 137–40, 144–50, Pls. Ia, Ib, IIb and IId; 1977: 118, 121–6, Figs 1, 5, 6, 10 and 16, Pls. XVI–XIX; also, on the Painted Chamber, see Henrickson 1983) were burnt down at the end of this level, according to excavations (Goff 1977: Fig. 10: D-F North Section, n. 47). The phase II tradition at Baba Jan, roughly relating to the seventh century BCE, is marked by a newly-introduced type of wheel-made mica-tempered pottery that is remarkably similar to that recovered at the Median complex of Nush-i Jan I[24] and Jameh-shuran IIB (Levine 1382 [2003]: 465, 467). Therefore, it makes sense to cautiously propose that this site may provide evidence about the Median expansion in the Central Zagros of this time. Examples similar to Baba Jan III ware were also found at the temple of Sorkhdom-e Lori (Van Loon 1957: 23–4), which nonetheless is dated imprecisely, and according to its cylinder seals, to a period between 900/850 BCE and 600 BCE (Goff 1978: 35).

It is possible that Ellipi also influenced, politically and culturally, the Poshtkooh area in the south and south-west given that the characteristic fine grey pottery ware discovered at the Iron Age III tombs in that area indicates links with the Baba Jan III painted pottery (Haerinck and Overlaet 2006b; cf. Goff 1978: 34). If so, the late Neo-Assyrian reliefs in the Poshtkooh[25] perhaps commemorated Assyrian incursions into Ellipi and beyond in the Poshtkooh, as the Assyrians could not invade the west of Kabirkooh without being confident about the Ellipian forces. Ellipi was probably bordered from the south-west by the country of Bīt-Bunakki, var. Bīt-Bunakku/Bīt-Burnaki. The polities of Raši/Araši (the former Harši of the post-Sargonic and Ur III texts, see n. 13), Bīt-Bunakki and the other fortified 'towns of the passes', mentioned in the Neo-Assyrian texts of the late eighth and seventh centuries BCE and located in the Poshtkooh area in the modern province of Ilam, experienced a contentious era in the seventh century of Elamite–Assyrian rivalry for dominance and the recurring rebellions of their populations.[26] According to these sources, Assyrian contingents perhaps reached the Poshtkooh's polities via the Kabirkooh passageway passing through Ellipian territory.

However, epigraphic data derived from studies on the Kalmakarra hoard, *trésor de Samati*, brought into light the existence of the later (c. sixth century BCE) local principality of Samati in the south-western areas of the Pishkooh around modern Poldokhtar (Mahboubian 1995; Bashash Kanzaq 1376 [1997]; 1379 [2000]; Khosravi et al. 2012; Salaris and Basello 2019: 83, 99–101; Henkelman 2003a: 214–27, Table 2). Also, the so-called Acropole texts from Neo-Elamite Susa referred to [BE]*pu-hu sa-ma-tip*, Samatian people (Vallat 1996; Henkelman 2003a: 203, 222). As the designation 'Ellipi' has not yet been acknowledged in local sources as the native land name, we cannot confidently decide whether the population and ruling dynasty of this state called themselves Ellipian or not. However, one might postulate that Samati of the Kalmakarra hoard denoted the Ellipians who by this time ruled southern Pishkooh on behalf of their Median overlords.[27] Given that the Ellipi state is last recorded around 660 BCE (Henkelman 2003a: 197), it is also possible that the Samatians formed a different dynasty, particularly as the documented onomastics of the rulers does not indicate a link between the two reigning lines (Diakonoff 1991: 16; Waters 2013: 483; Zadok 2013: 411; Salaris and Basello 2019: 83, 99–101; Bashash Kanzaq 1376 [1997]; 1379 [2000]). Moreover, the hoard discovered at the site of Chigha Sabz (18km north-west of the Kalmakarra cave) is also related to the Samatian kings (Vallat 1992; Gorris 2020: 196; Salaris and Basello 2019: 100; Potts 2016: 304, cf. Balatti 2017: ch. 5: n. 7).

As mentioned above, one of the northern regions neighbouring Ellipi was called Ḥarḥar. The country of Ḥarḥar is first mentioned in the Assyrian texts in the so-called Black Obelisk (RIMA 3, A.0.102.14 120–5), an inscription of Shalmaneser III (858–824 BCE) giving the account of his eastern campaign in 835 BCE. While here it is clearly distinguished from Media, later royal inscriptions assume Ḥarḥar, along with Araziaš/Upper Nartu and Bīt-Ramatua/Lower Nartu, a Median city. It was incorporated into the provincial system of the Neo-Assyrian Empire, being renamed Kār-Šarrukīn under Sargon II (721–705 BCE), and was made the centre of a province of the same name (Radner 2003: 38–40, 50–1). Assyrian sources are also quite informative in locating this polity in the Central Zagros, close to the Great Khorasan Road. As stated above, the northern Ellipian land of Bīt-Barrû was added to the province of Kār-Šarrukīn/Ḥarḫar by Senacherib (704–681 BCE) (RINAP 3/1: 63, § 28–30). Zakruti, a Median city according to the Kalḫu Annals of Tiglath-pileser III (745–727 BCE) (RINAP 1, 17: 5–7 and 39: 17–20a), bordered Ḥarḫar from the west according to the sixth Sargon II's campaign account in the inscribed Najafabad Stele (Levine 1972: 25; RINAP 2, no. 117). This source also, alongside Sargon's Annals, attests to the location of Kišesim, where the stele was erected (Reade 1995: 39; Gopnik 2011: 295), to the north of Ḥarḫar (Levine 1972: 39–41, ii 36–45; ARAB II: ii 10–11 and 56–7). As this stele is placed close to the Najafabad village of Asadabad County to the west of Hamadan, Kišesim is identified with the area between Asadabad and Kangavar Counties to the west of the Alvand range, with its eponymous centre at Godin II (Saeedyan and Firouzmandi 1395 [2016]: 73–4; cf. Radner 2013: 445; Alibaigi et al. 2018: 203–4, which assumed the region from Kangavar to Asadabad, Bīt-Ištar). Another Median city cited in the Najafabad Stele is Bīt-Sagbit. The sources from the reigns of Tiglath-pileser III (RINAP 1, 17: 1–4 and 47: 29–32) and Sargon II (Levine 1972: 39–40, ii 40–1) show that Kišesim and Ḥarḫar, alongside Gizilbunda, were neighbouring provinces of Bīt-Sagbit, which is probably identical with the earlier Median 'royal city' of Sagbita mentioned in the inscription of the Kalḫu stela of Šamši-Adad V (823–811 BCE) (RIMA 3, A.0.103.1 ii 34b–iii 36; Radner 2003: 40–1). The city is also suggested as being identical with the Achaemenid royal city of Hagmatāna (DB II.76; Kent 1950: 122), Greek Ecbatan (Medvedskaya 2002: 45–6). Hence, the most probable candidate for the location of this city is a northern area in the south of the modern Hamadan Province (Saeedyan and Firouzmandi 1395 [2016]: 76–8). These sets of evidence specify the location of Ḥarḫar/Kar-Šarrukin as being to the south of Kišesim/Kar-Nergal and to the north of Ellipi. Therefore, modern Nahavand, to the south of Hamadan, probably contained the Iron Age Ḥarḫar (Herzfeld 1968: 32; Reade 1978: 140, Fig. 1; 1995; 2013: 446; Saeedyan and Firouzmandi 1395 [2016]: 73–4).[28]

Before Senacherib added Bīt-Barrû to Ḥarḫar, Tiglath-pileser III had incorporated this Ellipian area into another Assyrian province in the Central Zagros, Bīt-Ḥamban (RINAP 1: 84, § i 5'–11'a). As mentioned, Bīt-Ḥamban, along with Namar/Assyrian Namri, was cited in earlier Mesopotamian documents as an important Kassite centre situated along the Great Khorasan Road. These passages indicate Bīt-Ḥamban's location to the west of Ḥarḫar and north-west of Bīt-Barrû and Ellipi (Medvedskaya 1999: 53). Therefore, it was probably situated in the east and centre of modern Kermanshah Province (Forrer 1920: 90; Herzfeld 1968: 13; Kinnier Wilson 1962: 113; Reade 1976: 139; 1978: 138–9; Medvedskaya, 1999: 53; Parpola and Porter 2001; Saeedyan 1397 [2018]: 112).

Parsua/Parsuaš was another centre in the highlands of the Central Zagros that Tiglath-pileser III conquered and annexed to the territorial holdings of his empire as an Assyrian province in 744 BCE (RINAP 1: KA: text no. 6 line 7-text no. 9 line 2-text no. 35 I 5–30). Assyrian royal inscriptions referred to this land from the mid-ninth to the late eighth century BCE (Potts 2016: 265). Generally, it is identified with an area from the north-west and north of the Mahidasht plain to the west of the Kurdistan Province of Iran around Lake Zarivar/Zirēbār near Marivan.[29] However, regarding its extent, some scholars limit it to the Kurdistan Province (Radner et al. 2020a: 85, 90–1; see also Radner et al. 2020b), while others support a vaster territory including the more southern areas in Kermanshah Province to the north and north-west of the Mahidasht plain (Levine 1974: 106–12, Fig. 2; Windfuhr 1974: 467; Reade 1995: 34–7; Parpola and Porter 2001; Imanpour 1382 [2003]: 30–9; Mollazadeh 1391 [2012]: 109–13; Yamada 2020: 182), as well as the north-east areas of this province and the adjacent areas in the south-east of Kurdistan Province (Alibaigi et al. 2018: n. 24) and east of Sanandaj (Forrer 1920: 90; Reade 1978: 139; Zimansky 1990: 14). Its capital is called Nikkur in the Neo-Assyrian sources (SAA 15: 36, letter 53; Radner 2003: 57, Table 7; Parpola and Porter 2001: 14, tab. 11; Zadok 2006). Nonetheless, the location of this city is still unknown (Radner 2003a: 57; Radner et al. 2020b: 106); given the possible location of Parsua in the north and north-west of the Mahidasht, Tappe[h] Kheibar is recommended for identification with the provincial capital Nikkur (Saeedyan 1397 [2018]: 118).[30]

As mentioned above, Zamua/Mazamua was the first land in the western Central Zagros that was incorporated into the provincial system of the Neo-Assyrian Empire around the mid-ninth century BCE given its strategic location. But it is attested in the Assyrian documentary evidence from the late tenth to the seventh century BCE, and although the same cannot confidently be said about other Assyrian provinces in the Zagros (Radner 2003: 62), Mazamua remained an Assyrian territory until the fall of the empire (Altaweel et al. 2012: 14; Yamada 2020: 167, 186–7, Table 1), albeit with periodic rebellions by several Zamuan kings (Klengel 1965: 358; Radner 2003: 39–40; Zadok 2005b; Altaweel et al. 2012: 12). As to its location, there is consensus on the Šahrazūr plain in modern Suleymaniyah having formed the core area of Zamua. Yamada (2020) argues that it extended eastward into the mountainous area behind the *chaîne magistrale* in the Penjwin and Marivan region in Iranian Kurdistan, as these highlands stood for what was called *māt Zamua ša bītāni*, the land of Inner Zamua (see also Levine 1989: 88; Altaweel et al. 2012: 13–14). However, Radner (Radner et al. 2020a: 91) maintains that, by the foundation of Parsua as another Assyrian province in 744 BCE, these eastern lands beyond the Hewrman/Uraman mountain range stretching to the Sanandaj area were incorporated into the territory of Parsua, despite keeping the ninth-century names of 'Zamua ša bītāni' and 'tâmtu ša Mazamua ša bētāni', and the 'Sea of Inner Mazamua', which is presumably Zirēbār Lake.[31]

Apart from the Najafabad Stele, another Neo-Assyrian relic in the Central Zagros is the Tang-e Var inscribed rock relief (Frame 1999; RINAP 2: no. 116), which is of great importance in terms of the reconstruction of the political and historical geography of the region in this era. The Tang-e Var relief and inscription were found by Ali Akbar Sarfaraz in 1968, about 50km south-west of the modern city of Sanandaj (Sarfaraz 1347 [1968]). On the basis of this inscription, we may assuredly locate Karalla in the area around the village of Tang-e Var (Parpola and Porter 2001: 11) where the relief was erected to commemorate the victory of a Neo-Assyrian king over the rebellious Karalla.[32] According to these two rock reliefs, we can also locate Allabria/Allapria, another Zagros state attested in the Neo-Assyrian sources. This land is attested in the Neo-Assyrian texts from the mid-ninth to the late eighth century BCE (Kinnier Wilson 1962; Zadok 2001: 95). Moreover, there are allusions to its capital, Paddira (Parpola 1970: 12 and 271), described as the easternmost point of the Assyrian empire (RIMA 3: 184, Shamshi-Adad V A.0.103.1, i. 7), while during Ashurbanipal's reign the town was part of Mannea, which was a region south-east of Lake Urmia centred around modern Saqqez, whose territory expanded towards Zamua during the first half of the seventh century BCE.[33] On the basis of these sources, Allabria was bordered by Parsua to the south and Karalla to the west, and was limited from the north and north-east by Mannea and Surikash – which was situated between modern Marivan and Baneh (Levine 1974: 114; 1977: 137, 145, Fig. 1; see also Balatti 2017: ch. 3: n. 32). Therefore, Allabria formed a buffer state between the Assyrian province of Parsua and Mannea (Zadok 2012) and may perhaps be sought in the Sanandaj valley to the east of Marivan and north-west of Sanandaj around Lake Zirēbār (Levine 1977: 145;

Brown 1979: 17; Parpola and Porter 2001: Pl. 11; Saeedyan 1397 [2018]: 81–2; Saeedyan and Gholizadeh 1398 [2019]: 124).

To the more eastern areas of the Central Zagros was located Median territory. The Assyrian sources, mentioning the name from the last third of the ninth century until the beginning of the seventh century BCE (e.g. Radner 2003: 37–9, n. 1 with a review of the bibliography), portray the western borders of Media as being in flux at different times (Diakonoff 1985; Radner 2003: 38; Dandamaev and Medvedskaya 2006; Roaf 1995). Despite this unclear picture, according to the localisation of some of the most important Zagrosian states and principalities mentioned above, we may still recognise that the western frontiers of the ninth-century Median petty kingdoms were limited to the intermontane plains of the Zagros, from the northwest by Mannea, from the west by Ḫarḫar, Kišesim and Gizilbunda, and from the south-west by Ellipi (Saeedyan and Firouzmandi 1395 [2016]: 74–9). Then, the western borders of the earlier Media were set up by the eastern areas of Alvand Mount, perhaps the ancient Silhazu (RINAP 1: Tiglat-pileser III 16; 17; 35; 41; 47), that is Hamadan city (Saeedyan and Firouzmandi 1395 [2016]), probably Sagbita of the ninth and eighth centuries BCE (see above), and the Malayer plain, possibly holding Zakruti and Ba'it-ili.[34] However, the Assyrian documents from the latter half of the eighth and the early seventh century BCE relate more lands in the Central Zagros, such as Ḫarḫar and Araziaš, to the country of Medes (Radner 2003: 39–40, 51). Notwithstanding Radner's doubts (Radner 2003: 51), such remarks indicate the gradual Median expansion during this period (Diakonoff 1985; Dandamaev and Medvedskaya 2006; Roaf 1995: Figs 22 and 23). The Assyrian kings of the eighth century penetrated more than their predecessors eastward into the Zagros highlands and perhaps beyond into the Iranian Plateau (Luckenbill 1926–7). Therefore, one may logically consider that they increasingly gained knowledge about the peoples and sociopolitical entities of the Central Zagros, particularly after the establishment of the new Assyrian provinces in the region (Balatti 2017: 330–1). Moreover, this interpretation rather accords with Herodotus' *Medikos Logos* (*Histories* I. 95–107) on the historical succession of the events associated with the formation of the Median state.[35] Despite the fact that the Neo-Assyrian sources remained somewhat silent regarding the Medes in the seventh century (Roaf 1995; Waters 2010: 63), it is the Babylonian sources of the Nabopolassar Chronicles (Grayson 1975: 90–6, Chronicle 3) and Nabonidus Stele (Schaudig 2001: 516, Babylon-Stele II 1'–41' and 523) that informed us that they not only became united under the king called Umakištar, Cyaxares of the Classical documents, but also formed an alliance with the Neo-Babylonians to pillage important Assyrian cities from 612 BCE onwards. This was done by conquering the heart of Assyria around 590 BCE (Curtis 1989: 52–4; Briant 2002: 22; Balatti 2017: 154–9; see also Roaf 2021 for the Hasankeyf Tablet, a recently discovered Late Assyrian land sale document with the name of Cyaxares, described as the Median king, ^{m}*ú-ba-ki-is-te-ri* ^{lú}*mat-a-a*).

Like its history, the archaeology of Media is a still-evolving field about which there is infrequent consensus (e.g. Genito 1986; 2005; Muscarella 1987; 1994: 57; Calmeyer 1987: 565–9; 1990; Sancini-Weerdenburg 1988; 1994; Brown 1988; 1990; Medvedskaya 1992; Stronach 2003; Liverani 2003; Razmjou 2005; Rollinger 2021 with more references). Such discussions are beyond the scope of this book, but here I present a brief, up-to-date review of the state of associated archaeological studies.

Tappe^{h} Nush-i Jan I and Godin Tappe^{h} II: 1–4 are attributed to Medes on the basis of their location in the Median triangle (Stronach 2003: Fig. 4) and their date, mid-eighth–seventh century BCE. At Nush-i Jan is an architectural complex, 'fort' as it is called, uncovered with segments with different secular (storage rooms and main columned hall) and religious (western and central temples) spaces (Stronach and Roaf 2007; see also Stronach 1969; Roaf and Stronach 1973; Stronach and Roaf 1978; Curtis 1984; 2005). Its buildings are dated to the mid-eighth–early seventh century BCE (Stronach and Roaf 2007; see also Curtis 1984). The structures of Godin Tappe^{h}, on the other hand, are identified as forming the base of a local ruler (Young 1969; Young and Levine 1974) and relate to the mid-eighth–mid-seventh century BCE (Gopnik 2011, Table 7.1; see also Gopnik 2003; 2005).

Since the excavations of Nush-i Jan and Godin, the cultural material examined at these two sites, mainly architectural components and features and pottery wares, have become the bases for identification of other Median sites. As Boucharlat (2020: 404) warns, however, this comparison has not always been done carefully, and in some cases has been done rather vaguely in terms of whether the sites are Median in the sense of period, polity or culture –to say nothing of the fact that we currently cannot be confident as to whether the Medes accounted in ancient Assyro-Babylonian texts were a homogeneous linguistic population or were made up of groups using different Iranian dialects/languages (Rollinger 2021: 339–40 with more references). These sites are situated in a quite extensive area from central Anatolia to the westernmost outlier of the Zagros range in the Hamrin valley, and from the Central Zagros to the western plains of the Iranian Plateau and around the piedmonts of the Kopet Dagh range and the Marv Oasis in southern Central Asia. Such an extent may serve to deter scholars and make them more cautious in deriving inferences on the basis of comparisons and relating partial cultural material to a certain ethnolinguistic group.

To the north-west, the archaeological site is explored of Kerkenes Dag, the largest pre-Hellenistic site on the central plateau of Anatolia. Kerkenes is located at the northern edge of the Cappadocia plain in Yozgat Province in the Central Anatolia Region of Turkey. Apart from some small-scale examinations in the early twentieth century (Schmidt 1929; Aydin 2004: 7), the main archaeological investigations at this site have been carried out in the course of the rather long-term Kerkenes Project led by Geoffrey and Françoise Summers, with the collaboration of David Stronach for nineteen seasons between 1993 and 2011 (Summers and Summers 2009: 3; Summers et al. 2011: 3; Dusinberre 2002: 19). These interdisciplinary fieldwork projects led to the discovery of a city from the Iron Age measuring 2.5km^2 and enclosed by a defensive stone wall seven kilometres in length with seven gates (Summers 2008b: 3; Summers et al. 2011: Figs 10 and 13). Here are uncovered several structures and spaces with different purposes: religious (Branting 2010: 44–7), palatial (Summers 1997: 92, Fig. 7; 2000a: 63, Fig. 7a; 2008a: 61; 2008b: 1; Draycott and Summers 2008: Plate 5), residential (Summers 2000a: 67–9; Summers et al. 2011: 32; Branting et al. 2011: 5–7, Fig. 95), commercial, and possibly military (Summers 2000a: 65), as well as those involving urban infrastructures such as reservoirs (Summers 2000a: 62, Fig. 6; 2008a: 62), and stables (Summers 2000a: 65; Summers and Summers 2009: 16, 18; 2010: 36–7).

Identifying Kerkenes Dag with Pteria, cited by Herodotus (*Histories*, I. 76), Summers assumes the late sixth century BCE as the most probable date for the site, although he does not rule out the possibility of its foundation in the previous century (Summers 1997; 2000a; 2008a; 2008b; see also Przeworsky 1929). Some of the archaeological evidence, in comparison to those items acquired at Gordion, among which are a bronze fibula and some pottery types, supports a date around 600 BCE (Dusinberre 2002: 20; Summers 2008b: 3). Summers first suggested that this site was a royal city founded and settled by a foreigner elite Median population (Summers 1997; 2000a: 58–60; see also Aro 1998: 250–4; Dusinberre 2002: 23–4; Brixhe 2008: 61; Draycott 2008: 58). However, their later excavations at Kerkenes led to a change in the excavators' opinion in this regard, as the city was most probably Phrygian (Summers and Summers 2003: 22–4; Summers et al. 2004; see also Strobel 1999; 2001: 53, n. 30; Liverani 2003: 6, n. 11; Roaf 2003: 19; Rollinger 2003a; 2003b: 322, n. 5). Bearing in mind that the artistic and architectural remains of Kerkenes Dag either have parallels inside Anatolia or are unique, there is no available sign of the direct influence of Media.[36] On the other hand, the material culture of Kerkenes Dag is closer to the Phrygian culture than to any other. Apart from the parallel Phrygian samples in central Anatolia and Phrygian inscriptions acquired at Kerkenes, the historical context of the Near East in this period supports a Phrygian identity for whoever founded this place. In this period, around the mid-sixth century BCE, Phrygian tribes had an opportunity to revive their rule and replace the former Gordion, destroyed between 830 and 800 BCE (Manning et al. 2001; cf. Muscarella 2003), with the strong Kerkenes in such a strategic position. This site is located 50km south-east of Boğazkale and 20km north-west of Alişar Hüyük. Thus, Kerkenes' Phrygians were possibly not isolated. Therefore, in my opinion, this city perhaps represents the Herodotean Pteria, a regional Phrygian centre that was conquered by the Lydians, who, by this time, c. 545 BCE, expanded their territories in the wake of the fall of Assyria and Urartu (Mohammdifar and Habibi 2017). Both the probable Phrygian character and the fate of the site are attested by its epigraphic and anepigraphic data and its ruins, which, after a short life, around half a century, were plundered and burned (Summers et al. 2011: 7).[37]

In the Central Zagros, Level III culture at Baba Jan is also related to the Medes by the excavator (Goff 1978: 41–2), while, as discussed above, both geographical and chronological considerations support an Ellipian identification. Furthermore, there are other sites in this region that have lately been excavated and called 'Median'. Tappe[h] Yelfān is among this group of archaeological sites, and is located 16km south-east of Hamadan County. Two seasons of salvage excavations at this tappe[h] were limited to its western foothill, where architectural remains, allegedly Median (Mollazadeh 1393 [2014]: 232–5, Figs 115, 127 and 128), were uncovered. Its pottery is related to a single period, the Iron Age III, and its plain buff ware tradition was considered similar to the assemblage of Nush-i Jan (Mollazadeh 1393 [2014]: 235–45, Figs 116–26). Mūsh Tappe[h] is also placed in Hamadan, 5km north of the renowned Tappe[h] Hegmatāne. However, compared to other sites of this group in the Zagros, Mūsh is not formed on the top of a high hill or tappe[h], but on a plain in Hamadan city. Four seasons of excavations have not completely unearthed the architectural remains, owing to the damaged condition of the site. Nonetheless, three long parallel rooms have been discovered, and, on the basis of the excavated test trench, some of the buildings were apparently filled by dried bricks and mud before being abandoned (Mollazadeh 1393 [2014]: 253, Figs 133–6). Most of the potsherds are of the common plain buff ware of the Iron Age III, but also some polished micaceous grey samples are reported (Mollazadeh 1393 [2014]: 253–4, Figs 136 and 137). The other site is Pā-Tappe[h]/Tappe[h] Gunespān, situated around 3km south-east of Malayer County. The plans of its buildings were partially reconstructed during six seasons of salvage excavations. Accordingly, a circular enclosure, of roughly 3m thickness, to the north holds five architectural spaces, among which are three long parallel rooms (Mollazadeh 1393 [2014]: 245–51, Figs 129–31). The uncovered pottery assemblage was classified and associated with the Iron Age III plain buff ware tempered with mica and quartz inclusion (Mollazadeh 1393 [2014]: 251, Fig. 132).

Another site is the so-called Median fortress (Kleiss 1970a: 133–68, Fig. 20; 1996b) located on the *Partherhangs*, Parthian slope, the mountain slope to the north-east of Darius I's *res gestae* and close to the Hellenistic Herakles Kallinikos monument at the important site of Bisotun, 33km east of Kermanshah city. This structure was excavated in 1966 (Kleiss 1996a: 7) and, alongside the pottery (Kleiss 1996b: Figs 3 and 4), is mainly dated according to a bronze triangular fibula of the eighth/seventh century BCE uncovered in its enclosing wall (Kleiss 1970: 174, Fig. 221, pl. 75; 1996b: 21, Fig. 2; Luschey 1974: 118, Fig. 11). Moreover, its construction with rectangular buttresses is compared to that of the fortress at Tappe[h] Nush-i Jan (Luschey 2013: 291). It has been postulated that this fortification locates Sikayauvatiš in the Nisāya district (DB I § 13) of Media, recorded in the adjacent Darius the Great's Bisotun inscription as the fortress of his Median rival, Gaumāta the Magia (DB I § 13, 1.58; Kent 1950: 118; Luschey 1968: 66–7; 1974: 118; 2013: 291; Kleiss 1996b). After the 1960s excavations carried out by the Tehran Branch of Deutsches Archäologischen Institut (DAS), Mehrdad Malekzadeh from the Iranian Center for Archaeological Research (ICAR) conducted excavations at this fortress in 2002. Subsequently, Karim Alizadeh (1382 [2003]) examined the ceramics of its different settlement phases and dated them to the Late Bronze, late Iron II and Iron III Ages, as well as the Achaemenid, middle and late Arsacid and Islamic periods. This study also showed that the micaceous temper is by no means exclusively typical of the Iron Age III pottery, and such an inclusion is observed in the pottery types of all the phases at the Bisotun fortress (Alizadeh 1382 [2003]: 92–4; see also Malekzadeh et al. 2014: 169; cf. Goff 1978: 30, 41). As Boucharlat (2020) has elaborately argued in his critical examination of the archaeological and topographic characteristics of Ulug Depe and the so-called Median forts all across the Iranian Plateau to Zagros, this might well be the case.

Ulug Depe is located in southern Turkmenistan, on the piedmont of the Kopet Dagh range between Namazga Depe and Altyn Depe. After the first three seasons of excavations, a fairly large building, probably around 1800m^2, was uncovered at the top of this tappe[h] and on a terrace called by the excavators the 'citadel'. This structure does not find an exact parallel in the first-millennium sites in its vicinity in Central Asia or even in the Iranian Plateau,[38] but instead shows clear similarities to some sites in the far more distant Central Zagros region, the fort of Nush-i Jan and storehouse of Godin II, along with the fort of Tell Gubba II[39] in the Hamrin basin in eastern Iraq (Boucharlat et al. 2005). Moreover, the wheel-made Iron Age pottery assemblage found in the Yaz II and III contexts of the Ulug Depe, in comparison to the collections of earlier periods, indicates a technological shift linked with a non-local tradition origin. According to the architectural similarities and a new ceramic tradition, therefore, it was at first suggested that the building perhaps functioned as an outpost of the Median realm which had supposedly expanded into Central Asia by that time (Briant 1984: 35–41; Boucharlat et al. 2005: 496). However, later, it turned out that the Ulug citadel was built around the ninth century BCE or even probably during the earlier period of Early Yaz II, thus over a century earlier than any foundation assumed to be Median in the Zagros or Iranian Plateau (Lecomte 2013: 170–80; Boucharlat 2020: 404). Therefore, although some comparable features relating to the architecture and site morphology are distinguishable between some of the sites, and not ubiquitously in all of them (Boucharlat et al. 2005, Table 1), the architectural differences between the Ulug building and the Zagros structures were pointed out, and the lack of homogeneity was emphasised even for the latter group of sites (Boucharlat 2020).

In all of the allegedly Median forts of the Central Zagros, the detected ceramic and architectural types are in some aspects comparable to those unearthed at Nush-i Jan I and/or Godin II. The location of these sites in or around (the latter the case with Bisotun's *die medische Festun*) the area called the Median triangle may persuade one to associate them with some sort of Median phenomenon of the Iron Age III. Nonetheless, the lack of absolute dating techniques, the limited scale of the excavations and the partial examination of architectural structures warn us about overlooking differences and making conclusions based on negative data that are hardly justifiable scientifically.

Whether or not the sites discussed above point to the extent of the Median state in the late seventh and early sixth century, holding an area from central or south-western Asia Minor in the west to southern Central Asia in the east and the Hamrin basin and the Southern or Central Zagros in the south, and whether or not the cultural materials indicate socioeconomic ties between these regions, the Achaemenid rise in the mid-first millennium BCE certainly brought all of the regions, and beyond, under a single political and administrative system.[40] In the area that forms the focus of this book, the age-old characteristic of ethnolinguistic diversity of the Central Zagros had lost its political echoes by this period, if not by the earlier Median era. By the time of the foundation of the first Persian Empire, the whole region, which had held the core area of the Median state, was incorporated into an imperial system as one of its most important economic, military and religious components. This historical landmark had repercussions for the Zagros highlands, where such a level of political disintegration as in pre-first millennium times never occurred again and some of these highlands held the position of political core areas, rather than peripheries, at least until the fall of the second Persian Empire, 650 CE.[41]

Nonetheless, the Achaemenids formed the largest empire of the ancient world to their times, they organised this huge realm, to put it in Tuplin's words, in the manner of 'a business of localising power to make it both more effective and in a way more palatable' (Tuplin 2011: 39–40). Cyrus the Great and his successor, Cambyses, conquered ancient states with long-established traditions of political geography, organisation, and royal tribute. Particularly in such countries, which had included vast and different regions/districts, these conquerors basically opted not to interrupt such arrangements.[42] Primary sources from Babylonia and Egypt under the Achaemenid rule corroborate this (Tuplin 1987: 123; Henkelman 2017: 149; Henkelman et al. 2017: XXV–XXVII with references). But the first of these political entities was the Median state, whose takeover by Cyrus provided him with (probably) large territories that could consequently improve his military assets and control over international roads and strategic passages, armed forces, and horses, along with financial resources. Hagmatāna, which was famous for its glamour, treasures and wealth, attested in the Neo-Babylonian, Achaemenid, Classical and Hellenistic sources (e.g. Grayson 1975: 106, Nabonidus Chronicle II. 1.4; Hdt., 1.98, 1.153, 3.64; Xen., *Cyr.* VIII. 6.22; see also Balatti 2017: 231–46 and 259; Henkelman 2017: 133, n. 130 with more references), retained its role in this period as one of the capitals of the empire – and Cambyses' favourite one (Tuplin 2011: 48–9). Its strategic location at the crossroads (de Planhol 2003: 605) of the Achaemenid realm was eminent too. It was situated on the so-called Great Khorasan Road that connected Mesopotamia to eastern Iran. Also, the Persian Gulf and Pārsa in the south were linked to the north via a royal road, accounted particularly in the travel-ration documents of the Persepolis Fortification Archive (PFA) (Hallock's Q category, that is) (Hallock 1969; 1978; see also Briant et al. 2008; Henkelman 2008a: 65–179), passing Gabae towards the more northern areas (Kuhrt 2014: 119–20) Hagmatāna (Henkelman 2017: 106, 131, 133, 134; Wiesehöfer 2001: 77, 144; Briant 2002: 189, 358, 737; Kuhrt 2014: 119–20; for the Parthian period, see Hausleiter et al. 2000: 1,315, Maps 93 and 94) and beyond (Plut., *Eum.* 16.1–2). The city was called, in Elamite terms in the Persepolis documents, Mataš and, less often, Agmadana/Akbaddana (Henkelman 2017: 106 and 198). Apart from other literary traditions (Schoff 1914: 29; Henkelman 2017: n. 130), the epigraphic data provided by the Persepolis tablets also reveal that Hagmatāna probably held, alongside a royal palace, a treasury and archive managing administrative matters of the satrapy of Media, which was perhaps similar to, but occupied a lower administrative level than, that of Persepolis (Briant 2002: 84–5; Kuhrt 2014: 114). Likewise, a number of Babylonian documents, from Cyrus' and Cambyses' reigns, are related to commercial transactions of the two influential merchant houses of Egibi, in Babylon, and Murašu, in Nippur, which refer to travels to Agmadanu following the (seasonal?) residence of the Achaemenid court in the city at the time (Briant 2002: 33, 738–40; Tolini 2011: 191–3; Henkelman 2017: 130). Apart from this city, which was the main seat of Media, the satrapy was subdivided into provinces/districts, *dahyāva*, among which Ragā, Nisāya, Kampadana and Asargarta – perhaps along with Razavanta-/Razumetanu/Razaundu (Henkelman 2017: 148) – are especially recorded in the lists of the inscriptions of Darius I and Xerxes.[43] Moreover, two fortresses, *didā*, of Media are noted in the Bisotun inscription: Sikayauvatiš

(DB I § 13 1.48–61) and the fortress of Hagmatāna (DB I § 13, DB II § 32 2.76, 77f.; see also Balatti 2017: 172–73). Ragā (DB III § 32. 2.70–8, § 36. 3.1–9) is widely identified with the Elamite Rakkan, Babylonian Ragā, Hellenistic Rhagae, Sasanian Ray and the contemporary Shahr-e Ray (Kent 1950: 205; Schmitt 2009: 60; Henkelman 2017: 13, n. 129). Located in Kampadana (DB II § 25. 2.27), the modern Bisotun was a religiously important site (Luschey 1968, Boyce 1982: 21–3), as is indicated by its Old Persian name, Bagastāna, place/seat of the god(s). It was, as discussed earlier, the location of a Median fortress which is identified by some scholars as the Sikayauvatiš fortress of the Nisāya district mentioned in the Bisotun inscription (Kleiss 1996b; Alibaigi et al. 2017: 203; cf. Saeedyan 1397 [2018]: 114). Bagastāna may also be considered the primary site for Darius I's accession according to the same inscription (Tuplin 2005), where the Achaemenid *rex triumphans* chose to set up the manifestation of his divine legitimacy and unequivoval power on a main east–west road and, according to a royal Near Eastern topos, with roots going back to the late third millennium BCE (Rollinger 2016). This place, further, held one of the most important royal paradises built along the major roads (Plut., *Art.* 25.1; see also Briant 2002: 739). Nisāya was a fertile plain in the Central Zagros, between Bagastāna and Hagmatāna, with rich pastures which were the nursery of the horse breed of the Nisaean mares, the Achaemenid royal herd renowned for its quality in the ancient Near East and even beyond in the Chinese (Wiesehöfer 2001: 147) and Graeco-Roman Worlds (Strab., XI. 13.7; Hdt., VII.40, IX.20; see also Briant 2002: 420; Balatti 2017: 225). As mentioned, this quality horse breed of the Zagros was one of the reasons for Assyrian raids in the region, but the accounts of the Greek and Latin texts (e.g. Plb., X. 27.1) accord with information recorded in the PFA in terms of the institutional scale on which the large royal herds were kept and reared here in the Achaemenid period (Henkelman 2017: 131). On the basis of the figures given in literary sources (Arr., *Anab.* VII. 13.1; Diod., XVII. 110.6), animal husbandry probably developed in more specialised forms in this era than in earlier times, beyond domestic pastoralism in areas with environmental capabilities for such a mode of economy. That said, this process had already begun in some areas of the Zagros highlands, at least since the late second millennium BCE when the pastoralist and agricultural modes of production were managed under the organisation of the Middle-Elamite state (n. 15). The scale of this involvement is a matter still to be determined, however.

This point leads us to the most important economic activity in the Central Zagros, at least from the Middle Chalcolithic period onwards: pastoralism. The presence of autonomous nomadic groups in the highlands of the Central and Southern Zagros regions is attested for Achaemenid and post-Achaemenid times (Briant 2002: 728–9; Salaris and Basello 2019: 85). The PFA tablets disclose an arrangement between the Persepolis administration and the pastoral groups living in some areas to the north and north-west of the purview of Pārsa (Henkelman 2013: 535; Balatti 2017: 180–9). Hence, we can to some extent examine the socioeconomic structure of these groups and the nature of their interactions with the imperial power. Thanks to these documents, we may learn about the contribution these peoples made to the imperial economy, via the exchange practice of livestock and pastoral products and the breeding of the royal herds within crown lands, *tage* (Wiesehöfer 2001: 266; Briant 2002: 420) or other pastures. Also, some of these peoples can be recognised as marappiyap, perhaps the Maraphians of Herodotus, and dappurap, perhaps the Tapyrians of Arrian (Balatti 2017: 272). The Achaemenid sources of the Persepolis archives and Bisotun inscription may even provide better information about the (state support for the) formation of tribal confederations, such as the Patishorians and Patišvariš, and their integration into the Achaemenid political system (Bahadori 2017). The Classical sources inform us better of the relationship of some of these groups with the central state (Kuhrt 2014: 115–16). They reveal a strategy that could secure the flow of commodities and information, under state supervision and control, via the strategic passages of royal roads passing through the Zagros ridges, for the Achaemenids themselves and their employees in the military and communications, *pirradazish* (Colburn 2013), or for diplomats and merchants, without any interruption being caused or trouble made by the inhabitants of the mountainous valleys and plains of the region, along with the military service of these peoples in the royal armies as required (e.g. Curt. IV. 12.10). In turn, the highlanders could keep their political autonomy, being exempt from paying tribute, and receive gifts and travel fees from the Great Kings who paid visits to them on their migration to Hagmatāna from Susa (Tuplin 1998) and via the Zagros roads. Arrian (III. 17.1–2, 6) records that the pastoralist Uxians of the mountains demanded that Alexander pay for his passage through 'Susian Gates' (Diod., XVII. 68.1) to Persia, according to their prior arrangement with the Persian kings (Strab., XV. 3.4). But these Uxians were only one of the mountainous groups who enjoyed such a prerogative in Achaemenid times (Strab., XV. 3.4; see also Briant 1982b: 57–112; 2002: 728–31). Strabo (XI. 13.6, XVI. 1.18), quoting Nearchus, and Arrian (*Ind.* 40.6–8) refer to the tribal groups of the Mardians next to the Persians, the Uxians (alongside the Elymaeans in the *Geography*) next to the Mardians, and the Cossaeans next to the Medes.[44] Arrian's narrative of the confrontation of the Uxians with Alexander is aligned with another story accounting (Strab., XVII. 111.4–6) for a later episode in the Diadochi period (323–281 BCE) that deals with a similar military campaign that took place in 317 BCE, and through a mountain road in the Zagros which was the alternative to the Susiana–Hagmatāna royal road (Briant 2002: 729). According to this passage, Antigonus I, who was struck by the Pasytigris after his battle against Eumenes, planned to head towards Ecbatana (Plb. X. 27.11) via this road. Ignoring the advice of Pithon, satrap of Media, about paying the Cossaeans of the area in order to use the path safely, he lost a large number of his men (Diod., XIX. 19.2–8; see also Briant 1973; Balatti 2017: 227–8, 288). These Cossaean peoples are probably called kušiyap in the Persepolis administrative documents (Henkelman and Stolper 2009: 287; Balatti 2017: 191–2, ch. 5: n. 204). Their mountains, Cossaea, are recorded in Media, to the south of Ecbatana; they were the neighbours of the Medes (Nearchus apud Strabo, XI. 13.6; Diod., XVII. 111.4), the Uxians (Nearchus apud Arrian, *Anab.* VII. 15.1) and the Susians (Plin., *Nat.* VI. 29.114, VI. 31.134) and served Darius III's army under the satrap of Media at Gaugamela (Curt., IV. 12.10). Therefore, their lands were most probably located in the Pishkooh area.[45] The route mentioned above was a rather more difficult but shorter alternative (Diod., XIX. 19.2) to the Achaemenid Royal Road recorded especially by Herodotus (5.52), yet, as discussed earlier (see n. 9), it had been under use since the Old Elamite period, starting at Urusagrig in southern Mesopotamia, heading north-east to Dêr, and passing thence through the Poshtkooh and Pishkooh areas to finally join the Great Khorasan Road. Possibly on account of the increasing importance of Hagmatāna, or possibly the earlier Median royal city of Sagbita/Bīt-Sagbit, during the first millennium BCE, the linking point of the roads shifted from the late third millennium Kimaš eastwards to there, a role played by the city during Achaemenid times and held for millennia (de Planhol 2003). Therefore, the topographic and environmental characteristics of the intermontane Zagros valleys, rare passageways and traversable roads through some of the ridges, along with the nomadic lifestyle of at least some of their inhabitants, were the main reasons for the Achaemenid kings granting those groups exclusive privileges.

The Elymaeans possibly enjoyed a similar type of arrangement. Although only recorded in Hellenistic sources (Salaris and Basello 2019: 89), we know that they inhabited the highlands to the east of the Susiana plain (Strab., XVI. 1.17; Plin., *Nat*. VI. 31.135) and west of the country of the Paraetaceni (Strab., XI. 13.6, XV. 2.8, XV. 2.14, XV. 3.12 and XVI. 1.18; Plin., VI. 29.116, VI. 31.131), a Minor Satrapy of Media Minor in the Achaemenid era located around modern Iṣfahan.[46] It was through this region that a royal road passed to connect Susiana to Paraetaceni (Strab., XV. 2.8, XVI. 1.8; Arr., *Anab*. III. 19.2) and Gabae (Diod., XIX. 34.7; Curt. V. 13.2; see also Henkelman 2008b: 311),[47] which was the location of a royal palace (Strab., XV. 3.3; Curt., V. 13.2; Plb., XXXI. 9.3), probably a treasury (Strab., XV. 3.3; See also Tuplin 1987: n. 76; Kuhrt 2014: 120; Henkelman 2008b: 305–6), and a station on another royal road between Pārsa to Hagmatāna portrayed in the Persepolis archives (Briant 2002: 358, 737; Henkelman 2008b). Strabo (XVI. 1.17) also located the Elymaeans to the south and south-west of the mountains of the Cossaeans and Media. Therefore, we can say that Elymaea comprised the strategic highlands to the east of the Susiana, the mountainous areas of the north-east of the modern Khuzestan Province and the adjacent province of Chaharmahal va Bakhtiyari to the west of Iṣfahan (Balatti 2017: 239–40, ch. 6: n. 133; see below).

However, regarding the social structure and economy of those societies, Greek and Roman texts present the Uxians (Arr., *Anab*. III. 17)[48] and Elymaeans (Strab., XVI. 1.18) as populations organised in two groups with the distinct identities of pastoralists of the mountains and agriculturalists of the plains, different from each other in all aspects of political, economic and social structures (see also Briant 1982a; Balatti 2017: 209–43; Salaris and Basello 2019). But as is argued by authorities (Tuplin 2010; Henkelman 2011: 8–9; Briant 2002: 729; Salaris and Basello 2019: 85, 92), and as the author of these lines indicates elsewhere (Habibi and Mohammadifar 2020; see Chapter 3, s. 3.6), this imprecise picture does not present the real state of affairs, but is a biased description and interpretation heavily loaded with propaganda and Greek topoi relating to modes of subsistence (Briant 1982a: 14–15) similar to those mentioned concerning an approach in the ill-informed ancient Mesopotamian sources in different periods (Kamp and Yoffee 1980; see above). Notwithstanding the Classical and Hellenistic representation of those peoples, the ethnographic studies on the ethnic groups in the Zagros areas indicated that these societies are political entities that include both farmer and pastoralist segments without socio-economic distinctions based on modes of subsistence (Barth 1953; 1961; Beck 1980; Black-Michaud 1972; Watson 1979; Digard 1981; Amanollahi-Baharvand 1367 [1989]). However, modern scholarship has in some cases perpetuated such a false division/opposition, which we cannot trace either in the partially remaining literature of the inhabitants (Hole 1978: 131) or in the texts of their neighbours, Urarṭian, Elamite and Achaemenid, with whom they had interacted (Balatti 2017: 327, also 36–9, ch. 2: n. 30; Salaris and Basello 2019: 85). Basically, the Zagros environment in different areas favours movement (seasonal pastoral nomadic or transhumant migrations) that would be sustained by the close socioeconomic bonds between the highlander agro-pastoralists and the groups settled in the adjacent lowland areas. Therefore, individuals and families could alter their way of life owing to various causes operating in different conditions, according to the social risk management strategies and social organisation of their group, without leaving tribal confederations or causing any change in their tribal identity that brought them together (Bradburd 1989; Rowton 1974; Cribb 1993: 16–17; see Chapter 1, s. 1.3, esp. n. 16).

The ancient Greek and Latin literature also discloses the development of arboricultural and agricultural activities in some areas of Media during Achaemenid and Hellenistic times.[49] The general support of the Great Kings for agriculture documented by Greek authors (Hdt., 3.117; Xen., *Ec.* 4.5; Plb., X. 28; Plut., *Art.* 25.1–2; Curt., VII. 2.22; Diod., XVII. 110.5, XIX. 21.2–4) is also corroborated by archaeological surveys in Fars, the Khârga Oasis of western Egypt, Babylonia and Bactria (e.g. Sumner 1986; Tuplin 2009: 111, n. 13; Kuhrt 2014: 118–19), the epigraphic data of the Persepolis administrative archive texts (Henkelman 2013: 535; Balatti 2017: 322–3), and palynological examinations in Fars (Djamali et al. 2010) that indicate projects aiming at the development of irrigation agriculture in some territories.

The Central Zagros areas were fully integrated into the political and administrative structures of the Achaemenid Empire. However, overall, this political shift did not basically change the economic and social aspects of life in the Zagros – at least not abruptly. Apart from the above-mentioned evidence concerning developments in agriculture, horticulture and animal husbandry in some areas, as discussed above, the Achaemenids probably adopted the former Median organisations centred at Hagmatāna. Although under the

Achaemenid satrap, provincial administrative subdivisions were handled by locals as before (e.g. Tuplin 2011: 50; Schütze 2017), as long as tributes were paid and the imperial order remained intact. On the other hand, the kings were perhaps inspired by an Assyrian (Balatti 2017: 94–5, 351) or Elamite (n. 15) strategy, and the nomadic groups from across the Pishkooh to the more southern areas in the Bakhtiyari highlands (to the north-east and east of the Susiana alluvial plains) were, with some contracts in terms of the indirect Achaemenid control of the region, basically autonomous in their internal affairs (Balatti 2017: 339, 344). As mentioned earlier, with the conquest of the Persian Empire by the Macedonian king Alexander III (336–323), this privilege was taken from the Zagros highlanders as the Macedonian conqueror subjugated the mountain-dwelling Uxians and Cossaeans (Arr., *Anab*. III. 17.1–2, 6, VII. 15.1–3; Diod., XVII. 111.4–6; Strab., XI. 13.6).[50] However, this new strategy apparently did not last long, since soon, during the Diadochi period and in 317 BCE, the Uxians of the mountains were documented by Diodorus (XIX. 17.2–3, 19.2–8) as being autonomous.[51]

Nonetheless, despite the short interval in the indirect control of the Zagros pastoralists happening as a result of the fall of the Achaemenid state, Alexander tried to revive the integrity of, and order in, his realm. He did so by retaining the Achaemenid institutions and administrative organisation that had been working (Wolski 1966; Wiesehöfer 2001: 105; Briant 1979; 2002: 876; 2009: 83; 2012: 187–8; Tuplin 2009: 109, 115; Olbrycht 2010: 353–9, 367; Jacobs 2011: 3/34; 2017; Strootman 2017: 181; Henkelman et al. 2017: XXXI); reassigning the local elites as the ruling class in different satrapies;[52] planning political intermarriages between himself, the Greek Nearchus and around ninety Macedonian companions with elite Persian women at Susa (Wiesehöfer 2001: 106–7; Briant 2002: 737; Olbrycht 2010: 360, 362; Potts 2016: 349 with more references); and adopting local culture himself and making his satrap Peucestas in Persis do so (Wiesehöfer 2001: 106–7).

After the uprisings that occurred across the empire before or upon Alexander's death, Media Atropatene was turned into the sovereign territory of the newly-established dynasty of Atropates, the former Achaemenid and Alexandrian satrap of Media (Strab., XI. 13.1; see also Wiesehöfer 2001: 107). Media proper, with its centre at Ecbatana, kept its prominence during the Hellenistic period (Briant 2002: 738–40). It had already played a crucial role at the heart of historical events of this era, in the account of the conquest of the Achaemenid territories and the Diadochi rivalries, holding a strategic location in terms of access to the eastern Iranian satrapies and the connection of northern Iran to Pārsa and the Persian Gulf.[53]

In 312 BCE, the Seleucid state was found in Mesopotamia, and soon, 309–308 BCE, Seleucus I Nicator took over Iran, overcoming Antigonos Monophthalmos. Then, Seleucus I gained control of the Asian part of Alexander's empire – except for those areas that remained in the hands of Chandragupta (Wiesehöfer 2001: 108; 2015: 75). Media became the seat of the Upper Satrapies[54] and remained so for over one and one half centuries until 147 BCE when the powerful Arsacid king Mihrdād I/Mithradates I dominated it (Assar 2004–5: 42–3, 53; Strootman 2017: 182–3; Balatti 2017: 238; cf. Debevoise 1938: 21). This event marked a significant point at which the Arsacid state developed into an empire and the Seleucid kingdom became a waning power, with the subsequent surrender of its seat at Babylonia to the same antagonist (141–138 BCE) (Debevoise 1938: 22–3, 42; Strootman 2017: n. 48).

The conquest of the Achaemenid realm brought about changes in the settlement patterns in the Central Zagros. The foundation of Greek and Macedonian colonies and the settlement of those populations in the region were totally new phenomena in the region, that had sociopolitical repercussions (Canepa 2014 with references). There are some remarks in the Graeco-Roman texts about Alexander's *poleis* establishments in the highlands after the forced pacification of the mountain inhabitants (Diod., XVII. 111.6; Arr., *Ind.* 40.8; Plb., X. 27.3), archaeological materials relating to Hellenistic foundations have been unearthed particularly in the areas around the path of the Great Khorasan Road in the Central Zagros. In Nahavand are found traces of the medium-sized excavated *polis* of Laodicea-in-Medi, which was perhaps founded in Antiochus I's reign (Ghirshman 1963: 19; Rahbar 1979; Rahbar et al. 2014; see Strab. XI.13.6). Here, an inscription from the year 193 BCE testifies to the centrally organised dynastic cult of the Seleucids, which was extended to include Laodice, the wife of Antiochus III (Wiesehöfer 2001: 109; Balatti 2017: 238, ch. 6: n. 127 with bibliography). Moreover, the partly man-made chambers of the Karaftō Caves in Divandarreh County, 20km west of Takab in northern Kurdistan Province, were used, if not cut, in the fourth or third century BCE according to an *in situ* Greek inscription dedicated to Herakles.[55] Another Greek inscription found in Media is at Bisotun, and similarly it asks for Herakles' protection and may clarify cultural interactions in this period (Canepa 2014: 19). In Bisotun, and at the gate of the walled enclosure of the so-called Parthian slope, Seleucus

Nicator, a Seleucid governor of the area, commanded the Herakles Kallinikos relief to be raised, accompanied by the Greek inscription which implies the dedication of this monument to Cleomenes, the last Seleucid viceroy of the Upper Satrapies, in 148 BCE, the last days of Seleucid rule in Media (Luschey 1996; Wiesehöfer 2001: 126; Strootman 2017: 184–5; Invernizzi 2020). Roughly a generation later, a similar project using the built environment of this prestigious site was carried out, this time by the Arsacid King of Kings Mihrdād II/Mithradates II (c. 124/23–88/87 BCE), who placed a relief near that of Darius and was followed later by other Parthians, perhaps King Vologeses and the local ruler Gotarzes, having two other rock reliefs carved at the sacred place.[56]

Furthermore, the Dinavar plain, in Sahneh County of Kermanshah Province, is likely the fertile Nisāya plain of Achaemenid and Hellenistic sources, given its geographical features as a fertile pastureland and its location between Bisotun and Hamedan (see above). Located in the heartland of Media, Dinavar was an important population centre in Sasanian–early Islamic times, being perhaps founded in the Seleucid period (Bosworth 1995: 416; Luschey 1996). Literary sources are informative in terms of relevant evidence from other areas of the Central Zagros (Balatti 2017: 263, ch. 7: n. 81 with references). The Hagmatāna palace decorations were partly stripped off during Alexander's conquest, and apparently the rest during the High Hellenistic age (Plb., X. 27.11; Diod., XVII. 80). However, the city was an important capital and mint in the Seleucid (Strootman 2017: 192) and Arsacid (Schoff 1914: 29; Wiesehöfer 2001: 128; Potts 2016: 377; de Planhol 2003: 605–6) periods. Built by Artaxerxes II, its temple of Anāhitā survived in the following eras, accounted in the Hellenistic sources as a temple devoted to Anaitis or Median Artemis (Strab., XI. 13.5; Plut., *Art.* 27.40; Plin., *Nat.* VI. 17; Isid. Char., § 6; see also Briant 2002: 738). A notable passage in Isidorus of Charax's *Stathmœ Parthicœ* states that Concobar, modern Kangavar adjacent to Dinavar, held an Artemis temple (§ 6; see also Vanden Berghe 1977: 182–4; 1984: 216).

In the southern areas of the Central Zagros, the pastoralist peoples appear in some episodes of Seleucid history. The Elymaeans appear in sources particularly during the latter part of Seleucid rule, which featured the challenges of confrontation with the two fresh and expansionist powers of the Romans and the Arsacids, and the subsequent financial crisis of the state. As discussed above, the Elymaeans were a group inhabiting the intermontane plains and valleys of the north-east of modern Khuzestan and the province of Chaharmahal va Bakhtiyari. The ethnonym Elymaea/Elymais is a Greek rendering of the ancient name of Elam, which was still in use in the Akkadian sources, as some scholars have clarified (Potts 2016: 370, 375, Table 10.2; Salaris 2017; Salaris and Basello 2019: 106). At Magnesia, the Elymaeans fought for Antiochus III in 190 BCE, alongside Cyrtian slingers (Liv., XXXVII. 40.1–14; see also Vanden Berghe and Schippmann 1386 [2007]: 20; Potts 2016: 368; Strootman 2017: n. 24; Balatti 2017: 235). However, the defeat, and the heavy tribute subsequently imposed by the Romans, probably drew the Seleucid king's attention to the treasures of a temple of Bel in Elymais (Vanden Berghe and Schippmann 1386 [2007]: 20; Potts 2016: 376 with bibliography). But the results of this campaign were disastrous for Antiochus as he was killed in 187 BCE in the course of the battle that was heated by the vigorous resistance of the Elymaeans (Strab., XVI. 1.18; see also Balatti 2017: 241, ch. 6: n. 139). Antiochus IV also risked a similar mission, invading Elymaea and its Artemis temple for despoil in 164 BCE – another failure for the Seleucid side, which paid the price with the king's life, apparently from a subsequent illness in Paraetaceni and at Tabae/Gabae (Plb., XXXI. 9; see also Wiesehöfer 2002; Potts 2016: 377–8; Balatti 2017: 243, ch. 6: n. 145 with further references). The Elymaeans perhaps founded their kingdom around this time (Stiehl 1959: 275; Tarn 1951: 466; Will 1967: 202; Sellwood 1983: 307) given some references in the Babylonian *Astronomical Diaries* to the plundering of Mesopotamia by Kammaškiri, that is Kamnaskires I, between 146 and 141 BCE (Shayegan 2011: 77, 98; Potts 2016: 348, Table 10.2; Balatti 2017: 246, ch. 6: n. 161 with references) and Strabo's passages (XI. 13.6, XVI. 1.18) about the alliance of the Cossaeans with those Elymaeans who were in conflict with the Susians and the Babylonians, although at an unspecified date. At some point, the Elymaean realm expanded to the alluvial plains of Khuzestan (Le Rider 1965: 352; Morkholm 1965: 127–8; Vanden Berghe and Schippmann 1386 [2007]: 26–36)[57] and, with its access to some strategic roads discussed earlier, the economy of the state was based on its control over international trade – similar to that of the adjacent Characene/Mesene (Wenke 1981: 306; Alizadeh 1985: 184; Vanden Berghe and Schippmann 1386 [2007]: 116; Salaris and Basello 2019: 81).

Archaeological excavations in the Bakhtiyari mountains to the north of Khuzestan at the modern Masjed-Soleiman and Bard-e Neshandeh (Ghirshman 1976 and 1978) and Kal-e Chendar in the Shami valley (Stein 1940: 141–59; Kawami 1987; Mathiesen 1992: 165–8; Messina and Mehr Kian 2014a; 2014b; Mehr Kian and Messina 2019) has unearthed complex structures on terraces, identified as sanctuaries[58] according to their monumental measures, architectural decorations and features such as altars or altar platforms, and anthropomorphic reliefs and inscriptions, and their environs – a cemetery in the case of Kal-e Chendar (Mehr Kian and Messina 2019). In the absence of absolute dating techniques, these buildings are related to Seleucid and Arsacid times (Vanden Berghe and Schippmann 1386 [2017]: 16, 22–3, 25; Sherwin-White 1984; Mehr Kian and Messina 2014a; 2014b; 2019; cf. Ghirshman 1978: 77, 89) according to epigraphic, iconographic and architectural features, and the stratigraphy of the sites. Notwithstanding the relative dating, the sanctuaries of Bard-e Neshandeh and Masjed-Soleiman in the mountainous Khuzestan are still the best candidates for the location of the Elymaean temples referred to in the Hellenistic sources.[59] This hypothesis may stand due to the inaccurate dating of the related sites and pending further discoveries in the region. Other archaeological data relating to the Elymaean dynasty include the subterranean tombs around Shushtar excavated at Golālak (Rahbar 1376 [1998]) and Dastuvā (Sarfaraz 1348 [1970]), as well as another one at Sāleh Dāvood on the west bank of the Karkheh River and 25km south-west of Dezful (Rahbar 1391 [2012]; see also Mousavi 2020). The excavators identified these tombs as the Elymaean royal tombs, which is a likely assumption in light of the location of the sites in Susiana and the numismatic and sigillographic evidence that was discovered, along with the decorative architectural features and the motifs designing the coffins representing Arsacid-period art with Hellenistic influences. Although the expanse of the territories under Elymaean control, which changed over the course of their rule (162/161 BCE–224 CE), is still a subject of debate, the Susiana plain, according to the numismatic data, was under Elymaean rule for a time, particularly from the mid-first century CE onwards until the advent of the Sasanians (Kahrstedt 1950: 39–40; Vanden Berghe and Schippmann 1386 [2007]: 9; Wenke 1981: 306).

Elymaean rock reliefs make up another category of evidence carved in the mountains to the north-east/east of the Khuzestan lowlands according to ancient Iranian royal traditions.[60] These monumental remains are particularly informative in terms of the history of the dynasty and the nature of its political relationship with the Seleucid or Arsacid kings,[61] the expansion of its realm in different periods, the political and social structures of the state, and the artistic and religious traditions of the groups settling these highlands. Nonetheless, apart from the limited epigraphic data some of these remains provide (see Henning 1952; Bivar and Shaked 1964), the stylistic and technical aspects of the iconography of these reliefs have been the main focus in their examination. Several different interpretations of the depicted scenes and various identifications of their figures have been presented,[62] and as a result the proposed dates vary in most of the cases (see Vanden Berghe and Schippmann 1386 [2007]). However, these rock reliefs generally cover an era between the latter half of the second century BCE and the first quarter of the second century CE.

2.4 INTEGRATION INTO THE SASANIAN EMPIRE

By the time of the establishment of the Sasanian Empire in 224 CE, semi-autonomous states such as Elymaea stood no chance of ruling. Ardašīr-i Pābagān and his successors organised a hierarchically centralised political structure in which the territories were governed according to well-defined imperial administrative organisation and were therefore under the direct control of the central Sasanian state.[63]

In terms of administrative and political geography, the Sasanian era may be divided into two main sub-periods: early Sasanian (from the foundation of the state in 224 CE up until the second enthronement of Kawād I in 499 CE) and late Sasanian (from the sixth to the first half of the seventh century).[64] However, this does not connote a revolutionary change in all aspects of these structures. Despite the dearth of data, some stable features through the whole era are still reported.[65] That said, the administrative reforms initiated by Kawād I and continued by his son and successor, Husraw I (531–579) (e.g. Gyselen 2001a; 2001c; 2019: 4, 333–4), established a new era in terms of the territorial divisions and administrative organisations of the state.

The main sources available for the earlier phase, which basically reflects the situation in the late Arsacid era (Wiesehöfer 2020a: 482), are epigraphic data from the third and fourth centuries derived from the monumental inscriptions of Šābuhr I (ŠKZ, see Huyse 1999) and Kirdīr (KKZ, see Gignoux 1971; 1991; MacKenzie 1989) on the Ka'be-ye Zardošt (lit., Ka'ba of Zoroaster) at Naqsh-e Rostam and that of Narseh in Paikuli (NPi, see Herzfeld 1924; Skjærvø 1983; 2006; Cereti and Terribili 2014), along with some official seals and seal impressions, while for the later part of the period the key sources for such studies are archives of different sorts of seals (or seal impressions on bullae) from judicial-religious and civil administrations that appeared in the sixth century (Gyselen 2019: 4, 8). Several of these territorial institutions from Sasanian times can be traced back to the Achaemenid and Arsacid periods. Yet other organisations were founded and territories created *ex nihilo* in the Sasanian era, especially during the process of the sixth-century territorial rearrangements (Gyselen 2019: 251).

Following the terminology of the hierarchal, territorial division identified and documented according to administrative seals by Gyselen (1989; 2019), I present here a brief state-of-the-art historical geography of the Central Zagros and the arrangement of its areas at the four levels[66] of *kust* (grande région), region, province and canton. As wide and diverse as the area under examination, its different sectors were divided into distinct administrative divisions.

Māh, m'd/m'dy, is attested as a region either by the early Sasanian epigraphic sources, for example ŠKZ (§ 2–3), or later numismatic evidence (Gyselen 2019: 141–2). This toponym is also documented by the late sigillographic data, but only as part of the provincial names of Māh-kust-ī-Nēmāwand and Māh-kust-ī-Wastān, which were located in the region of Māh but whose administrative precinct may be determined only relatively given the uncertainties regarding the location of the most of their cantons (Gyselen 2019: 145). Attested by the administrative seals of the sixth–first half of the seventh century, ten cantons of Māh-kust-ī-Nēmāwand have so far been identified, only two of which can be confidently located: Šābuhr-xwāst near the current Khorram-abad in Lorestan (Le Strange 1905: 201; Schwarz 1969: 922) and Nēmāwand, the modern Nahavand, which held the status of *šahrestān*, provincial capital (Gyselen 1989: 53–4; 2019: 144, 459). Yet apart from these, Kangāvar, Harsīn, Alištar, Borğūerd, Karağ and Nīmvar were probably other cantons of this province (Gyselen 2019: 144). Moreover, Rāmīn, a small late Sasanian town mentioned in Islamic sources (Gyselen 2019: 155), was located close to Nēmāwand (Daryaee 2002: 57: Modi has suggested its possible identification with War ī wahrāmāwand of the *Šahrestānīhā-ī Ērānšahr*). Māh-kust-ī-Wastān, probably centred on Wastān (Old Pers. Bagastāna), around the present-day Dinavar, was another Māh province, an *ōstān* whose *ōstāndār* administration is attested (Gyselen 2019: 138). Although their Middle Persian names are not yet known, Dinavar, Kermanshah[67] and Mahidasht in the modern Kermanshah Province certainly belonged to Māh-kust-ī-Wastān (Gyselen 1989: 54; 2019: 145).

However, as Gyselen (2019: 141) argued, the territory of the third-century Māh extended well beyond these two provinces. In the same area, to the north and west of Māh-kust-ī-Wastān, were located the two neighbouring provinces of Walaxšfarr and Ērān-āsān-kar-Kawād.

Chaumont (1974) indicated that historical sources often associated Walaxšfarr with Hulwān (see also Ferdowsi, 8.492; Jullien, F. 2004: 175; Gyselen 2019: 225). The *ōstāndār* administration of Ērān-āsān-kar-Kawād is attested, and is also most probably to be identified with the area around Hulwān.[68] Moreover, Māsabādān was another *ōstān* of Māh whose locality was to the south of Māh-kust-ī-Wastān and west of Māh-kust-ī-Nēmāwand according to the administrative seals (Gyselen 1989: 54; 2019: 154; see also Plin., *Nat.* VI. 31.134–5). Its *šahrestān* is more accurately located around the modern Shīrvān in Ilam Province (Le Strange 1905: 202; Kettenhofen 1993), to the west (according to Gyselen 2019: 154) of the Seymareh River.

As mentioned above (n. 64), Hamadān is among the few regions whose *šahrab* administration is attested for both early and late Sasanian times. As is brilliantly discussed by Gyselen (2019: 97–102; see also Gyselen 1989: 50–1; 2001b; 2011), Hamadān *šahr* was in the early stages of the Sasanian period adjacent to the region of Abhar, but around the middle of the sixth century they were perhaps united as two provinces of the region of Hamadān and renamed Hamadān-kust-ī-šahrestān and Hamadān-kust-ī-Abhar respectively.[69] Of the cantons of Hamadān-kust-ī-šahrestān attested by the available administrative seals, so far only Hamadān-frāx-kar, as the province's *šahrestān*, can be identified with the modern city of Hamadan (Gyselen 2019: 102). Notably, Lake Zarrōmand, Av. Zarənumant, mentioned in the *Greater Bundahišn*, XII. 2 and 10 (Cereti 2007: 56, 63) and attested by administrative sigillography (Gyselen 1989: 50–2), was also located in the Hamadan region.

The inclusion of the more southern areas of the Central Zagros in the adjacent regions of Spahān and Hūzestān is possible. The Synods (Chabot 1902) accounted the Māh dioceses of Masabadan/Māsabādān, Balasphar/Walaxšfarr, Hamadan/Hamadān and Nēhāvand/Nēmāwand, the latter two of which perhaps also included Abhar and Wastān respectively (Kettenhofen 1993; Gyselen 2019: 142).[70] Nonetheless, these texts recorded the bishopric of Beit Mihraqāyē, Mihragān-kadag, in the ecclesiastical province of Bēth-Huzāyē (Gyselen 2019: 114). As is also the case with Spahān, one may nonetheless consider that the Synods do not inevitably reflect the official administrative geography of the Sasanian Empire. That said, the southern neighbour of Māsabādān, Mihragān-kadag, probably also with provincial status, is among the cases whose attribution to either of the regions of Māh and Hūzestān is yet to be revealed (Gyselen 1989: 55; 2019: 159–60). In the Islamic historiography, the centre of Mihrajānqadhaq is Seymarah (Le Strange 1905: 202;

Yuosofvand and Karamzadeh 1399 [2020]: 154–6). Given the information from these sources and the parallel rich archaeological evidence studied in the course of the salvage archaeological pro-jects conducted over the past decade, the most probable candidate for the location of this provincial centre is the Pishkooh area, the border area of Lorestan and Ilam Provinces in the Seymareh valley.[71] Mihragān-kadag was the home town of Hormazdān, known as Hormizdān in the Syrian *Chronicle of Khuzestan/Guidi* (Nöldeke 1893: § 32, n. 4; Rezakhani and Bavandpour 1395 [2016]: § 15; Jullien, F. 2009), who was the brother-in-law of Husraw II and the maternal uncle of Šērōye (Dinavari 1960: 129) and, according to Ṭabari (1375 [1996]: V. 1,883–90 and V. 1,895–903; see also Shapur Shahbazi 2004; Morony 2012: 209–10), one of the noble generals of the Sasanian army (= Ērān-spāhbed?) who fought against the Arab Muslims in Mesopotamia and Hūzestān. Although Mihragān-kadag is mentioned alongside the Hūzestān on an *āmārgar* seal and this may imply that the latter did not include this province in the late Sasanian period, the available data are still far from sufficient to assure one that it was incorporated into Māh (Gyselen 2019: 159–60).

To the other edge of the southern areas of the Central Zagros high-lands in Chaharmahal va Bakhtiyari Province, recent excavations at Tappe[h] Bardnakōn have brought about the identification of a sig-nificant late Sasanian site (Khosrowzadeh et al. 2020a). Given the administrative bullae archive including seal impressions from various administrations of different provinces in the regions of Hūzestān, Pārs and Spahān, Tappe[h] Bardnakōn locates an inter-regional administra-tive centre of that period with long-distance political and economic interactions. Also, the sigillographic data derived from the large corpus of 559 clay sealings studied by Rika Gyselen (Khosrowzadeh et al. 2020b; 2020c) indicated that this settlement was then located in the canton of Rāwar-kust-ī-rōdbār, which was part of the province of Gay, ancient Gabae, in the region of Spahān. This specifies that the Sasanian region of Spahān, in the west, included the whole lower Zāyandeh-rōd basin in the Chaharmahal area to the middle of the present-day province of Chaharmahal va Bakhtiyari.[72] Wherever the region of Pahlaw is cited, in either the early royal Sasanian inscriptions of ŠKZ (§§ 2 and 30) and NPi (§§ 5, 10, 16, 32, 74 and 86) or the Islamic literary sources (see Ghodrat Dizaji 2016: 44), Spahān, with its *šahrestān* at Gay (*Šahrestānīhā-ī Ērānšahr* § 53; see also Gyselen 2019: 200), was in all cases part of it. However, it is notable that Pahlaw is not accounted in KKZ (Gignoux 1971; 1991; MacKenzie 1989) and instead, Spahān is recorded as a distinct region, a status which it retained through the sixth-century reforms (Gyselen 2019: 168 and 199). Moreover, the extent of Pahlaw in the later phases was different from in the late Arsacid and early Sasanian periods (Ghodrat Dizaji 2016 and Tafażżolī 1999: 158). That said, given the present state of knowledge, it remains open to question whether, in the early Sasanian period, the region of Pahlaw included the canton of Rāwar-kust-ī-rōdbār to the west of Gay or whether this area belonged to Māh.

Also, the highlands of the Central Zagros belonged to two distinct *kust*, Kust-ī-xwarbārān and Kust-ī-nēmrōz. The quadripartition of Ērānšahr,[73] and consequently of the *Ērān-spāhbed* administration, happened in the sixth century in the territories named after the four cardinal points – except for the north, for which the term 'Ādurbādagān' replaced Abāxtar, north, out of ideological considerations (Gyselen 2019: 8, 127, 334; Rezakhani 2021: 242–3). Along with sigillographic materials, the key data concerning the four *kust* and their extent may be acquired from the roughly contemporary literary sources of the *Šahrestānīhā-ī Ērānšahr* (Daryaee 2002; see also Markwart 1931; Hedāyat 1321 [1941]a; 1321 [1941]b; Cereti 2020) and the *Ašxarhac'oyc'*, the seventh-century *Armenian Geography* of Ananias of Širak or pseudo-Movsēs Xorenac'I, whose information about Ērānšahr was particularly derived from source(s) in Middle Persian (Širakac'i 2003; see also Hewsen 1992; Markwart 1901; Greenwood 2011; 2018). However, these documents bear different opinions regarding territorial divisions, and hence they place some of the same areas of the Central Zagros in different *kust*.

While both the *Šahrestānīhā-ī Ērānšahr* and the *Ašxarhac'oyc'* attributed Spahān and Gay to the Kust-ī-nēmrōz and located Ray in the Kust-ī-Ādurbādagān, Hamadān, whose location was to the northwest of Spahān and west of Ray, was erroneously considered part of the East Side, Kust-ī-xwarāsān, by the Armenian document (Gyselen 2019: 134–5, 138). However, the *Šahrestānīhā-ī Ērānšahr* (§ 26) located Hamadān in the west, Kust-ī-xwarwarān/Kust-ī-xwar<ō>frān. Furthermore, given the facts regarding the administrative ties between the region of Hūzestān and Mihragān-kadag provided by the sigillographic sources of the sixth–first half of the seventh century, Gyselen considers Mihragān-kadag under the Kust-ī-nēmrōz, Side of the South, even though Anania Širakac'i placed Mihragān-kadag in the Kust-ī-xwarwarān, Side of the West (Gyselen 2019: 130–3 and 138). Also worthy of mention is that, on the basis of the fact that the canton of Rāwar-kust-ī-rōdbār was part of the region of Spahān, the Kust-ī-nēmrōz at least included, in the west, the eastern part of the modern province of Chaharmahal va Bakhtiyari in the Zagros highlands.

2.5 CONCLUSION

In this chapter, along with the brief review of the historical geography and long-term sociopolitical processes as far as the available sets of evidence allow, we may here stress some key factors particularly influential in the formation of cultures and development processes experienced across the areas of the Central Zagros. The microenvironments of this vast region provided rather different natural conditions for the attraction/construction of various ethnic groups with their distinct social organisations, ways of life and economies. Therefore, it is crucial to consider that the term 'Central Zagros' is an overarching geographical designation for a vast mountainous area made up of several zones with different environmental conditions.

As regards the prehistoric Late Bronze and Iron Ages or the historical era, the political disintegration – particularly for the times before the first millennium BCE[74] – and ethnic diversity of the region are discussed according to cultural materials and literary sources of different sorts. Nonetheless, the ethnolinguistic entities may scarcely be identified merely on the basis of archaeological materials. This quick examination of the available data concerning the historical geography of the Central Zagros during the third–first millennia BCE pictures the diverse demographic (and multi-ethnic?) structure of the region during the Bronze and Iron Ages. Local perspectives are under-represented in the studies conducted on the basis of literary sources, as these documents mainly represent a Mesopotamian or Graeco-Roman perspective. The associated states propagating or supporting these perspectives were, most of the time, in political and/or economic rivalry with those in the highlands. Even if not biased, in many cases these texts present an inaccurate image, for instance about ethnonyms such as 'Elamites', 'Gutians', 'Lullubians' and 'Šimaškians', invented by the traditions articulating particular historical accounts and calling several distinct peoples by a single name. Archaeological projects designed to address the issue of the identification of the location and extent of the political entities mentioned above are still mainly lacking. As stated, these different territories may barely be traced archaeologically. However, the intermontane plains and valleys across the region hold numbers of important, yet unexcavated sites that are identified in the course of reconnaissance surveys and whose size and surface material are promising.[75] Future excavations at such sites may lead to the discovery of epigraphic material of different sorts, potentially shedding light on the administrative and political structure of central western

Iran from the turn of the third millennium BCE up until the coming to power of the Achaemenids.[76]

The diversity of economic foundations and subsistence modes involves another main cultural aspect of the region in different eras, that is, the significant role of pastoralism, either transhumant or nomadic. The presence of nomadism in different areas and regular (seasonal?) movements and migrations to the adjacent lowlands led to the long-standing socioeconomic interactions and, subsequently, intertwined bonds between the populations of these regions.[77] This historical process has implications for the notion of the Central Zagros as a region closely linked to its adjacent areas in different aspects and not an isolated mountainous area. Therefore, instead of limiting the dimorphic social structures to 'the border areas', which are hard to define concretely, and perpetuating the topos of ancient literatures regarding the 'contentious relations within the cultural dualism between the highlands (the Iranian Plateau) and the lowlands (Susiana)' (Salaris and Basello 2019: 91–2, 97–8), perhaps it is more proper to consider the common sociocultural traits on a larger geographical scale in both the highlands and lowlands as geographically distinct settings yet closely connected due to the discussed cultural features and environmental and topographic conditions (see Chapter 1, s. 1.3 and Chapter 4). The pastoralist peoples of the highlands, however, were capable of overthrowing the powerful Mesopotamian states, and were influential enough to guarantee their independence and be exempt from paying tribute during the time of the Achaemenid Great Kings. Furthermore, we may be able to distinguish the patterns of political behaviours and contextualise domestic politics in their long-term historical and cultural milieu of formation process. Incorporation of the Zagros nomads into the Sasanian royal armies, accounted in some Middle Persian and Arabic books of early Islamic times (see Chapter 3, s. 3.6 and n. 26), probably happened according to an ancient tradition which can be traced back at least to the Achaemenid period, when these groups were to some extent integrated into the royal economy and provided military service for the Achaemenids based on particular arrangements between the two parties.

This point brings us to two other key factors of Central Zagros geography and topography: the mountainous environment, and strategic location. The obstacles to free movement in this region are of several varieties, among which are arduous mountains, bottlenecks and narrow valleys, harsh climatic conditions, dangerous animals, limited resources for people and their flocks and equids, bandits and brigands, canals and wide and fast-flowing rivers, and a limited number of safe crossing points. As discussed, the Central Zagros holds few roads with proper conditions such as can be regularly used for communication between Mesopotamia and the Iranian Plateau and beyond. Of these ancient roads, some, as mentioned earlier, may be reconstructed from the plethora of historical evidence, literary, archaeological and ethnographic. One of these is the Bronze Age road leading from southern Mesopotamia at Urusagrig and Dêr to the Central Iranian Plateau through the Central Zagros (see Chapter 2, ss. 2.2, 2.3). The Pārsa-Hagmatāna royal road via Gabae is another important ancient road running through the region which is recorded in the travel-ration documents of the PFA (see Chapter 2, s. 2.3). Two other routes, cited in the documents of the Hellenistic and Arsacid periods, along with medieval sources, connected the Susiana and Ramhormoz Plains to the Işfahan area and northern Fars via the Bakhtiyari and Chaharmahal areas (see Chapter 2, n. 47; Chapter 4, ss. 4.5, 4.5.1). The dearth of proper paths, and the topographic features of this region, provided the groups inhabiting its intermontane valleys and plains with the potential for controlling its inter-regional roads, and the opportunity for taking advantage of the strategic location of the highlands. These populations could noticeably impact the flow of information and the passage of caravans and armies, and this was among the main reasons for their appearance in the Babylonian and Graeco-Roman texts in different historical episodes from the third millennium BCE to the Diadochi and Hellenistic eras. The key role these roads played is also noticeable from the close proximity to them of some major settlements of different periods. The most important contemporary cities of the region are also among those that owe their formation partly to their location at the crossroads of such networks.

This study may also help us to understand the built environment of the region and the religious and royal importance that some sites held among local populations for millennia. Bisotun was one of the heritage sites whose landscape was used in royal and religious projects by different dynasties in the period from the first millennium BCE to the first millennium CE. Bagastāna was the main site of Darius I's propaganda. He had his statement at this site on the Great Khorasan Road carved in Elamite and Babylonian, along with Old Persian, not only to impress the locals but also to convey a particular historical account internationally, according to an age-old topos in ancient Near Eastern royal ideologies. This 'wide perspective' may prove handy in terms of the historical reconstruction and interpretation of some historical events and important decisions made by political actors and leaders during Late Antiquity. Acting like Ardašīr II (379–383 CE) had done, and naming it Māh-kust-ī-Wastān, the late Sasanians chose the same area of Bisotun during a time of transition, ambitious polities and turmoil (see e.g. Wiesehöfer 2009; 2010) for their investiture rock reliefs and magnificent ayvāns, rather than Fars, which held their predecessors' monumental buildings and state-supported art works.[78] This shift is parallel with the changes that occurred in Sasanian political ideology. The big picture, therefore, may help us to understand the political transformations and economic developments that happened in the region during this period.

NOTES

1. On the historical geography of the Central Zagros in the third and second millennia, see Hallo 1957–71; 2005; Henrickson 1984; Schacht 1987; Steinkeller 1988; 2007; Eidem 1990; 1993; Potts 1994; Frayne 1997; 1999; 2008; 2011; Schrakamp 2012, among others. And regarding the Neo-Assyrian Zagros, for example, see Schrader 1878; Streck 1898; 1899; 1900; Billerbeck 1898; Forrer 1920; Speiser 1928; Herzfeld 1968; Levine 1972; 1973; 1974; Reade 1978; 1995; Brown 1986; Zimansky 1990; Reade 1995; Lanfranchi 1995; Brown 1979; Medvedskaya 1999; 2000; 2002; Zadok 2000; 2002a; 2002b; Radner 2003; Fuchs 2004; Maniori 2008; 2010; 2014; Alibaigi et al. 2012; 2016; Alibaigi and MacGinnis 2018; Balatti 2017: 51–118; Saeedyan 2018.

2. This geographical term remained in use in Babylonia up until the Hellenistic period. For its usage in the Babylonian documents of the time of Cyrus II onwards, see Balatti 2017: 160–3.

3. See also Eidem 1992: 51; Balatti 2017: 7, 10, ch. 1: n. 36 with more references; and for an earlier attestation in a Lagaš document dating to the time of the Gudea dynasty, see RTC 249: col. iv, line 8; cf. Steinkeller 2018: 299–301.

4. For example, Levine 1972: line 32; see also Klengel 1965: 365; Wäfler 1975: 267; Zadok 2005b; Ahmed 2012: 77. Radner prefers Mazamua: Altaweel et al. 2012: 12; Radner 2017: 211; Radner et al. 2020a: n. 7; cf. Medvedskaya 2000; Yamada 2020. See also below.

5. The rock relief of Darband-i Gawr in the region, in the Qara Dagh range roughly 35km south of Solaymaniyah (Strommenger 1963), relates to the Ur III period (Boese 1973: 15–25; Postgate and Roaf 1997: 152; Eppihimer 2009: 259–62).

6. For different forms of this toponym in a time span from the Early Dynastic to the Neo-Assyrian periods, see Ahmed 2012: 230–1.

7. Aɴnubanini, King of Lullubum, is mentioned in the Haladiny inscription of the king Iddi(n)-Sîn (col. i, lines 51–2). This shows that the two

kings were probably contemporaries and in rivalry over controlling the Zagros Gates (Ahmed 2012: 255, 258, 264–5; cf. Walker 1985: 186, 189–90. See also the next note).

8. The gorge Pāy-e Tāq, c. 3km above Sarpol-e Zohāb, is one of the rather rare easy paths through the Zagros ranges, called hence the Zagros Gates, *Zagri Pylæ* (Ζάγρου πύλαι; cf. Strabo, *Geog.* XI. 13.8; see also Herzfeld 1968: 11; Levine 1974: 3–4; Steinkeller 2013a: 310, n. 108; Kessler 1998: 92; Potts 2020: 56: for its later different names). The pass was a pivotal part of an inter-regional road that connected central Mesopotamia with the Iranian Central Plateau and beyond. This significant road was used through the ages, probably from Early Dynastic times onwards (Rawlinson 1839: 34; Radner 2003: 42; Dandamaev and Medvedskaya 2006; Gentili 2012: 165–6; Steinkeller 2013a: 304–12; 2018: 191–5, Fig. 2; Balatti 2017: 66–7). The route was called the Great Khorasan Road in medieval times (Le Strange 1905: 9), as being the Near Eastern section of the inter-continental road renowned as the Silk Road (Roaf 1995: 56–7, Fig. 22).

9. This road was part of the later Royal Road, the Achaemenid imperial network connecting Susiana and Sardis (Hdt., *Histories* 5.52). But by then this route had been in use for a long time, as it is attested in the Early Dynastic sources discovered at Abū Ṣalābīḫ and Ebla (Frayne 1992: 58–60; see also Gentili 2012: 165–6, n. 6; Potts 2016: 81, 244).

10. Seidl (Shaffer et al. 2003: 35–6, 39), tentatively and from a philological point of view, assigned the former to the end of the Ur III period, more probably to the early phase of the Old Babylonian period. This time span accords with the date proposed for other Simmurian inscriptions of Bētwate (Al-Fouadi 1978; Collon 1990; Frayne 1990: 708–16; 1992: 635; 1997; Shaffer et al. 2003: n. 125: for a brief review of different opinions in this regard; for Iddi(n)-Sîn's inscriptions, see Ahmed 2012: 250–85; cf. Frayne 1990: 708, 712–13).

11. Edzard et al. 1977: 4–5. Cf. Lambert 1972: 74, who has recommended the site of Deh-Now on the Susiana plain. See also Schacht 1987: 175.

12. Such a situation is examined for this area in the Sasanian period (see Chapter 3).

13. The other branch of this route, taking a general northward direction, joined the Great Khorasan Road in the Central Zagros. This route, from Dêr (modern Badrah), possibly headed for Harši (modern Ilam County), Kimaš (modern Islamabad-e Gharb, formerly Shahabad-e Gharb), from where it continued along the long-range Khorasan Highway to Hurti (modern Kermanshah; for the identification of the three latter toponyms of post-Sargonic and Ur III documents and also the trajectory of this road, see Steinkeller 1988; 2013a: 304–12, Fig. 2; cf. Lafont 1996: 87–93; Frayne 1999: 159–61; Steinkeller 2018: 191, which situated both Kimaš and Hurti on the Hamadan plain) and Šimaškian lands (see below) towards the Central Iranian Plateau.

14. Steinkeller 2013a: 302–3; 2018: 195; Ahmed 2012: 61–2. For references to him in Susa and Ur III sources, see De Graef 2015: 294–6; Sallaberger and Schrakamp 2015: 25; Steinkeller 2014b: 287.

15. The discovery of materials from the late Middle-Elamite period on the eastern and north-eastern peripheries of the Susiana plain towards the Central Zagros highlands and the Central Iranian Plateau, at Kul-e Farah and Shkaft-e Salmān in the Izeh valley, that is ancient Ayapir (Vallat 1993: 26–7), Qal'e-geli/Tall-e Afghān in Lordegan and Sūleqān near Shahrekord and on the road to Izeh, parallels the data reported from Susiana to Anšan and the northern shores of the Persian Gulf, which may indicate new construction projects in this era (Stolper 1984: 41; Potts 2010; 2016: 244; Henkelman 2011: n. 24). This explanation may accord with the idea of Šutrukid imperial expansionism (Potts 2005: 9–10; Petrie 2005; Álvarez-Mon 2013: 221, n. 50), but at the same time it may be considered an *argumentum ex silentio* justified by an adverse inference drawn from the dearth of systematic field projects, particularly in the Bakhtiyari highlands and the intermontane plains of the Chaharmahal area to the east of Susiana. It is worth mentioning that, recently, a late Middle-Elamite administrative archive, including around forty inscribed clay tablets, was discovered in the Kohgiluye area to the south of the Bakhtiyari highlands. Apparently, preliminary studies of this corpus have already provided, *inter alia*, interesting information concerning Middle-Elamite state organisation and control of pasturelands and farms and the engagement of the kingdom in the management of both pastoralism and agriculture in its highland territories (Sallaberger and Henkelman 2022; see also Atayi 1397 [2018] for the accidental discovery of the administrative archive from Tappe[h] Goštāspi and the total destruction of the site).

16. The 160 extant *narû* steles that document royal land grants across the territories under Kassite rule are quite informative in this regard (Slanski 2000: 98; see also Potts 2017: 346–7).

17. However, the anthroponomical data derived from the Choghā Gavāneh archive do not present any Kassite features (Abdi and Beckman 2007; Gentili 2012). This implies that around the early eighteenth century BCE the region was not yet populated by Kassite speakers (Potts 2017: 354; 2020: 59–60). In view of this, the Kassites are not recorded among the peoples who inhabited the Central Zagros in Sargonic and Ur III sources (Zadok 2005a).

18. MacGinnis 2020; Dandamaev and Medvedskaya 2006. For these interactions, see Rigg 1942; Wright 1943; Levine 1977; Muscarella 1986; Lanfranchi and Parpola 1990; Rollinger 1999; Radner 2003; Liverani 2003.

19. Radner (2017: 211) prefers the Mazamua reading, while Yamada (2020: 179–81) claims that both names, Zamua and Mazamua, are correct, as they are variant appellations referring to the same land

but in different periods – the latter from the Shalmaneser III onwards. In fact, according to a remark in the account of Sargon II's eighth campaign – 'the land of Lullumī that they call the land of Zamua' (RINAP 2: Sargon II, no. 65) – this name was the original designation used by the natives of the land (Klengel 1988: 166–7; Altaweel et al. 2012: 12; Yamada 2020: 167–8; see also below).

20. Cf. Yamada 2020: 179, which suggested an earlier time in the reign of Ashurnasirpal II.

21. ARAB 2: II.I.6: lines 32–4, II.IV.183; RINAP 1: no. 5: l. 10; RINAP 2: no. 117 (= Levine 1972: 38–9: ll. 31–2); SAA 15: 36–7, 54: 7'–11'; see also Reade 1978: 139–40; 1979: 179; Oded 1979; Kessler 1986: 68; Fales 1996: 7; Radner 2003: 50; Roaf 1995; Balatti 2017: 67, 70; Yamada 2020: 183–4; generally, on the Assyrian policy of deportation, see Rollinger 2018: 427–8; and for the different strategic concepts of the Neo-Assyrians in north-western Iran, see Lanfranchi and Rollinger 2021: 59–60.

22. ARAB II: 49, line 97 and 52, line 99; see also Medvedskaya 1999: 64; Dandamaev and Medvedskaya 2006, who limited it to the north of Šimaški, which they presumed was in the modern-day valley of Khorram-abad.

23. For the most comprehensive introduction to the site and its excavated material in the Metropolitan Museum of Art, see Muscarella 2013: 389–458. See also Schmidt et al. 1989: 50–7; Potts 2013: 211–12; 2016: 304; Parpola and Porter 2001: 5, where it is considered the state's capital; cf. Balatti 2017: 264–5.

24. Goff 1968: 124–5; 1970: 152–3; 1977: 105; 1978: 29–30, 36, where it is referred to as Baba Jan II Imported Ware. See also Brown 1979; Stronach 1978a on the related pottery in Tappeʰ Nush-i Jan. See also below.

25. The rock relief of Heydarabad-e Mishkhas is related to one of the last powerful Assyrian kings in the seventh century – Sennacherib, Essarhaddon or Ashurbanipal (Alibaigi et al. 2012). Shkaft-e Gulgul is also believed to show an Assyrian king of the same era (Vanden Berghe 1973b; Grayson and Levine 1975; Van der Spek 1977, which regards Esarhaddon as the most probable; cf. Reade 1977, who claims it belonged to an Assyrian commander, probably in Assurbanipal's reign).

26. For analysis of the sources, see Balatti 2017: 138–43. On the location of Bīt-Bunakki, see Zadok 1985: 48; Miroschedji 1986: 212, suggesting a location around modern Dehloran; Potts 2016: 263; cf. König 1938: 338; Young 1967: 13; Parpola and Porter 2001: 7, map 11/C3, who locate it in the Pishkooh; and for Raši/Araši, consult Balatti 2017: ch. 5: n. 8 with references.

27. Cf. Balatti 2017: 147, who takes the references to the Samatians in the Neo-Elamite administrative texts from Susa as indications of the political sovereignty of Elam over them.

28. Nonetheless, it is noteworthy that, as with many other Zagrosian toponyms of the early half of the first millennium BCE (see e.g. Herzfeld 1968; Levine 1974; Rollinger 1999; Zadok 2002), different authorities have presented a variety of opinions regarding the location of Ḥarḥar, and it is still a disputed matter in the field (for an alternative suggestion and bibliography, see Alibaigi et al. 2016).

29. Cf. Zadok 2001: 30; 2012, who tends to locate it in the northern reaches of the west of Lake Urmia. Also, Saeedyan (1397 [2018]: 116–18) and Yamada (2020: 181) considered the Penjwin and Marivan areas in the west as far as Sanandaj in the eastern parts of the consecutive Karalla and Zamua and beyond Parsua.

30. Alibaigi et al. 2016 suggested the large settlement of Tappe[h] Kheibar (Malekshah) in the north-west of Mahidasht, Rawansar County, for the identification of Ḥarḥar's centre, according to the criteria of its size, its rich Iron Age III surface material, its shape and surroundings, its location near the Great Khorasan Road, and comparison with the rock relief representation of the city's conquest by Sargon II at Khorsabad.

31. Speiser 1928: 19; Zadok 2005b; Yamada 2020: 182; Potts 2021 with bibliography; cf. Medvedskaya 2000: 436 and 442, who suggests Urmia.

32. This Assyrian king is identified by the majority of scholars with Sargon II (Frame 1999: 35; Radner et al. 2020a: 84; Yamada 2020: 182; Balatti 2017: 78). Cf. Reade 1977 and Curtis 1389 [2010]: 19, which haver between Tiglath-pileser III and Sargon II.

33. Zadok 2012; for the historical geography of this state, see Levine 1974: 113–16; Brown 1979: 9–16; Mollazadeh 1388 [2009]: 49–51.

34. Solving the Assyrian issue, Media, in the late seventh and the first half of the sixth century BCE, exploited the power vacuum to expand its control beyond central western Iran, perhaps in the Southern (Dandamaev and Lukonin 1989: 58–61; Wiesehöfer 2001: 2; Potts 2016: 289; cf. Briant 2002: 22; Henkelman 2003a: 210–11) and Northern Zagros – maybe to around central Anatolia (*Histories* I.72; n. 36; cf. Rollinger 2003a and 2003b), in the west beyond the Tigris and along the Lesser/Lower Zab (Langdon 1912: Nabonid: nos 1 and 8; Beaulieu 1989: nos 1 and 15). Despite the dearth of evidence on the northern and eastern frontiers of Media (e.g. Tuplin 2004: 235; Waters 2010: 66–7), the Median realm probably included the areas beyond the Central Zagros mountains to the east, perhaps around Mount Damavand (RINAP 1, 47, obv. 1–4 and 52, 1–4; ARAB II: ii 82; 96; 97; 50; cf. Dandamaev and Medvedskaya 2006; Roaf 1995: Fig. 23; Curtis 1389 [2009]: 25; Potts 2016: 289). This may also be discerned through Achaemenid sources (Schmitt 2009: 60, DB § 32 C). Note that here the Assyrian Mount Bikni (e.g. Tadmor 1994: 74–5, Kalḫu Ann. 16, 9) is identified with Mount Damavand (Winkler 1889: 1, xxvii, n. 3; Billerbeck 1898: 93; Streck 1900: 369; Eilers 1954: 309; Young 1967: 13, n. 12; Medvedskaya 1992: 78;

Reade 1995: 40; Parpola and Porter 2001: 45–6; Zadok 2001: 114; Radner 2003: 49, n. 63; Dandamaev and Medvedskaya 2006; Curtis 1389 [2010]: 18–19; Saeedyan and Firouzmandi 1395 [2016]: 81–2; Balatti 2017: ch. 3: n. 134), while some other scholars suggested the Alvand mountain range (e.g. Levine 1974; Brown 1979: 19–21; 1986: 116; 1988: 84; Genito 1986: 63; Muscarella 1987: 109, n. 3; 1994: 57–8; Young 1988: 13, n. 31).

35. This text is the earliest and most important related historical account, although its historical credibility has been questioned in terms of its chronological framework and its reliance on oral traditions (e.g. Helm 1981; Christensen 1933a: 234; Sancisi-Weerdenburg 1988; 1994; Briant 2002: 25–7, 31–2, 34; Rollinger 2003a; 2010; Henige 2004 with bibliography).

36. The Audience Hall of the Palatial Complex at Kerkenes (Summers 2000a: 63, Fig. 7a; Draycott and Summers 2008: Plate 5) may be comparable to the columned halls discovered at Nush-i Jan I and Godin II, but such pillared structures are by no means exclusively Median. They have been unearthed at earlier, non-Median sites in Anatolia, Armenia and north-west Iran, such as at Altintepe, Erebuni, Bastam, Hasanlu IV, Qalaichi and Ziwiye (Ünal 1988: 1,481; Dyson 1989: Fig. 11; Mo'tamedi 1376 [1997]; Kargar 1383 [2004]: 231–2; Forbes 1983: Figs 6, 12, 31, 32; Boucharlat 2020: 413, 415; see also Beckman 2010: 85–6), and also in the southern coastal areas of the Persian Gulf in the United Arab Emirates, at Rumeilah (Boucharlat and Lombard 2001) and Muweilah (Magee 2001, cf. Muscarella 2008, who relate the building to the seventh century BCE or even later), before the formation of the Median state (Gopnik 2010: 196).

37. Also, in Turkey, further to the south-west and around Adıyaman city, rescue excavations, led by the French, were carried out at the archaeological site of Tille Höyük between 1979 and 1990 (French 1982; 1983; 1984a; 1984b; 1985a; 1985b; 1986a; 1986b; 1988; 1991; 1992; French et al. 1982). The fieldwork brought about the discovery of an architectural complex at the latest level of the site, X, dated to the Iron Age, which is comparable to structures at Zagros, such as Hasanlu IVb, Nush-i Jan I, Godin II and Baba Jan II in different respects (Blaylock 2009: 173–200, 210). Therefore, Tille has been related to the Neo-Babylonian/Median period (Roaf 1990: 203; Roaf 1995: 65–6; Makinson 1999: 375; Summers 1998: 405–6; Summers 2000b: 192; Tuplin 2003: 365; Dan 2020), and to the presence of Medes in Anatolia (Roaf 1995: 65–6; Summers 1998: 405–6; Saeedyan and Gholizadeh 1398 [2019]). On the other hand, the final reports of the excavations of this settlement phase date level X and its buildings to the Achaemenid period on the basis of the stratigraphy of Tille (Blaylock 2009 and 2016).

38. The western areas of the Central Iranian Plateau, particularly around Qom and Tehran, have recently turned into a hub for the archaeology

of the Iron Age. Although the grand mud-brick platform of Tappe[h] Sialk on the upper level of the southern mound, Sialk VI, had been unearthed in the 1930s (Ghirshman 1939), it was once again examined in the course of the Sialk Reconsideration Project under the leadership of Sadeq Malek Shahmirzadi (1382 [2003]). On the basis of its pottery (Fahimi 2003) and painted bricks (Nowrouzzadeh 1381 [2002]; Saeedyan 1398 [2019]: 308–9, Fig. 14), this structure is related to the Iron Age II and III (tenth–seventh centuries BCE) (Ghirshman 1939; Malekzadeh 1383 [2004]: 60–82). In Kashan area, 11km west of the city of Kashan, the archaeological site of Gholām Tappe[h]-ye Ja'far-ābād is also studied, and has provided Sialk VI material culture and disturbed mud-brick architecture decorated with bricks painted with geometric motifs (Gol-Mohammadi et al. 1393 [2014]; Saeedyan 1398 [2019]: 310, Fig. 16). Another important site of this era with rich archaeological data is Tappe[h] Ozbaki, which is located more to the north, in Savojbolagh County and 5km south-west of the old city of Hashtgerd. Yousef Majidzadeh excavated this site over six seasons between 1998 and 2005, which led to the study of settlement phases from the late seventh/early sixth millennium BCE to the mid-first millennium BCE. Among these phases is the Iron III level, IV, that is called 'Median fortress', referring to a fortification measuring around 1,000m² with seventeen distinct architectural spaces, assumed to be Median on the basis of a comparison between its architectural elements such as three parallel rooms, a staircase and recessed niches, along with pottery, and elements at Nush-i Jan (Majidzadeh 1379 [2000]: 38–49, Figs 1–3; 1380 [2001]: 4, 40, Map 1; 1389 [2010]a: 227–30; 1389 [2010]b; Boucharlat et al. 2005: 486; Mollazadeh 1393 [2014]: 286–301; Saeedyan 1398 [2019]: 319–20). Qom is another key area for the concentration of sites related to this period. Here, for twelve seasons from 2003 (Sarlak 1389 [2010]; 1390 [2011]), excavations at Tappe[h] Qoli-Darvish, located on the south-western edge of the outskirts of Qom, unearthed interesting evidence mainly relating to the Iron Age I and II, notably a structure built on three platforms all of whose spaces were intentionally filled and sealed by mud brick and chaff-tempered mud mortar (Sarlak and Malekzadeh 1384 [2005]; Saeedyan 1398 [2019]: 307). Also, the motifs of the painted bricks found at this site (Malekzadeh and Naseri 2013: Fig. 4; Saeedyan 1398 [2019]: 306–7, Fig. 13) are similar to those of Sialk and Shamshirgah (Sarlak and Malekzadeh 1384 [2005]: 54; Sarlak 1388 [2009]: 97). Zar Bolagh and Vasun-e Kahak are two other sites in this area, 45km north and south of Qom respectively. Excavations at these yielded the discovery of two single stone structures which were systematically filled and sealed before being abandoned. The former, at Zar Bolagh, was filled with shale and splinter and covered by two walls, one made of stone and the other consisting of 8-to-10m-thick mud brick founded by mortar. According to its potteries, related to the late buff ware horizon, this structure is dated to the Late Iron Age (Malekzadeh 1382 [2003]; Malekzadeh et al. 2014). Built with slabs and shale with clay mortar, the building of Vasoun was also deliberately filled with mud and sealed by a wall made of mud and stone chips (Malekzadeh 1383 [2004]: 43–6). However, during the survey conducted at this site only twenty coarse potsherds were found, which are apparently associated with the plain buff ware of Iron Age III (Mollazadeh 1393 [2014]: 305). Another important site of this horizon in the Iranian Plateau is Shamshirgah, situated around 20km south-east of Qom city. Its architectural relics, mainly built with stone and mud mortar, are assumed to be a fortress according to their defensive position and topography (Fahimi 1382 [2004]; 1389 [2010]; Mollazadeh 1393 [2014]: 308). The building is related to Iron Ages II and III on the basis of its pottery (Kleiss 1983; Fahimi 1382 [2004]) and fairly numerous painted bricks, with comparable examples at Qoli Darvish and Sialk (Malekzadeh and Naseri 2013; Saeedyan 1398 [2019]: 310, Fig. 15). Shamshirgah is also identified as the settlement of those buried in the cemetery of Tappe[h] Sarm, 700m south-west of Shamshirgah (Fahimi 1382 [2004]: 64–5; Kavosi and Sarlak 1398 [2019]). Tappe[h] Sarm is considered contemporary with the main settlement of Shamshirgah given the presence of ceramic types comparable with those from Sialk B cemetery (Fahimi 1382 [2004]: 61). In accordance with architectural elements comparable with those uncovered in some of the Iron Age II and III sites in the Zagros, the region containing the above-mentioned sites in the Iranian Plateau is called eastern Media by some scholars (e.g. Sarlak and Malekzadeh 1384 [2005]; Malekzadeh and Naseri 1384 [2005]; Malekzadeh 1385 [2006]). Nonetheless, the dates are not confidently set, and nor are these sites homogeneous archaeologically.

39. The level II at Tell Gubba held three major architectural features (Postgate and Watson 1979: 172–3). Although firstly dated to the Achaemenid period, the plan of the large building of this phase is comparable to that of the Nush-i Jan complex (Oguchi and Matsumoto 2001: 14). For further publications discussing the stratigraphy and materials of this site, see Fujii 1981; Ii 1988; 1989; 1990; 1993 and Margueron 1999: 20–39, Figs 1–8.
40. This control was indirect in some intermontane sections of the Zagros (see below).
41. Apart from the royal centre of Hagmatāna, the Zagros highlands were the core areas for the formation of the Mannean, Ellipian and Elymaean states in the first millennium BCE.
42. Tuplin 1987: 140; Wiesehöfer 2001: 76; 2015: 69–73; Briant 2002: 412; Olbrycht 2010: 355. See Högemann 1992 and Briant 2002: 391, 400, 411 for an analysis of the available data regarding Darius' changes to prior administrative structures. Further, on the adaptation/

integration of local systems in/into the Achaemenid imperial administration, see Jacobs 2011; Henkelman 2017.

43. Jacobs 2011: 1–2/34; Tuplin 1987: 113; Kent 1950: 55. For other
scholarly opinions about the meaning of *dahyu*, see Wiesehöfer 2001:
165; Jacobs 2011: 3. Also, the term *eparchy* is mentioned in the
Graeco-Roman sources (Diod., XIX. 44.4), and is probably identifiable
with *medinah* in the Aramic and Hebrew documents from contemporary Egypt, according to Briant (2002: 737–8).

44. Strabo (XI. 13.3 and XV. 3.1) also mentions the Cyrtians of Media
Atropatene and Persis, who were already recorded (Plb., V. 52.5) as
slingers in the army of Molon, the Seleucid satrap of Media and the
viceroy of the Upper Satrapies (see Potts 2016: 354–5; Balatti 2017:
ch. 6: n. 120 with references; Strootman 2017: 198: on Molon and his
revolt). As Potts (2014: 120–4) disclosed, this term is the Greek variant
of the generic noun *kurd*, which was used to refer to herders in general,
regardless of the ethnolinguistic background of those groups. Such
usage continued in Sasanian–early Islamic times (see Chapter 1, s. 1.3;
cf. Brunner 1983: 766–7).

45. See Reade 1978; Schmitt 1993; Briant 1976: 174–5; Balatti 2017:
192, 220–31, ch. 6: n. 91. Regarding the identification of the C/Kissia,
which was the Greek term synonymous with Elam in the Classical
sources of the Achaemenid period (e.g. *Hist*. III. 91.4), and its distinction from C/Kossaea in the Classical and Latin sources, see Nöldeke
1874: 174–5; Salaris and Basello 2019: 87–8, n. 40; Potts 2016: 332–3,
368–70 with bibliography.

46. Jacobs 2011: 9–10/34; Balatti 2017: 240, ch. 6: n. 135; cf. Henkelman
2008b: 311, who locates it 'immediately north of Pasargadae'; see also
the next note.

47. Gabae has long been identified with the area around modern Iṣfahan
(Hoffmann 1880: 132, n. 1130; Weissbach 1910a, 1910b; Brunner
1983: 752; Hausleiter et al. 2000: 1,316, 1,317; Potts 2016: 366, 375).
This identification is mainly supported by the strong evidence for the
location of the region of the Parthian G'b, Mid. Pers. Gay (Gyselen
2008; 2019: 84; Henkelman 2008b: 311) in this area. However, following an earlier suggestion by Hinz (1970: 1036), Henkelman (2017:
n. 143; 2008b: 312) recently proposed a more southward area, around
the Izad-khwast/Abadeh plain, for the Achaemenid Gabae, according to the Persepolis archives introducing it within the jurisdiction of
Pārsa's administration and its economic sphere, Strabo's description
(XVI. 1.18) of its availability from the Susis road, and Henning's
(1957) linguistic analysis of the name Gaba- as denoting 'valley'.
Henkelman dismisses the later data backing the Iṣfahan location,
inferring that these sets of evidence denote either the survival of the
name Gabae for a different area or the expansion of Gabae north-
wards during post-Achaemenid times. Although such changes in the

administrative divisions are attested for some areas, such as Parthia, Mid. Pers. Pahlaw, over time (Ghodrat-Dizaji 2016; more generally, see Gyselen 2019: 333–4), there are no available data supporting such a later geographical shift or expansion for Gabae. Moreover, examination of the sigillographic material unearthed at the newly-discovered archaeological site Tappe[h] Bardnakōn (Khosrowzadeh et al. 2020a), carried out in the course of the collaboration between Rika Gyselen and this author and the excavators, was very informative. In particular, the epigraphic data read by Gyselen brought about the identification of the hitherto-unknown canton of 'Rāwar-kust-ī-rōdbār' in the province of Gay in the late Sasanian period, located to the west of modern Isfahan around the central areas of the modern province of Chaharmahal va Bakhtiyari (Khosrowzadeh et al. 2020b; 2020c). This proves that the late Sasanian province of Gay in the Spahān region (Gyselen 2019: 199–200), at least, included the whole lower basin of the Zāyandeh-rōd River, a part of which is the Chaharmahal area (for early Islamic times, see Henning 1977: 178, n. 1). The historical road that is called Atābaki in medieval sources (Ibn Battuta 1371 [1993]: 241) was an inter-regional route that connected Khuzestan to Isfahan via the Bakhtiyari and Chaharmahal areas. Archaeological surveys in the region led to the recognition of some remaining parts of this road dated to the Sasanian era – given the majority of the related sites on it – (see Chapter 4; see also Khosrowzadeh and Habibi 2015; Mehrkiyan 1997: n. 12) and its mainly paralleling the contemporary Izeh–Shahrekord highway – before the recent construction of the Karun-4 Bridge, which led to the waterlogging of some parts of this road. The formation of important settlements of the late Middle-Elamite period, such as Qal'e-geli/Tall-e Afghān in Lordegan and Sūleqān around Shahrekord (see n. 15), was perhaps related to the presence and use of this route in that era too. Probably, this was the road that led to the Achaemenid Gabae and that is recorded in the Graeco-Roman sources in the Hellenistic period. On the basis of his excavations, Ghirshman (1976: 79–80) postulated the existence of a Seleucid garrison at Masjed-Soleiman, which was along 'an important route leading north towards Gabiene with its capital Gabae/Tabae' (Potts 2016: 366–7). The road headed from Susa towards the north-eastern piedmonts of Khuzestan and, passing Izeh and Masjed-Soleiman, led to the Bakhtiyari highlands and the Chaharmahal intermontane plains, to finally reach Paraetaceni and Gabae (Ghrishman 1976: 79–80; Vanden Berghe and Schippmann 1386 [2007]: 11; Petrie 2005; Salaris and Basello 2019: 81; see also map in Rawlinson 1839).

48. For an analysis of the data given by the Classical texts regarding the location of the Uxians around the Fahliyan plain between Khuzestan and Fars, see Briant 1982b: 220; Salaris and Basello 2019: 89, n. 54 with references.

49. See Balatti 2017: 323 for a review of these documents, and 289–90 for agriculture, viticulture and arboriculture in the Zagros during the first millennium BCE.
50. Notwithstanding Strabo's quoting of Nearchus (XI. 13.6), the Elymaeans are not mentioned in the accounts of Alexander historians, which might be interpreted as a sign indicating that Alexander did not confront them and their lands (Salaris and Basello 2019: 89).
51. See Schmitt 1993. For a review of Alexander's encounter with the Zagros peoples according to the historians of Alexander, see Balatti 2017: 205–26.
52. Among many, one may mention Atropatene and Oxydates in Media, Oxathres in Paraetaceni, the Persian aristocrats under Peucestas in Persis, Mazaeus in Babylon and Mithrines of Sardes in Sardis (Briant 1985; 2006; Shayegan 2007; Olbrycht 2010: 353, 362).
53. Darius III stopped at Hagmatāna, expecting forces from eastern Iran to join him to refresh his armies after the Gaugamela battle – so had Artaxerxes II done prior to advancing towards Babylonia in 401 BCE (see Briant 2002: 629, 738–40; Colburn 2013: 47). Alexander, after conquering the city, left reliable assets, either in terms of *strategoi* or as part of the royal treasures that had been seized at Susa and Persepolis, at Ecbatana (Briant 2002: 739). The city was also the base for the revolt of Eumenes against Antiochus III in 222–220 BCE (Vanden Berghe and Schippmann 1386 [2007]: 19).
54. Jacobs 2010: 94–6; Wiesehöfer 2015: 75; Strootman 2017: 185, 198. See also Sherwin-White and Kuhrt 1993 regarding Seleucid rule in the Upper Satrapies.
55. Stein 1940: 339; Bernard 1980; von Gall 1978; 2010; Rougemont 2012: n. 75; 2013; Callieri and Askari Chaverdi 2013: 694; Balatti 2017: 280. See Zournatzi 2016 for a brief review of the functions proposed for the rock-cut spaces; Miraskandari and Chaychi Amirkhiz 1398 [2019] on the recent excavations of the 'Floor C' by Iranian archaeologists.
56. Debevoise 1938: 150–2; Von Gall 1996: 85–8, Abb. 1, Tafel 13–14; Kleiss 1970: 147–9, Abb. 13; Wiesehöfer 2001: 121, 126; Tuplin 2009: 115 with more references. See Invernizzi 2020 for the Seleucid-Arsacid period rock reliefs at Bisotun and Sarpol-e Zohāb. Also in this area, west of Kermanshah, Moradi recently (2019) published a new inscribed rock relief discovered in the present-day town of Javanrood and dated to the late Arsacid era according to palaeographic, stylistic and iconographic criteria.
57. According to Strabo (XI. 13.6, XVI. I.18), the realm of the Elymaean state also included Gabiane, Korbiane, Massabatice (Mid. Pers. Māsabādān, Arabic Māsabadhān and Latin Massabatene) and Mihragān-kadag (Syrian Bēt Mihraqāyē and Arabic Mihrajānqadhaq). The latter two districts are located in the Poshtkooh and Pishkooh areas on the basis of the late antique sources (see below).

58. Consult Messina and Mehr Kian 2014b: 448, which, at Kal-e Chendar, proposes this function only for the structures on the so-called Stein Terrace.

59. Vanden Berghe and Schippmann 1386 [2007]: 22; cf. Herzfeld 1932: 39, who proposes Susa. See also Tarn 1951 for the Elymaean Artemis-Nanaya temple of Antiochus IV's reign.

60. For a brief review of the history of the discovery of these reliefs, see Mehrkiyan 1997.

61. Especially the relief of Hung-e Azhdar/Nowrouzi as the earliest of the Elymaean reliefs discovered so far (Vanden Berghe and Schippmann 1386 [2007]: 39–45, 104; Messina and Mehr Kian 2010; Messina 2015).

62. For instance, see Haerinck 2003 regarding Tang-e Sarvak II, NE side, with more references.

63. Christensen 1933b; see also Gyselen 2019: 14–15; cf. Pourshariati 2008, who rejected the Christesenian opinion on the concentrated structure of the political system of the state for most of the Sasanian period in favour of an unconcentrated dynastic confederacy system – an idea, however, that has its own deficiencies (Daryaee 2010b; Payne 2014). However, it is notable that, in particular, Rika Gyselen's studies of the primary Sasanian sources have led to the reconstruction of the administrative structures of the empire and also of such structures after its fall – in the post-Sasanian era at least until the mid-eighth century in the territories south of the Caspian Sea, and around 695 in the reign of the Umayyad 'Abd al-Malek in the rest of the once-Sasanian realm – and to clarification of the point that this system underwent rather extensive reforms in terms of its military, economic and fiscal structures, initiated by Kawād I after his return to the throne in 499 (among many of her monumental works, see Gyselen 1989 and 2019. See Wiesehöfer 2020b for further bibliography and a concise, but precise, review of her later book; see also Habibi 1401 [2022]). See also Huyse 1994: 329; Daryaee 1995; 2002: 11–14; 2003: 43; Gariboldi 2015; cf. Gignoux 1984: 25–7, which challenged the idea of the quadripartition of the empire.

64. For a more comprehensive sub-periodisation of the Sasanian era according to various factors, see Wiesehöfer 2014; see also Shayegan 1999; 2003: 369–72; 2013: 805–7.

65. Among which are the *šahr* status of Hamadān and Gay, which are both attested in the third (ŠKZ § 48) and sixth centuries (for detailed discussion, see Gyselen 2001b; 2008; 2011; 2019: n. 4, 84, 97–102, 200, 333; Khosrowzadeh et al. 2020b: 85, 92; cf. Huyse 1994: 329, which emphasised the profound changes that happened in the administrative organisation of the late Sasanian Empire).

66. The hierarchy is composed of five levels according to the available sets of evidence, yet the fifth category, which is the largest zone, a 'very

large region' (très grande région), does not apply to the geographical scale of the focus of this book.

67. Arabic Qermīsīn from the early Islamic period up until the thirteenth century (Le Strange 1905: 187; Schwarz 1969: 480–1; Hausleiter et al. 2000: 1,318, Map 93).

68. Kettenhofen 1993; Gyselen 1989: 45–6; 2019: 68–9: between Šahrazūr, Mid. Pers. Syārazūr, and Hulwān, perhaps at Qasr-e Shīrīn; cf. Hedāyat 1321 [1941]b: 172, n. 3: between Garmegān and Nōdšīragān; Hausleiter et al. 2000: 1,317, Map 93, which suggested the modern Harsin in Kermanshah Province. Gyselen (2019: 69, 225) points to another hypothesis, that Walaxšfarr and Ērān-āsān-kar-Kawād made up a single province before Kawād I's changes in the area in the early sixth century. Accordingly, Walaxšfarr was a foundation of an Arsacid King of Kings named Walaxš, given that the province was recorded as a diocese by the Synods in 424 CE, under the Syrian name of Balašparr (Chaumont 1974: 82–4; Kettenhofen 1993; Gyselen 2019: 142), that is, before the only Sasanian king of that name (r. 484–488 CE). Later on, the Sasanian king Kawād I renamed it, giving it the honorary title of Ērān-āsān-kar-Kawād, having commanded reestablishment projects there, as recounted by some Islamic literary sources and parallel numismatic evidence.

69. Cf. Huyse 1994: 328–9, speculating about another hierarchical arrangement for the two areas, that is, a status between the levels of province and canton.

70. For more information about the Christian populations of the Central Zagros, either Ērānian converts or An-Ērānian deportees, in the late antique Christian literature, see the *Chronicle of Khuzistan* (Guidi 1903; Nöldeke 1893; Rezakhani and Bavandpour 1395 [2016]) and *Martyrdom of Pethion: Adurhormizd, and Anahid* (Bedjan 1897; Sims-Williams 1985; Payne 2010: 27–92).

71. The Sasanian monumental structures have been examined in this area, at the sites of Barz-e Qawāleh/Ramāvand (Hourshid and Mousavi Haji 2015; Hassanpour 2015; Hasanpour et al. 2016; Karamian and Farrokh 2017), Rouhe (Niakan 2019) and Dareh-shahr (Stein 1940: 206–8; Lakpour 1389 [2010]; Sa'adati and Naseri Somei 2019). See also Hasanpour et al. 2016; Mohammadifar and Tahmasebi 2014; Niakan 2015a, 2015b. However, the relative dating of the architectural types and features used in these projects is problematic, if not sketchy. As recent fieldwork projects in the Seymareh River basin have indicated, such architectural conventions and ceramic traditions in this area continued rather persistently through Late Antiquity. Being examined recently, some important sites are consequently related to Sasanian–early Islamic times (Lakpour 1389 [2010]; Feizi et al. 2012; Sa'adati and Naseri Somei 2019; Mohammadifar 2014). For a comprehensive examination of the archaeological materials of this

period in the neighbouring Abdanan County, see Chapter 3. Regarding the chahār-ṭāqs, mainly fire-temples, of the Sasanian period in the Central Zagros, particularly in the Pishkooh and Poshtkooh areas, see Schippmann 1971; Vanden Berghe 1977; Mo'tamedi 1371 [1992]; Mehrafarin and Ahmadi Hedayati 1381 [2011]; Mohammadifar and Motarjem 2012; Vandaee and Jafari 2012; Moradi 2016; Moradi and Keall 2019; Yousefvand and Miri 1398 [2019]; Khosravi et al. 2018 with more references.

72. Given the dearth of evidence for early Sasanian times, we are not confident whether it was also the case in the earlier phases of the period. However, it is worth noting that some Hellenistic sources regard this area in the upper Karun River basin as part of Media (e.g. Plin. *Nat.* VI. 31.136).

73. In fact, the administrative, military and fiscal changes that occurred in terms of the quadripartition were designed for Ērān, and An-Ērān was excluded. The distinction between Ērānšahr and An-Ērānšahr (the land of non-Iranians, roughly corresponding to the lands of the Caucasus) is already mentioned in the third-century inscription of Narseh at Paikuli and those of Kirdīr in Sar Mašhad and on the Kaʻbe-ye Zardošt (thanks to Rika Gyselen for noting this point; see Gyselen 2019: 12, 127; see also n. 62).

74. From this time onwards, different areas of the Central Zagros, as a former peripheral region of the Elamite and Mesopotamian states, became the core area of important kingdoms such as Media, Ellipi and Elymaea. These areas also held an important inter-regional status in Late Antiquity. Needless to say, such a transformation of the status of a region over time and with the changes in political and socioeconomic conditions can be studied in many cases. Ancient Fars provides another instance of this phenomenon. Persis, the birthplace of two Persian Empires holding Anšan as one of the most important Proto-Elamite and Elamite centres, was a peripheral area in the Arsacid Empire (Wiesehöfer 2019).

75. For example, the late Middle-Elamite sites of Qal'e-geli and Sūleqān in Chaharmahal va Bakhtiyari Province and settlements from the early half of the first millennium BCE in Hamadan Province.

76. Up until that time, we may still regard the BAMI as one of the most important research projects carried out in the Central Zagros (see above). This project continued regularly for a fifteen-year period and succeeded in providing a general perspective on cultural trends in the Pishkooh and Poshtkooh areas from the Chalcolithic period up to Islamic times, regardless of the discussions about demography and political organisation. Archaeologists, consequently, identified varied cultural phases and zones in the region under examination during different periods. As to the zones, for instance in the rather small geographical limits of the Poshtkooh, they distinguished three distinct

areas, north-western, south-eastern and central, that were culturally linked but still had different ceramic traditions in the early third millennium, ED II/early ED IIIa in the standard Mesopotamian chronology (see e.g. Haerinck 1986: 61–8).

77. Such regular movements between the winter and summer quarters are observed in different areas, among which one may mention the migrations between the Diyāla/Sirwān plain and the Hamrin basin; between the upper and lower Sirwān/Diyāla River valley and western Kermanshah; between the Bakhtiyari area, to the west and south of Chaharmahal va Bakhtiyari Province, and northern-eastern Khuzestan; between the Lorestan highlands and Dehloran's Dasht-'Abbās plain and lower Abdanan's Kalāt and Mourmouri plains; and between upper Abdanan and Dehloran and the Jebel Hamrin. Despite the modern political boundaries, the areas reaching towards the western Zagros region are closely linked to the adjacent highland system of the Central Zagros Mountains to the east and north-east and the alluvial lowlands to the south and south-east, thanks to the long-standing historic route systems and major pathways, with a history going back at least to the Early Dynastic period, nomadic connections along the wider inter-regional highland–lowland system, and trade and economic ties. In this case, inter-regional economic interdependence between these regions has led to cultural interaction, political subjugation and economic exploitation.

78. See Habibi, in press. One may also recall Husraw II's building projects of royal palaces, fire-temples, gardens and hunting fields at Qasr-e Shīrīn and the nearby Hawesh Koori. Moreover, the stone structure of Tāq-e Garrā may belong to the same era. This building is erected at the Pāy-e Tāq pass, which itself is the location of the well-known ancient *Zagri Pylæ*, the Zagros Gates, around Sarpol-e Zohāb (Dehpahlavan et al. 1397 [2018] with bibliography; see n. 8). Also, Canepa (2018), especially by examining architecture, visual culture and built environment in Pārs, indicates how the Sasanians utilised previous Near Eastern royal ideologies and ancient legacies and reshaped heritage landscapes to construct a royal identity mainly representing their role and image as legitimate and divine.

3 A System at the Edge of Chaos: Abdanan in the Sasanian Period

3.1 INTRODUCTION

The purpose of this chapter is to study human–environmental interaction in the Abdanan region during the Sasanian period. Accordingly, after introducing the human and natural geography of Abdanan and reviewing its archaeological literature, I describe the different categories of 106 Sasanian sites (Map 3.2) in the region under study. Then, using the Arc GIS programme, I evaluate the relationship between different environmental variables and the location of Sasanian sites to analyse spatial models of the regional distribution of these sites. The reasons for the establishment and continuation of the settlements and subsistence strategies are among focal points in this examination. It should be noted that there are cases of related sites that are assumed as a single complex point in the maps to prevent distortion of spatial analysis. Furthermore, the spatial distribution patterns and concentration of different types of sites are investigated. Note also that no geomorphological information on the region is currently available.

3.2 GEOGRAPHY OF ABDANAN

3.2.1 Natural geography

Abdanan, a county in Ilam Province, is located to the west of the folded Central Zagros Mountains, between N32°53' latitude and E47°30' longitude and N32°883' latitude and E47°500' longitude. Abdanan is an intermontane plain with an area of 2617km², which consists of three districts, Markazi, Sarab-e Bagh and Mourmouri,

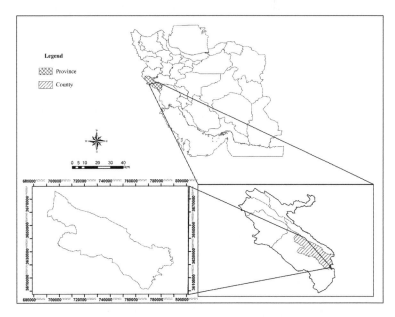

Map 3.1. Location of Abdanan County on the map of Ilam Province on map of Iran. (Source: author)

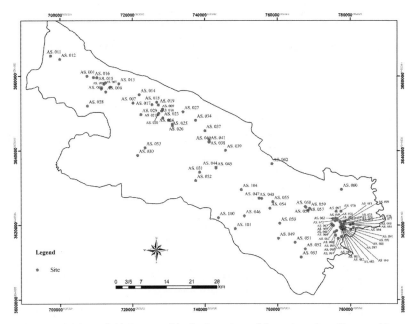

Map 3.2. Map of Abdanan with the location of Sasanian sites discussed in Chapter 3. (Source: author)

and its neighbouring counties are Dare-shahr, to the north and east; Dehloran, to the west of Ilam Province; Andimeshk, to the south, in Khuzestan Province; and Pol-dokhtar, to the south-east, in Lorestan Province (Map 3.1). This region is located between the mountain ranges of Kabirkooh, to the north and east, and Dinarkooh, Siahkooh and Dalpari to the south and west. Another important geographical characteristic of the county's location is that it is adjacent to the lowlands of Dehloran and Susiana to the west and south. Given this situation, there are two different types of climate in Abdanan. On the one hand, the northern, north-western and western parts of the county are mountainous areas that constitute the major part of the region. With an average elevation of 1,500m a.s.l., these areas have a mountainous climate, with an average annual precipitation of 400mm, and Zagros steppe vegetation in the montane forests and pastures. On the other hand, the eastern and south-eastern areas of the region include alluvial plains such as Mourmouri, Kalāt and Mōlāb, which are connected, without major geographical barriers, to the Khuzestan plains and through Dinarkooh Mountain to Dehloran, which is geographically part of southern Mesopotamia. Located on the parallel latitude lines of lowlands, each of these plains, with an elevation range of less than 300m a.s.l., has a dry climate with an average annual precipitation of around 200mm and dry steppe vegetation (Abdollahi and Sadeghi-Rad 2010: 21–31; Moradi 2005: 2).

3.2.2 Human and historical geography

Ilam Province is part of a region that was called Hossein-abad-e Poshtkooh up until 1935. Poshtkooh region bordered Lorestan and Khuzestan to the east, Khuzestan to the south, Iraq to the west and Kermanshah to the north (Shishegar 2005). In 1928, the initial core of Abdanan city was formed by resettling nomads as part of a compulsory sedentarisation plan.[1] Ethnologically, the population of this county consists of Lor, Lak and Kurd groups (Abdollahi and Sadeghi-Rad 2010: 37–9). Regarding historical geography, we have to mention that little information is available on the region during pre-Sasanian periods. Nonetheless, we know that Abdanan had been part of Elam territory (Potts 2016: 14–15). To be more precise, the Poshtkooh region including Abdanan was part of Awan, which is mentioned in the Mesopotamian texts from the mid-third millennium, Godin III: 6 period in the Central Zagros chronological terms, and the Mesopotamian phase from ED II–III, onwards (Potts 2016:

90–1; Vallat 1993; see Chapter 2, s. 2.2). No written document relating to Elamite civilisation has been acquired from this region. However, the Old Babylonian copies of Old Akkadian royal inscriptions (C7 caption c; Sargon 2a, 2b) relating to the third and second millennia BCE (Gelb and Kienast 1990; Sallaberger and Westenholz 1999: 38; Potts 2016: 92–3; Van Dijk 1978; Frayne 1992: 71) mention a place the name of which is transliterated as URU_XA^{ki} or Arawa and recognised as Dehloran (Michalowski et al. 2010: 105–8; Frayne 1992: 71; Steinkeller 1982).[2] In addition, de Miroschedji suggested that the location of the Neo-Elamite Bīt-Burnakki (Luckenbill 1924: 88; see Chapter 2, s. 2.3), mentioned in the Babylonian Chronicles (iii.10–11), should be considered somewhere around Dehloran (de Miroschedji 1986: 215; Potts 2016: 263). In the Achaemenid period, the north-west area of Susa, modern Lorestan and Poshtkooh, was called *Cissia*, the land of the *Cassai*. However, it seems that the area played a minor role in the political culture of the Achaemenid Empire (Michalowski et al. 2010: 111). The connection of this region to Elam is attested as late as around 900 in the Syriac codex 354, kept in Paris's *Bibliothèque Nationale*, and in the table of Elias of Damascus, where Mehraqān-qadaq is mentioned as part of the ecclesiastical province of Elam (Potts 2016: 425). Herzfeld (1968: 15–16) has suggested that Poshtkooh was part of the country of *Nesæan* horses mentioned by Strabo (XI.13.7, XVI.1.18) as one of the countries on the path of Alexander's campaign. However, as discussed in Chapter 2.3, this is unlikely as the Nisāya district of the Bisotun inscription was located between Bisotun and Hagmatāna, that is, probably, the Dinavar plain. In the third century CE, the *Res Gestae Divi Saporis* mentions Māh as part of the territory that Šābuhr I called Ērānšahr, the domain of the Iranians (Hyuse 1999: 22–3; Daryaee 2002: 3–4; see Chapter 2, s. 2.4). In the early Islamic period, Ilam divided into two separate regions: the northern one, with its centre in Shirvan, called Māspazān, and the southern region with its centre probably in the Seymareh, modern Dare-shahr, named Mehraqān-qadaq. Mentioning these regions, historical documents of this period contain some information on their climatic, geographical and ethnic characteristics (Abi-Ya'qub 1977: 43–4), as well as accounts of the regional conquests by Muslim Arabs (Al-Balādhori 1866: 125–6). The late antique ecclesiastical authors also provide interesting information about the Christian population of the Central Zagros under Sasanian rule. The East Syrian hagiographical texts show how the once *An-Ērānian* Christian deportees reached the level of landowners and Sasanian officials (Payne 2015:

59–92; Fiey 1970: 372–3). In particular, *Martyrdom of the Captives* (Bedjan 1891: 323–4) has recorded how the population deported from Beit Zabai participated in the development of the irrigation agriculture of Masabadan/Māsabādān, the neighbouring region of the contemporary Abdanan. To involve themselves in the economy of the region, they changed the natural landscape of the region but also made their mark on the built environment of the Iranian highlands by founding structures such as shrines, along with the related rituals and (hi-)stories to which their identities were attached (Payne 2015: 68, 77).

3.3 EARLIER RESEARCH

Between 2000 and 2010, six seasons of archaeological surveys were undertaken in Abdanan County (Motarjem and Mohammadifar 2000; Mohammadifar and Motarjem 2001; Moradi 2005; Ahmadi 2008; Javanmardzadeh 2010; Abdollahi 2011). However, apart from two articles on the Jōliyān fire-temple, the site AS.035 (Mohammadifar and Motarjem 2012) and the Posht-Qal'e castle, AS.021 (Sadeghi-Rad and Zargoush 2015), no archaeological information about Abdanan has been published so far. Studying the archaeological data acquired from the systematic total coverage and high-intensity surveys, in 2014, I led a structural survey involving random sampling and with a focus on the spatial distribution of the Sasanian-period material culture in the region.

3.4 CATEGORIES OF THE SITES UNDER STUDY

The Sasanian archaeological data of Abdanan is rich not only quantitatively but also qualitatively. The diverse categories of sites provide proof of this point (Map 3.15). They are introduced here one by one.

3.4.1 *Large settlements*

This category consists of the sites of AS.027, AS.034, AS.050, AS.105, and the two complexes of AS.040–AS.041 and AS.101–AS.102–AS.103. These sites formed in vast plains with the potential for cultivation. The important characteristic of these settlements is clearly their considerable size, ranging from six to 10ha with a surface covered by remains of architectural structures (Figures 3.1–3.11). These ruins include AS.027 and the complex of AS.101–AS.102–AS.103, with relics of various buildings in the

Fig. 3.1. A sample of the architectural remains on AS.027, view from north.
(Source: author)

Fig. 3.2. AS.027, view from south. (Source: author)

form of their foundations and some walls around one metre in
height (Figures 3.1, 3.8, 3.9). Notably, each of the sites AS.105
and AS.034 had originally been part of the complexes containing a
settlement and a castle, in the case of the former, and a settlement,
castle and fire-temple in the case of the latter. The sites of this
category are dated to the Sasanian period on the basis of ceramic
samples acquired from them (see Chapter 5, s. 5.3),[3] as well as the
archaeological data from their neighbouring sites in the cases of
AS.034 and AS.105.

Fig. 3.3. AS.034, view from south. (Source: author)

Fig. 3.4. AS.040, view from east, on AS.041. (Source: author)

Fig. 3.5. AS.041, view from west, on AS.042. (Source: author)

Fig. 3.6. AS.050, view from west. (Source: author)

Fig. 3.7. AS.101, view from east. (Source: author)

Fig. 3.8. Architectural remains on AS.101, view from north. (Source: author)

Fig. 3.9. Architectural remains on AS.102, view from west. (Source: author)

Fig. 3.10. AS.103, view from west. (Source: author)

Fig. 3.11. AS.105 on the western slope of Kāse Māst Mountain, view from south.
(Source: author)

3.4.2 Sedentary sites

Another category of Abdanan's archaeological sites is made up by the sedentary sites of AS.001, AS.003, AS.004, AS.005, AS.007, AS.008, AS.015, AS.022, AS.023, AS.051, AS.052, AS.054, AS.055, AS.056, AS.057, AS.058 and AS.060. Besides their smaller size, the other feature of these sites making them distinct from the sites related to the large settlements category is their shape. The members of the category of sedentary sites in the northern highlands of Abdanan are as level as the farms where they are mostly found, while in the eastern and south-eastern lowlands of the county they are shaped in the form of mounds, in some cases with several cultural layers (Figures 3.12–3.18). Generally, the sites of this category are located in the places that have the capacity for agricultural exploitation, besides access to pastures. The shape and environmental setting of

Fig. 3.12. AS.023, view from east. (Source: author)

Fig. 3.13. AS.051, view from west. (Source: author)

Fig. 3.14. AS.052, view from south-west. (Source: author)

Fig. 3.15. AS.054, view from north. (Source: author)

Fig. 3.16. AS.055, view from west. (Source: author)

Fig. 3.17. AS.056, view from south. (Source: author)

Fig. 3.18. AS.057, view from north. (Source: author)

these settlements and the archaeological materials recovered from them attest to their permanent nature.

3.4.3 *Nomadic sites*

Nomadic sites are another category of archaeological sites recognised in Abdanan. This category includes the sites of AS.002, AS.006, AS.009, AS.010, AS.013, AS.014, AS.016, AS.017, AS.028, AS.029, AS.030, AS.031, AS.032, AS.033, AS.037, AS.44, AS.045, AS.053, AS.061, AS.062, AS.064, AS.065, AS.066, AS.067, and AS.069–AS.099. It is notable that the concentration of the camp-sites is in the eastern part of the county. The available evidence for recognition of the economic modes of nomadic and transhumant pastoralism consists of the recovered material culture such as architectural remains of campsites (Figures 3.22–3.29), spatial distribution of sites (see below), ethnological evidence of the exploitation of the area as the traditional place of *Beirānvand* nomads' winter camps, regional environmental characteristics such as the favourable climatic conditions of the eastern part of Abdanan in autumn and winter compared to those of the neighbouring highlands of Ilam and Lorestan, and the rich pastures of the area in those seasons. Furthermore, several temporary settlements are discovered across the other parts of the region and generally within a short distance from sedentary sites. These sites are another type of temporary camps shaped in the hillsides where ample pasture is accessible but the soil is not agriculturally suitable. Apart from the geographical features of their location (Figures 3.19–3.21), the small size of these sites

Fig. 3.19. AS.002, view from west. (Source: author)

Fig. 3.20. AS.009, view from south. (Source: author)

Fig. 3.21. AS.010, view from west. (Source: author)

Fig. 3.22. Foundations of architectural structures on AS.066, view from
north-west. (Source: author)

Fig. 3.23. AS.072, view from north-west. (Source: author)

Fig. 3.24. AS.074, view from north-east. (Source: author)

Fig. 3.25. Foundations of architectural structures on AS.074, view from south. (Source: author)

and particular archaeological finds such as the forms and limited quantity of ceramics indicate that this type of temporary site can be attributed to transhumant pastoralist camps. It seems likely, however, that they were bases for a multi-resource economy in which, besides animal husbandry, a range of stable agricultural activities might be practised (Khazanov 1994: 23). Accordingly, while groups settled

Fig. 3.26. AS.083, view from north-east. (Source: author)

Fig. 3.27. AS.098, view from east. (Source: author)

permanently, elements of them, as herders, could leave to travel short distances from these campsites (see also Chapter 1, n. 13).

3.4.4 *Castles*

This category includes AS.019, AS.021, AS.036, AS.042 and AS.106. With their thick defensive walls,[4] these castles were erected at strategic points on mountain picks, overlooking the surrounding plains and settlements. Another common characteristic of these structures is their clear association with the adjacent vast and medium

Fig. 3.28. Foundations of architectural structures on AS.098, view from north. (Source: author)

Fig. 3.29. AS.099, view from west. (Source: author)

settlements located quite close to them. These attached settlements are the respective AS.009, AS.022, AS.034, AS.043 and AS.105. The castle AS.036, especially, along with its adjacent sites, presents an interesting case of the particular landscape of a Sasanian city in the region, consisting of different parts such as a castle, fire-temple, residential section and agricultural fields, each of which earned a specific space according to its function in the complex. The strategic position of this site (Map 3.2; Figure 3.36) indicates its military importance. The structure is placed on the mountain that reaches from the north and via a narrow path to the only corridor across the northern mountains of the area. Besides, from other sides, this castle gets to the Jōliyān plain with a very high gradient. Towering high over the plain, it offers spectacular views over the settlement of Jōliyān (AS.034) and the northern passageway passing through the massive mountains to the plain. As expected, the pottery sherds from castles belong to large vessels produced for storage purposes. These sites vary in size, and while the area of AS.042 is only 232.5m, AS.021 measures 8,450m. The other three castles, AS.019, AS.036 and AS.106, are consecutively 2,750m, 4,200m and 4,500m in area. The representatives of this category are dated to the Sasanian period according to their architectural characteristics (Figures 3.30–3.44),

Fig. 3.30. Part of the architectural structures remaining in AS.019, view from east. (Source: author)

Fig. 3.31. AS.019, view from south-west. (Source: author)

Fig. 3.32. Position of the castle of AS.021, view from east. (Source: author)

Fig. 3.33. North-west view over the plain, river and village of Posht-qal'e from AS.021. (Source: author)

Fig. 3.34. AS.021, the north-eastern U-shaped corner towers and one of the rounded buttress towers, view from east. (Source: author)

Fig. 3.35. Position of the castle of AS.036, view from south. (Source: author)

Fig. 3.36. South view over the plain, fire-temple and large settlement of Jōliyān from AS.021. (Source: author)

Fig. 3.37. Part of the architectural structures remaining in AS.042, view from north. (Source: author)

Fig. 3.38. Part of the architectural structures remaining in AS.042, view from south. (Source: author)

Fig. 3.39. Western and northern remains of the walls and architectural structures inside the castle of AS.106, view from south. (Source: author)

Fig. 3.40. Part of the southern wall of the castle of AS.106, view from south-west. (Source: author)

Fig. 3.41. South-west view over the plain of Panj-berār from AS.106.
(Source: author)

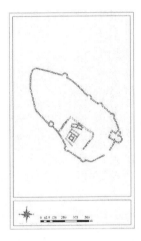

Fig. 3.42. Plan of AS.021. (After Sadeghi-Rad and Zargoush 2015, Plan 2).

Fig. 3.43. Plan of AS.036. (After Mohammadifar and Motarjem 2001, Plan 19)

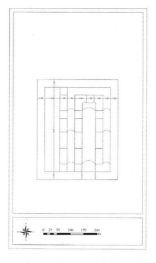

Fig. 3.44. Plan of AS.042. (After Mohammadifar and Motarjem 2001, Plan 28)

and to comparative examination of their archaeological materials – particularly pottery wares (see Chapter 5, s. 5.3) – and those of their neighbouring contemporaneous counterparts.

3.4.5 *Manor houses*

Two other sites of AS.39 and AS.100 are assigned to another category of archaeological sites in Abdanan named as manor houses. Geographically, these sites are located at the central part of Abdanan region. This group of sites is distinguished according to the architecture reminiscent of these sites (Figures 3.45–3.51), which is evidently larger than the regular architecture and on a monumental scale, absence of defensive structures, easy access to either site, and their location in the neighbourhood of large settlements – respectively, the complexes of AS.040–AS.041 and AS.101–AS.102–AS.103. These manor houses are dated to the Sasanian period on the basis of their architectural remains and pottery sherds (see Chapter 5, s. 5.3), and the remains of their large, adjacent, Sasanian settlements.

3.4.6 *Fire-temples*

This category includes the sites of AS.018, AS.026, AS.035 and AS.048, all in the central plain of Abdanan. The close location of AS.026 and AS.048 to the respective forts of AS.024–AS.025 and

Fig. 3.45. AS.039, view from south-east. (Source: author)

Fig. 3.46. AS.039, view from south-west. (Source: author)

Fig. 3.47. Part of the architectural structures remaining in AS.039, view from north-west. (Source: author)

Fig. 3.48. AS.100 beside the dirt road of Seyyed Habib Shrine, view from south-west. (Source: author)

Fig. 3.49. Part of the architectural structures remaining in AS.100, view from south-west. (Source: author)

Fig. 3.50. Part of the architectural structures remaining in AS.100, view from south. (Source: author)

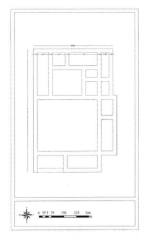

Fig. 3.51. Plan of AS.039. (After Mohammadifar and Motarjem 2001, Plan 24)

AS.047 is an indication of the association between these categories (see Map 3.15 for the spatial association of the location of fire-temples in relation to other categories of sites). Similarly, the two other fire-temples were constructed near the castles AS.019 and AS.035. Also noteworthy is that AS.035, the Jōliyān fire-temple (Figures 3.56–3.58), has remained in a better condition than the rest of the fire-temples found in Abdanan, even though it has been almost completely dug up in clandestine excavations and its cultural deposits are completely disturbed. This fire-temple is the surviving part of a larger structure consisting of four stone walls and piers of, respectively, 6m and 2m thickness, surrounded by a 1.5m wide vestibule[5] (Figure 3.64). The size and architectural features of the Jōliyān fire-temple[6] imply the probable importance of the population centre of Jōliyān (AS.034). Apart from this particular example, according to surface evidence, other remaining fire-temples of Abdanan, that is S.018 and AS.026, lack a vestibule and any space other than the central chahār-ṭāq part – unless prospective excavations prove otherwise. These two structures measure 64m and 56m in area, covered by the pillars of the chahār-ṭāqi. As to the ruins of AS.048, it is not currently possible to recognise a clear pattern in the distribution of the abundant scattered architectural remains with cobblestones with plaster mortar. Nonetheless, as the experts from the local office of the Ministry of Heritage, Handicraft and Tourism assured us that the four piers of a chahār-ṭāqi not long ago stood at the top of the mound, we opted to mention the site and to date it according to its typical Sasanian pottery sherds and the architectural materials of the ruins that were commonly used in the Sasanian buildings of Abdanan and its adjacent areas, such as Sasanian complexes in Dare-shahr County and the Seymareh River basin (see Chapter 1, s. 1.4; Chapter 2, n. 71). Generally, dating of these sites is according to their architectural features (Figures 3.52–3.58), and comparative examination of the pottery sherds recovered from them with material from their neighbouring Sasanian sites (see Chapter 5, s. 5.3).

3.4.7 *Forts*

Five other Abdanan sites fall into the category of forts. These are AS.011, AS.012, AS.024, AS.025 and AS.047. Constructed with rubble and cobblestones with a plaster mortar, these structures were erected on the natural hills of the county. As expected, they are

Fig. 3.52. AS.018, view from west. (Source: author)

Fig. 3.53. Remaining parts of the four piers of AS.018, view from south-east. (Source: author)

Fig. 3.54. Part of the architectural structures remaining in AS.026, view from south-east. (Source: author)

Fig. 3.55. Remaining parts of the south-eastern and north-eastern piers of AS.026, view from east. (Source: author)

Fig. 3.56. Position of AS.035 on a natural hillock, view from north. (Source: author)

Fig. 3.57. Four piers of AS.035, view from south-west. (Source: author)

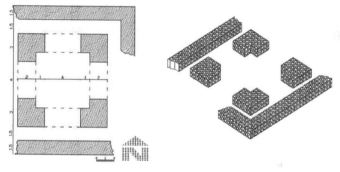

Fig. 3.58. Plan of AS.035. (After Mohammadifar and Motarjem 2012, Plan 1)

strongly related to the main roads and passageways[7] of the region (see below). In terms of size, this category is not homogeneous and comprises the fortlets of AS.024 and AS.025, with respective areas of 292.4m and 121m, and the forts of AS.011 and AS.012, which are much larger, 15,000m in area. Moreover, the area of the fort of AS.038 measures 3,600m. This category also includes AS.047, whose size cannot be estimated given the quite damaged state of the ruins on the rather high mound. Differentiation between the forts and the other category of defensive structures in Abdanan, castles, is not based on the size of the representatives of each category, but according to their geographic location, environs, spatial distribution and relation to other sites, rate of accessibility, and surface materials. As for the functions of the castles, such as as a space for storing surplus agricultural yields, they are, compared to forts, richer in terms of surface material. Unlike castles, the forts are categorised according to their close connection to roads. The fact that they are not near settlements of large or medium size distinguishes them from castles, which are a component of urban built environments and are closely linked to settled populations and an agriculture-based economy (see Map 3.15 for the spatial distribution of the categories and their overlap). In the case of the forts, however, a strong association can be observed with the main roads of the area and its strategic regional passageways (Map 3.16, Chapter 3, s. 3.6). The fortlets of AS.024 and AS.025, with a view to the south-east and east, overlook one of the most important roads of Abdanan, which connects the lowlands of the east and south of the region to its mountainous area and, by reaching to the Kabirkooh mountain ranges, to the farther regions of the Central Zagros. Similarly, the fort AS.047 with its view towards the south, south-west and west, offers remarkable views over an eastern–western road in the central plain of the county.

The presence of the Sasanian fort of Seyrom-shāh on the northern side of the Kabirkooh pass in the neighbouring region of Dare-shahr, the historical Seymareh, posits the hypothesis that this strategic pass through the mountain ranges of the Central Zagros was under use and control in this period. Seyrom-shāh fort (Figure 3.59) is placed on the peak a hill 40m in height on the eastern shoreline of the Seymareh River between N33°20′23.54″ latitude and E47°9′4.81″ longitude. From the south and south-east, it offers a view over the Ramāvand plain, holding the important Sasanian city of Ramāvand or Barz-e Ghawāleh, its fire-temple, and an illustriously stucco-decorated palace/manor house (Karamian 2015; Niakan 2015).[8] Seyrom-shāh has an irregular rectangular plan oriented in a north-east–south-west direction, with a length of 97.5m and width of 38m on its north-eastern flank and a width of 23.5m on the south-western side (Mohammadifar 2010: 52). Following the traditions of this era, the fort has contemporary parallels in the adjacent Abdanan in terms of its architectural material, features and design.[9] Therefore, apart from the note about the interrelation between forts and fire-temples in Abdanan, strategic inter-regional roads[10] could have a major impact on the positioning logic of the construction of these defensive structures. The architectural remains (Figures 3.60–3.64), ground plans (Figures 3.65–3.66) and defensive character of these sites, as well as the pottery sherds recovered from them (Chapter 5, s. 5.3), have formed the bases for recognition of their function and date.

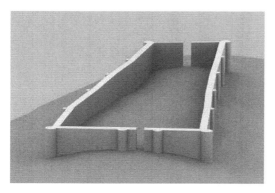

Fig. 3.59. 3D reconstruction of the Seyrom-shāh fort, view from north-east. (After Mohammadifar 2010)

Fig. 3.60. AS.024, view from west. (Source: author)

Fig. 3.61. Part of the architectural structures remaining in AS.024, view from south. (Source: author)

Fig. 3.62. AS.025, view from south-east. (Source: author)

Fig. 3.63. AS.047, view from south. (Source: author)

Fig. 3.64. Part of the eastern wall of AS.047, view from east. (Source: author)

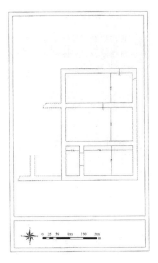

Fig. 3.65. Plan of AS.024. (After Mohammadifar and Motarjem 2001, Plan 15/1)

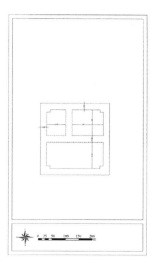

Fig. 3.66. Plan of AS.025. (After Mohammadifar and Motarjem, 2001, Plan 15/2)

3.5 SASANIAN SETTLEMENT PATTERN IN ABDANAN

As mentioned above, the purpose of this chapter is to study the spatial distribution of the Sasanian sites in Abdanan. To reach this goal, besides understanding the cultural specifications of the region under exploration in this period, one has to analyse the interaction between the human and environmental variables of its habitat

(Anschuetz et al. 2001: 188–9). The foundation of the studies that have aimed to identify the patterns between sites and environmental factors and land use is the hypothesis that people prefer to locate their settlements as close as possible to the most important resources for their subsistence strategies (Banning 2002: 32). Accordingly, the quantity of the relationship between such factors and settlement patterns is evaluated. Those variables are distance and position of the sites relative to roads, rivers and near neighbours, and elevation ranges, land use, vegetation, and erosion condition of the place holding archaeological sites, along with the type of climate influencing these.

3.5.1 Distance from roads

Concerning this variable, the sites divided into three categories. Accordingly, 11.6 per cent of them are located in the zone of less than 500m distance, and 37.7 and 50.7 per cent of the sites are situated in distance zones of 500–1,000m and 1,000–1,500m respectively (Map 3.3).

Path modelling is one of the most challenging research topics within spatial analysis in archaeology. Over the past decade, there has been considerable progress in this regard. The use of path modelling in landscape archaeological research, nevertheless, is

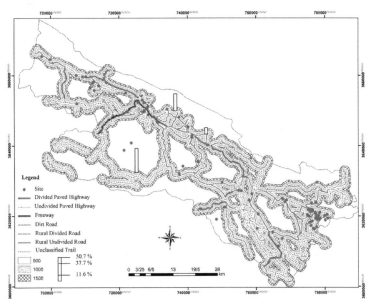

Map 3.3. Location and ratio of sites in relation to roads. (Source: author)

still relatively limited (Polla and Verhagen 2014: 3). However, studying roads and the quality of exploitation of natural passageways has played a considerable role in spatial analyses. As roads provide the opportunity for socioeconomic relationships between different human groups, they may also reflect either the determinism of different ecosystems or the struggle of people overcoming natural barriers limiting them (Khosrowzadeh and Habibi 1394 [2015]: 107). Movement constitutes landscape. It is an essential act of weaving places into the web of landscape, making it real for the people themselves. People also carry objects, moving them into new positional and relational contexts with other things, and they create new material encounters and traces through movement (Mlekuž 2014: 5). Todays, the majority of GIS-based network analyses concern road networks, and attempt to answer questions concerning network structure or typology, the location of particular facilities – usually archaeological sites – on the network, and the routing of information, goods, or people through those networks (Conolly and Lake 2006: 237–9). Furthermore, regional, archaeological surveys provide important insights into the debate over the crucial roles of trade and communication in the development of early states (Wilkinson 2000: 240). This point is even more significant in the spatiotemporal horizons under examination in the present research. Abdanan holds the infrequent safe passageways of the arduous Kabirkooh mountain range. According to historical documents and the geographical situation of Abdanan County, we know that one of the most important linking roads between Mesopotamia and the Central Zagros region, and consequently beyond to the Central Iranian Plateau, passed through this region. This is the road introduced by Herodotus as the Royal Road between Sardis and Susa (5.49; Evans 1982: 69), passing Mesopotamia via the Jebel Hamrin district into Dehloran, Abdanan and the north-western portion of Khuzestan, through Der and Kimsar, towards Susa (Potts 2016: 81; see also Chapter 2, s. 2.5 and n. 9). However, as Frayne (1992: 58–9) specified, such a route had been in use at least since Early Dynastic times.[11] Later, in the Assyrian documents of the early first millennium, since 858 BC and by Shalmaneser III (Obel.1.190; see also Herzfeld 1968: 23–4, 222), this Babylon–Hagmatāna road is called *Simesi pass*. The important communicative role of this natural route continued through history, and it is attested in the early Islamic documents as the main road between Baghdad and Hamadan (Ibn Khordādbeh 1992: 24–63; Abi-Ya'qub 1977: 43–4). The most important border of the Sasanian Empire was the western one, commercially and politically, and the Sasanian kings of kings could not ignore the location of Abdanan in the first great fold of Zagros, after Jebel Hamrin, to the east of Mesopotamia. Therefore, apart from all supposedly regional functions of the roads of Abdanan during this period, one may also consider them in an inter-regional context.

3.5.2 *Distance from rivers*

In this section, we discuss the distance of the archaeological sites from rivers, under three categories of sites with a distance of less than 500m, between 500 and 100m, and 1,000–1,500m, which respectively include 10.5, 41.7 and 47.7 per cent of the sites (Map 3.4).

'Next to the energy of sun, water is the most essential prerequisite for life on earth' (Vink 1983: 44). In recent years, water has become an important subject in landscape archaeology. As an inseparable part of any landscape, this element is fundamental for human life and any kind of human–environment interaction. As water is the blood of organic organisms and essential for any kind of production, its possession and control are usually regarded

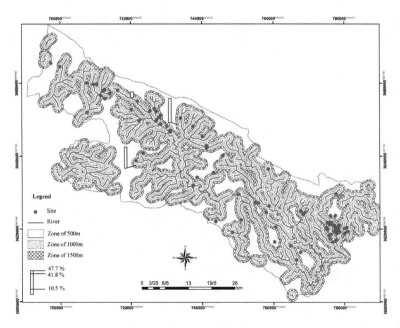

Map 3.4. Location and ratio of sites in relation to rivers. (Source: author)

as the main symbols for monopolisation, democracy, and the fair management and distribution of resources. Water politics has been under examination in the social sciences for a long time, indicating the capabilities of this environmental variable in respect of power distribution and its influence on groups (Strang 2008: 123). It may be an important factor in the formation of dendritic models of the spatial distribution of sites. Therefore, this element can act as a cause behind the establishment of social hierarchy (Banning 2002: 161–3). Given the undeniable impact of water resources in ecosystems on all aspects of human life, it is critical to study them. In the recent years, this emphasis has led to evaluation of this environmental factor in regional spatial analysis (Peterson 2008: 256). Regarding the water resources of the region under study, Abdanan, with a large number of rivers and springs, is one of the richest areas of Ilam Province. Literally meaning 'water supply', the name of this county reflects the same fact. Furthermore, archaeological data in the neighbouring area of Dehloran have shown a long history of the management of water resources and usage of canals from the Choga Mami Transitional (CMT) phase (Wilkinson 2000: 251).[12] In particular, the available evidence about the imperial investment of the Sasanians in the irrigation system and construction of canals in the adjacent areas of south-western Iran and southern Mesopotamia points to the huge scale of water management planning during this period. The monumentality of some of the Sasanian hydraulic landscapes in southern Mesopotamia, south-western Iran, the Gorgan plain and Fars, in the form of different types of canals designed according to the economic and political policies of the central state and the environmental and topographic settings of each region, points to the imperial level of such practices.[13] Nevertheless, we may consider that not all the water management projects relating to the Sasanian period inevitably imply such a scale. As discussed, the studied archaeological data about the Sasanian-era expansion of the hydraulic landscapes in the Dehloran plain (Neely 1974; 2011; 2016) are aligned with the literary sources of the East Syrian hagiographical tradition (Bedjan 1891: 323–4). However, we have no evidence that might lead us to refer such activities to a political authority rather than to the local state. The same implication seems to be sensible in respect of the Mianab plain of lowland Susiana too (Moghadam and Miri 2003). Therefore, it is important to acknowledge the challenge of recognising the nature and scale of the infrastructural developments even for different areas inside single geographical zones, whether it be the highlands of the Central

Zagros or its neighbouring lowlands of Khuzestan. Regarding the region under study, although there is no available data for the empirically tested material from Abdanan, according to the above-mentioned macro-regional evidence from the adjacent areas around Abdanan, one may not rule out the possibility of the same condition appertaining during the Sasanian period. In this regard, archaeological data can also be of use to some extent. In the central plain and eastern areas of Abdanan in particular, where environmental conditions are closer to those of the lowlands of Khuzestan and Dehloran, around the settlements of AS.022, AS.034, AS.057 and AS105, alongside the fort AS.037, canals are documented and irrigation agriculture has been practised. A more intensive research design in Abdanan, aimed at exploring these inter-site activities and establishing the origins of channels (Jotheri 2018), will probably lead to similar results.

3.5.3 *Elevation of the sites above sea level*

According to this factor, the relationship between the location of Sasanian sites and their elevation is illustrated in two types of maps: a Digital Elevation Model (DEM), which properly displays different elevation ranges of the region, and a sectioned map (Maps 3.5–3.6).

Three zones of elevation of less than 500m, between 500 and 1,000m, and between 1,000 and 1,500m contain 49.9, 32.3 and 13.72 per cent of the sites respectively. It is notable that no Sasanian site within the zones with elevation ranges of between 1,500 and 2,000m and 2,000 and 2,500m has been found. Elevation ranges form thermal centres with different temperatures. They are influential on various features of ecosystems, such as air pressure, radiation, temperature,[14] annual precipitations, diversity of animal and vegetation species, and the time-span of growth seasons, and consequently on the differently adopted subsistence strategies of various societies all around the world. In addition, as the impact of elevation on visibility is definite (Lock et al. 2014; Winterbottom and Long 2006: 1357), this factor can determine the levels of resource accessibility, quantity/quality of interaction between human groups, and visual and the cognitive potentials/limits of those groups. Located between two different geographical zones of alluvial plains and intermontane highlands, Abdanan displays a diverse character according to altitude and is a proper case for examining such influences.

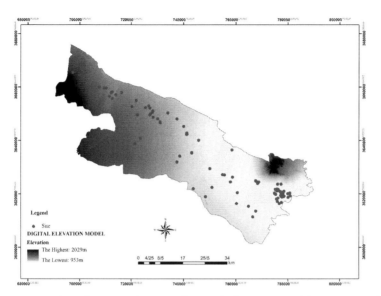

Map 3.5. Location of sites on the map of Digital Elevation Model. (Source: author)

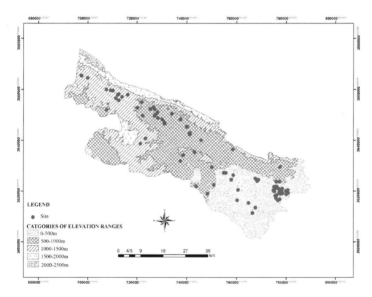

Map 3.6. Location of sites in relation to elevation. (Source: author)

3.5.4 Types of land use

In this section, we divide the Sasanian sites into distinct groups on the basis of the factor of land use. According to this variable, the strong majority of the sites, 95 per cent, are found in areas with rich and steppe pastures with dispersed trees. Two other categories are

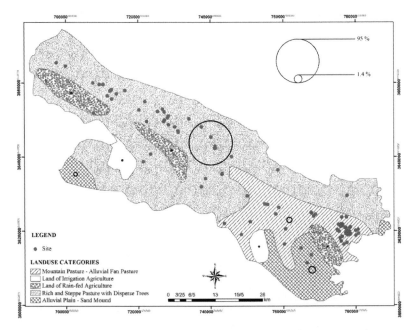

Map 3.7. Location and ratio of sites in relation to land use. (Source: author)

alluvial plains–sand mounds and mountainous pastures–alluvial fan pastures, each of which contains 1.4 per cent of the sites under study in Abdanan. In addition, each of the categories of lands featuring irrigation and rain-fed agriculture contains around one per cent of the sites (Map 3.7).

The undeniable practical and political significance of land has frequently made it the centre of struggles over its use and control (Rhind and Hudson 1980: 3). Land use is closely associated with the economy of the people exploiting specific lands. Among the main changes made by humans to our planet are the diversion of half of the fresh water, half of all plant productivity, and the modification of around half of the lands for our own purposes (McGill 2015: 38). From an ecological viewpoint, land use is the manifestation of the ecosystem management of our species in order to meet some of its needs (Vink 1983: 13). However, uses of land and other production factors in an economy are the outcomes of numerous observations. Lands under the exploitation of human groups are inextricably admixed with the history, ideology and economy of those populations. To know how a particular land is exploited and shaped/reshaped in a specific period, it is necessary to identify who has used it. Nonetheless, the proprietary land use analyses in the social sciences have demonstrated that the local landholders are usually the ones who have the vaguest criteria regarding the related process of decision-making and the possible alternatives (Denman and Prodano 1972: 17–19). The specific use of a land by individuals is usually part of the unconscious process of acculturalisation they experience in their societies. People gain a particular image/concept of the land they have settled on and exploited in relation to its natural landscape, alongside the built environment. In other words, land use is construed in the habitus under whose influence they live.[15] Another factor potentially impacting this relationship is the regional plans according to which decision-makers at an upper level in the social organisation, local or central states, exercise authority to design policies regarding land use in each region as a constituent part of a larger unit. In light of the monumental projects practised in different territories of the Sasanian Empire, therefore, besides the local culture, it is also important, in the present examination, to consider the bigger picture and role of state management and planning. Abdanan has vast pastures owing to its rich water resources. Although, in some parts of the central plain, the soil is rich enough for irrigation agriculture, groups are mostly using small-scale rain-fed agriculture besides the exploitation of pastures.

3.5.5 Land vegetation

In studying the vegetation of the places containing the Sasanian sites in Abdanan County, we observe eleven distinct categories featuring different kinds of vegetation. Accordingly, 37 per cent of the archaeological sites are located in the grassland zone. The farmlands involving rain-fed and irrigation agriculture also contain 37 and 12 per cent of these sites, respectively. In addition, 12 per cent of the sites are found in the forest zone and around one per cent of them are located in pastures of average quality (Map 3.8).

'Vegetation is any plant cover in which a number of plant species have adapted to the growth conditions with regard to the combination of the plant species as well as to their spatial arrangements' (Vink 1983: 61). Dictionary definitions which usually describe vegetation as plants collectively are inadequate, as vegetation is an integral part of an ecosystem and cannot be understood without analysing its role within that ecosystem (Kent and Coker 1992: 1). Comprising competing plant communities, this factor depends on the environment and its effects, too. Therefore, a plant community and its environment may have to be treated in combination as a

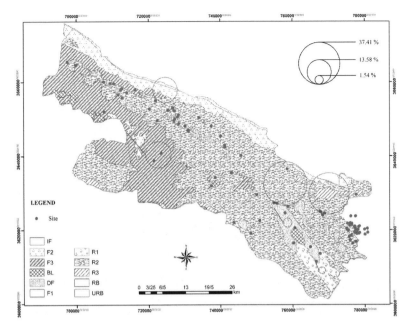

Map 3.8. Location and ratio of sites in relation to vegetation. (Source: author)

unit (Küchler 1967: 17–18). By environment here, we mean the notion of a very complex system of different interrelated organisms integrated within a spatial unit. Therefore, to analyse any environment, it is vital to consider the transformative force of living organisms in their ecosystem. This concept underlies the cultural aspect of environment marked by anthropogenic modifications. Regarding vegetation and land use, these processes of human modification are evaluated exploring 'conversion to pasture, cropland, tree plantations, urbanisation, and secondary vegetation'.[16] Thus, we should consider that the very concept of vegetation, beside its natural character, embraces a cultural notion. Vegetation is an important factor in settlement locating. This factor plays a focal role in determining the basic diet, subsistence strategy and economy of groups. Binford (2001), in his modelling based on hunter-gatherer societies and environmental conditions, discusses how the scale of nomadism, that is the number of movements in a year, is related to the availability of a stable amount of food, due to population increase. Therefore, one may expect that the regions with rich vegetation have the potential to attract human groups with different subsistence strategies. Influenced by diverse climate conditions and having a proper soil for allowing plants to flourish in many areas, vegetation in Abdanan is considerably diverse, making the adoption of an agro-pastoral compound economy possible.

3.5.6 *Distance from other sites*

In relation to this factor, we consider six separate categories of sites. Thus, 68 per cent of the sites are located within a zone of distance of less than 500m from the nearest neighbour, 10 per cent are found in the distance range 500m–1,000m, and 7.77 and 12.22 per cent of them respectively are situated in the 1,000–1,500m and 2,000–3,000m zones (Maps 3.9–3.10).

Study of the distance of archaeological sites from their closest neighbour and their position with regard to other sites plays a focal role in regional, spatial analyses. Apart from the fact that analysis of this factor can demonstrate the spatial organisation of sites, it may offer us an opportunity to examine socioeconomic systems, the spatiotemporal processes of these systems, and inter-group relationships and borders in large-scale regional patterns. Analysis of this variable has been considered from the first days of settlement pattern archaeology. For instance, we can mention how application of the central-place theory (Christaller 1966) of human geography resulted

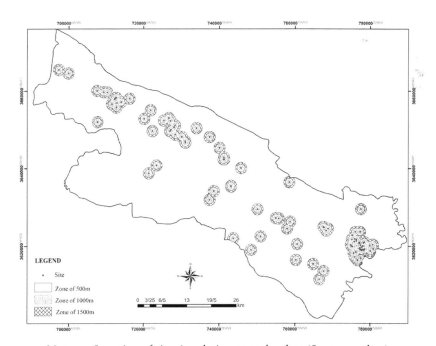

Map 3.9. Location of sites in relation to each other. (Source: author)

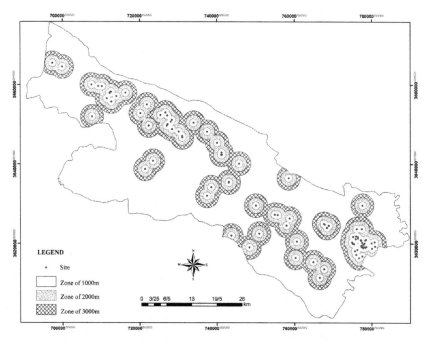

Map 3.10. Location of sites in relation to each other, within the distance zones
of 1,000m. (Source: author)

in successful analysis of the archaeological data acquired from the
alluvial plains of southern Mesopotamia and south-western Iran
(Adams 1965; 1981; Adams and Nissen 1972). In recent years, and
because of the development of distributional models of spatial analysis in landscape archaeology, research in this area has progressed and
entered a new stage with more accurate interpretations. However, it
should be noted that, due to the interwoven nature of cultural and
natural factors behind the settlement patterns, it is not always easy
to determine the related settlement systems.

As regards the sites under examination, they have a high level
of integrity, which can be a sign of their strong mutual depend-
ency. The regional settlement pattern consists of related but distinct
models. This point is especially distinguishable when we compare
the distribution pattern of the sites in the eastern part of Abdanan
with that of the other sites of the county. The archaeological sites
of eastern Abdanan are distributed in a concentrated clustered
pattern that indicates intensive interaction among the members of
clusters. On the other hand, other sites in the central plain and
mountainous parts of the region are arranged in a linear-dendritic

pattern. The buffer map of the sites with distance zones of 1,000m (Map 3.10) demonstrates these patterns more clearly.

3.5.7 *Erosion level of the sites' soil*

In this section, we divide the Sasanian sites of Abdanan into five categories. Accordingly, 45.8 per cent of the sites are located in the zone of low erosion and 8.3 per cent of them appear in the zone of relatively low erosion. Other zones, of average erosion, relatively high erosion and high erosion, contain 16.6, 19.7 and 9.3 per cent of the sites respectively (Map 3.11).

In this section, we study the impact of soil erosion as an environmental factor in the sites' placing. Undoubtedly, the properties and potentials of soil have a direct influence on the food production and economic growth and decline of human groups. However, in evaluating this variable, it is necessary to study the erosional processes that happened after the period under examination as well, otherwise the impacts of this variable in the analysis can be misleading. In Abdanan, the important point is that apart from the depositional process connected with the mountains around the county, the concentration of human activities in the central plain has increased

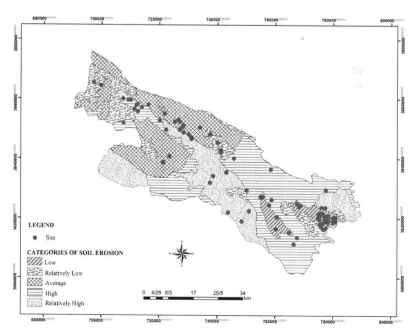

Map 3.11. Location of sites in relation to soil erosion. (Source: author)

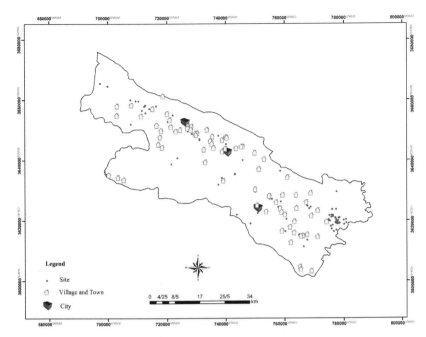

Map 3.12. Location of sites in relation to contemporary population centres.
(Source: author)

soil erosion in this particular area. The central plain holds the most important contemporary centres of population in the region (Map 3.12), which is an indication of the related modern processes. However, according to the general distribution of the Sasanian sites, they are concentrated in the areas within the zones of low or relatively low soil erosion.

3.5.8 *Position of sites according to climate types*

In the examination of the location of sites according to different climate types, five distinct categories are considered. Accordingly, 47.4 per cent of them are located in the dry climate zone, and the semi-arid zone encompasses 3 per cent of the sites. In addition, severe semi-arid and average semi-arid zones contain 46.3 and 3 per cent of these sites respectively. It is notable that no Sasanian sites have been found in the mild humid climate zone of Abdanan (Map 3.13).

Climate, as an influential intermediate in human–environment interaction, is a basic subject in landscape research. A number of variables such as precipitation, air pressure, humidity, temperature and wind are considered under this heading (Vink 1983: 35).

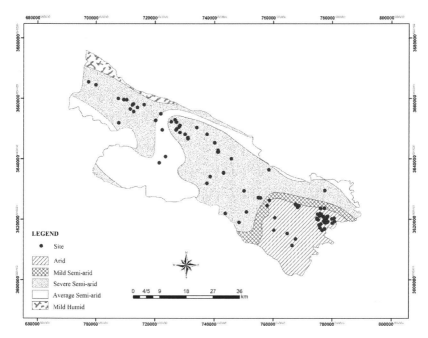

Map 3.13. Location of sites in relation to types of climate. (Source: author)

Different combinations of these variables form discrete climate types, each of which has dominated some parts of the world. Besides the point that climatic conditions in a given area are influenced by environmental conditions such as elevation and latitude, climate forms the flora and fauna of a region. Consequently, the economic and political systems of any society are partly shaped in response to climate conditions. The cultural influence of this factor is so great that sometimes the cultures of various human groups in a vast geographical area[17] are grouped under one overarching term which implies the general dominant climate type in those regions, such as 'Mediterranean culture' or 'the culture of dry regions'. Nonetheless it is clear that the impact of climate on human societies has considerably decreased with modern technological advances, although this does not mean that climate influence has nowadays been rendered insignificant. The heated public debate on climate change taking place at international level is a fact that demonstrates this point. The climate of Abdanan is discussed above, yet it is important to note that, partly due to the diverse climate types in the region, a dichotomy in the distribution pattern of the sites is recognisable. According to the other variables discussed above, this pattern is applicable to the observed differences between the sites of dry, eastern Abdanan and the others formed under the influence of the semi-arid climate of the rest of the region.

3.6 EVALUATION

Cultural evolution has followed different paths. After diffusion from Africa, societies separated from each other and lived out different cultural histories. We face different sets of paths that began their generation on the same foundation (Renfrew 2006: 225). Hence, one may assume that the cultural process experienced in the highlands of the Central Zagros is different from those experienced in the lowlands of Mesopotamia and Khuzestan. However, as ethnographic and archaeological evidence has demonstrated, the interwoven interaction and transportation networks of people, materials and information between these neighbouring regions attest that they should not be construed as oppositional territories, but as complementary.[18]

Due to their diversity, strategic significance and marginality, mountainous regions are often very special environments. Mountain contexts are of great importance for people living in the highlands or the areas neighbouring them, not only on account of their rich natural resources and great biodiversity but also because of their unique sociocultural dynamics whose development has tended to be via means placed, often, far away from the centres of political power. This marginality can also extend to the movement within these regions where mountain ranges, due to their natural configuration, regularly constitute mighty obstacles and play a central role in strategy, commerce and travelling (Marrieta-Flures 2014). In analysing the settlement pattern of Abdanan in Sasanian times, besides the environmental variables cultural factors are also taken into consideration. The strategic situation of the region in the first great fold of Zagros to the east of southern Mesopotamia grants this region military importance. The location of this region is significant from another aspect, too. Abdanan is located between the lowlands of south-western Iran, southern Mesopotamia,[19] and the highlands of the Central Zagros. This location was bound up with cultural interactions which played a focal role in the formation of the specific cultural identity of the region in the Sasanian period. Examination of the related material culture has demonstrated this phenomenon.[20] In light of its proper environmental capabilities and ecological potentialities, holding strategic passageways and providing for the requirements of its inhabitants,[21] Abdanan is a region highly suited to attracting human groups. The varied environment

of the Central Zagros and south-western Iran lends itself to different types of land use across the sedentary and mobile spectrum of
subsistence modes. The lowland plains and montane valleys make
up the majority of the agriculturally productive areas which, besides
the slopes and foothills, also hold rich pasturelands. Seasonal movements of pastoralists and semi-sedentary groups between highlands
and lowlands are explored in many ethnographic studies (Hopper
and Wilkinson 2013: 36; see Chapter 2, n. 77). It was the geographical position of Abdanan, between the lowlands of Khuzestan and
the Central Zagros Mountains, such as the Kabirkooh mountain
range, that brought about such diversity. The practice of different
subsistence strategies in the spatiotemporal horizons under study
is reflected in the archaeological material and the related spatial
distribution. As mentioned above, we may identify different types of
pastoralism in Abdanan during the Sasanian era. Pastoral nomadism set its centre in the eastern part of Abdanan and transhumance
placed it near the sedentary sites, particularly in the central plain.
Moreover, practising of the agriculture-based economy is recognisable in the irrigation or rain-fed types of agriculture around the
large settlements, such as AS.034, AS.102–AS.103 and AS.105; the
sites of average size, such as AS.022 and AS.023; and the small
ones, AS.051, AS.055 and AS.057. This diversity is also demonstra-
ble from another viewpoint, that is, evaluation of the concept of
sites' richness (Banning 2002: 138–9), and according to the number
of the categories of sites. In the GIS programme, the spatial statis-
tics index of the standard deviational ellipse distribution enables us
to evaluate the concentration of sites in general, and that of each
category of sites in particular (Maps 3.14–3.15). Accordingly, it
is specified that, during the Sasanian period, sedentary sites were
concentrated in the central plain more than in preceding times.
Consequently, they had better access to environmental capacities
such as roads, water resources, proper soil and rich pastures. There
is an overlap among the spatial organisation of the categories of
castles, sedentary sites and large settlements. According to the visibility concept,[22] the aspect layer of the region is also studied, (Map
3.16) and hence it is noted that forts are directly connected to the
most important linking routes of the region. The forts are concentrated in the northern part of the central plain, where they hold the
main regional passageways of Abdanan as well. This determines
the role of roads as an important factor in the location of these
structures. Bearing in mind the strategic position of the region,
this model of distribution makes sense. Also noteworthy is that,

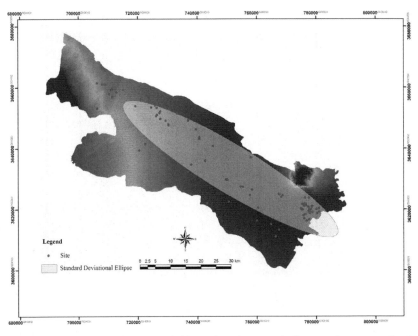

Map 3.14. Standard deviational ellipse distribution of all sites. (Source: author)

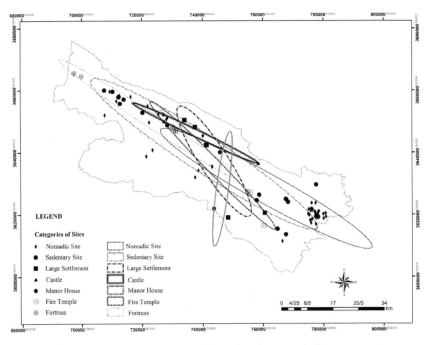

Map 3.15. Standard deviational ellipse distribution of all site categories.
(Source: author)

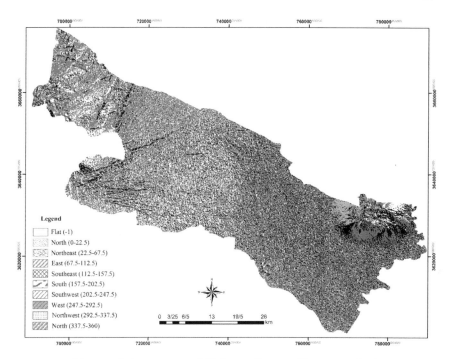

Map 3.16. Aspect map of Abdanan County. (Source: author)

according to the spatial pattern of nomadic sites, particularly in the eastern part of the county, the roads variable was not as important as water resources for the location of these campsites. The sites identified as manor houses are not frequent, a fact that makes evaluating their spatial concentration challenging. That said, it seems likely that their location was connected with their neighbouring large settlements. The same would also be true for fire-temples, except they are also closely associated with the forts.

The regional spatial distribution of Sasanian sites in Abdanan demonstrates the interwoven correlation of settled and nomadic sites, particularly in the northern part of the region. This prevents us from considering these parts of society as opposing. The observed associations between highlands and alluvial plains and among nomads and settled groups in the ethnological and archaeological evidence lead us to reconsider the traditional concept of the gap between people with different subsistence strategies, which is an echo of the first interpretations of the ancient society of Mesopotamia (Kamp and Yoffee 1980). Ethnic groups which, as political entities, include farmer-herder sectors are proofs of the weakness of such a model in the interpretation of the vertical/enclosed pastoral nomadism of the Central Zagros throughout different eras. On the basis of the constant relationship between and links among nomads and settled people, such a division existed neither in the peoples' minds nor in their partially remaining literature (Hole 1978: 131). Since these groups were interwoven in a dimorphic society, there was probably no distinct territory of nomads or settled agriculturists. For the most part, some or all of the pastoral pastures were located in the surrounding areas of cities or settlements (Paulette 2013: 135), and the group, politically speaking, was under the control of a larger entity which had its centre in a city.[23] Therefore, there is no reason to look for such a presumed distinction in the archaeological material in this case. The enclosed nomadism concept, suggested by Rowton (1974) for Zagros pastoral nomadism, implies a situation in which, as relationships between groups are close, symbiosis appears. Here, sociopolitical interaction among nomads and settled peoples is an outcome of a physical environment that demands seasonal movements and the close interaction of the populations with different modes of subsistence (see Chapter 1, s. 1.3). The spatial organisation of Sasanian sites in the Abdanan region, moreover, demonstrates the position of some campsites with a likely function related to transhumance located near settlements. This picture conforms to the compound economy model, designed for the maximum exploitation of such a diverse ecosystem. The considerable increase in the number of Sasanian sites in Abdanan (Graph 3.1), attested by all the archaeological surveys in the region, specifies the population growth and successful economic system in the county during this period. Recent research projects undertaken in the provinces of Ilam, Kermanshah and Lorestan[24] confirm a similar phenomenon, according to which the number of Sasanian sites increased in all types of cities,[25] villages

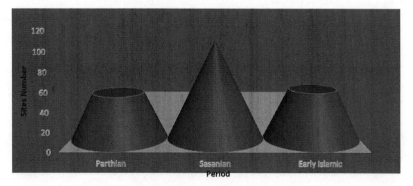

Graph 3.1. Chart showing the number of Parthian, Sasanian and Early Islamic sites in Abdanan. (Source: author)

and castles.[26] Development of the agricultural lands, as an important fiscal source, was critical for the Sasanian central state (Whitcomb 2014: 212). On the basis of their economic politics, the Sasanians developed the structures of water management such as weirs, dams, water-powered mills, canals, and irrigation systems in different territories of the empire (Adams 1962; 1965; 1981; 2006; Adams and Hansen 1968; Wenke 1975–6; 1981; 1987; Kim 1991; Hole 1979: 209; Simpson 1996; 2000; 2003; Neely 1974; 2011; 2016; Moghaddam and Miri 2003; Hopper and Wilkinson 2013; Hartnell 2014; Boucharlat 2015; Khosrowzadeh and Habibi 1394/2015; Lawrence and Wilkinson 2017: 6–7; Alizadeh and Ur 2007; Alizadeh 2014; Ur and Alizadeh 2013; Sauer et al. 2006: 138–51; Sauer et al. 2008: 156–65; Sauer 2017; Omrani Rekavandi et al. 2013; de Gruchy and Jotheri 2019; Soroush 2019). As discussed above, evidence for such activities is studied in Dehloran and Khuzestan in southwestern Iran, Hamrin and Diyāla in Mesopotamia, and Mughan and Gorgan Plains on the northern borders of the Sasanian Empire, to mention some cases. Such findings help to explain the population growth documented for some of the regions in this period. To study conditions in Abdanan, however, we need to consider the strategic location of the county, too. The increase in the number of forts and castles in Abdanan is related to the security of the passageways and roads, which were particularly limited, and were important for the local or central state in the northern mountainous areas of Abdanan. The Sasanian-period appreciation of the Central Zagros region is noticeable as one considers the foundation of the new cities in the region (see Chapter 2, s. 2.4), and the socioeconomic developments traced archaeologically, especially for the later part of the period, in areas such as Seymareh, Dare-shahr and Abdanan. One can postulate that the region underwent a growth, militarily and politically, from the reign of Husraw II (591–628) onwards, especially by the time of crisis in the western border of the empire and the decline of security in its capital.

It is hard to identify evidence that implies opposition to the mainstream culture through the partial material culture at archaeologists' disposal, but it is worth mentioning that the ceramic data for the region are quite homogeneous.[27] On the other hand, as mentioned above, the spatial pattern of the Sasanian sites' distribution in Abdanan County does not present a single settlement model, but apart from the dendritic model as the dominant pattern in the region, the eastern part of the county provides a clustered distribution model. It seems likely that, in spite of all the links which can be assumed in the enclosed nomadism system among the settled and nomad groups, eastern Abdanan's nomads constructed their distinct model of distribution according to their priorities in terms of the factors of intra-group relationships, security considerations, and the availability of flat land, pasture and water. On the basis of their subsistence strategy and social system, nomads represented a sub-culture in the Abdanan society of this period. Probably, therefore, without their being a serious threat to the local or central state, these people's military[28] and economic potential could be exploited and, without an exclusive territory, they could perhaps enjoy a level of independence as reflected in historical documents of earlier times (Hole 1978: 161; Daryaee 2009: 40–1).

In light of the data discussed, the dimorphic social system of Abdanan in the Sasanian period experienced a population growth that happened at an inter-regional level. This transformation probably ensued as a result of state-level planning and investment and the economic system adopted with regard to ecological conditions. On this inter-regional scale, one may recognise a positive correlation between the size of the system and the rate of its complexity (Binford 2001: 317–18; Johnson 1982). Here, we can point to the sub-systems of the region under study according to the available data. The natural ecosystem, comprising various environmental factors, is apparently the first of them to be considered. The political organisation,[29] with elites[30] and local Sasanian aristocrats (*āmārgar, šahrab, mow, driyōšān-jādaggōw-ud-dādwar* and so forth, as is mainly sigillographically attested for Mihragān-kadag, see Chapter 2, s. 2.4) managing the society, is another, characterised by its landscape signatures such as castles, fortifications, manor houses, and large settlements that could not be exploited except with capital investment. Another to mention is a net of different modes of subsistence represented by groups such as farmers, transhumant pastoralists (*dahigān* and *wāstariyōšān*) and artisans (*hutuxšān*),[31] alongside pastoral nomads (*kurd*) of eastern Abdanan. The associated site spatial organisation appears in the distribution models of sites all across the region. The ideological sub-system is also recognisable in light of the remains of centres such as fire-temples (*ātaxš kadag*) and gravestones (*dahmag*).[32]

According to the complex adaptive systems model,[33] in the evolutionary process from which those systems proceeded, sub-systems, with their special organisations and procedures, formed at a higher level as interwoven networks interacting with each other that shaped simultaneous hierarchies and general systems. Interaction and information flux within the system provide the adaptive self-organisation capability. In the state of self-organisation, social organisations are balanced, with a high level of potential for reaction and dynamic information process, and the system is set on the border between stability and chaos that is called by Packard the edge of chaos (Packard 1988a; 1988b; see also Jones, B. 1997). The non-linear causality and complexity of the interaction among different parts, which are characteristics of these systems, make it difficult to predict the outcome of the system-level behaviours by analysing their constituents. In other words, the scale and direction of the shift of the system hardly match the scale and direction of the phenomenon that caused it (Bernabeu Auban et al. 2012: 24). The mentioned evidence for the population growth and economic development of the mid-first millennium has been studied in territory ranging from Syria to parts of southern Mesopotamia, and in Iran, from its south-westernmost plains in Khuzestan Province to the Mughan plain at the north-western edge of the country, and beyond in the southern Caucasus in the Mil plain and at Bardha in the Republic of Azerbaijan, as well as in the Central Zagros and Fars regions and on the northern Persian Gulf coast around the Bushehr area (Adams 1962; 1965; 1981; 2006; Adams and Hansen 1968; Wenke 1975–6; 1981; 1987; Kim 1991; Simpson 1996; 2000; 2003; Neely 1974, 2011, 2016; Moghaddam and Miri 2003; Kennet 2007: 110; Potts and Roustaei 2009; Hopper and Wilkinson 2013; Hartnell 2014; Boucharlat 2015; Khosrowzadeh and Habibi 1394/2015; Lawrence and Wilkinson 2017: 6–7; Alizadeh and Ur 2007; Alizadeh 2014; Ur and Alizadeh 2013; Alizadeh et al. 2015: 126, Fig. 14, Tab. 3: the highest pre-medieval demographic growth in the Rāmhormoz region in Parthian and Sasanian times; Sauer 2017: 14–15; Wordsworth and Wencel 2018; al-Jahwari et al. 2018; Panahipour 2019). Such data determine the condition of a general inter-regional system at the edge of chaos. By the time, the exploitation of land has reached a considerably intense level. This situation did not last for long, however, since, according to the climate fluctuations of the Late Antique Little Ice Age from the early sixth century (Alizadeh et al. 2021 with references) and the socioeconomic crisis of the Early Medieval period, most of these areas entered an era of demographic and fiscal decline in which population levels and pressure on land resources were meagre in comparison to their apogee in the Sasanian period (Wilkinson 2000: 250; Whitcomb 2014; Alizadeh et al. 2021).

3.7 CONCLUSION

The diverse geography of Abdanan has provided the required conditions for the formation of different subsistence strategies and, hence, a compound economy. Apart from this, the strategic situation of the county is important. These two potentialities found a proper context for exploitation in the Sasanian period. By this time, the rivalry, economic and military, between the Sasanian and Roman/Byzantine Empires was followed by the large-scale imperial investments and the consequent intensification of pressure on land resources in some regions. Given its strategic situation holding important roads and passageways, along with its diverse character both socially and naturally, Abdanan was among the Sasanian territories that experienced unprecedented demographic growth ensuing from the more efficient resource management. Although a general pattern for the state-level management and investment in different parts of the empire may be inferred, these areas are dispersed, and the cause, nature and scale of the plans in each of them are distinct. Therefore, we need to be aware of the danger of generalising and to be careful in interpreting data from sample areas and making comparisons. The grounded interdisciplinary analysis of different sets of evidence relating to Abdanan in the Sasanian period indicates the particular character of its socioeconomic development, yet given the amount of the available data we cannot confidently determine the level of the political power behind it. Notwithstanding the historical and archaeological evidence indicating the imperial projects of the Sasanians in neighbouring regions, in Abdanan we may not rule out the role of local authorities. However, through the formation of new cities with their related socioeconomic features and structures, and in connection with nomadic centres, Abdanan during the Sasanian period underwent a new experience in the spatial distribution and settlement location that had its roots in the dimorphic social system and compound economy adopted with regard to the maximum exploitation of environmental resources. In a larger context, Abdanan perhaps was part of an inter-regional plan in which confrontation with social change was an inevitable outcome. It might be through this process that the population growth and equilibrium of the connected sub-systems of Abdanan in the Sasanian period, as part of a larger system, turned into the population decline of post-Sasanian times.

NOTES

1. See Amanollahi-Baharvand 1989: 232–53 for a succinct description of this plan and its consequences for the nomadic tribes of Iran.
2. In particular, it is identified as the archaeological site Musiyan (Carter and Stolper 1984: 212) and Tell Farrokh-abad (Frayne 1997: 233).
3. See Chapter 5 for illustrations and tables relating to the pottery sherds discussed in this chapter.
4. In the case of AS.021, with eight towers mounted at regular intervals and rectangular embrasures.
5. See Mohammadifar and Motarjem (2012) for the description and comparison of this fire-temple.
6. Apart from other factors such as rich archaeological materials, the size of the settlement, its adjacent castle, and the suitable environment of the Jōliyān plain for agriculture.
7. This book assumes that ancient roads follow similar paths to those of their modern counterparts. In both sample areas, various sets of evidence indicate the overlap of main ancient and modern routes. The terrain and topographic features, environmental conditions and geographical location of the arduous mountain ranges and intermontane valleys of the Central Zagros restrict communication networks and prevent free movement owing to several diverse obstacles (Chapter 2, s. 2.3). The limited number of traversable roads and infrequent safe passages is also reflected in Graeco-Roman sources (see Chapter 2, s. 2.3). These texts, too, signify the close association of the roads with the pastoralist highlanders of the region. As discussed, in these areas the Zagros environment favours movement and imposes seasonal pastoral nomadic or transhumant migrations. Ethnographic evidence (Chapter 2, n. 77; Chapter 4, s. 4.5.1) and historical documents (Wahrāmān, 42: 58; see Chapter 1, s. 1.3) point to the regular use of certain paths by nomads for seasonal migration. Archaeology may throw more light on the matter. The long-held seasonal migration networks of contemporary pastoral nomads in Farsan County mirror the spatial model of Sasanian settlement distribution to some extent (Chapter 4, s. 4.5.1). Also, some remaining parts of the historical road, called in medieval documents the Atābaki Road (Ibn Battuta 1371 [1993]: 241), were documented in archaeological surveys of Farsan County and dated to the Sasanian period according to the majority of the related sites on it (see Chapter 4). The route mainly paralleled the contemporary Izeh–Shahrekord highway (Chapter 2, n. 47). The location of important settlements of different eras (Chapter 2, n. 15) and Sasanian forts (Chapter 3, s. 3.4.7, Map 3.15) along the main roads of the consecutive Farsan and Abdanan areas is another indication of the lasting use of the main roads throughout history. Moreover, apart from the Classical and Hellenistic sources, indeed, administrative records of different

traditions and times, such as the Akkadian and Babylonian tablets and the Persepolis and the Tappe[h] Bardnakōn archives, indicate the continuous use of some routes, for example the so-called Great Khorasan Road, over millennia (Chapter 2).

8. For identification of the location of the Seymareh valley in the Sasanian province of Mihragān-kadag see Chapter 2, s. 2.4, and, for parallel archaeological evidence, see Chapter 2, n. 71.

9. It is built with rubble and cobblestones with a plaster mortar, and its plan followed the topographic features of the hill on which it stands. The details, such as four U-shaped corner towers and the main entrance flanked by rounded buttress towers, are comparable with those of AS.036 and AS.106 in Abdanan. Beyond the Central Zagros, Fulayj, a recently excavated Sasanian fort near Suhar on the Batinah Coast of Oman, provides an interesting case similar to these structures in terms of both architectural materials and features (al-Jahwari et al. 2018: 727–8, with more references).

10. See the section 'Distance from roads' in this chapter.

11. According to a list of toponyms that, as mentioned above, refers to URU_XA^{ki} on the path of the road (Frayne 1992: 58–9).

12. The CMT phase is considered to be between the late Samarra and early Ubaid periods in the Mesopotamian plains, c. 5000 BCE (Shaw and Jameson 1999: 160; for more information, see Oates 1987a, 1987b; Calvet 1987).

13. Such as the monumental Canal of Nahrawan in southern Iraq or the Shadorwan bridge of Shushtar in south-western Iran (Adams 1962; 1965; 1981; 2006; Adams and Hansen 1968; Wenke 1975–6; 1981; 1987; Sauer et al. 2006; Sauer et al. 2015; Wilkinson and Rayne 2010; Wilkinson et al. 2015: 408; Hartnel 2014; Lawrence and Wilkinson 2017; de Gruchy and Jotheri 2019; Soroush 2019).

14. In the case for mountainous areas, not only for those areas themselves but also for their neighbours (Vink 1983: 35).

15. For the notion of 'habitus' and the theory of its dynamic coincidence with 'field' according to Pierre Bourdieu's ideas, see Dyke 1999; Taylor 1998; Maton 2010.

16. Land that was disturbed but allowed to regrow (McGill 2015: 39).

17. Albeit problematically and unprofessionally.

18. See Hopper and Wilkinson (2013) for the parallel settlement-population fluxes between Susiana, Rām-Hormuz and Dehloran in the Prehistoric periods and between south-western Iran and southern Mesopotamia in the historical periods. Also, see Carter and Wright (2010) for similarities between the ceramic samples of Dehloran and southern Mesopotamia in the Early Dynastic phases and in the Achaemenid period; see Habibi and Heidari (1393 [2014]) for the same observation about the collections acquired from the Central Zagros and south-western Iran in the Sasanian period.

19. If we consider Dehloran as a part of southern Mesopotamia.
20. See Chapter 5.
21. For inter/intra-regional interactions and their political and commercial purposes.
22. For more information on this subject, see Lock et al. 2014; Winterbottom and Long 2006: 1,357.
23. In contrast to what is known about horizontal/open nomadism.
24. All as parts of the Central Zagros region (Boucharlat 2015).
25. Such as the large settlements of AS.034, and the complex of AS.101–AS.102–AS.103 in Abdanan, and Dare-shahr and Sargandāb in the neighbouring areas of Abdanan (Mohammadifar 2014).
26. Such as AS.019, AS.021, AS.036 and AS.106 in Abdanan, and Seyrom-shāh in the Seymareh valley (Mohammadifar 2014).
27. See Martin (2013: 96–191) for the study of sub-cultures in archaeology.
28. As mentioned earlier, some evidence regarding this point is available in written documents (Ibn Balxī 1984: 168; Cereti 1995: 7.9).
29. For the organisation of the society of the Sasanian Empire, see Daryaee 2009: 39–68.
30. On the regional scale, in Abdanan, it might include grandees (*wuzurgān*), the gentry (*āzādān*), a regional military commander (*naxwār*) and commanders of the forts (*argbed*).
31. These three groups formed most of the regional population settled in cities (*šahr, šahrestān*) and villages (*rustag, deh*) of different sizes.
32. This sub-system is related to the class of priests (*āsrōnān*) and the administrations of *mowūh* and *mowbed*. Given the different types of Abdanan's fire-temples with or without vestibules and other probable spaces, here it might include *hērbedān* (priests attending the fires), *dastûrān* (expert theologians), *dāwarān* (judges) and *radān* (learned priests).
33. For more information on CAS models, see Bernabeu Auban et al. 2012; Zurlini et al. 2008.

4 *Pastoral Nomadism in the Iranian Highlands during Late Antiquity: The Case of Farsan*

4.1 INTRODUCTION

Chapter 4 focuses on the process and factors behind the landscape-related and sociopolitical transformations that occurred in the Farsan region in Late Antiquity. As part of the Bakhtiyari highlands, Farsan County provides different environmental settings from Abdanan as discussed in the previous chapter. Although the cultural processes in the mountainous areas with a height of over 2,000m above sea level, such as Farsan County, are distinct from those of other geographical zones, yet, as discussed above (Chapter 1, s. 1.3), the topographic and climatic features of the Central Zagros have led to long-standing socioeconomic bonds between its inhabitants and the populations of the adjacent lowlands. However, archaeologically, these highlands are largely overlooked, particularly in terms of historical eras. That said, the recent fieldwork projects in the Farsan region have created a rather rare opportunity to investigate the long-term socioeconomic transitions scientifically, and to distinguish the various cultural and natural variables influential in these developments. Therefore, the geography of the region is here discussed first. Then, the general settlement system of Farsan is briefly examined in order to study the regional patterns of the Sasanian sites' spatial distribution in their long-term context and against their backdrop in pre-Sasanian times. The focal points explored in this chapter are the recognition of the general historical settlement systems and models, the evaluation of the processes of transformation in the built environment and modes of subsistence over time, and the factors behind these in the period under examination. In this process, the data acquired from the multi-period intensive Farsan Survey project in 2007, along with excavations at the significant site of Tappe^h Bardnakōn in two seasons in 2017 and 2018, are examined. Although of the 216 sites identified in the course of the survey thirty-six relate to the Sasanian period, we only consider the categories of settlement, tappe^h, hilltop, and sherd scatter – twenty-nine sites – in studying the distribution patterns, so as to prevent distortion of regional, spatial analysis. However, the other sites, which are cemeteries and a road situated along or on the top of the mountains, will be presented separately. The technique used for dating the sites identified in the survey is based on examining the cultural materials and comparing them with the specimens unearthed, in particular, in the course of the excavations of Tappe^h Bardnakōn, but also of other Sasanian sites of the Zagros and neighbouring regions (see also Chapter 5).

4.2 GEOGRAPHY OF FARSAN COUNTY IN THE BAKHTIYARI AREA

The Bakhtiyari highlands are made up of the area running from the mountainous Khuzestan, north to north-east of Susiana, to the western and central areas of the province of Chaharmahal va Bakhtiyari. Geologically, this area is situated in the Sanandaj-Sirjan Zone and is mainly made up of Cretaceous limestone. Chaharmahal va Bakhtiyari Province (E 49°34′ N 31°9′–E 51°26′ N 32°49′) is delimited to the north by Iṣfahan and Lorestan Provinces, to the west by Khuzestan Province, and by the respective provinces of Iṣfahan and Kohgiluyeh va Boyer-Ahmad to the east and south (Map 4.1). The topographic orientation of the province follows the general direction of the north-west-to-south-east-tending Zagros Mountains. The highest area is the Zardkooh subrange of the Central Zagros Mountains, with several peaks well above 4,000m a.s.l. The elevation of the lands, between 4,548m and 1,800m a.s.l. (Zendeh-del 1377 [1998]: 24), hence decreases as one moves towards the eastern and south-eastern areas of the province, where, also, the largest alluvial flatlands of Chaharmahal va Bakhtiyari Province, with the potential for agricultural exploitation, are formed. These highlands include many narrow intermontane valleys, ravines, and small and medium-size enclosed plains that hold rich natural resources particularly in terms of seasonal pastures and perennial rivers. The Kārōn and Zāyandeh-rōd, the two most important rivers of the Iranian Plateau, source from the Kouhrang area and the Zardkooh range to the north-west of Chaharmahal va Bakhtiyari. The former is the longest and the only navigable river of Iran, which, by receiving other powerful

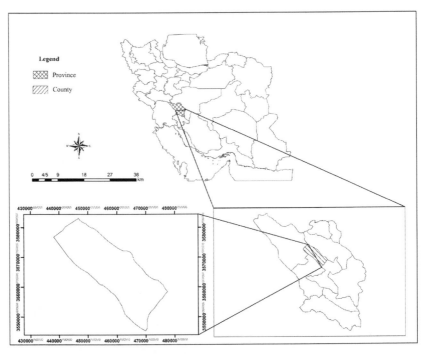

Map 4.1. Location of Farsan County on the map of Chaharmahal va Bakhtiyari Province on map of Iran. (Source: author)

currents such as the Bāzoft, Armand, Khersān, Vanak, Shimbār and Šūr-e Lāli in its upper basin, finally heads towards the south-west to join the Arvand-rōd at the Iran–Iraq border and reach the Persian Gulf, feeding the Susian lowlands. The latter, Zāyandeh-rōd, is the largest river in the Central Iranian Plateau, which from its Zardkooh upspring at the Kouhrang Tunnels and Dams runs eastward towards its lower basin in the Chaharmahal and then Isfahan areas, to finally pour into the salty Gāvkhōni Lake and marshes to the south-west of Isfahan plain and on the edge of the central desert of Iran. Apart from the rich natural resources providing for rather large-scale pastoralism, horticulture and dry farming in areas, these highlands make possible both the regional connections through the valleys and inter-regional communication between different natural and cultural zones of the Central Iranian Plateau, Central Zagros and Southern Zagros ranges and the lowlands of south-western Iran and Fars, via Kohgiluyeh va Boyer-Ahmad, containing rare and strategic passages through the Zagros ridges of the region.

Located roughly in the centre of this province, the area of Farsan County, the region under examination, measures 558km². Farsan is located in the Imbricated Zone of the Zagros Thrust Belt in the geological zone of Sanandaj–Sirjan in the Central Iranian Micro-Continent (E 50°20′ N 32°15′–E 50°30′ N 32°25′). Farsan County is bordered by Kouhrang County from the north and north-west, Ardal County from the west, and the respective Borujen and Shahrekord Counties from the south and east (Map 4.1). It contains a district with the two rural areas of Mizdej-e 'Oliyā, that is Upper Mizdej, and Mizdej-e Soflā, Lower Mizdej, and its centre is the city of Farsan. This county is topographically made up of an enclosed central plain, and a system comprising several small and narrow valleys and bot-tlenecks between different mountains surrounding the county. The central Farsan plain is geologically featured with terrace and debris flow of piedmont and the valley system of the region (Map 4.2). Among its most important mountains are the ridges of Sāldārān in the west and south-west, Lākhersān in the south-west, and Chōbin in the north and north-west, whose highest peak is Jahānbin Mount with 3,332m a.s.l. The main faults of the region are also in the higher-altitude ranges of the county, along with the south-eastern areas of the Farsan plain (Map 4.3). Measuring 20km long and 6km wide, the plain of Farsan has an elevation of just over 2,000m a.s.l., and, although largely flat, it is slightly depressed in its centre (Map 4.8). The general slope of the region is north–south, yet there is also an east–west orientation accounting for the surface water direction from west to east. These water resources are rich, and along with the average yearly precipitation of 545mm, the main rivers of the county are the Gorgak, Bābā-Heydar and Pireghār. On account of the above-mentioned environmental features, the area has historically been one of the main population centres of the Bakhtiyari nomadic tribes.[1] The main Bakhtiyari clans of Farsan are called Bābādi, Haft-langeh, Sanjari pastoralists, and Behdārvand (Āhanjideh 1378 [1999]: 360; Sa'idyan 1388 [2009]: 33).

4.3 EARLIER RESEARCH

Apparently, the earliest archaeological fieldwork carried out in Chaharmahal va Bakhtiyari Province were the excavations of Jahāngir Yāsi from the Archaeological Center of Iran at the pre-historic site of Tappe[h] Eskandari of Hafshejān to the south of Shahrekord in 1968, carried out with the purpose of delimiting the artificial deposits expanse. However, unfortunately, there is no extant report of this project (Norouzi 1388 [2010]: 162). The main step in this early stage of archaeological study of the province was taken by

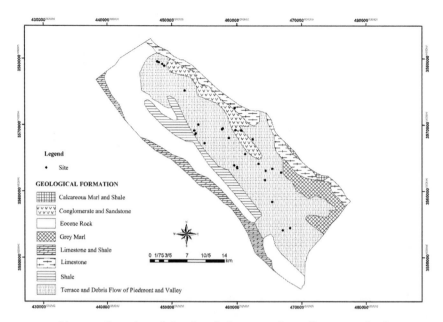

Map 4.2. Location of sites in relation to geology. (Source: author)

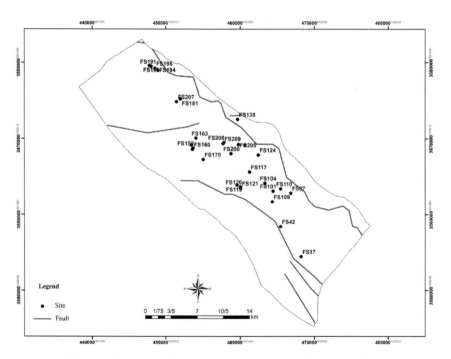

Map 4.3. Location of sites in relation to faults. (Source: author)

the American archaeologist Allen Zagarell in the 1970s. Following his reconnaissance surveys of 1974, 1975 and 1978 in the plains of Khān-Mirzā, Emām-Qeis, Gandomān, Choghākhor, Lordegan, Bārez, Sheyvand, Qal'e-madrese, Dehdez, Helō-Sa'd and Bolghār along the main roads from Lordegan to the west and Shahrekord, opening the test trenches at the important sites of Qal'e-Rostam, Gerd-chellegāh and Qal'e-geli of Lordegan threw some light on the chronological sequence of the prehistory of the province, particularly in its south-eastern and eastern areas (Zagarell 1975; 1982a; 1982b; Nissen and Zagarell 1976). The Neolithic pottery of Qal'e-Rostam was later analysed and published by Reinhard Bernbeck (1989; see also Gebel 1994). Also, some data on the Chalcolithic era of the Bakhtiyari highlands have been published, based on both Nissen's and Zagarell's (Dittmann 1986) and on newly undertaken (Khosrowzadeh 2015) surveys.

Nevertheless, Farsan County remained archaeologically unknown until the revival of archaeological activities during the last three decades in the form of reconnaissance surveys in the overlooked areas and salvage excavations at the sites under immediate threat of destruction (Roustaei 2010; Khosrowzadeh and Bahrami-nia 1391 [2012]; Habibi and Khosrowzadeh 2014; Esmaeali Jelodar 1393 [2014]; Esmaeali Jelodar and Zolqadr 1393 [2014]; Azadi 2015; Roustaei 1394 [2015]; Norouzi and Heydari Dastenaei 1397 [2018]; Mortazavi and Heydari Dastenaei 1398 [2019]).[2] In 1994, 1999 and 2005, Ja'far Mehr Kian was appointed by the Iranian Center for Archaeological Research (ICAR) to lead the excavations at the monuments of Khān-evy at the Darkesh-varkesh Pass, 7.5km to the south of Jōneqān city in Farsan County. Consequently, the arched stone structures were identified as a medieval caravanserai on the Atābaki Road, which was founded in the Ilkhanid period but remained under use until the Qajar period. However, apparently some artefacts point to the earlier settlement phases at the site in Parthian and Sasanian times. Mehr Kian also carried out a survey at the Darkesh-varkesh pass that led to the identification of some prehistoric sites. The findings from these works, nonetheless, are still to be published. Moreover, Aliasghar Norouzi, also from ICAR, opened some test trenches at the Pireghār Tunnel in Deh-cheshmeh village, and close to Tappe[h] Bardnakōn, in the course of the salvage excavations of this tunnel in 2014, whose results are also yet to be published.

As mentioned above, Farsan Survey project, led by Alireza Khosrowzadeh in July and August 2007, brought about the discovery of 216 sites ranging from the Middle Palaeolithic to the late Islamic period. According to the geographical position and topographic features of the region, the fieldwork was planned on the basis of 1/25,000 maps and employed intensive method surveying of different areas on foot and random sampling of sites. However, some small parts of the central plain could not be explored properly as these areas were then densely covered by vegetation due to the high level of underground water near the surface (Khosrowzadeh 2010: 318). In terms of their shape and morphology, generally speaking seven different types of sites may be recognised here, settlement, tappe[h], hill-top site, nomadic site, cemetery, building, and cave and rock-shelter, while the most prevalent category is the temporary sites of sherd/flint scatters (Khosrowzadeh 2010; Khosrowzadeh 1391 [2012]; Habibi and Heydari 1393 [2014]; Khosrowzadeh and Habibi 1394 [2015]).

By the time ten years had elapsed after the survey, the considerable scale of destruction at the site of Tappe[h] Bardnakōn, in form of several illegally-dug ditches at its peak, made salvage excavations at this significant settlement urgent and necessary. Therefore, Alireza Khosrowzadeh (Shahrekord University) and Aliasghar Noruzi (ICAR) initiated excavations in 2017, followed by their second season in the following year. Bardnakōn is situated approximately 2.4km south-east of Deh-cheshme village around the western edge of the central plain of Farsan and beside the Pireghār River (E 50°34′13.69″ N 32°12′42.17″). This site is formed on an oval-shaped circular natural hill 150m in diameter and with a height of 30m above the surrounding plain (Figure 4.1). Its main settlement phase dates from the Sasanian era, yet pottery samples from the Chalcolithic, Elamite, Achaemenid and Parthian periods have also been discovered among the surface materials, as well as some prehistoric lithics. Given the large extent of clandestine excavations, the cultural deposits of Tappe[h] Bardnakōn are disturbed and the excavators had limited options in terms of the locations of trenches. Therefore, the excavations were limited to the small rather undamaged part of the tappe[h] on its southern slope, which is also less steep than other flanks of this mound (Figure 4.2). The fieldwork procedure at Bardnakōn was conducted according to the identification of cultural deposits. If over 20cm of the deposits was unearthed without any visible change, the classification method of deposits could proceed on the basis of arbitrary vertical levels. In order that the deposits and features could be described in as precise a manner as possible, each was given a locus number. The two 10 × 10m trenches of A and B were dug into this area to the

Fig. 4.1. Aerial view of Tappe[h] Bardnakōn from the south-east.
(Source: Khosrowzadeh et al. 2020a, banner photo)

final southern edge, with 24 and 48 loci documented in each respectively. Two plastered 2.5m-thick walls that are north–south- and east–west-tending, and three narrow corridors with a north–south orientation within the east–west-tending wall, were uncovered at Trench A. Furthermore, in the other trench, B, the lower course of one wall and parts of another with a north-east–south-west orientation were unearthed (Figure 4.3).[3] The air-dried, chaff-tempered mud bricks that were uncovered are of four sizes: 40 × 40 × 10cm and 37.5 × 37.5 × 7cm from the walls in Trench A, and 40 × 40 × 8cm and 50 × 50 × 10cm from the spaces in Trench B. Despite the controlled excavations, the stratigraphy of Tappe[h] Bardnakōn may scarcely be examined scientifically given the disturbed condition of the cultural layers. Moreover, the limited extent of the excavations currently prevents us from making conclusive remarks about the plan of the architectural structures (Khosrowzadeh et al. 2020a: 223–4; Khosrowzadeh et al. 2020c: 166–8). However, at present, this author tentatively proposes a chahār-ṭāq plan with ambulatories composing a fire-temple with different spaces and functions, for Bardnakōn's buildings. This hypothesis is put forward on the basis of the uncovered plan (Figure 4.4) and materials (see Chapter 1, s. 1.4). The important corpus of 559 clay sealings are among the findings whose epigraphic, iconographic and technological traits follow the late Sasanian artistic, royal, administrative and political conventions. In particular, the archive of twenty-two administrative

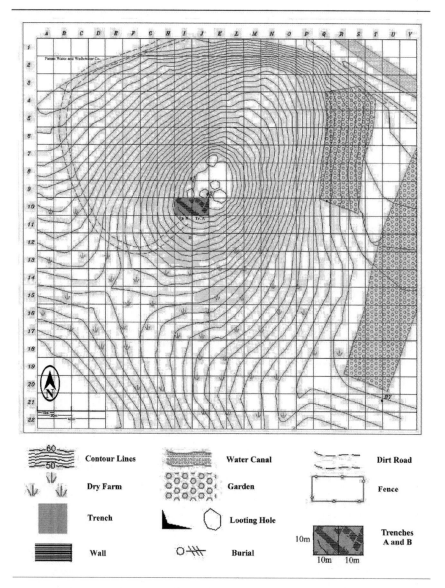

Fig. 4.2. General map of Tappe^h Bardnakōn with the location of the Trenches A and B (Source: Khosrowzadeh et al. 2020b, Figure 4)

bullae that Rika Gyselen and this author studied in collaboration with the excavators of the site (Khosrowzadeh et al. 2020b; 2020c) is informative. As the clay sealings were all, apart from sixteen specimens that were discovered among the surface materials, uncovered at Trench B (Figure 4.3), one may logically assume

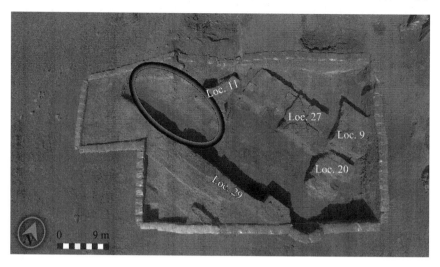

Fig. 4.3. Photograph of the excavated area of Tappe^h Bardnakōn indicating the unearthed architectural structures, related loci, and concentration findspot of clay bullae. (Source: Khosrowzadeh et al. 2020a, Figure 4)

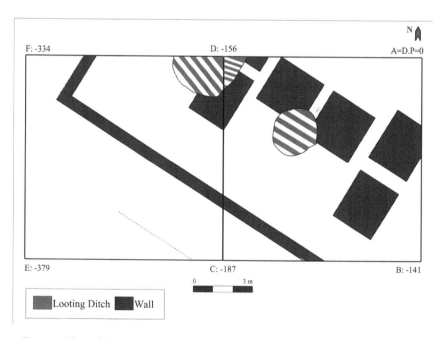

Fig. 4.4. Plan of the excavated architectural structures specifying the location of walls and ditching holes. (Source: Khosrowzadeh et al. 2020a, Figure 5)

that the excavations at this trench located a repository at Tappe[h] Bardnakōn where the used sealings were kept. This point is backed up by the administrative seal impressions of the archive, representing the place as the hitherto-unidentified administrative centre of the late Sasanian canton of Rāwar-kust-ī-rōdbār located in the province of Gay in Spahān region (Khosrowzadeh et al. 2020b: 87). Moreover, large assemblages of glass and metallurgical slags and fragments of glassware and metal tools (Khosrowzadeh et al. 2020a: Figs 13, 14, 18 and 19) indicate the industrial production that had taken place at the site. Also, the pottery classification and typology specifying the storage jars as the most common pottery form in this assemblage (see Chapter 5), along with some tools such as a sickle (Khosrowzadeh et al. 2020: Fig 18f) and quernstones (Khosrowzadeh et al. 2020a: Fig 17), attest to agricultural activities at this place (Khosrowzadeh et al. 2020a: 230). Finally, the ceramic spindle whorls discovered here (Khosrowzadeh et al. 2020: Fig 20c) point to some kinds of animal husbandry. That said, despite the damage cused by clandestine excavations, large-scale scientific fieldwork projects at Tappe[h] Bardnakōn are necessary to make known the socioeconomic aspects of life at the place and disclose the function of its building before further destruction of its cultural deposits.

4.4 SETTLEMENT SYSTEMS AND LONG-TERM PROCESSES OF LANDSCAPE TRANSFORMATION IN FARSAN COUNTY

As discussed above, sites from different eras and of various types are found in Farsan County. The earliest group of them, from the Palaeolithic era, are made up of nine caves, rock-shelters and open sites. By the Neolithic period, the sites may be categorised into two kinds of permanent hill-top sites formed on the natural hills and temporary or nomadic sherd/flint scatters with no visible relief. This change represents a landmark in the cultural landscape history of Farsan, as these two site types persisted as the main characteristics of the region's built environment throughout the ages to come, with spatial distribution shifts and demographic fluctuations in different eras. The same holds true for the general settlement patterns and key factors of site location through the ages until Late Antiquity. Accordingly, the sites are mainly located along the mild slopes of the mountains surrounding the Farsan plain and in the side valleys of the region where the perennial rivers, along with rich soil in some areas, are easily available. However, the central Farsan plain was avoided and remained largely inhabited, as in these times the central plain was marshy due to the high level of its underground water close to the ground and its chiefly flat topography which is rather depressed in the centre. Such a marshy condition is currently visible in the county in the areas to the west and north-west of Jōneqān city, around the villages of Choqā-hast and Kowrān, particularly around the Farsan River. This environmental condition is also attested in the southern areas of the larger neighbouring Shahrekord plain, where is called Margh (lit. 'the meadow'), and was marshy until roughly fifteen years ago when global warming and drought caused the underground water level to drop.[4]

After reaching its prehistoric peak with thirty-five sites in the Chalcolithic period, a trend also confirmed for other areas in Chaharmahal va Bakhtiyari Province (Zagarell 1982a) and the larger Central Zagros in Hamadan and Kermanshah Provinces (Balmaki 2013), the number of sites remained stable through the following eras until around the last quarter of the first millennium BCE, averaging twenty-five per period (Graph 4.1). Yet the numbers are highest (thirty-eight) for the sites of late Seleucid–Parthian times (Graph 4.1). Moreover, the most commonly occurring type of sites in this period were the stone-heaped cemeteries, although cemeteries had already become rather more frequent, alongside hill-top sites, in the preceding Achaemenid period. Furthermore, in this period, together with the continuity of the former site location along the foothills and piedmonts around the central plain and in the valleys

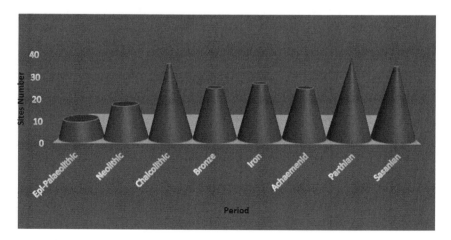

Graph 4.1. Chart showing the number of the sites discovered in Farsan County per period. (Source: author)

of the region, as an unprecedented phenomenon in the settlement patterns of Farsan, few settlements were found in the Farsan plain *ex nihilo*. As discussed in Chapter 2.2, in late Seleucid–Parthian times, Chaharmahal va Bakhtiyari Province was a territory of the Elymaean kingdom and part of its trade-based economy. Located along the important inter-regional communication roads of the province through the arduous Zagros ridges, the Farsan region partly owed its developments during the Elymaean period to its strategic location (see also Chapter 2, s. 2.4).

4.5 THE SASANIAN SETTLEMENT PATTERN IN FARSAN

Apart from the twenty-nine Sasanian sites whose spatial distribution is examined here (see Appendix 2), six cemeteries and a road relating to this period are also identified in the Farsan Survey project. The site of FS.025 partially locates the historical Atābaki Road (Figures 4.5 and 4.6), mentioned by medieval sources (Ibn Battuta 1371 [1993]: 241), which linked the south-western lowlands to

Fig. 4.5. Remaining part of the Atābaki Road across the cliffs of Sāldārān Mount, view from south. (Source: Habibi 1390 [2012]: Figure 4)

Fig. 4.6. Remaining part of the Atābaki Road in Sāldārān Mount, view from north. (Source: Habibi 1390 [2012]: Figure 5)

the Central Iranian Plateau, Iṣfahan plain. The road was related to the Sasanian era in light of the dating of the majority of the related sites on it (see Chapter 5), along with prior excavations in the earlier deposits and settlement phases of the Ilkhanid caravanserai of Khān-evy on the road which are reported from Parthian–Sasanian times (Chapter 4, s. 4.3). As per the historical accounts of the road and its course through the region, and according to the geographical position and topographic features of the Farsan area, the intensive method of survey led to the partial identification of this stone-paved road in its difficult passages through the narrow valleys along the foothills of the Sāldārān Mount, 10.3km south-west of Jōneqān, mirroring the contemporary Izeh-Shahrekord highway (see Chapter 2, n. 47; see also Khosrowzadeh and Habibi 2015; Mehrkiyan 1997: n. 12).

The cemeteries mostly belong to a single funerary tradition according to which roughly circular, stone-heap tumulus-shaped structures are arranged in groups of burials in isolated locations and along a line on the crests of the mountains (Khosrowzadeh 2010: 318–19. Figures 4.7 and 4.8). In the local Bakhtiyari dialect this type of cairn is called *chol*. The exact size of each burial cannot be estimated because of their disturbed condition caused by clandestine excavations. However, even if the estimate is inaccurate, the area covered with scattered rubble

Fig. 4.7. FS.187, a *chol* burial on a high mound to the south of Veys-ābād village, view from north. (Source: Habibi 1390 [2012]: Figure 48)

stones is taken as an indication of the measures of the structures. Their key concentration is on the mountains around Jōneqān city, and chief among them is the cemetery of Chahār-dōl Mountain (the sites between FS.043 and FS.056. Figure 4.8). These cairn burials are located on the northern and southern slopes of this mountain between 2.2km and 2.9km south of Gōshe village. Also in this area are *chol* burials (FS.005–FS.008), discovered on the bedrocks of the western and southern slopes of Jahānbin Mountain, to the north-east of the Sarāb-bakān valley. Moreover, the mountain called both Ālmāqāji (in the local Turkish dialect) and Kōh-e cheshme-ye kāse-kīse (in the local Bakhtiyari dialect), 4.5km south-west of Jōneqān, holds a group of over fifty burials on its south-eastern to western slopes (FS.082). However, such funerary remains are also found in the more northern areas of the county. From 3.1km and 3.4km north of Farsan city and on the rather low mountains of the western and eastern piedmonts of the valley of Darre hanā bālā (lit., Upper Hanā Valley), these types of cemeteries were documented during the survey (FS.140–FS.144). Finally, four similar *chol* burials were discovered around Bābā-Heydar and to the south of Veys-ābād village as well (FS.184–FS.187) (see also Appendix 2. Figure 4.7). Worthy of mention is that the

Fig. 4.8. FS.056, a *chol* burial on the slope of Chahār-dōl Mountain, view from east. (Source: Habibi 1390 [2012]: Figure 20)

occurrence of archaeological material on the surface of the cemeteries and their surroundings is quite low, and even non-existent in some cases, perhaps partly because the great majority of them are looted and disturbed. Therefore, they are dated on the basis of a comparison of the pottery wares acquired from some of them and their adjacent sites, as well as the morphology and shape of the burials themselves. However, opinions regarding the date of such burial structures vary greatly (see e.g. Boucharlat 1989; Huff 1999: 351; Khosrowzadeh 2014: 31–3; Bendezu-Sarmiento and Jafari 2018).

Furthermore, a rock-cut niche, FS.199, is listed among the Sasanian sites of Farsan County. It measures 1.60 × 0.90 × 0.70m and is carved into the cliffs of a rather high mountain situated 1km north-east of Kovānak village. Yet the cliff that used to hold this tomb is detached from the mountain cliff and is at present partly broken (Figure 4.9). These types of burial remains are distributed all across the Bakhtiyari area and are called in that dialect *bard-e gōri*, lit., 'entombment stone' (cf. Heidary and Hosseini 1394 [2015]: 302). This type perhaps represents a continuation of the chamber tombs that are to be traced back to the Achaemenid period, and their funerary tradition was most probably Zoroastrian or associated

Fig. 4.9. FS.199, a *bard-e gōri* rock-cut funerary structure, on the foothill of a rather high mountain to the north-east of Kovānak village. (Source: Habibi 1390 [2012]: Figure 53)

with it. The specimens in the Bakhtiyari are comparable to the late Sasanian funerary remains of the inscribed rock-cut niches discovered in Fars Province, according to whose epigraphic information they were called *daḥmag* in Middle Persian, New Pers. *dakhme* (Cereti and Gondet 2015 with references). This term itself backs up the links with Zoroastrian burial customs (Frye in Stronach 1978b: 163; cf. Cereti and Gondet 2015: 378). The niches in the Bakhtiyari area, in the provinces of Khuzestan and Chaharmahal va Bakhtiyari, along with one attested in Abdanan County of Ilam Province (see Appendix 1: AS.046), are less elaborate than those in Fars, as the samples of the former set discovered to date lack Middle Persian inscription (for an example with a probably later Arabic inscription, see Heidary and Hosseini 1394 [2015]: 304, Figs. 8 and 9) and almost all decoration on their façade or surrounding cliffs.

Following the methods used in Chapter 3, here the spatial distribution of Sasanian sites in the forms of tappe[h] (Figures 4.10 and 4.11) and sherd scatter sites (Figures 4.12 and 4.13), dated on the basis of the comparative examination of ceramics and architectural remains (see Chapter 5), is studied.[5] Accordingly, the relationship between

Fig. 4.10. FS.104, Tappe^h Sāleh, view from north. (Source: Habibi 1390 [2012]: Figure 24)

Fig. 4.11. FS.200, Tappe^h Panj'ali, view from north-west. (Source: Habibi 1390 [2012]: Figure 54)

Fig. 4.12. FS.159, āb-sefīd (2) sherd scatter, view from south. (Source: Habibi 1390 [2012]: Figure 40)

Fig. 4.13. FS.087, Dareh-jenni (1) sherd scatter, view from north-west. (Source: Habibi 1390 [2012]: Figure 22)

the human groups and their ecosystem is examined by assessing the interaction between the Sasanian sites and environmental variables. Therefore, we may consider the role played by these variables, along with cultural factors, in site location and hence in the regional economy and its social structures. This in turn enables us to reconstruct the cultural and natural settings of the formation and continuity of settlement patterns in Sasanian Farsan, contextualise them within the long-term settlement systems, and recognise their processes of transformation in the period under study. Those variables considered here are the distance and position of the archaeological sites relative to roads, rivers and nearby neighbours, and elevation ranges, land use, and vegetation of the places holding these sites.

4.5.1 *Distance from roads*

In this section, we discuss the distance of the archaeological sites from roads, under three categories of sites with distances of less than 500m, between 500 and 1,000m, and between 1,000 and 1,500m, which respectively include 65.51, 31 and 3.44 per cent of the sites (Maps 4.4 and 4.5).

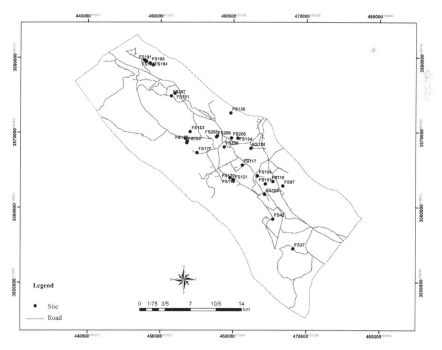

Map 4.4. Location of sites in relation to roads. (Source: author)

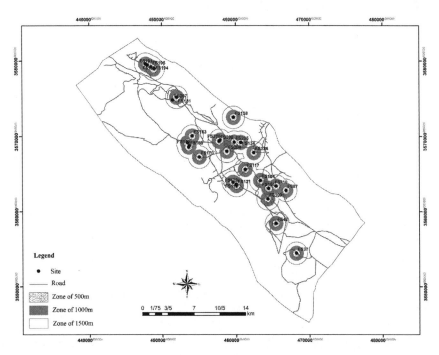

Map 4.5. Location of sites in relation to roads. (Source: author)

The main historical roads passing the highlands of Chaharmahal va Bakhtiyari Province were two paths split in the Lordegan plain that is to the south of the province and adjacent to Izeh County of Khuzestan Province. One road, the medieval Atābaki Road, turned from Lordegan to the north and north-east and, passing through Ardal and Farsan Counties, ran towards the Chaharmahal plains to finally reach the Iṣfahan area. The other, from Lordegan, headed to the east towards Borujen County to reach the southern areas of Iṣfahan Province, around Shahreza, and lead to the northern Fars, the Abadeh and the Izad-khwast area (see also Chapter 2, n. 47). In Khuzestan, some branches of these roads headed, from Izeh, south towards Ramhormoz and Ahvaz, and some lead, from Izeh and Masjed-Soleiman, west on the way to Dezful and Susa. The trajectories are somehow verified by the sigillographic archive of Tappe[h] Bardnakōn. As discussed, the administrative bullae of this corpus attest to the long-range administrative and political interactions between the canton of Rāwar-kust-ī-rōdbār, Tappe[h] Bardnakōn in modern Farsan County, the provincial capital of the region of Spahān, Gay, and other centres in the region of Hūzestān, precisely its provinces of Rām-Ohrmazd (Ramhormoz), Ohrmazd-Ardašīr

(Ahvaz), and Weh-Andiyok-Šābuhr (around Dezful), and the region of Pārs, the province of Īg (Khosrowzadeh et al. 2020b and 2020c). One may infer that these administrative connections perhaps disclose the Sasanian-period operation of those inter-regional roads linking the regions of Khuzestan, Iṣfahan and northern Fārs via modern Chaharmahal va Bakhtiyari Province.

As mentioned above (see Chapter 4, s. 4.4; Chapter 2, s. 2.2), the topography of this province in the Central Zagros ranges and the communication roads it provides through the mountains constituted an important factor with regard to the economic and political developments that occurred in Farsan in different eras. This is particularly confirmed for the times from the late first millennium BCE onwards. Literary data and archaeological evidence concerning the economy of the Elymaean state are informative in this regard. But this point is clearer in the Sasanian period as per the site location factors and spatial distribution. Thus, the Sasanian sites are mostly concentrated in the central plain, and nineteen of them, that is just over 65 per cent, are at a distance of less than 500m from roads.

Characterised with mobility, despite its rate, also one may suppose that the modes of subsistence and lifestyles associated with nomadism have played crucial roles in constituting and maintaining the inter-regional networks – the passage of groups, the flow of information and the exchange of products and artefacts. The allusions by Hellenistic sources to the control of different pastoralist highlanders over the main Zagros roads testify to this point in the Achaemenid, Diadochi and Seleucid periods (see Chapter 2, s. 2.2). It is worth mentioning that there is a degree of overlap between the spatial model of Sasanian settlement distribution across Farsan County and traditional, seasonal migration roads used by the Bakhtiyari nomads (Khosrowzadeh and Habibi 1394 [2015]). The typology and comparison of the Sasanian pottery of Farsan have also verified this point, presenting close similarities to the contemporary assemblages discovered from Khuzestan and Fars regions (Habibi and Heydari 1393 [2014]; see Chapter 5).

4.5.2 *Distance from rivers*

As regards this variable, the sites are divided into three categories. Accordingly, 51.72 per cent of them are located in the zone of less than 500m distance, and 20.68 and 27.58 per cent of them are situated in the distance zones of 500–1,000m and 1,000–1,500m respectively (Maps 4.6 and 4.7).

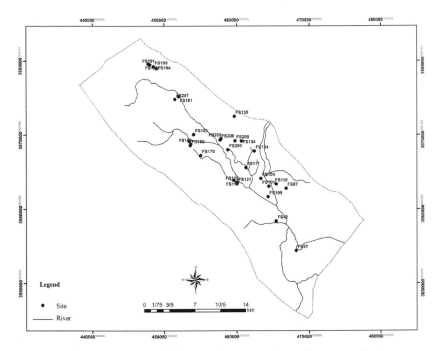

Map 4.6. Location of sites in relation to rivers. (Source: author)

There are many permanent springs and rivers around the central enclosed plain of Farsan which attracted populations from prehistoric times to Late Antiquity. Sites, either permanent settlements or temporary camps, were located particularly to the east and west and in the several side valleys of the plain favouring access to these water resources, along with rich pastures, for modes of subsistence and economy based on pastoralism and rain-fed agriculture. As mentioned above, notwithstanding its rich water resources, the marshy environment of the central plain had up until the recent past been preventing extensive agricultural activities and settlements in the area. In the Sasanian period, however, most of the sites were founded on the Farsan plain. Moreover, fourteen Sasanian sites, over 49 per cent of the total number, are located over 500m away from the rivers. Therefore, the practice of water management structures and techniques such as canals and irrigation systems, attested for several Sasanian territories (see Chapter 3, ss. 3.5.2, 3.6), is quite possible in some areas of the plain during this era. Nonetheless, the projects adopting a geo-archaeological approach, such as those carried out in south-western Iran (see n. 4), are required to scientifically clarify the conditions in the region in antiquity. It is worth noting that the

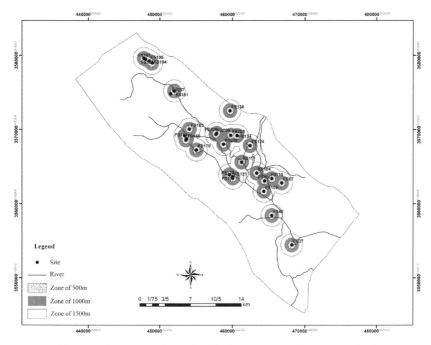

Map 4.7. Location of sites in relation to rivers. (Source: author)

spatial distribution pattern still shows a noticeable interdependence with rivers in this period (fifteen sites with a distance range of under 500m from rivers), and some sites were situated according to the traditional site location systems in the narrow valleys and foothills around the central plain.

4.5.3 Elevation of the sites above sea level

As regards this factor, the relationship between the location of Sasanian sites and their elevation is illustrated in a Digital Elevation Model (DEM) map (Map 4.8). The zone of 2,000–2,111m contains 48.27 per cent of the sites. Yet each of the two categories of 2,111–2,222m and 2,222–2,333m includes only 6.89 per cent (two sites) of the total figure. Moreover, the sites at the highest altitude were located in the two groups with elevation ranges of between 2,333–444 and 2,444–555m. The former zone held 13.79 per cent of the sites, while 24.13 per cent of them were discovered in the latter.

The high altitude of the county, which is over 2,000m a.s.l. in its lowest areas on the Farsan plain, is a determining factor in terms of the climate conditions of the region. The Farsan plain is surrounded by

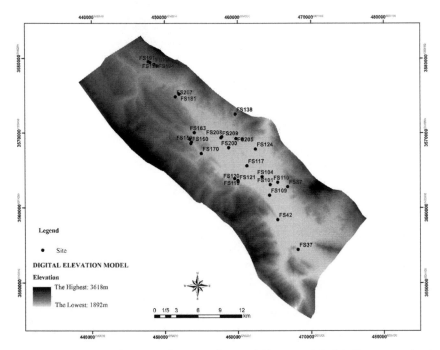

Map 4.8. Location of sites on the map of Digital Elevation Model. (Source: author)

high mountains that are oriented from north-west to south-east. This high average altitude exerts an influence on the environmental features of the county. The high air pressure, rather high yearly precipitation in the country, and long cold winters, along with its rather small size, lead to the flora and fauna species in Farsan County being rather limited.

Roughly half (fourteen) of the Sasanian sites are located in the lowest elevation zone of the region, a substantial change compared to earlier times. Notwithstanding this shift towards the lower central plain, still the second most inhabited elevation zone is encompassed by seven sites found in the lands inside the side valleys with an altitude ranging from 2,444 to 2,555m. While the rest of the sites, eight, are formed in the three categories between these two highest and lowest populated zones, this distribution largely represents a dichotomous model in terms of site location preference and the factor of elevation in the region.

4.5.4 *Types of land use*

In this section, we divide the Sasanian sites of Farsan County into distinct categories on the basis of the function of the lands holding

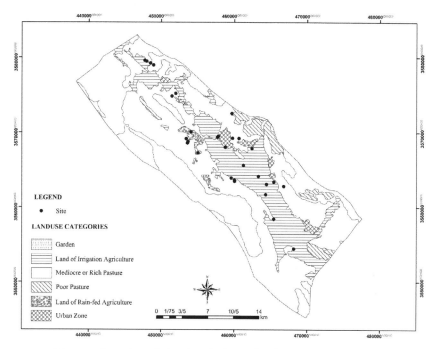

Map 4.9. Location of sites in relation to land use. (Source: author)

them (Maps 4.9 and 4.10). Accordingly, 46.5 per cent of the sites are located in the lands involving irrigation agriculture and the mediocre or rich pastures contain 42.79 per cent of them. Moreover, 7.2 and 3.5 per cent of these sites are discovered in two other land-use categories, respectively, lands of rain-fed agriculture, and poor pastures.

As argued in the previous chapter (Chapter 3, s. 3.5.4), examination of the formation and distribution of archaeological sites according to this factor can be informative. Land use is closely linked to the economic preferences and modes of subsistence of groups, and its study may be helpful for a better understanding of those groups' perceptions of their habitat's natural landscape. Therefore, the built environment and their exploitation of natural resources could be construed as sets of strategies that are adaptive to the ecosystem. As with the discussion about the distribution of the Sasanian sites in Farsan County according to elevation zones, the variable of land use signifies two main groups of site location in this region. The most populated group, comprising fourteen sites, favoured the central plain lands with the potential for irrigation agriculture. The other group includes two fewer sites, with a preference for higher-altitude lands containing quality pastures. This spatial model indicates two

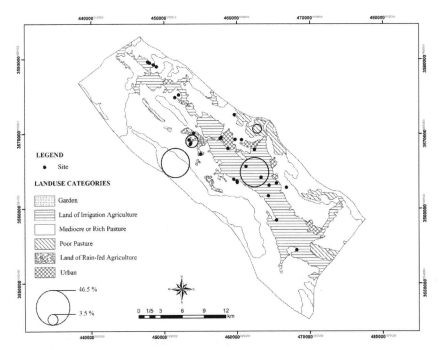

Map 4.10. Ratio of sites in relation to land use. (Source: author)

modes of economy and lifestyles associated with agriculture and pastoralism. Meanwhile the other categories, of rain-fed agriculture and poor pastures, with only three sites collectively, probably played a complementary role in this dichotomous structure, besides the more specialised forms of irrigation agriculture and nomadic pastoralism. Therefore, besides the traditional mode of economy of the region in earlier eras, which depended heavily on pastoralism and limited rain-fed agriculture, the agriculturally-based economy was developed on the Farsan plain during the Sasanian period.

4.5.5 Land vegetation

To evaluate the sites' location according to the land vegetation variable, five categories are considered, in two of which Sasanian sites are found: 85.7 per cent of the archaeological sites are located in the grassland zone, and the rest, 14.3 per cent, are located in rain-fed agriculture farmlands (Maps 4.11 and 4.12).

It was mentioned above that the rather small size of Farsan County, and some environmental features such as high altitude, poor and pebbly soil in some areas, long winters and cold days, have led to the

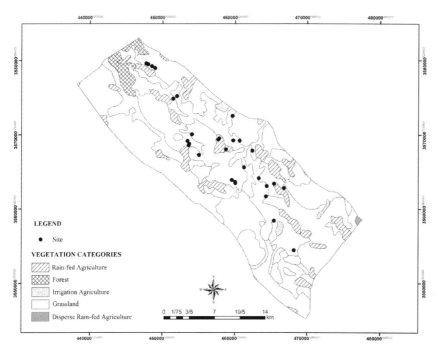

Map 4.11. Location of sites in relation to vegetation. (Source: author)

limited vegetation types in the county. Therefore, the region is only sparsely forested and the main vegetation categories are pasturelands, gardens, and wheat and barley farms. But as was argued in Chapter 3 (s. 3.5.5), the notion of vegetation and its types in different areas is not solely a natural trait but is also a variable underlying a cultural notion, given the long-term processes of anthropogenic modifications in environments, and by extension in vegetation. The fact that the vast majority of the Sasanian sites of Farsan (twenty-five) are located in the lands covered by grassland indicates their substantial role in the subsistence of the inhabitants of the region, more precisely in pastoralism of different sorts. The main vegetation category in the Farsan plain is grassland, which leaves small areas for other categories, among which only the lands with the vegetation type associated with rain-fed agriculture contain (four) Sasanian sites.

4.5.6 *Distance from other sites*

In respect of this factor, we consider four separate categories for the archaeological sites under study: 55.17 per cent of the sites are located within a zone of distance of less than 500m to the nearest neighbour,

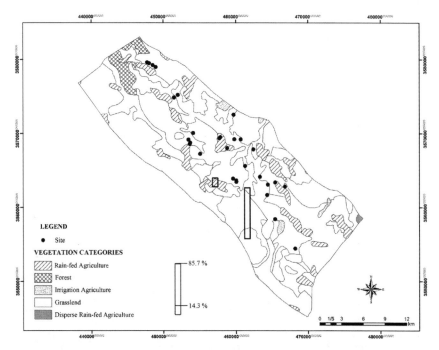

Map 4.12. Ratio of sites in relation to vegetation. (Source: author)

27.58 per cent are found in the distance range 500m–1,000m, and 6.89 and 10.34 per cent of them are situated in the 1,000–1,500m and over-1,500m zones respectively (Map 4.13).

Investigation of the position of archaeological sites in relation to their contemporary counterparts may clarify the rate and the mechanisms of their economic and political interaction and help us to recognise the social organisation and complexity of those societies. Examination of this factor can also enable us to explain the models of regional settlement patterns. While just over 82 per cent of the Sasanian sites across Farsan County are situated at a distance of less than 1,000m from their adjacent sites, the distance zone of sixteen of them is under 500m. This indicates the high levels of interdependence between them. The shift in site location and spatial distribution towards the lower Farsan plain is discussed above. This was accompanied by the growth of the settlement hierarchy through the foundation of some main settlements such as FS.119 (1.5ha) and FS.163 (4ha) and the complex of the mounds of FS.208 and FS.209 (4ha). FS.119 is called Tappe[h] Bardnakōn and, as discussed above, locates an administrative centre of the late Sasanian canton of Rāwar-kust-ī-rōdbār in the province of Gay in the region of Spahān. In this

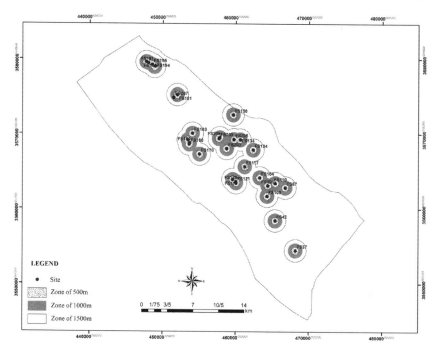

Map 4.13. Location of sites in relation to each other. (Source: author)

period, the increased hierarchy of the sites constituted networks of settlements where the top level (the above-mentioned sites) with their satellite sites, such as FS.87 (temporary site. Figure 4.13), FS.109, FS.110 (temporary site?), FS.120, FS.121, FS.134, FS.158 (temporary site?), FS.159 (temporary site?) and FS.160, were interconnected via middle-range settlements (such as FS.117, FS.124, FS.170 and FS.205). In the case of Tappe^h Bardnakōn, the establishment of this site had repercussions for the regional settlement system of the region, leading to higher levels of interaction and a more complex settlement organisation. Accordingly, the peripheral settlements of this centre (FS.120 and FS.121) which were located closely around it at a distance of less than 500m, together with other freshly founded (FS.117 and FS.087) or resettled (FS.104 (Figure 4.10), FS.109 and FS.124) sites, linked different site clusters in the central plain (Khosrowzadeh and Habibi 2015: 112–13; Khosrowzadeh et al. 2020a: 232).

4.6 EVALUATION

Geographical location, and the environmental and topographic features of Farsan County, provided certain opportunities in this region for hosting populations, at least from the Middle Palaeolithic era onwards. Generally, as discussed, the settlement systems of Farsan were formed by the nature of the human–environment relationship across the region, which was mainly based on pastoral economies of different types. Accordingly, the spatial distribution of material culture followed an overall pattern in which the groups inhabited the several narrow side valleys and foothills surrounding the central plain of Farsan, with sherd/flint-scattered sites basically making up the built environment, particularly in prehistory. The long-term processes of the settlement system and the changes it has experienced over time are discussed above. Generally, encompassing the long timespan between the Palaeolithic and late Seleucid eras, the first episode of the history of Farsan's cultural landscape mainly featured a dominantly pastoral landscape with campsites founded along the mild mountain slopes. The second episode, including late Seleucid–Parthian times, was a transitional era of demographic growth and a slight shift in long-lasting dominant site location preferences through the foundation of some sites in the lower altitude ranges of the central plain. Yet it was during the following episode of the Sasanian period, our chronological focus, that the settlement patterns of the county were transformed considerably.

In Sasanian times, the sites were concentrated in the Farsan plain. Moreover, while their total number does not show meaningful change relative to the preceding period, the sites are generally larger. The rate of spatial concentration of them in the lower central plain (an unprecedented phenomenon) is echoed by the fact that roughly half, 49 per cent, of these sites were not under use in the Parthian period. Also worthy of mention is that 31 per cent of them were founded from scratch, and the rest, 17.28 per cent, were resettled after a long post-prehistoric period of abandonment. In terms of the settlement patterns, the spatial distribution of the Sasanian sites situated around the central plain in the higher-altitude zones of the valleys of Farsan was, as in earlier times, in a linear pattern and in close connection to the roads and rivers of the area (Map 4.14). But the spatial organisation of the sites in the central plain is distinguished, as it is an arrangement in clusters of sites of different size in three hierarchical levels and with high levels of interaction. That said, it should be borne in mind that, except for Tappe[h] Bardnakōn which is excavated, the size of the sites is estimated merely according to the surface materials scattered on and/or around them, and is itself subject to natural and artificial interventions over time.

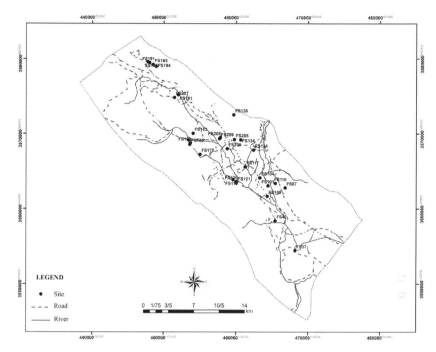

Map 4.14. Location of sites in relation to roads and rivers. (Source: author)

Also, notwithstanding the intensive methods practised in the Farsan Survey project, most likely some of the archaeological sites are not documented. One may assume different scenarios for this, among which are the sites being already completely destroyed, buried under the alluvial deposits of the surrounding mountains, valleys and ravines in the central plain, or simply overlooked by the archaeological team.

The mountains and foothills of the Central Zagros hold a substantial portion of the population of Iran. The main economic activity of the various peoples inhabiting the different micro-environments of the region has historically been associated with animal husbandry, whose types differed under various circumstances. The different modes of pastoralism, nonetheless, could be exercised simultaneously and in a single area (see Chapter 1, n. 16; Chapter 3). However, pastoralism, along with other economic modes, has generally been practised on different scales through the ages: village-based (which can be traced long back into prehistory), historic contractual, and, later, specialised nomadic. Settlement patterns, historical documents and natural features indicate that Farsan County has, historically, been a hub for animal husbandry in the so-called highlands of

Bakhtiyari, which is named after one of the two largest nomadic confederations of Iran.

The Sasanian period is an era of socioeconomic transformation in this county. Particularly since the sixth century, the Sasanian Empire experienced administrative and political reforms leading to changes in the economic structures and built environment of some territories (see Chapter 3, with references). The changes that occurred in the long-standing settlement system of Farsan in this era signify socioeconomic shifts in terms of the modes of economy of the inhabitants of the region and their complex social structures. Along with vertical nomadism, an agriculture-based economy developed beyond the limited dry farming of earlier eras. Nevertheless, agricultural development in this period did not undermine the traditional pastoralist foundation of the region's economy. On the one hand, a large majority (87.5 per cent) of the sites located in the lands with an elevation range below 2,222m a.s.l. are permanent sites. On the other, the higher altitudes largely hold nomadic campsites (92 per cent, see Appendix 2). It is also interesting that the location of the temporary sites and *chol* burials is mainly adjacent to the modern Bakhtiyari nomads' campsites, called *vārgah* in their dialect. Therefore, the spatial distribution of these sites somewhat mirrors the traditional seasonal migration routes of the local nomads towards Kouhrang County and Khuzestan Province. These changes indicate a pattern in terms of land use. However, drawing political and social implications from these sets of evidence is problematic. Neither is any local political border confidently discernible according to the distinct settlement patterns, and nor do these patterns and the transformations of the settlement system suggest sociocultural differences in terms of the identity of the groups with distinguishable lifestyles and modes of subsistence. Apart from the presence of temporary sites in the central plain and sedentary settlements in the surrounding foothills, this settlement system was formed in order to attain higher levels of economic efficiency of the natural system. Notwithstanding their different economic structures, pastoralist and agriculturalist groups of the region, with their campsites or sedentary settlements, were in close interaction with each other in the rather small area of Farsan. As discussed above (Chapter 2), such links in the Central Zagros highlands were not typical of a particular era, yet the scale of relationships varied under different circumstances and on the basis of the specialisation rate of groups in specific modes of subsistence.

Evidence about contractual pastoralism in the Achaemenid period and the related developments in the sense of nomadic pastoralism has already been discussed. Also, literary data about the incorporation of nomadic groups of the Central Zagros in the imperial armies of the Achaemenids and Sasanians have been presented (Chapter 2). Therefore, it makes sense to look for such relationships between the nomadic populations of Farsan and the Sasanian state and its authorities in the archaeological materials argued above. Apart from the local nomads and agriculturalists, the presence of official authorities and representatives of the Sasanian state is reflected in material culture. The *mowūh* administration of the canton of Rāwar-kust-ī-rōdbār, that is, modern Farsan County, at its centre, Tappe[h] Bardnakōn, and perhaps other centres of lower administrative rank in the county, regulated financial exchanges and tax matters in the canton and facilitated official inter-regional economic and political relations with other cantons and provinces according to the rules and official legal procedures of, and under the control of, the Sasanian state. Technological progress, political developments, and, perhaps, rather large-scale projects with investment by the local authorities under the central state's supervision, made possible the more effective exploitation of the natural resources and ecosystem services of the Farsan plain in terms of agricultural structures and access to main roads in this period. Availability of irrigation lands was a crucial factor for the site location of settled agriculturalists (46.5 per cent of the total sites in this case), while pastoral nomads founded their camps on the lands of rich or mediocre pasture (42.79 per cent, see Map 4.10). But access to the roads was essential to either group given that 95 per cent of the sites are located at a distance of less than 1km from them (Map 4.5). The material culture of this period, including clay sealings (*supra*) and ceramics (Chapter 5), indicates the inter-regional role of this region, particularly in the late Sasanian period. No trace of defensive barriers, forts, fortresses or even fortlets has been discovered in the spatiotemporal horizons under examination. This absence of defensive infrastructures probably specifies strong levels of security of the region and its roads, which in turn shows the successful hegemonic presence of local authorities and Sasanian administration in Farsan. The strategic location of Farsan County in the Central Zagros (geographically) and the region of Spahān (administratively) and between different areas played an important role in economic developments during the Sasanian period. As discussed above, this is echoed in the settlement patterns, with access to roads one of the key factors in site location all across the region.

4.7 CONCLUSION

Lands with elevation ranges of over 2,000m a.s.l. are mountainous areas with particular natural features and topographic conditions. They provide distinct opportunities for, and, contrarywise, challenges to, human life and the formation processes of cultures. The Bakhtiyari highlands in the Central Zagros are such areas, with natural features different from those of the neighbouring Central Iranian Plateau and Khuzestan lowlands. Focusing on the spatial distribution of archaeological materials in Farsan County in the province of Chaharmahal va Bakhtiyari, this chapter has provided another case study, apart from Abdanan County in Chapter 3, on the regional socioeconomic transition during Late Antiquity, in this case in the southernmost part of the Central Zagros, and again a strategic area between different geographical and cultural zones. To contextualise the Sasanian-period sociopolitical milieu of Farsan in *longue durée*, the data relating to palaeoclimate (Chapter 1, s. 1.1.1), long-term settlement systems and models (*supra*) and the historical geography of the region (Chapter 2) were examined. I argued that the changes reflected in the settlement patterns and material culture of the region in the Sasanian period had roots in the transformations in terms of political changes and social complexity.

Following the local political developments and population growth in the Parthian period, Farsan experienced further sociopolitical transformations in the Sasanian era. Through the foundation of an administrative centre, Rāwar-kust-ī-rōdbār, the region participated in economic and political spheres according to the formal legal standards and regulations of the central Sasanian state on an inter-regional scale, and facilitated interactions between Spahān in the Central Iranian Plateau (Gay province) and south-western and southern plains in the regions of Hūzestān and Pārs (Ohrmazd-Ardašīr, Rām-Ohrmazd and Weh-Andiyok-Šābuhr and Īg provinces). This was accompanied by noticeable changes in the spatial distribution of sites, leading to the transition of the long-standing settlement system of Farsan. The transformation of settlement patterns and the associated models showed that the growth of larger sedentary settlements on the central Farsan plain than in earlier times depended on agriculture-based economy. The development of agricultural

infrastructures could not take place without fairly large-scale projects with investments backing agricultural economies against the
ancient pastoral backdrop of the region. The Sasanian-period cultural landscape of Farsan was mainly formed by the close interaction
of its sedentary and nomadic groups as reflected in the built environment and cultural material. Therefore, the main feature of this
socioeconomic milieu was the symbiosis between pastoral nomads
and the settled agriculturalists. The regular economic exchanges and
social relationships between the pastoral nomads of Farsan (and its
neighbouring Kouhrang County) and the farmer groups of either
the county itself or the towns and villages of the Chaharmahal area
and Iṣfahan to the east are attested up until the very recent past
(Chapter 1, s. 1.3, n. 17). It is also interesting to note the overlap
between the location of the majority of temporary sites and that of
the modern Bakhtiyari campsites. In Late Antiquity, the traditional
pastoral nomadism, with a limited range of dry farming, together
with irrigation agriculture, enabled better exploitation of the natural
resources and potentialities of the county, among which its strategic
location and the operation of its important communication roads
were also significant. This picture accords well with the late Sasanian
administrative system, and with the landscape transformations
and economic and infrastructural developments attested in various
territories under the Sasanian rule.

NOTES

1. These centres were mainly part of the summer quarters, *sardsir*, of the
   Bakhtiyaris, yet, as was noted over a century ago by Lesān-al-saltaneh
   Sepehr (1386 [2007]: 15), the area around modern Nāqān city of the
   Farsan County has historically been used as the winter quarters of
   some of the Bakhtiyaris who would migrate from their summer quarters
   in the Choghākhor area in the adjacent Borujen County. This is still the
   case today.
2. It is noteworthy that the undertaken works have mainly yet to be published.
3. Making an educated guess as to the overall plan of the structures uncovered at Tappe[h] Bardnakōn based on a comparison of the parts unearthed
   with other buildings that contained such archives and have been excavated at other sites, it is probable that these spaces were parts of a fire-
   temple with ambulatories. Needless to say, we need to wait for further
   excavations unearthing the architectural remains.
4. Gasche 2007 argued, on the basis of literary sources, that the southern alluvial lands of Khuzestan were not inhabited until the late first

millennium BCE. See also Gasche 2005, distinguishing the differences between the modern and ancient paths, branches, canals and coastal lines of the Kārōn, Karkheh and Jarrāhi Rivers, and the northern shorelines of the Persian Gulf in south-western Iran according to remote sensing and geological data.

5. Information about each of the sites is presented in Appendix 2.

5 *Sasanian Pottery from the Central Zagros: Interactive Local Traditions*

5.1 INTRODUCTION

This chapter examines the Sasanian pottery wares of the Central Zagros region, a subject that has largely been overlooked. Pottery makes up the most abundant material in archaeological findings generally. Needless to say, our knowledge of the types and features of and changes in ceramics throughout different eras assists us to reconstruct ancient societies in terms of chronology, intercultural interactions, and economies and modes of production. Hence, we study the assemblages discovered from the excavations and surveys in the two sample areas under examination in this book and their adjacent region in the Central Zagros. Moreover, the Sasanian collections published from other territories of the Sasanian realm are considered by way of comparison. These examples have been acquired from several fieldwork projects:

In Khuzestan:

- excavations at Shāōr Palace (Boucharlat and Labrousse 1979)
- surveys in Miānāb of Shushtar ('Āli and Khosrowzadeh 1385 [2006])
- surveys in Susiana (Wenke 1975–6)
- surveys in Izeh (Eqbal 1976)

In Fars:

- excavations at Hajiabad (Azarnoush 1994)
- excavations at Qasr-i Abu Nasr (Whitcomb 1985)
- excavations at Tal-i Malyan (Alden 1978)

In the north of the Central Iranian Plateau:

- excavations at Chāl-tarkhān of Rey (Kleiss 1987)

In the north-east of the Central Iranian Plateau (Labbaf Khaniki 1387 [2008]):

- excavations at Gorgan plain at Tureng-tepe (Lecomte 1987)
- excavations at the Great Wall of Gorgan (Priestman in Omrani Rekavandi et al. 2008; see also Priestman 2013b and Daghmehchi et al. 2022)
- excavations at Merv (Puschnigg 2006a, 2006b, 2008)
- surveys of Damghan (Trinkaus 1986)

In the south of the Central Iranian Plateau (Lamberg-Karlovsky 1970: 6–22; Kennet 2002, 2004).

In the west and north-west of the Central Iranian Plateau

- excavations at Tappe^h Bardnakōn (Khosrowzadeh et al. 2020a)
- excavations at Qal'e Seyrom-shāh (Mohammadifar and Tahmāsebi 1393 [2016])
- excavations at Khorheh (Kleiss 1985)
- excavations at Tafresh (Kleiss 1999)
- surveys in Māh-neshān (Khosrowzadeh and 'Āli 1383 [2004])

In southern Mesopotamia:

- excavations at Tell Abu Sarifa (Adams 1970)
- excavations at Tell Mahuz (Venco Ricciardi 1970)
- excavations at Kish and Barghutiat (Langdon and Harden 1934)

In northern Mesopotamia:

- the Salvage Project around the Eski Dam/former Saddam Dam (Simpson 1996)

On the northern and southern coasts of the Persian Gulf:

- surveys and excavations in Bushehr (Whitcomb 1987)
- surveys and excavations in Ras al-Khaimah (Kennet 2004)
- surveys and excavations at Kalba (Phillips 2008)

Generally, this examination is undertaken primarily with respect to the form of the vessels, especially the shape of their rims. The selection criteria for the examples found from the fieldwork projects in the sample areas are the possibility of reconstruction of the complete form of vessels, and the diagnostic and typical attributes of some sherds. Hence, the rims, bases, decorated potsherds, leads, handles and plain bodies were the priorities in order of high to low. The study mainly provides a qualitative typological assessment of the Sasanian ceramic repertoire of the Central Zagros, with the aim of reaching a preliminary understanding of the formative processes of the pottery types and a relative dating. The classification is taxonomic (Rouse 1960: 313; Shepard 1985: 224–5), following the structured method (Orton et al. 2007: 78–9). 'Class' is the expression used to refer to a group of examples that are categorised on the basis of their resemblances in terms of overall form, and by other sets of characteristics including geometric shape and technical attributes. This does not mean that all the members of a class possess completely similar forms and measures; rather, they display intra-class distinctions, particularly in terms of the shape of the rim and, in some cases, size. On the basis of these differences, each class is subdivided into separate 'types'.

Apart from the classification, and comparison and typology of them, the simple presentation of the samples is of foremost importance given the present state of Sasanian archaeology (see the next section).

5.2 SASANIAN POTTERY

The need for systematic studies of Sasanian pottery is a widely acknowledged issue in Sasanian archaeology that still remains to be tackled (e.g. Whitcomb 1987: 47; Boucharlat and Haerinck 1991: 305; Azarnoush 1994: 183; Kennet 2002: 153; Schippmann 1383 [2004]: 133). The situation in the field of Sasanian ceramic is the outcome of several causes, including: the usually disturbed condition and complexities of Sasanian urban contexts (Boucharlat and Haerinck 1991: 305); art-historical approaches to the material culture (Puschnigg 2006a: 3–5); the geographical differences and local character of the pottery of this period (e.g. Huff 1986: 302); the constant occurrence of some types all through either the late Parthian and early Sasanian or the late Sasanian and early Islamic periods (Boucharlat and Haerinck 1991: 306); the continuity of some forms throughout the whole Sasanian era (Azarnoush 1994: 240);

methodological issues regarding the excavations of Sasanian strata, particularly prior to around the last quarter of the twentieth century (Puschnigg 2006a: 3–8); and disregarding of the publication of the data on them, or only their brief presentation, because of a focus on earlier layers (Azarnoush 1994: 183 and 240; Freestone 2008: 3; Tāj-bakhsh and Azarnoush 1392 [2013]: 220; Puschnigg 2006a: 3–8), along with the dearth of published data from many territories.[1]

In the Sasanian period, various industries were organised, more fully than before, in industrial centres specialising in a certain industry and related production (Ghirshman 1978: 441–2; Schippmann 1386 [2007]: 96–7; Daryaee 1383 [2004]: 107; Christensen 1933b). Concerning the ceramic of this era, authorities have claimed that it lost its status as an elite commodity compared to in earlier times, and that this role was undertaken by other materials such as gilded silver vessels and seals (Schippmann 1383 [2004]: 166; Huff 1986: 307; Trinkaus 1986: 49–50; Puschnigg 2008: 37). However, as per the current state of knowledge, we may still take a more conservative position regarding such a general proposition for all the territories. At least, so far as the organisation of production is concerned, there are sets of evidence indicating the concentrated production of some wares in particular areas (Langdon and Harden 1934; Ricciardi 1970: 430; Wenke 1975–6; Seyyed Sajjadi 1989; Potts 1998; Kennet 2002; 1393 [2014]: 72, 199; De Cardi 2008; Pace et al. 2008; 'Āli and Khosrowzadeh 1384 [2015]). Needless to say, this organisation was, in terms of scale, smaller than that for silk textiles and precious metal vessels. Nevertheless, the trend of increasing specialisation in production was not exclusive to the latter group of industries. From the profession list of Dēnkard, it may be inferred that there were at least three sorts of pottery makers (Tafazzoli 1974: 193–6; see also Simpson 1997: 79 for hints in the Babylonian Talmud). Moreover, the inscribed pithoi reported from some early Sasanian sites such as Tepe Yahya, period I, IA (Lamberg-Karlovsky 1970: 8–9, Fig. 3: m; Frye in Lamberg-Karlovsky 1970: 131) and Qal'e Dokhtar of Firuzabad (Huff and Gignoux 1973) challenge the above-mentioned statement regarding the status of ceramic vessels in the Sasanian period. In particular, Gignoux presented a vase of Qal'e Dokhtar whose epigraphic data indicate its probable function in the Zoroastrian ritual of haoma (Huff and Gignoux 1973: Abb. 26, 148–9, Taf. 44, 1).

Another quality widely attributed to Sasanian ceramic in general is local distinction across regions (Huff 1986: 302; Simpson 1997: 74, 79; Hozhabri 1380 [2001]: 384; Labbaf Khaniki 1387

[2008]: 163–4; Mohammadifar and Tahmasbi 1393 [2014]: 150; Habibi and Heydari 1393 [2004]; Puschnigg 2008; Mousavi and Daryaee 2012: 1,091–2; Priestman 2013a). In other words, pottery of this period is represented by variations in section and decoration, and technical attributes that give a distinct/local character to the assemblages of different regions, and hence it should be examined on the basis of separate studies in each cultural zone. Some types were produced and distributed in particular areas, among which one may recall TURQ/Turquoise Glaze in southern Mesopotamia and south-western Iran (Langdon and Harden 1934; Wenke 1975–6; Simpson 1997: 75 and 79; Kennet 2004: 35–8 and 96; 'Āli and Khosrowzadeh 1385 [2006]: 1385), TORP/Torpedo-shaped Jars in areas on the Persian Gulf southern coast, southern Iran and southern Mesopotamia (Kennet 2002; 2004: 85), Namord Ware in south-eastern Iran and the shores of the Oman Sea (Seyyed Sajjadi 1989; Potts 1998; Kennet 2002; Khosrowzadeh and Sarlak 1397 [2018]), and die-stamped potteries with Sasanian leitmotifs in late Sasanian northern Mesopotamia, according to the excavations at Khirbet Deir Situn (Simpson 1996; 1997: 79, Fig. 5; 2013).

As mentioned above, the presentation, classification, typology and comparison of the collections discovered in the areas under examination provide a better understanding of Sasanian ceramic from the Central Zagros in general, and of its local varieties in particular. This may further shed light on the cultural interactions across the highlands and with their adjacent regions. The aims of this study, therefore, are also to specify whether the pottery types followed local examples or whether they were primarily common wares distributed in larger areas beyond the Central Zagros; and to determine to what extent this pottery reflects the continuity of pre-Sasanian traditions. Therefore, the prototypes and earlier samples of some forms will also be explored, together with the comparison of contemporary collections. But firstly, they are classified here on the basis of their overall forms, rim shapes and section thickness, and then their comparative chronology is discussed.[2]

5.3 SASANIAN POTTERY FROM ABDANAN: AT THE BORDER OF TWO DISTINCT CULTURAL ZONES

In this section, a total of 185 samples are classified, which were acquired from the Sasanian sites of Abdanan County in the course of its surveys.

5.3.1 Jars

Jars[3] (Figure 5.1: 1–30, Graph 5.1) constitute one of the most common classes in this collection. They were discovered in rather diverse forms and are categorised into the two general types of necked jars and jugs. Necked jars constitute the most frequently occurring type of the class. Their fabric has, for the most part, medium mineral inclusions – sand, limestone and calcite – and their colour ranges from buff to pinkish buff, pink and red. All the samples are wheel-made. The texture is usually compact and coherent as a result of being exposed to proper firing temperature and conditions. However, 40 per cent of the samples were fired insufficiently and their fabric organic inclusions are not burnt well. Furthermore, a few of the ceramics are covered in slip or monochrome alkaline greenish blue glaze on either side (some jugs), and some are decorated with incised parallel horizontal wavy or straight lines or the stamped motif of concentric circles on the exterior (some necked jars).

5.3.2 Large jars

This class[4] (Figure 5.2: 1–25, Graph 5.2) is presented typologically in two groups, necked and neckless. The fabric colour is mostly orange or red, but in some cases brownish red, reddish buff, orange buff, green and grey. Approximately half of the large jars have a coarse texture. Their inclusion is mainly mineral, with some organic materials in some examples. All the sherds are wheel-made and have smooth surfaces. On the other hand, the majority of them are not exposed to proper firing temperature and have an irregularly fractured texture. Apart from some specimens of the necked type with horizontal grooves and bands on their necks and shoulders, most of the sherds are plain wares with no slip or decoration.

5.3.3 Pots/cooking pots

Having considerable diversity in terms of their forms, these closed-mouth jars[5] (Figure 5.2: 26–31, 5.3: 1–8, Graph 5.3) are classified as forming two groups, pots (Figure 5.2: 26–31) and small pots (Figure 5.3: 1–8), on the basis of their measures. The majority of them have an orange fabric, yet some brownish red, grey and greenish buff are also present. Moreover, most of the samples of this type were not fired properly and around half of their fabrics are coarse,

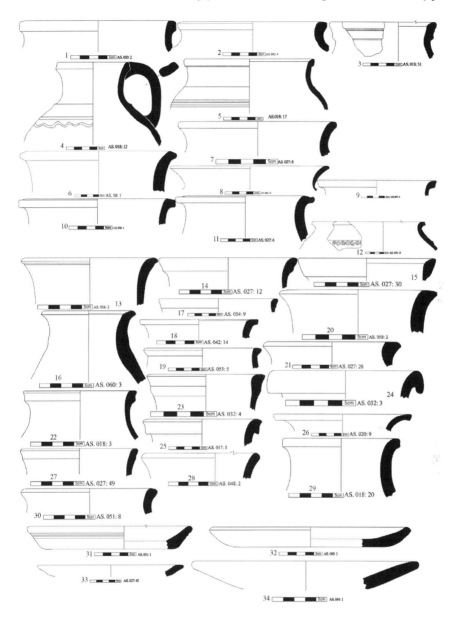

Fig. 5.1. Sketches of the ceramic types of Abdanan: necked jars (1–12), jugs (13–30) and dishes (31–4). (Source: author)

with frequent air holes. These ceramics are wheel-made and have smooth surfaces and compact textures whose fabric inclusions consisted of mineral elements of sand, calcite and limestone. Moreover, the great majority of them lack any slip or decorative design.

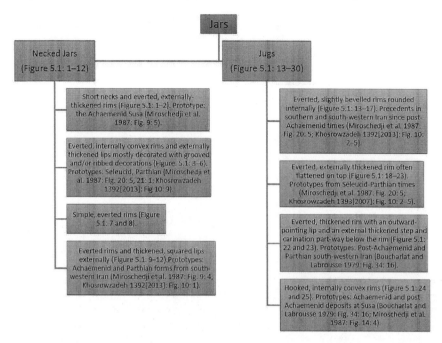

Graph 5.1. Classification chart of jars in the Abdanan collection. (Source: author)

5.3.4 *Bowls*

Bowls[6] (Figure 5.3: 9–44, 5.4: 1–27, Graph 5.4) make up the most common class in the Sasanian ceramic collection of the Abdanan region, which is itself categorised into three groups: large bowls (Figure 5.3: 9–28), bowls – the most common type in the Abdanan collection (Figure 5.4: 1–27) – and beakers (the majority of glazed wares in the collection (Figure 5.3: 29–44)), mainly on the basis of the size of the samples. Fabric colours are mostly orange, buff and red. These wheel-made vases are, in general, well-fired and have medium fabrics with compact textures. Nonetheless, most of the large bowls were not exposed to proper firing conditions and their fabrics are coarse with frequent medium and small air holes. Approximately 25 per cent of these sherds are covered with a buff slip. This class is decorated, in unusual examples of the large bowls with rims troughed on top, with incised and appliquéd lines and finger-trailing horizontal rope pattern; and in one of them, with a greenish blue glaze; and in the bowls type, with appliquéd S-twist cordons; and in four samples, with a greenish blue or olive-green glaze; and in nine beakers, with a greenish blue or green glaze.

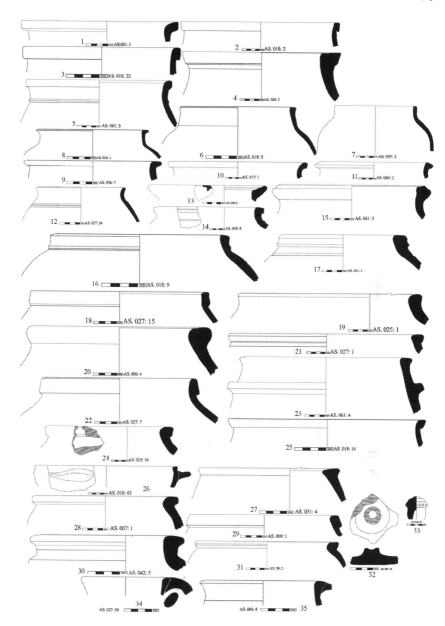

Fig. 5.2. Sketches of the ceramic types of Abdanan: necked large jars (1–15), neckless large jars (16–25), pots (26–31), lids (32 and 33) and pitchers (34 and 35). (Source: author)

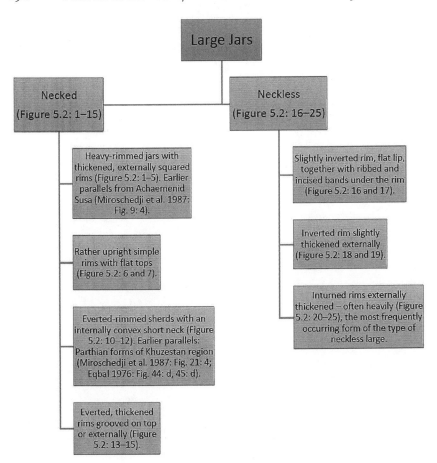

Graph 5.2. Classification chart of large jars in the Abdanan collection. (Source: author)

5.3.5 Pitchers

Two examples of this form[7] are represented in this collection. These handled vases have everted, externally thickened rims, orange buff fabrics with mineral inclusions, and a smooth surface shaped using a pottery wheel (Figure 5.2: 34–5).

5.3.6 Dishes

The fabric colours of the four dishes[8] of this assemblage (Figure 5.1: 31–4) are orange, beige and grey, and they have mineral inclusions of sand, limestone and calcite. These wheel-made vases have medium bodies, about half of which are well-fired, and have a compact and

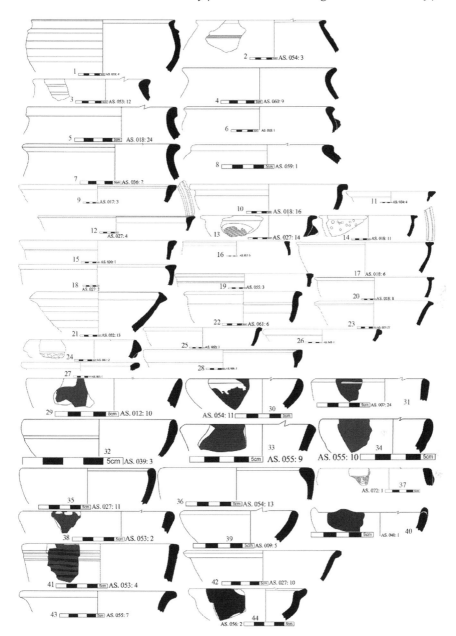

Fig. 5.3. Sketches of the ceramic types of Abdanan: small pots (1–8), large bowls (9–28) and beakers (29–44). (Source: author)

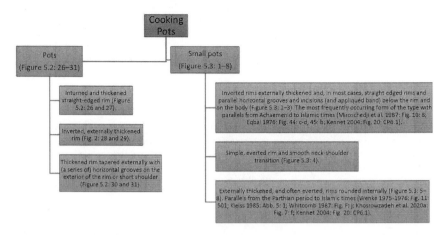

Graph 5.3. Classification chart of pots/cooking pots in the Abdanan collection. (Source: author)

coherent texture. One of the dishes (Figure 5.1: 31) has traces of thin slip on either surface, and the other (Figure 5.1: 34) is decorated with parallel horizontal incised lines on the exterior below the rim. The first two examples of this type have flaring rims with rounded lips and the other two are featured with slightly everted rims.

5.3.7 Basins

Two examples of basins[9] (Figure 5.4: 42–3) have orange buff and greenish buff fabrics with inclusions of sand grains of fine to coarse sizes, along with organic materials – chaff. The specimens are wheel-made and have medium bodies. The first vase has a flaring, lid-seated rim and the next one an upright, thickened rim with a rounded lip.

5.3.8 Ceramic parts in the Abdanan collection

Apart from the classification provided mainly on the basis of pottery forms and according to rim shapes, here the other ceramic parts of the Abdanan collection are briefly presented.

In this assemblage are two lid examples (Figure 5.2: 32–3) which are perhaps associated with large jars. Handles (Figure 5.5: 22–9) are another ceramic component of this collection, with types of single strand (Figure 5.5: 22–3), oval (Figure 5.5: 24), and blind loops with upturned triangular sections (Figure 5.5: 25–8). The latter handle type is probably related to the class of pots/cooking pots. Also noteworthy is that this type may also be considered a type of lug handle, but these examples are different from the horizontal lug handles reported from

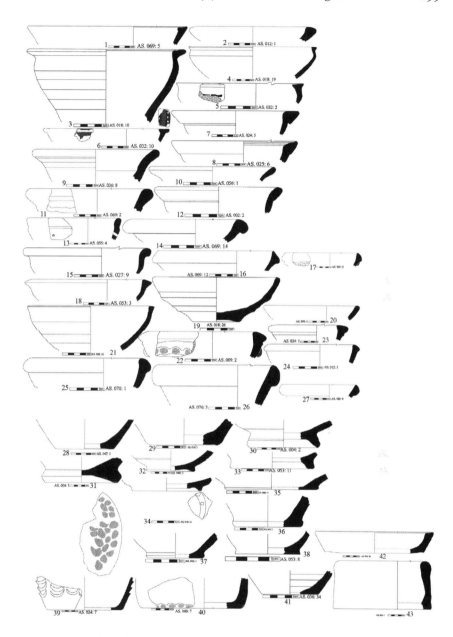

Fig. 5.4. Sketches of the ceramic types of Abdanan: bowls (1–27), bases (28–41) and basins (42 and 43). (Source: author)

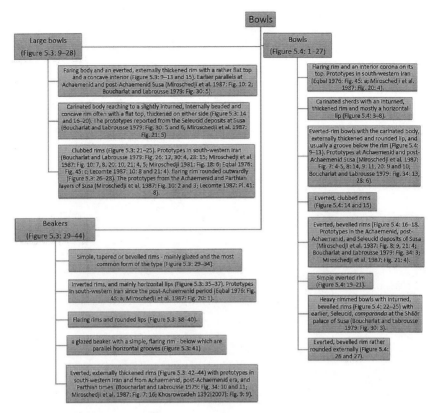

Graph 5.4. Classification chart of bowls in the Abdanan collection. (Source: author)

contexts dated to the ninth and tenth centuries at Samarra, Susa, Istakhr and Pasargadae (Whitcomb 1985: 52) or earlier assemblages (e.g. Overlaet 2003: 77, Figs 54, 56 and 57; Lamberg-Karlovsky 1970: Fig. 5: D and O), in the sense that the triangular sections of the Abdanan samples, along with similar specimens reported from Farsan County as the other area under examination here (Khosrowzadeh et al. 2020a: Fig. 7: a), are upward-pointed. This author argues that Abdanan's blind loop handle is a local type from the Central Zagros region in the Sasanian period, whose precedents are reported at Qal'eh-i Yazdigird (Keall and Keall 1981: Fig. 16: 6, 36, 27: 19). Also notable is that the forms with a hole in their upper section discovered at Tureng-tepe, phase VI A (Lecomte 1987: Pl. 60: 13), and Qasr-i Abu Nasr, phases 2a–2b (Whitcomb 1985: fig. 54: c), are to some extent comparable with our examples, yet they had roots in a distinct tradition going back continuously to Achaemenid and Parthian times (Whitcomb 1985: 119).

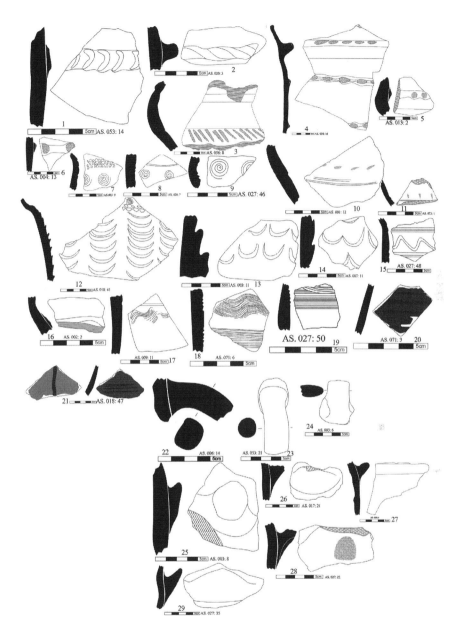

Fig. 5.5. Sketches of the ceramic types of Abdanan: body parts (1–21) and handles (22–9). (Source: author)

Another ceramic part of the Abdanan collection is made up of different base types (Figure 5.4: 28–41) of concave flat (Figure 5.4: 28–9), concave disk (Figure 5.4: 30–4), disk (Figure 5.4: 35–8) and flat (Figure 5.4: 39–41). Moreover, there are bodies in this assemblage (Figure 5.5: 1–21) that have decorations of various types: ribbed and pinched (Fig. 5: 1–3), ribbed and finger-impressed (Figure 5.5: 4–6), stamped (Figure 5.5: 7–9), grooved and impressed (Figure 5.5: 10–11), scaled and stamped (Figure 5.5: 12), scaled (Figure 5.5: 13 and 14), appliquéd (Figure 5.5: 16), combed (Figure 5.5: 17–19) and glazed (Figure 5.5: 20 and 21). It is worth mentioning that comb decoration is attested, in cases that show a highly skilled manner, by assemblages uncovered at various Sasanian sites (e.g. Langdon and Harden 1934: 124; Whitcomb 1985: Fig. 43: g-h-k, 45: a, 50: g-i-m-n; Azarnoush 1994: Fig. 180: t; Simpson 1996: 100).

5.3.9 Discussion

The Sasanian ceramic assemblage of Abdanan presents some local features that might be typical of the Sasanian pottery repertoire in the Central Zagros region. The stamped decoration of concentric circles is of the motifs, occurring alone or along with scaled decoration, that designed jars unearthed at Sargandāb, Dare-shahr and Abdanan. The handle type of blind loops with upturned triangular sections is another example of such traits. Apart from Abdanan, it is discovered in the Dare-shahr area and indicates a distinctive diachronic process in this cultural zone. Furthermore, given the local mines of gypsum and limestone in the mountains of this region, the majority of the sherds in this collection have inclusions of limestone and calcite. Worthy of mention is that the impressed scaled decoration of jars reported in Iran from central and south-eastern areas, particularly Kerman, was also common in the Central Zagros in this period. In the latter region, this certain type of decoration is found from Sargandāb, Kangavar, Dare-shahr, Seyrom-shāh and Abdanan. It was perhaps used since the early Sasanian period and its prototype was unearthed at Qal'eh-i Yazdigird.

Notwithstanding the local features, many of the pottery forms in this assemblage have parallels from all across the Sasanian realm. However, the correlation is higher with the contemporary collections found in the neighbouring areas of the Central Zagros and south-western Iran cultural zones, particularly in the case of the bowls. This fact is also indicated by the presence of the turquoise-glazed ware (mainly beakers), produced in southern Mesopotamia and south-western Iran, in the Abdanan assemblage. Examination of the background of these forms reveals the pre-Sasanian precedents of them in south-western Iran. Therefore, overall, this collection provides information about the continuity of earlier ceramic traditions of this area in Sasanian times in the Abdanan region, despite the fact that the contemporary parallels of many forms have not inevitably been discovered in the adjacent areas. The close correlation with the samples from the Central Zagros and south-western Iran makes sense, considering the geographical location of Abdanan and the administrative and political conditions applying in the era (see Chapter 2, ss. 2.3, 2.3.1; Chapter 3, s. 3.2.2). On the one hand, Abdanan was a part of the Poshtkooh area and connected from the north and north-east to other areas of this region, and on the other, it reached eastwards to the Khuzestan south-western lowlands, almost without natural barriers.[10]

5.4 THE SASANIAN POTTERY OF THE BAKHTIYARI HIGHLANDS AND ITS SOCIOECONOMIC IMPLICATIONS

The primary purpose of this section is to present the Sasanian ceramic collection that was acquired from the archaeological fieldwork projects carried out in Farsan County. The classification, comparison and analysis of these materials along with the assemblages discovered from the adjacent cultural zones and other territories of the Sasanian realm may also provide a relative understanding of the (inter-)regional socioeconomic relations of the inhabitants of this area in the Sasanian period. Indeed, before the excavations at the late Sasanian administrative centre of Tappe[h] Bardnakōn, certain data about the Sasanian pottery in Farsan County to the south-eastern edges of the Central Zagros were not available – a challenge yet to be tackled in many other territories. But currently, thanks to the study of the examples uncovered in the deposits of this tappe[h], we may offer a more confident presentation of the Sasanian samples collected in the surveys of the county.

Therefore, as with the examination and comparison of the Abdanan collection (*supra*), here the Farsan assemblage of Sasanian pottery is studied. The Sasanian ceramic of Farsan is technically made up of a group of simple wares that is further categorised into typological classes and types according to the attributes of overall form and rim shape.

5.4.1 Jars

The most frequently occurring class in the Sasanian collection of
Farsan relates to jars (Graph 5.5), and is itself subdivided into three
distinct types, necked (Figure 5.6: 1–28, 31–5), neckless (Figure 5.6:
36–41) and jugs (Figure 5.6: 42–8). Necked jars constitute the most
common type of this class. The fabric of most of the jars has one of
the colours of buff, orange buff and reddish orange, while some are
in other tints, including reddish buff, cream buff, grey buff, orange,
light brown, red, beige, reddish brown and light brown. The fabric
texture is usually medium and its inclusions are sand, calcite, grit and,
in some cases, gravel. Apart from two samples produced by hand, all
the jars are wheel-made and have a smooth surface. The majority of
them are also well-fired and their fabrics are compact. A noticeable
number of examples of this class have slips in buff, brown, cream
and orange colours, and two of their outer surfaces show traces of
an all-over thin wash cover. The kinds of decoration used in some
cases include comb motif; incised lines and grooves; and appliquéd,
parallel, horizontal or wavy lines – with finger-impressions on some
examples (Figure 5.6: 1–28, 31–48).

5.4.2 Dishes

The Abdanan collection of Sasanian ceramics includes a dish
(Figure 5.6: 49) with a carinated body, bevelled rim and low ring
base. The specimen has a buff fabric with inclusions of sand and fine-
to-large particles of limestone and its texture is medium. This hand-
made dish lacks slip on its interior but has wavy combed decoration.

5.4.3 Bowls

The class of bowls (Figures 5.6: 50–3, 5.7, 5.8: 1–8, Graph 5.6)
is subdivided into two general types, large bowls (Figures 5.7,
5.8: 1–8) and bowls (Figure 5.6: 50–3), on the basis of size; the
former type is more common and its rim shapes are diverse. Most of
the fabric colours of this class are orange, orange buff and buff,
together with some cases of light orange, reddish orange, light
buff, grey buff, light brown, reddish brown, light green and beige.
The majority of the fabrics are medium, and, as inclusions, they
include fine to rather large particles of limestone, sand and grit,
along with organic materials such as chaff in some sherds. All the
examples are wheel-made. Apart from some grey to black cores, the

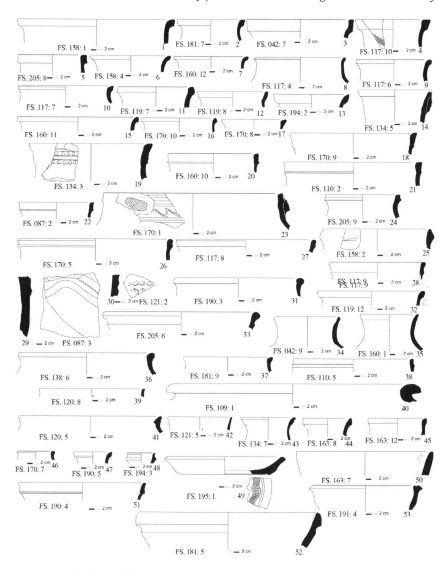

Fig. 5.6. Sketches of the ceramic types of Farsan: necked jars (1–28, 31–5), body parts (29 and 30), neckless jars (36–41), and jugs (42–8), dishes (49) and bowls (50–3). (Source: Habibi 1390 [2012])

majority of these vases are well-fired and have compact and hard textures. Furthermore, most of them lack any slip, yet a number of the examples of the class have traces of buff, reddish buff, brownish buff and cream slip. Their decorations are bound to some vases with incised parallel lines motifs.

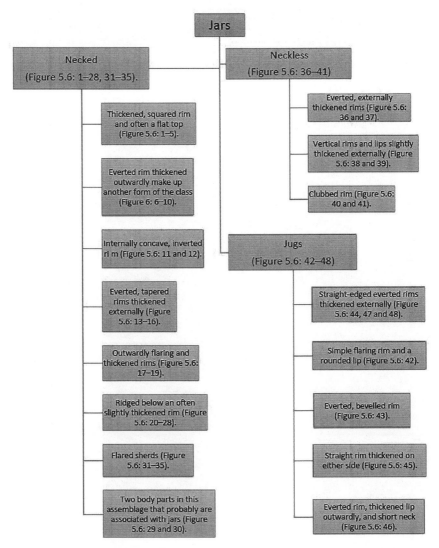

Graph 5.5. Classification chart of jars in the Farsan collection. (Source: author)

5.4.4 Pots/cooking pots

A noticeable amount of the sherds in the Farsan collection of Sasanian ceramics are related to the class of cooking pots (Figures 5.8: 9–30, 5.9: 1–11, Graph 5.7). Although diverse in terms of form, pots establish a rather homogeneous group in the sense that the technical features of the majority of them are as follows. Fabric colours are usually reddish brown, and in some cases grey, orange and brownish orange. Core and inner and outer margins of most of the sherds are

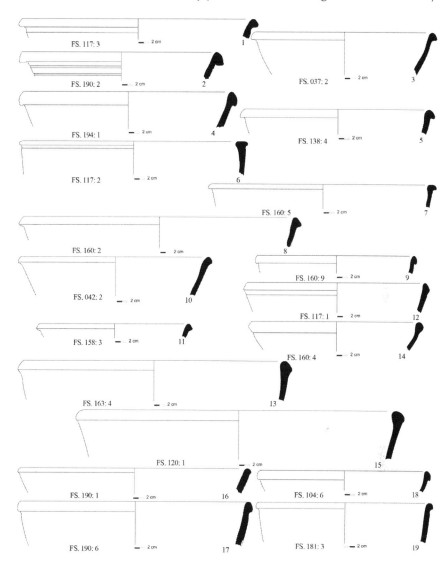

Fig. 5.7. Sketches of the ceramic types of Farsan (large bowls). (Source: Habibi 1390 [2012])

black. These examples are all wheel-made, with smooth outer surfaces and compact fabrics that have sand and grit inclusions. Apart from some with slips of buff, greenish buff, cream buff and brownish orange colour, the majority of the vases lack slip. The decoration is often parallel straight, wavy and zigzag incised lines on the body, except in the case of a small pot with a horizontal groove below the rim. Also, a few vases are ribbed on the shoulder, including a pot with

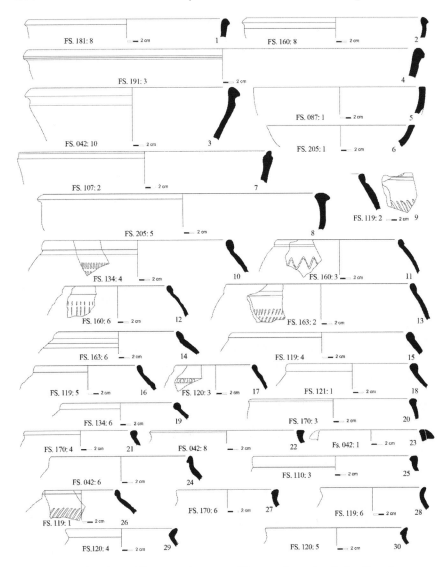

Fig. 5.8. Sketches of the ceramic types of Farsan: large bowls (1–8) and pots (9–30). (Source: Habibi 1390 [2012])

two parallel horizontal ribs and two small pots with a single rib on the shoulder. Moreover, one example has pinched decoration on the exterior too. These vases were made for cooking. The production of the cooking pots of the Farsan collection in the Sasanian period, as well as those of Khuzestan, took place according to earlier examples in terms of either their forms or technical features, hence indicating the continuity of Parthian-period traditions in this area.

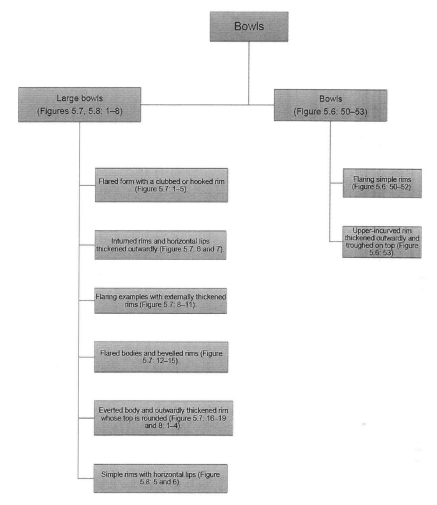

Graph 5.6. Classification chart of bowls in the Farsan collection. (Source: author)

5.4.5 *Large jars*

The fabric colour of the class of large jars (Figure 5.9: 12–27, Graph 5.8) is commonly orange buff, orange and red, yet there are also some in light orange, reddish orange and brown. The fabrics are mostly medium but in some cases they are coarse. Their inclusions are sand, grit and fine-to-large particles of limestone, along with, in a few samples, gravel and organic materials such as chaff. They are wheel-made and have smooth surfaces, and, apart from some examples with core hues of between grey and black, are fired properly. Half the members of this class are covered with slips in buff, orange buff, reddish buff and

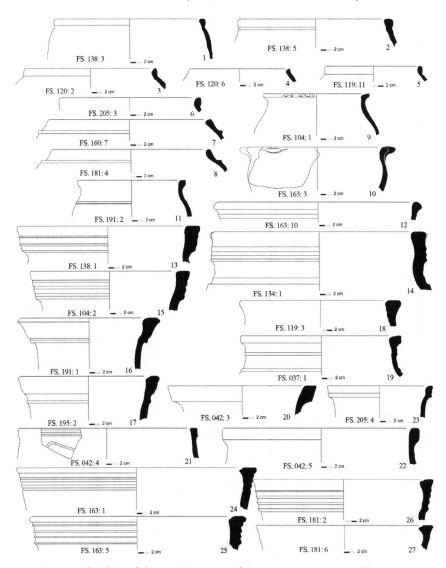

Fig. 5.9. Sketches of the ceramic types of Farsan: pots (1–11) and large jars (12–27). (Source: Habibi 1390 [2012])

brownish orange. In terms of decoration, some of the large jars have incisions and ribs below the rim or, in a few cases, on the neck.

5.4.6 Discussion

The typological analysis of the Sasanian potteries of the Farsan collection points to the similarities between this repertoire and those studied in the cultural zones of south-western Iran, the Central

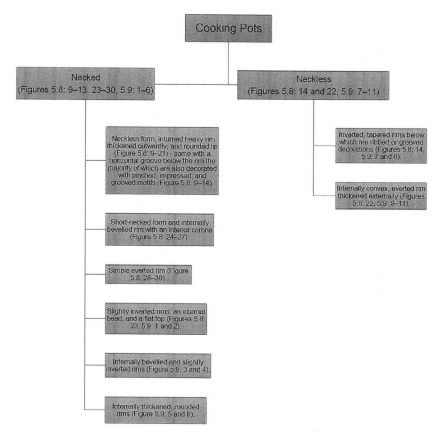

Graph 5.7. Classification chart of pots/cooking pots in the Farsan collection. (Source: author)

Zagros and Fars more than other Sasanian territories. This indicates the interactions between the Farsan region and those areas. This point makes sense given the strategic location of Farsan between the Central Zagros, the Central Iranian Plateau and the south-western lowlands of Iran, and the archaeological and historical attestations, such as the historical Atābaki Road, regarding the engagement of Farsan County in inter-regional relations (see Chapter 2, n. 47 and Chapter 4, s. 4.5). As expected, the cultural interactions reflected in the ceramic assemblage under examination partly mirror the situation pictured by the archaeological materials unearthed in the late Sasanian deposits excavated at Tappe[h] Bardnakōn of Farsan, including ceramics, but most importantly its administrative bullae archive (Khosrowzadeh et al. 2020a; Khosrowzadeh et al. 2020b; 2020c). The corpus signifies the economic and political roles of this place as an administrative centre located in the canton called

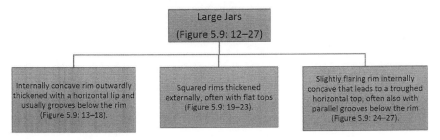

Graph 5.8. Classification chart of large jars in the Farsan collection. (Source: author)

'Rāwar-kust-ī-rōdbār' in the Spahān region. Accordingly, this happened on an inter-regional scale between the regions of Spahān, Hūzestān and Fārs. The limited overlap of the conclusions derived from the examination of ceramic and administrative bullae collections of Farsan is mainly due to the limited available knowledge about Sasanian ceramic in some areas (see above). Currently, we possess scarcely any knowledge in this regard concerning the Isfahan area.

5.5 CONCLUSION

Bringing together the collections of Sasanian pottery from the sample areas under examination within the Central Zagros geographical zone, this chapter has presented original data according to classification, typological analysis, and comparison (see Appendix 3) of the ceramic specimens. Given the geographical location of two Abdanan and Farsan Counties as two intermediary areas in the Central Zagros region, this study has not only examined the local nature of Sasanian ceramic particularly in this region, but may also cast light on the continuity or disruption of earlier traditions in either area and its interactions with the adjacent cultural zones in Sasanian times.

Accordingly, the continuity of earlier traditions is noticeable on an inter-regional level, reflected for instance in the forms and decorations of the classes of cooking pots and bowls in the sample areas and in south-western Iran. On the other hand, another noticeable point is that there are features that occur only in some areas of the Central Zagros and not in the whole region. For example, one may recall blind loops with upturned triangular sections, certain decorative motifs such as stamped concentric circles and scaled bodies, or technical attributes. This suggests that a certain rate of diversity might be traced even in a single geographical zone, that is, here, the Central Zagros region. That said, many forms have undeniable parallels reported from widely separated sites across the Sasanian realm. Therefore, we may define the distinct disposition of the Sasanian pottery of the areas under examination mainly on the basis of decorative and technical attributes. However, the present state of the field evidently limits this analysis. Further works, particularly publication of assemblages uncovered in well-dated contexts, are required to shed light on the matter and falsify/verify current speculations. As discussed earlier, Sasanian ceramic is a problematic subject, for various reasons. The dearth of excavated contexts and – even more rare – published strata relating to the Sasanian period considerably limits the possibility of determining the sequence and chronology of different pottery wares and of precisely dating them to a certain phase of this era. Therefore, more advanced examination of the Sasanian ceramic repertoire of the Central Zagros, perhaps using different quantitative and more scientific methods, is required, but this is a matter that is dependent on further excavations of Sasanian strata and their publication. This is a serious challenge that future research should address.

Another suggestion for future research on Sasanian ceramic may be made here. In light of the precise definition of pottery classes presented for some regions so far, consideration of form as the more basic (and stable) aspect of pottery wares may enable us to provide general classes for wider geographical areas that are not inevitably located in a single cultural zone. Currently, this can help us to progress the field given our present state of knowledge.

NOTES

1. For the history of archaeological research on the Sasanian sites in general and on Sasanian ceramic in particular, see Huff 1986; Boucharlat and Haerinck 1991: 305–6; Puschnigg 2006a; 2006b: 3–9; Mousavi 2008; Mousavi and Daryaee 2012.
2. For comprehensive description and comparisons see Appendix 3.
3. Here, the designation 'jar' is accorded to a group of samples with or without handles whose forms contain the geometric shapes of hyperbola-ellipse or ellipse-truncated cone or ring-truncated cone. The proportion of the rim diameter to the height of this class is over ½ (Labbaf Khaniki 1387 [2008]: 148). Jug is also a type of this class with the same proportions, only in smaller measures than jars. This type contains one of the combinations of cylindrical-ring, truncated conical-semi-circular, and truncated conical-ovoid shapes and usually has a short neck leading to an internally concave rim.

4. In the present study, the class of large jars is defined by pottery forms with the geometric shape of an ellipse or sphere (for the neckless type), or combinations of truncated cone-ellipse or truncated cone-semi-circle or cylinder-ellipse (for the necked type). The proportion of rim diameter to height of this class is over ½. The difference between jars and large jars, apart from some of their geometric shapes, is in their overall size and the thickness of the body.

5. Cooking pots have spherical or elliptical shapes or, in less common cases, a truncated conical-spherical combination of shapes, and the proportion of rim to height in them is between ¾ and 1. These vases mostly have an overall spherical form with a closed mouth and an inverted rim. However, in some less frequently occurring forms the rims are everted.

6. 'Bowl' is a general form designed with one of the geometric shapes of semi-circle, skull cap, truncated cone and ring (Labbaf Khaniki 1387 [2008]: 148). Large bowls are similar, yet with larger measures, and have a rim diameter of over 30cm and a thicker body. Also, beakers are produced with the same geometric attributes, but the rim diameter of this type is less than 10cm and the body is finer than in other types of the class of bowls.

7. 'Pitcher' may be defined as a deep vase similar to a bottle, but distinct from that due to its taller neck, which has a rim diameter to overall height proportion of around ½. Pitchers are usually composed of the geometric shape combinations of hyperbola-semi-circle or hyperbola-truncated cone, together with a handle.

8. The class of dishes is made up by shallow vases that are in the shapes of a ring, usually with a flat base.

9. Basins have the same attributes as dishes in terms of form and geometric shape, but are larger and produced with thicker bodies.

10. Despite being officially a part of Ilam Province, nowadays the Abdanan region is mainly linked to the adjacent counties of Khuzestan Province through socioeconomic relations.

6 Conclusion. The Multifaceted Landscape of the Central Zagros during the Sasanian Period and Its Socioeconomic Transformation

Long before the formation of world empires and Sasanian rule in the Iranian world, the Central Zagros region had been inhabited by various groups. The highlands attracted populations by providing proper circumstances, with enough precipitation for dry farming and even irrigation agriculture in some areas, with ample water resources and rich soil for arboriculture and viticulture; with rich pasturelands for animal husbandry; and with access to strategic passageways through the mountains for involvement in regional exchange, trade and banditry. The diverse ways of life and modes of subsistence are reflected as traditions in various micro-environments of the region in later documents, both Iranian and Graeco-Roman. The intermontane plains and valleys of the region developed their various local kingdoms in the Iron Age. These different political entities were later united under the Median kings and Achaemenid Great Kings. However, archaeological data and literary evidence indicate that the diverse socioeconomic structures across the Central Zagros continued despite the political changes. Groups with different subsistence strategies were acknowledged by the central states. From the royal city of Hagmatāna to a number of towns, villages and nomadic centres across the highlands, each played its role in the imperial and royal economies and armies.

The cultural landscape of the Central Zagros, in cases such as Bagastāna, and its strategic roads were essential to the domestic policies of the Iranian empires and their kings, who invested in exploitation of the heritage of the former and in safe access to the latter. Therefore, in the vicinity of Median and Achaemenid relics of Bisotun, both the local rulers and the Kings of Kings of post-Achaemenid and Arsacid times tried to link their names and images to the ancient cultural topos and the religious values attached to the heritage site. These kings also realised the significance of local highlanders and their rulers in confidently securing the ancient roads crossing through different areas of the Central Zagros. In light of its particular topography and strategic location, the Central Zagros region has a limited number of safe inter-regional paths with proper conditions for regular use. Linking the Central Iranian Plateau to south-western Iran, the Persian Gulf and Mesopotamia and beyond, these roads and crossing spots have been used for millennia, and hence, the inhabitants of the region, especially nomads, were fairly well acquainted with them. Therefore, communication, information flow and product transportation could be controlled or disrupted by these populations. The states handled the situation through the arrangements either of granting exclusive privileges to the highlanders (the Achaemenids) or conceding high rates of independence to the Elymaean kingdom (the Arsacids).

The Sasanian built environment of the Central Zagros was a multifaceted landscape made up of long-held human niche construction and contemporary adoptive formation processes, in accordance with either the varied natural setting of the Central Zagros or the late antique zeitgeist of the Near East, that is, the socioeconomic milieu, religious movements, and political geography and domestic and foreign policies of the Sasanian central state. The different aspects of this environment constituted various types of landscape, not only in terms of geographical features but also culturally. Religious landscapes are echoed in the settings of temples, burials and institutions. They were associated with Zoroastrianism (e.g. fire-temples and *bard-e gōri* rock-cut niches), and probably with Christianity, Zurvanism, Mithraism, Mazdakism and Manicheism. Political landscapes are mainly imperial signatures in the natural environment that reflected the authority and hegemonic presence of the central power of the Sasanian state, or its representatives, in the form of monuments marked with royal symbols, hunting grounds, administrative centres, defensive structures and manor houses. Economic landscapes, on the other hand, are the locales altered by activities related to the subsistence of groups, and their instances are to be sought in forms such as pasturelands, agricultural fields, irrigations systems and gardens. Moreover, heritage landscapes are essentially hybrid environments with natural and man-made sectors involved with the cultural, communal memory and constructed values of the societies of their environs, and might well be related to different cultural aspects. Hence they could imply interwoven layers of the religious, political and economic notions of all three types of cultural landscapes mentioned above. Heritage sites, together with political landscapes, reflect the political ideology of the Sasanian Empire in its different stages. One may also point to residential landscapes that held urban, rural and temporary campsite areas and the associated socioeconomic structures of the populations attributing a sense of home to them. Therefore, this complex built environment could offer a variety of opportunities to the imperial power, together with its local client states. They contributed to Sasanian political culture from various perspectives, and were exploited by the political base of authority for economic and military purposes, and certainly for gaining legitimacy and securing political hegemony. In the Sasanian era, the potentials of the region for state-level propaganda were not overlooked by the kings. They built monuments along western Central Zagros's ancient roads and passages. By this time, the area of the Achaemenid Bagastāna was called Wastān, the province of Māh-kust-ī-Wastān. Not far from the sacred mount of Bagastāna/ Wastān, Husraw II revived the royal art of rock relief, after over two hundred years, commissioning monumental projects next to the earlier Sasanian investiture scenes and in the larger ayvān of the modern Tāq-e Bostān, the favourite spot of the Sasanians for such a purpose outside their motherland, Pārs.

The sample areas studied here are case studies of intermediary zones. The cultural materials of Abdanan and Farsan Counties in the Sasanian period indicate their role between the different regions of Central Zagros and south-western Iran, and, in the case of the latter, the Central Iranian Plateau. Notwithstanding the particular topographic conditions of the Central Zagros, the close socioeconomic interactions prove that Abdanan and Farsan were not geographically isolated areas and impenetrable highlands sheltered between arduous mountains, as is sometimes assumed for mountainous areas. The strategic location of both of the sample areas, their inter-regional roads, and nomadic populations, along with the central Sasanian geographical and political administration, were all factors incorporating this phenomenon. In this regard, enclosed nomadism, as a historical mode of subsistence in the Central Zagros, perhaps played a main role in association with the domestic policies of the central and local state in this era. Therefore, to understand the economy and sociopolitical milieu of these areas, and probably of the whole late antique Central Zagros, it is crucial to consider the role of pastoral nomadism together with more sedentary economies and ways of life. Information about the rates of integration of the nomads inhabiting the mountainous plains and valleys of the Central Zagros into the socioeconomic structures of the Sasanian state is not abundant yet is still discernible. Although it was not an unprecedented arrangement in Iran, according to literary sources the forces of nomads, *kurd*, were part of the Sasanian armies. Some Middle Persian texts also attest to the regulation of the seasonal migration of nomads in Sasanian law. Despite the several distinctions between the overall spatial distribution of material culture and the organisation of settlements in Abdanan and Farsan Counties in the Sasanian period, these phenomena are also comparable, in the two sample areas, in some respects. A main common instance is the incorporation of different subsistence strategies based on pastoralism, either nomadic or transhumant, and agriculture, both dry and irrigation, which is reflected in the regional settlement systems and related archaeological materials in both of the counties. As revealed by the concept of enclosed/vertical nomadism, the long-held seasonal migration of pastoral nomads imposed by the environment of the intermontane areas has brought about socioeconomic interdependence between highlands and lowlands and groups with different modes of subsistence. These links were formed for purposes of adaptation to environmental conditions and better exploitation of natural resources in a wide area, and flexibility in the less predictable climate of the highlands. Particularly in the case of natural disasters, these relationships could ensure the survival of herds, and of the nomadic groups. The close ties developed by inter-regional interactions make up a characteristic cultural feature of the region that could lead to the formation of identities for social groups including segments with distinct ways of life and modes of subsistence attested by anthropological studies, as well as the Classical and Hellenistic sources. The remains of the architectural type of courtyard/compound homesteads of different sizes which have an association with pastoralism, either nomadic or transhumant, are ethnographically attested and are archaeologically reported at late antique sites both in the Zagros highlands, in Abdanan County and the northern Sirwān/Diyāla River valley, and in their adjacent lowlands, in the Dehloran plain and Hamrin Basin. These structures are concrete indications of the above-mentioned inter-regional movements and links. The pottery types of the mountainous valleys and plains of Farsan and Abdanan in the Central Zagros that are comparable to those wares traditionally made and used in south-western Iran constitute another set of evidence for such a phenomenon.

This might to some extent account for another common cultural aspect of these two areas: the apogee of the population rate in the Sasanian period. As already discussed, the close socioeconomic links between groups with different economic structures on a local or even an inter-regional scale could be beneficial to all of the parties. Such a system could be in balance with natural conditions and provide the necessities for the survival of the inhabitants in the micro-environments of the region, ultimately leading to demographic growth. The rise in the number of sites, the emergence of defensive structures, manor houses, and fire-temples in the Abdanan region, the overall larger size of settlements, the shifts in their spatial organisation, and the increased complexity of their systems in comparison with earlier times, along with the foundation of an inter-regional administrative centre in Farsan County, are among the factors that indicate economic developments in the agricultural and pastoral sectors of societies in either sample area, under the organisation of political authorities. Hence, in this process the role of the central Sasanian state must not be overlooked. Apart from the expansion of agriculturally based settlements and the strong presence of transhumant and nomadic pastoralism in contrast to preceding eras, the adoption of the traditions and formal procedures of the Sasanian state signifies the point. Chahār-ṭāq, associated with official Sasanian Zoroastrianism, generally represents a prominent plan for Sasanian religious architecture that is examined at all sorts of Sasanian sites of royal complexes and manor houses, and in the settings both related and unrelated to settlements across the Sasanian realm. Apart from the the three 'Great Fires of State', with Ādur Gušnasp of Media being securely located at Takht-e Soleiman, some of these structures perhaps hosted the Bahrām Fires, *Ātaxš-ī Warhrān*, sometimes even founded by the *šāhānšāh* himself as Šābuhr I's Ka'be-ye Zardošt inscription relates, or by high religious authorities such as *mōbedān mōbed* or the *hērbed* of the Sasanian court and royal sphere, as Kirdīr's Ka'be-ye Zardošt inscription reveals, all across the empire, in Ērān or An-Ērān. Several of these fire-temples are also reported from Abdanan. Moreover, the possibility of this occurring at the large settlement of Tappe[h] Bardnakōn in Farsan cannot be ruled out. Nonetheless, before clandestine excavations damage the structures of this site even more, further seasons of systematic excavations urgently need to be carried out with the aim of uncovering the architectural spaces completely. This is the only way to determine whether the building complex at this centre was a kind of chahār-ṭāq. Nevertheless, we are already reasonably well-informed concerning the role played by this site in the late Sasanian Empire. Especially in light of the administrative sigillographic archive of Tappe[h] Bardnakōn, at this administrative centre, the central Sasanian state managed and controlled socioeconomic matters not only in this area, the canton of Rāwar-kust-ī-rōdbār of the province of Gay in the region of Spahān, but also on an inter-regional scale between the different geographical zones of the Central Zagros, the Central Iranian Plateau, and south-western and southern Iran. These procedures were carried out according to the political and official legal and judicial regulations operating across the territories of the Sasanian Empire from the sixth century onwards. Compared to in earlier times, the more structured administrative and political system of the Sasanian state, at least in the later phase of its rule, enabled it to oversee such matters both at the core and in the more peripheral areas of the empire, which in turn made its taxation efficient across different territories according to their economic potentials. The same holds true also for the Central Zagros, a region of prominent interest to the Sasanians in different economic, military, political and cultural respects. Indeed, a vital part of this process was the high level of territorial control and state investment and planning for the organisation of settlements and infrastructural development according to various conditions such as topography, natural resources, and the geographical features and location in different territories of the Sasanian realm.

The grounded interdisciplinary regional analysis of the archaeological, historical, sigillographic and ethnographic data in Abdanan and Farsan demonstrates the overall distinct material culture and settlement systems and patterns of these areas, in light of their different environmental settings, geographical features and location, and administrative status in the territorial organisation of the Sasanian state. This point denotes the varied character of the socioeconomic transition in the Sasanian realm, not only in different territories but also inside the single geographical zone of the Central Zagros, mostly considered as a single platform for the formation and development of local homogeneous cultural processes. However, the regional variations in the geographical zone of the Central Zagros, which is constituted by different micro-environments, may not be ignored in the wake of highlighting the similar cultural formation processes and economic bases. The parallel sets of data studied in other parts of the late antique Middle East signify the varied dynamics behind the changes occurring in this period. Processes of nucleation of dispersed settlements into larger population centres are examined in different geographical zones such as the Farsan region, east of the River Jaghjagh in eastern Syria, northern Khuzestan, and, probably, the Rāmhormoz plain, a phenomenon utterly different from the rise in rural settlements in the Abdanan region, Mughan Steppe in East Azerbaijan Province and Mil Steppe in the Republic of Azerbaijan, or the otherwise militarised landscape of the Gorgan plain. Therefore, in a region such as Farsan, where a degree of continuity in the settlement patterns and number of sites from the Parthian era is recognised, the late antique transformation is reflected in the growth of the settlement hierarchy and the more complex settlement system, the increased rate of change of site location, and the main factors in that process, along with the size of settlements. Another instance for the diverse disposition of socioeconomic developments is represented by the different organisation of hydraulic landscapes in the Gorgan plain and the lowlands of southern Mesopotamia and south-western Iran. Moreover, one may recall the distinct linear barriers of Khandaq-e Shapur in southern Mesopotamia and the northern frontiers of the Gorgan Wall in north-eastern Iran and the Ghilghilchay and Derbent Walls in the Caucasus. The dynamics behind these re-organisations and transformations include, but probably are not limited to, urban development; agricultural yield raise and pastoralist product increase; natural resource management, particularly in the forms of structures such as irrigation systems, canals, aqueducts, dams and watermills; defensive landscape reinforcement, according to the types of threat and geographical conditions of (principally) borderlands but also the inner territories of the Sasanian realm on the strategic inter-regional roads and passageways; and climate-fluctuations adaptation associated with Late Antique Little Ice Age conditions (see Chapter 1, s. 1.1.1). The scale, nature and dynamics of settlement system shifts, infrastructural developments and demographic shifts in various territories differed. The minor importance of Eastern Arabia for international trade in the Sasanian period was probably the reason for the absence of the major investment projects that are otherwise documented for some other areas, such as southern Mesopotamia, by archaeological works and historical accounts. Therefore, archaeological studies of Eastern Arabia in this era indicate the decline in population and economic activity. Another comparable pattern is to be discerned in the Sasanian–Roman frontier zone in north Syria. Here, in comparison with the northern Sasanian borderlands, there are no traces of rural settlement rise, as is the case in the Mughan steppe, or landscape militarisation, as in the Gorgan plain, but instead important urban trade hubs between the two empires such as Nisibis were fortified. Each of these cases, therefore, needs to be analysed in its context. That said, in a broader context, they were indications of a shifting historical phenomenon which, rather than representing a gradual evolution of long-held niche construction on a local level, was a systematic transformation with complex processes behind it and, at its core, was associated with the planning framework and landscape investment of an imperial power.

Appendix 1 List of Archaeological Sites Examined in Chapter 3

Name	Size	Type	Type of archaeological data
AS.001	220×160m	Sedentary site	Dispersed architectural remains with rubble stone, and ceramics.
AS.002	75×60m	Nomadic site	Scattered sherds and rubble stones.
AS.003	60×50m	Sedentary site	Scattered sherds.
AS.004	130×80m	Sedentary site	As AS.003.
AS.005	85×50m	Sedentary site	As AS.001.
AS.006	120×80m	Nomadic site	As AS.001.
AS.007	75×70m	Sedentary site	As AS.003.
AS.008	85×60m	Sedentary site	As AS.003.
AS.009	30ha	Nomadic site	Scattered sherds and rubble stones with plaster mortar.
AS.010	50×35m	Nomadic site	As AS.003.
AS.011	100×150m	Fort	Ceramics, architectural remains with rock rubble, cobblestones and plaster mortar.
AS.012	100×150m	Fort	As AS.011.
AS.013	30×18m	Nomadic site	As AS.003.
AS.014	15×2m	Nomadic site	Scattered sherds and foundations of architectural structures.
AS.015	70×30m	Sedentary site	As AS.003.
AS.016	120×80m	Nomadic site	As AS.003.
AS.017	300×100m	Nomadic site	As AS.003.
AS.018	8×8m	Fire-temple	As AS.001.

Name	Size	Type	Type of archaeological data
AS.019	50×55m	Castle	As AS.011.
AS.020	1.5ha	Graveyard	Storage jar sherds, cobblestones and a piece of human bone.
AS.021	130×65m	Castle	As AS.011.
AS.022	4.5ha	Sedentary site	As AS.011.
AS.023	500×700m	Sedentary site	As AS.003.
AS.024	17.20×17m	Fort	As AS.011.
AS.025	11×11m	Fort	As AS.011.
AS.026	8×7m	Fire-temple	Architectural remains with cobblestones and z plaster mortar.
AS.027	7ha	Large settlement	As AS.011.
AS.028	50×60m	Nomadic site	As AS.003.
AS.029	50×30m	Nomadic site	As AS.003.
AS.030	400×100m	Nomadic site	Scattered sherds and cobblestones with plaster mortar.
AS.031	40×30m	Nomadic site	As AS.003.
AS.032	200×70m	Nomadic site	As AS.030
AS.033	300×100m	Nomadic site	As AS.003.
AS.034	6.5ha	Large settlement	Ceramics, glasses, architectural structures, and foundations with cobblestones and plaster mortar.
AS.035	11×11m	Fire-temple	As AS.034.
AS.036	70×60m	Castle	As AS.034.
AS.037	80×70m	Nomadic site	Pottery sherds and a blade.
AS.038	60×60m	Fort?	As AS.034
AS.039	31.1×20.6m	Manor house	As AS.038.
AS.040	3ha	Large settlement	As AS.003.
AS.041	5ha	Large settlement	As AS.030
AS.042	15.5×15m	Castle	As AS.038.

Name	Size	Type	Type of archaeological data
AS.043	10ha	Large settlement	As AS.038.
AS.044	60×50m	Nomadic site	As AS.003.
AS.045	200×150m	Nomadic site	As AS.003.
AS.046	70×40cm	*Bard-e gōri* rock-cut niche	Rock-cut funerary structure.
AS.047	?	Fort	As AS.041.
AS.048	30×26.5m (the area at the top of the mound covered with scattered architectural remains)	Fire-temple	As AS.032.
AS.049	67×38m	Fire-temple?	As AS.032.
AS.050	8ha	Large settlement	Dispersed ceramics, blades, flakes, bricks, and cobblestones with plaster mortar.
AS.051	3ha	Sedentary site	Dispersed ceramics, architectural remains with cobblestones and plaster mortar, and a lithic core.
AS.052	50×50m	Sedentary site	Ceramics and lithics.
AS.053	20×20m	Nomadic site	Scattered sherds and flint blades.
AS.054	30×17m	Sedentary site	As AS.041.
AS.055	150×200m	Sedentary site	Dispersed ceramics, cobblestones, blades, flakes and cartridge-shaped cores.
AS.056	49×44m	Sedentary site	As AS.030.
AS.057	149×113m	Sedentary site	As AS.055.
AS.058	40×43m	Sedentary site	Dispersed ceramics and cobblestones.
AS.059	5×5.60m	Rock-shelter	Dispersed ceramics, blades, flakes and cores.

Name	Size	Type	Type of archaeological data
AS.060	300×200m	Sedentary site	Ceramics, glasses, iron clinkers, architectural structures, and foundations with cobblestones and plaster mortar.
AS.061	60×20m	Nomadic site	Scattered sherds and foundations of architectural structures with cobblestone.
AS.062	20×15m	Nomadic site	As AS.061.
AS.063	11×13m	Cave	As AS.003.
AS.064	30×25m	Nomadic site	As AS.061.
AS.065	35×30m	Nomadic site	As AS.060.
AS.066	10×20m	Nomadic site	As AS.061.
AS.067	47×40m	Nomadic site	As AS.061.
AS.068	14×16m	Cave	As AS.061.
AS.069	27×25m	Nomadic site	As AS.061.
AS.070	55×40m	Nomadic site	Scattered sherds and foundations of architectural structures with cobblestone and mortar plaster.
AS.071	40×15m	Nomadic site	Scattered sherds, a blade, an iron ring, and foundations of architectural structures with cobblestone.
AS.072	40×20m	Nomadic site	As AS.061.
AS.073	23×23m	Nomadic site	As AS.061.
AS.074	23×23m	Nomadic site	As AS.061.
AS.075	85×30m	Nomadic site	As AS.061.
AS.076	30×26m	Nomadic site	As AS.061.
AS.077	20×17m	Nomadic site	As AS.061.
AS.078	24×18m	Nomadic site	As AS.061.
AS.079	60×30m	Nomadic site	As AS.061.
AS.080	33×32m	Nomadic site	As AS.061.
AS.081	40×25m	Nomadic site	As AS.061.

Name	Size	Type	Type of archaeological data
AS.082	25×18m	Nomadic site	As AS.061.
AS.083	1,500×800m	Nomadic site	Scattered sherds, glasses and iron clinkers.
AS.084	300×300m	Nomadic site	As AS.003.
AS.085	40×20m	Nomadic site	Scattered sherds, blades and flint cores, and foundations of architectural structures with cobblestone.
AS.086	18×20m	Nomadic site	As AS.034.
AS.087	50×20m	Nomadic site	As AS.061.
AS.088	25×25m	Nomadic site	As AS.061.
AS.089	50×30m	Nomadic site	As AS.061.
AS.090	25×15m	Nomadic site	As AS.061.
AS.091	120×115m	Nomadic site	As AS.085.
AS.092	450×250m	Nomadic site	As AS.061.
AS.093	25×25m	Nomadic site	As AS.061.
AS.094	30×23m	Nomadic site	Scattered sherds, hand-mills, and foundations of architectural structures with cobblestone.
AS.095	42×31m	Nomadic site	As AS.061.
AS.096	46×27m	Nomadic site	As AS.061.
AS.097	25×22m	Nomadic site	As AS.061.
AS.098	40×35m	Nomadic site	As AS.061.
AS.099	115×100m	Nomadic site	Scattered sherds and a glass.
AS.100	210×100m	Manor house	As AS.034.
AS.101	450×450m	Large settlement	As AS.034.
AS.102	80×40m	Large settlement	Scattered sherds, a brick, blades and flint cores, and architectural structures with cobblestone and mortar plaster.

Name	Size	Type	Type of archaeological data
AS.103	90×40m	Large settlement	As AS.102.
AS.104	55×22.5m	Caravanserai	As AS.034.
AS.105	6ha	Large settlement	As AS.034.
AS.106	60×75m	Castle	As AS.060.

Appendix 2 List of Archaeological Sites Examined in Chapter 4

Name	Size	Type	Type of archaeological data
FS.015	10×10m	*Chol* burial	Disturbed structure with rubble stones of different sizes.
FS.016	10×10m	*Chol* burial	As FS.015.
FS.017	5×5m	*Chol* burial	As FS.015.
FS.018	5×5m	*Chol* burial	Scattered sherds and disturbed structures with rubble stones of different sizes.
FS.019	10×6m	*Chol* burial	As FS.018.
FS.025	?	Stone-paved road	Structures of pebbles and cobblestones.
FS.037	100×80m	Settlement	Scattered sherds, partial bones and a stone mortar.
FS.042	150×80	Temporary site?	Scattered sherds, two blades and a bronze tallow burner.
FS.043	5×5m	*Chol* burial	As FS.018.
FS.044	4×4m	*Chol* burial	As FS.018.
FS.045	10×10m	*Chol* burial	As FS.018.
FS.046	5×5m	*Chol* burial	As FS.015.
FS.047	20×20m	*Chol* burial	As FS.015.
FS.048	12×12m	*Chol* burial	As FS.015.
FS.049	10×10m	*Chol* burial	As FS.015.
FS.050	5×5m	*Chol* burial	As FS.015.
FS.051	9×9m	*Chol* burial	As FS.015.
FS.052	15×15m	*Chol* burial	As FS.015.

Name	Size	Type	Type of archaeological data
FS.053	10×10m	*Chol* burial	As FS.015.
FS.054	8×8m	*Chol* burial	As FS.015.
FS.055	?	*Chol* burial	As FS.015.
FS.056	15×15m	*Chol* burial	As FS.015.
FS.082	?	*Chol* cemetery	Bricks, one pottery sherd and disturbed structures of over fifty graves with rubble stones of different sizes.
FS.087	100×80m	Temporary site?	Pottery sherds.
FS.101	100×100m	Settlement	As FS.087.
FS.104	100×150m	Settlement	Pottery sherds and four blades.
FS.109	100×70m	Settlement	Pottery sherds and a blade.
FS.110	80×70m	Temporary site?	Pottery sherds.
FS.117	100×100m	Settlement	Pottery sherds, glassware and a pestle.
FS.119	100×150m	Settlement	Plastered bricks, pottery sherds, bullae, gemstones, blades, glassware, a coin, and stone and metal tools.
FS.120	70×70m	Settlement	As FS.087.
FS.121	120×80m	Settlement	As FS.087.
FS.124	150×150m	Settlement?	As FS.087.
FS.134	70×70m	Settlement?	As FS.087.
FS.138	150×100m	Temporary site?	Pottery sherds and a pestle.
FS.140	8×8m	Three *chol* burials	As FS.015.
FS.141	5×5m	*Chol* burial	As FS.015.
FS.142	8×8m	*Chol* burial	As FS.015.
FS.143	9×9m	*Chol* burial	As FS.015.
FS.144	7×7m	*Chol* burial	As FS.015.
FS.158	60×50m	Temporary site?	Pottery sherds and a piece of glass.

Name	Size	Type	Type of archaeological data
FS.159	100×70m	Temporary site?	Pottery sherds and blades.
FS.160	100×70m	Temporary site?	Pottery sherds, blades and two pieces of glassware.
FS.163	200×200m	Settlement?	Pottery sherds, blades, pestle, mortar, pieces of glassware and a millstone.
FS.170	80×150m	Temporary site?	As FS.015.
FS.181	20×20m	Temporary site?	As FS.158.
FS.184	13×13m	*Chol* burial	Disturbed structure with rubble stones of different sizes, and one pottery sherd.
FS.185	12×12m	*Chol* burial	As FS.015.
FS.186	7×7m	*Chol* burial	As FS.015.
FS.187	13×13m	*Chol* burial	As FS.015.
FS.190	100×100m	Temporary site?	As FS.158.
FS.191	100×80m	Temporary site?	As FS.110.
FS.194	80×80m	Temporary site?	As FS.110.
FS.195	100×100m	Temporary site?	As FS.110.
FS.199	160×90×70cm	*Bard-e gōri* rock-cut niche	Rock-cut funerary structure.
FS.200	100×50m	Settlement	Pottery sherds and blades.
FS.205	100×100m	Settlement	As FS.110.
FS.207	100×150m	Temporary site?	As FS.110.
FS.208	150×120m	Settlement	Pottery sherds and a partial quern.
FS.209	70×60m	Settlement	As FS.110.

Appendix 3 Catalogues of the Pottery Specimens Examined in Chapter 5

Table 5.1 Description of Figure 5.1

No.	Site Identifier	Description (1. Manufacture 2. Firing 3. Fabric Colour (Core Ext. Int.) 4. Inclusion 5. Finish 6. Decoration 7. Exterior Coating. Colour. Treatment 8. Interior Coating. Colour. Treatment)	Reference	Notes
1	AS.003: 2	1. Wheel 2. High-fired 3. Orange 4. Stone and sandy grit with occasional fine limestone particles 5. Coarse	Boucharlat and Labrousse 1979: Fig. 27: 2; Alden 1978: Fig. 5: 2; Whitcomb 1985: Fig. 51: z; Adams 1970: Fig. 6: cc; Whitcomb 1987: Fig. D: g	Early Sasanian. With a slight profile difference.
2	AS.042: 4	1. Wheel 2. Well-fired 3. Orange buff, greenish buff, orange buff 4. Stone and sandy grit, occasional fine limestone particles 5. Medium	AS.018, 24; AS.036, 2. Alden 1978: Fig. 5: 2; Azarnoush 1994: Figs 174: m, 190: b; Phillips 2008: Fig. 13: 1; Adams 1970: Fig. 5: p; Wenke 1975: Fig. 13: 705; Trinkaus 1986: Fig. 20: 1	Hajiabad examples have larger rim diameters.

3	AS.018: 31	1. Wheel 2. High-fired 3. Grey, orange buff, buff 4. Stone and sandy grit 5. Medium	Whitcomb 1987: Fig. D: cc; Azarnoush 1994: Fig. 174: l; Mohammadifar and Tahmāsebi 1393 [2016]): Fig. 12: S.S.24; Kennet 2004: Fig. 35: type 58	With a slight form difference from the SMAG type.
4	AS.018: 12	1. Wheel 2. Well-fired 3. Red 4. Stone and sandy grit with lime particles and chaff 5. Coarse 6. A horizontal rib on the neck, two horizontal straight and wavy grooves on the shoulder	Khosrowzadeh et al. 2020a: Fig. 6: I; Stronach 1978b: Fig. 123: 6; Keall and Keall 1981: Fig. 15: 21; Khosrowzadeh et al. 1399 [2020]: Fig. 10: 3; Venco Ricciardi 1970: Fig. 90: No. 25; Alden 1978: Fig. 6: 1–2; Langdon and Harden 1934: Fig. 1: 23; Adams 1970: Fig. 6: be; Wenke 1975: Fig. 12: 602; Trinkaus 1986: Fig. 20: 10	Sherds of Pasargadae and Damghan lack handle.
5	AS.018: 17	1. Wheel 2. Well-fired 3. Buff, orange 4. Stone and sandy grit with fine lime particles 5. Medium 6. A horizontal rib on the neck, parallel horizontal grooves on the shoulder	Stronach 1978b: Fig. 123: 5; Azarnoush 1994: Figs 184: b, 190: d; Langdon and Harden 1934: Fig. 3: 12; Adams 1970: Fig. 5: s; Whitcomb 1985: Fig. 44: a; Wenke 1975: Figs 10: 401, 13: 716; Mohammadifar and Tahmāsebi 1393 [2016]): Fig. 5: S.S.57.	With a slight rim diameter difference.
6	AS.058: 1	1. Wheel 2. Well-fired 3. Red 4. Stone and sandy grit 5. Medium	Azarnoush 1994: Fig. 184: b; Venco Ricciardi 1970: Fig. 94: No. 74; Trinkaus 1986: Fig. 19: 7	Tell Mahuz sample has a smaller rim diameter.

Table 5.1 (continued)

No.	Site Identifier	Description (1. Manufacture 2. Firing 3. Fabric Colour (Core Ext. Int.) 4. Inclusion 5. Finish 6. Decoration 7. Exterior Coating. Colour. Treatment 8. Interior Coating. Colour. Treatment)	Reference	Notes
7	AS.027: 8	1. Wheel 2. Well-fired 3. Orange 4. Stone and sandy grit with fine and large lime particles 5. Medium	Azarnoush 1994: Fig. 164: a; Langdon and Harden 1934: Fig. 3: 8; Whitcomb 1985: Fig. 46: j; Phillips 2008: Fig. 13: 6; Trinkaus 1986: Fig. 20: 1; Kennet 2004: Fig. 37: type 58.	The form and technical attributes of the SMAG type are slightly different.
8	AS.042: 11	1. Wheel 2. High-fired 3. Greenish buff 4. Sand with chaff 5. Medium	Whitcomb 1985: Fig. 44: d	The compared specimen has a smaller rim diameter.
9	AS.007: 3	1. Wheel 2. High-fired 3. Orange 4. Fine grit 5. Medium 7. Slip, light brown	AS.001: 3; Whitcomb, 1985, Fig. 44: c; Wenke, 1975, Fig. 13: 707; Whitcomb, 1987, Fig. D: x	The example from Qasr-i Abu Nasr is burnished and the sample from Bushehr is glazed.
10	AS.006: 1	1. Wheel 2. High-fired 3. Orange 4. Stone and sandy grit with fine limestone particles 5. Medium 7. Slip, buff 8. Slip, buff	Alden 1978: Fig. 6: 12; Azarnoush 1994: Fig. 190: I; Whitcomb 1985: Fig. 19: d	With a slight profile difference.

11	AS.027: 6	1. Wheel 2. Well-fired 3. Orange 4. Stone and sandy grit with fine limestone particles and chaff 5. Coarse 7. Slip, buff	Lamberg-Karlovsky 1970: Fig. 3: D; Whitcomb 1985: Fig. 19: d	With different decoration.
12	AS.018: 15	1. Wheel 2. Well-fired 3. Orange 4. Stone and sandy grit with fine limestone particles and chaff 5. Coarse 6. A row of stamped concentric circles on the shoulder 7. Slip, buff.	Lamberg-Karlovsky 1970: Fig. 3: N; Azarnoush 1994: Fig. 164: a; Phillips 2008: Fig. 12: 3; Adams 1970: Fig. 5: p; Simpson 1996: Fig. 3: 7; Kennet 2004: Fig. 35: type 81	The example from Kalba is burnished and the parallel from Tepe Yahya is plain.
13	AS.056: 3	1. Wheel 2. Well-fired 3. Buff, green 4. Sand 5. Medium 7. Glaze, green 8. Glaze, green.	Stronach 1978b: Fig. 123: 7; Azarnoush, 1994, Fig. 164: c; Boucharlat and Labrousse 1979: Fig. 27: 8; Whitcomb 1985: Fig. 19: d	The parallels lack glaze.
14	AS.027: 12	1. Wheel 2. Well-fired 3. Orange 4. Stone and sandy grit with fine lime particles 5. Medium 7. Slip, buff.	Lamberg-Karlovsky 1970: Fig. 6: G; Khosrowzadeh et al. 2020a: Fig. 6: h; Azarnoush 1994: Fig. 163: a, 174: b; Alden 1978: Fig. 6: 10; Whitcomb 1985: Fig. 16: c, 47: d; Wenke 1975: Fig. 10: 408; Simpson 1996: Fig. 3: 3; Whitcomb 1987: Fig. G: o; Mohammadifar and Tahmasebi 1393 [2014]: Fig. 12: S.S.21; Kennet 2004: Fig. 37: type 76.	With a slight profile distinction. Different technical attributes from the SMAG type.

Table 5.1 (continued)

No.	Site Identifier	Description (1. Manufacture 2. Firing 3. Fabric Colour (Core Ext. Int.) 4. Inclusion 5. Finish 6. Decoration 7. Exterior Coating. Colour. Treatment 8. Interior Coating. Colour. Treatment)	Reference	Notes
15	AS.027: 30	1. Wheel 2. Well-fired 3. Orange 4. Stone and sandy grit with fine lime particles 5. Medium	Azarnoush 1994: Fig. 164: a, 174: l; Alden 1978: Fig. 6: 12; Whitcomb 1985: Fig. 47: d; Wenke 1975: Fig. 10: 408; Simpson 1996: Fig. 3: 3; Whitcomb, 1987, Fig. G: o; Kennet 2004: Fig. 37: type 76.	As AS. 027: 12.
16	AS.060: 3	1. Wheel 2. Well-fired 3. Orange 4. Stone and sandy grit with fine lime particles 5. Coarse	AS.058, 3; Venco Ricciardi 1970: Fig. 94: No. 69; Langdon and Harden 1934: Fig. 3: 8; Whitcomb 1985: Fig. 46: l, 48: q; Kleiss 1985: Abb. 5: 18; Kennet 2004: Fig. 37: type 58.	Handled parallels from Qasr-i Abu Nasr. Different technical attributes from the SMAG type.
17	AS.054: 9	1. Wheel 2. Well-fired 3. Orange 4. Stone and sandy grit 5. Coarse 8. Slip, buff.	Boucharlat and Labrousse 1979: Fig. 27: 10; Whitcomb 1987: Fig. H: cc	Smaller rim diameter of Shāōr Palace specimen.
18	AS.042: 14	1. Wheel 2. High-fired 3. Greenish buff 4. Sand with fine lime particles and chaff 5. Coarse.	Whitcomb 1985: Fig. 47: e	Larger diameter from the parallel.

19	AS.055: 5	1. Hand 2. High-fired 3. Red 4. Stone grit and chaff 5. Coarse 8. Slip, buff.	Phillips 2008: Fig. 12: 5; Whitcomb 1985: Fig. 43: f; Wenke 1975: Fig. 13: 707; Kleiss 1987: Abb. 5: 6	Different decoration.
20	AS.058: 2	1. Wheel 2. Low-fired 3. Grey 4. Stone and sandy grit and limestone particles 5. Coarse.	AS.060, 3; Azarnoush 1994: Fig. 189: l; Kennet 2004: Fig. 37: type 58.	With a slightly different form from the second parallel.
21	AS.027: 28	1. Wheel 2. Low-fired 3. Grey, light grey, buff 4. Stone and sandy grit and fine limestone particles 5. Medium.	Venco Ricciardi 1970: Fig. 94: No. 73; Langdon and Harden 1934: Fig. 3: 8; Whitcomb 1985: Fig. 47: e	
22	AS.018: 3	1. Wheel 2. Well-fired 3. Reddish buff, buff, reddish buff 4. Sand with chaff and fine limestone particles 5. Medium.	Lamberg-Karlovsky 1970: Fig. 5: C; Alden 1978: Fig. 6: 10; Azarnoush 1994: Fig. 174: l; Whitcomb 1985: Fig. 16: c; Lecomte 1987: Pl. 61: 12; Simpson 1996: Fig. 3: 3; Puschnigg 2006a: 7.10; Mohammadifar and Tahmāsebi 1393 [2016]): Fig. 12: S.S.24; Khosrowzadeh et al. 1399 [2020]: Fig. 8: 3; Kennet 2004: Fig. 35: type 58;	With a slightly different form from the last two parallels, and a taller neck than the Merv example.
23	AS.032: 4	1. Wheel 2. Well-fired 3. Buff 4. Stone and sandy grit 5. Medium, 7. Glaze, blue 8. Glaze, blue.	Azarnoush 1994: Fig. 174: l; Khosrowzadeh et al. 1399 [2020]: Fig. 6: 2; Wenke 1975: Fig. 10: 408	The parallels lack glaze.
24	AS.032: 3	1. Wheel 2. Well-fired 3. Orange 4. Stone and sandy grit with lime particles 5. Medium.	Khosrowzadeh et al. 1399 [2020]: Fig. 1: 5; Kennet 2004: Fig. 37: type 58.	The first parallel is glazed.

Table 5.1 (continued)

No.	Site Identifier	Description (1. Manufacture 2. Firing 3. Fabric Colour (Core Ext. Int.) 4. Inclusion 5. Finish 6. Decoration 7. Exterior Coating. Colour. Treatment 8. Interior Coating. Colour. Treatment)	Reference	Notes
25	AS.017: 5	1. Wheel 2. High-fired 3. Red 4. Sand with lime particles and chaff 5. Medium 7. Slip, buff.	Lamberg-Karlovsky 1970: Fig. 3: B and C; Alden 1978: Fig. 6: 17; Azarnoush 1994: Fig. 174: b; Whitcomb 1985: Fig. 16: f, 43: I; Phillips 2008: Fig. 9: 1; Boucharlat and Labrousse 1979: Fig. 27: 10; Lecomte 1987: Pl. 61: 12; Kleiss 1999: Abb. 5: second from bottom right; Whitcomb 1987: Fig. E: c; Khosrowzadeh et al. 1399 [2020]: Fig. 8: 3; Kennet 2004: Fig. 35: type 58.	With a slightly different form and profile.
26	AS.020: 9	1. Wheel 2. High-fired 3. Orange 4. Sand with lime particles 5. Medium 8. Slip, buff.	Eqbal 1976: Fig. 45: e; Whitcomb 1985: Fig. 44: d; Keall and Keall 1981: Fig. 13: 32	
27	AS.027: 49	1. Wheel 2. Low-fired 3. Buff grey, buff, buff grey 4. Stone and sandy grit with lime particles 5. Medium 8. Slip, buff.	AS.027: 30; Azarnoush 1994: Fig. 174: l; Whitcomb 1985: Fig. 16: a; Wenke 1975: Fig. 10: 408; Khosrowzadeh et al. 2020a: Fig. 6: j; Kennet 2004: Fig. 37: type 76.	With a slightly different form from the SMAG type.

28	AS.048: 2	1. Wheel 2. Low-fired 3. Orange, grey, orange 4. Stone and sandy grit with lime particles 5. Medium.	Lecomte 1987: Pl. 41: 10, 55: 15; Whitcomb 1987: Fig. G: f; Alden 1978: Fig. 5: 2; Venco Ricciardi 1970: Fig. 94: No. 69.	
29	AS.018: 20	1. Wheel 2. High-fired 3. Red, orange, orange 4. Sand with lime particles 5. Medium.	AS.018: 3; Venco Ricciardi 1970: Fig. 94: No. 69; Langdon and Harden 1934: Fig. 3: 12; Whitcomb 1985: Fig. 47: e, 19: d; Simpson 1996: Fig. 3: 3; Kennet 2004: Fig. 37: type 58.	A slightly different form and technical attributes from the SMAG type.
30	AS.051: 8	1. Wheel 2. High-fired 3. Orange 4. Sand with lime particles 5. Coarse.	AS.027, 8; Alden 1978: Fig. 5: 2; Azarnoush 1994: Fig. 174: k; Whitcomb 1985: Fig. 19: c; Langdon and Harden 1934: Fig. 3: 8; Kleiss 1985: Abb. 3: second from top; Trinkaus 1986: Fig. 20: 1; Kennet 2004: Fig. 37: type 58.	As AS. 018: 20.
31	AS.001: 1	1. Wheel 2. Well-fired 3. Beige 4. Stone and sandy grit with lime particles 5. Medium 6. Parallel horizontal grooves below the rim.		
32	AS.009: 3	1. Wheel 2. Low-fired 3. Grey, orange, grey 4. Stone and sandy grit with lime particles and chaff 5. Medium.	Mohammadifar and Tahmāsebi 1393 [2016]): Fig. 9: S.S.79.	

Table 5.1 (continued)

No.	Site Identifier	Description (1. Manufacture 2. Firing 3. Fabric Colour (Core Ext. Int.) 4. Inclusion 5. Finish 6. Decoration 7. Exterior Coating. Colour. Treatment 8. Interior Coating. Colour. Treatment)	Reference	Notes
33	AS.027: 43	1. Wheel 2. High-fired 3. Orange 4. Stone and sandy grit with lime particles 5. Medium.	AS.064: 1; Mohammadifar and Tahmāsebi 1393 [2016]): Fig. 9: S.S.34; Khosrowzadeh et al. 1399 [2020]: Fig. 1: 3.	The last parallel is glazed.
34	AS.064: 1	1. Wheel 2. High-fired 3. Orange, orange buff, orange buff 4. Stone and sandy grit with lime particles 5. Medium. 7. Slip, buff.	AS.027: 43; Khosrowzadeh et al. 1399 [2020]: Fig. 1: 4; Mohammadifar and Tahmāsebi 1393 [2016]): Fig. 9: S.S.34	AS. 027: 43.

Table 5.2 Description of Figure 5.2

No.	Site Identifier	Description (1. Manufacture 2. Firing 3. Fabric Colour (Core Ext. Int.) 4. Inclusion 5. Finish 6. Decoration 7. Exterior Coating. Colour. Treatment 8. Interior Coating. Colour. Treatment)	Reference	Notes
1	AS.001: 3	1. Wheel 2. Well-fired 3. Orange 4. Grit with limestone particles 5. Medium. 7. Slip, buff 8. Slip, buff.	AS.007: 3; Keall and Keall 1981: Fig. 16: 36; Alden 1978: Fig. 6: 12; Whitcomb 1985: Fig. 42: I; Wenke 1975: Fig. 10: 405; Whitcomb 1987: Fig. D: x	Different decoration.
2	AS.018: 2	1. Wheel 2. Well-fired 3. Reddish buff 4. Sand with limestone particles and chaff 5. Coarse.	AS.018: 14; Azarnoush 1994: Fig. 184: d, 186: c; Whitcomb 1985: Fig. 42: g; Kleiss 1987: Abb. 12: 8, 14; Trinkaus 1986: Fig. 14: 13	With a slight profile difference.
3	AS.018: 23	1. Wheel 2. Low-fired 3. Grey, red, brown 4. Sand with limestone particles 5. Coarse.	Azarnoush 1994: Fig. 184: d; Whitcomb 1985: Fig. 44: g; Wenke 1975: Fig. 8: 304, 13: 716; Kleiss 1987: Abb. 12: 8	With a slight profile difference.
4	AS.024: 3	1. Wheel 2. Low-fired 3. Grey, red, brown 4. Sand with limestone particles 5. Coarse.	Whitcomb 1985: Fig. 42: g; Keall and Keall 1981: Fig. 13: 7	The parallels are decorated.

Table 5.2 (continued)

No.	Site Identifier	Description (1. Manufacture 2. Firing 3. Fabric Colour (Core Ext. Int.) 4. Inclusion 5. Finish 6. Decoration 7. Exterior Coating. Colour. Treatment 8. Interior Coating, Colour. Treatment)	Reference	Notes
5	AS.061: 3	1. Wheel 2. Well-fired 3. Orange 4. Stone and sandy grit 5. Coarse 6. Horizontal groove on the neck–shoulder transition	Azarnoush 1994: Fig. 190: b; Phillips 2008: Fig. 12: 3; Whitcomb 1987: Fig. H: aa	With a larger rim diameter.
6	AS.018: 5	1. Wheel 2. High-fired 3. Brownish red 4. Stone and sandy grit with chaff and limestone particles 5. Medium.	Lamberg-Karlovsky 1970: Fig. 6: M; Stronach 1978b: Fig. 124: 9; Whitcomb 1985: Fig. 16: d; Adams 1970: Fig. 5: s; Keall and Keall 1981: Fig. 14: 18; Trinkaus 1986: Fig. 19: 6	The first three examples are handled.
7	AS.055: 2	1. Wheel 2. Low-fired 3. Reddish buff, grey buff 4. Grit 5. Medium.	Whitcomb 1985: Fig. 16: d; Adams 1970: Fig. 5: s; Keall and Keall 1981: Fig. 19: 14	The first parallel has handle and horizontal grooves.
8	AS.054: 1	1. Wheel 2. Low-fired 3. Orange, grey 4. Stone and sandy grit with limestone particles 5. Medium.	Lamberg-Karlovsky 1970: Fig. 5: K; Wenke 1975: Fig. 10: 405, 13: 707; Whitcomb 1985: Fig. 42: b, 43: d.	The last parallel, with a slight profile difference, is decorated.

9	AS.036: 7	1. Wheel 2. Well-fired 3. Dark grey 4. Stone and sandy grit with lime particles 5. Coarse 7. Buff slip 8. Buff slip	AS.036: 2; Langdon and Harden 1934: Fig. 3: 8; Kleiss 1985: Abb. 3: second from bottom; Whitcomb 1987: Fig. D: d; Trinkaus, 1986, Fig. 18: 6	
10	AS.017: 1	1. Wheel 2. Well-fired 3. Red 4. Stone and sandy grit with lime particles and chaff 5. Coarse 7. Buff slip 8. Buff slip	Azarnoush 1994: Fig. 174: m; Whitcomb 1985: Fig. 47: q; Simpson 1996: Fig. 3: 7; Kleiss 1985: Abb. 3: second from top; Whitcomb 1987: Fig. H: aa.	Smaller rim diameters of Hajiabad and Ahram area specimens.
11	AS.060: 2	1. Wheel 2. Well-fired 3. Orange 4. Stone and sandy grit with lime particles and chaff 5. Coarse 7. Buff slip 8. Buff slip	Whitcomb 1987: Fig. I: p; Azarnoush 1994: Fig. 184: a.	Susa example, with a slight profile difference, has a smaller rim diameter.
12	AS.027: 24	1. Wheel 2. Well-fired 3. Green 4. Stone and sandy grit with chaff 5. Medium.	Lamberg-Karlovsky 1970: Fig. 3: O and 5: G; Azarnoush 1994: Fig. 174: m, 184: c; Kleiss 1985: Abb. 3: fourth from top; Adams 1970: Fig. 5: p; Simpson 1996: Fig. 3: 6; Trinkaus 1986: Fig. 13: 1; Kennet 2004: Fig. 37: class LISV	The first parallel is plain.
13	AS.048: 5	1. Wheel 2. Well-fired 3. Green 4. Stone and sandy grit 5. Medium 7. Green glaze 8. Green glaze.	Labrousse 1979: Fig. 30: 4, 28: 2; Azarnoush 1994: Fig. 174: h; Adams 1970: Fig. 6: ay	The rims of the parallels lack groove.

Table 5.2 (continued)

No.	Site Identifier	Description (1. Manufacture 2. Firing 3. Fabric Colour (Core Ext. Int.) 4. Inclusion 5. Finish 6. Decoration 7. Exterior Coating. Colour. Treatment 8. Interior Coating. Colour. Treatment)	Reference	Notes
14	AS.054: 4	1. Wheel 2. Low-fired 3. Orange buff, grey. 4. Stone and sandy grit with limestone particles 5. Medium 6. Horizontal grooves on the exterior of the rim and neck.	Azarnoush 1994: Fig. 188: f; Simpson 1996: Fig. 3: 7; Kleiss 1999: Abb. 5: first from top; Keall and Keall 1981: Fig. 12: 2	The parallels lack the externally grooved rim.
15	AS.061: 5	1. Wheel 2. Well-fired 3. Red 4. Stone and sandy grit with lime particles 5. Coarse	Simpson 1996: Fig. 3: 7; Keall and Keall 1981: Fig. 11: 28	The first parallel lacks the troughed rim.
16	AS.018: 9	1. Wheel 2. Well-fired 3. Orange 4. Stone and sandy grit with chaff 5. Medium 6. Parallel horizontal grooves on the neck–shoulder transition area	Azarnoush 1994: Fig. 174: n, 188: f; Adams 1970: Fig. 5: q; Wenke 1975: Fig. 13: 705; Khosrowzadeh et al. 1399 [2020]: Fig. 9: 4.	With a slight profile difference.
17	AS.041: 3	1. Wheel 2. Well-fired 3. Orange, buff, orange 4. Grit with lime particles 5. Coarse 6. Horizontal ridge on the neck, and groove on the shoulder.	Azarnoush 1994: Fig. 188: f; Wenke 1975: Fig. 12: 603; Adams 1970: Fig. 5: r; Trinkaus 1986: Fig. 18: 3.	The last two parallels are plain.

18	AS.027: 15	1. Wheel 2. Well-fired 3. Orange 4. Stone and sandy grit with chaff 5. Coarse 7. Slip, buff, 8. Slip, buff	AS.032: 8; Adams 1970: Fig. 5: r; Wenke 1975: Fig. 12: 610.	With a slight profile difference.
19	AS.025: 1	1. Wheel 2. Well-fired 3. Orange 4. Stone and sandy grit with limestone particles 5. Coarse	Phillips 2008: Fig. 13: 1; Azarnoush 1994: Fig. 185: j; Alden 1978: Fig. 5: 3; Adams 1970: Fig. 5: q; Wenke 1975: Fig. 11: 504, 13: 705; Keall and Keall 1981: Fig. 14: 19; Trinkaus 1986: Fig. 12: 18; Barfi et al. 1391 [2012]: Fig. 8: 4.	The first two parallels are decorated.
20	AS.006: 4	1. Wheel 2. Well-fired 3. Orange 4. Stone and sandy grit with limestone particles 5. Coarse	Azarnoush 1994: Fig. 190: e; Venco Ricciardi 1970: Fig. 94: No. 75; Adams 1970: Fig. 6: ce; Wenke 1975: Fig. 11: 503; Khosrowzadeh et al. 1399 [2020]: Fig. 9: 6; Mohammadifar and Tahmāsebi 1393 [2014]: Fig. 6: S.S.180: 6; Kennet 2004: Fig. 35: type 81.	The second and last parallels have smaller rim diameters. The Tell Mahuz sample is glazed.
21	AS.027: 1	1. Wheel 2. Well-fired 3. Red 4. Stone and sandy grit with chaff 5. Coarse	Alden 1978: Fig. 5: 9; Azarnoush 1994: Fig. 190: e; Wenke 1975: Fig. 8: 302; Eqbal 1976: Fig. 46: m; Keall and Keall 1981: Fig. 11: 19; Trinkaus 1986: Fig. 13: 10.	The rim diameter of the first parallel is larger and the last sample's is smaller.

Table 5.2 (continued)

No.	Site Identifier	Description (1. Manufacture 2. Firing 3. Fabric Colour (Core Ext. Int.) 4. Inclusion 5. Finish 6. Decoration 7. Exterior Coating. Colour. Treatment 8. Interior Coating. Colour. Treatment)	Reference	Notes
22	AS.027: 7	1. Wheel 2. Well-fired 3. Orange 4. Stone and sandy grit with lime particles 5. Medium	Whitcomb 1985: Fig. 46: m; Langdon and Harden 1934: Fig. 1: 8.	
23	AS.061: 4	1. Wheel 2. Well-fired 3. Orange, green buff, orange 4. Stone and sandy grit with limestone particles 5. Coarse 6. Appliquéd ridge 7. Slip, buff, 8. Slip, buff	Khosrowzadeh et al. 2020a: Fig. 7: c; Wenke, 1975, Fig. 12: 602.	With a slight profile difference.
24	AS.025: 19	1. Wheel 2. Well-fired 3. Orange 4. Stone and sandy grit with lime particles 5. Medium 7. Slip, buff	Wenke, 1975, Fig. 8: 302; Mohammadifar and Tahmāsebi 1393 [2014]: Fig. 6: S.S.185; Kennet 2004: Fig. 35: type 81.	With different technical attributes from the last parallel.
25	AS.018: 14	1. Wheel 2. Well-fired 3. Reddish brown 4. Grit with lime particles 5. Coarse.	AS.018: 2; Azarnoush 1994: Fig. 186: c; Whitcomb, 1985, Fig. 44: g.	With a slightly different form from the Hajiabad example.

26	AS.018: 63	1. Wheel 2. Well-fired 3. Reddish brown 4. Stone and sandy grit with lime particles 5. Coarse.	Whitcomb 1985: Fig. 51: ee, 54: j.	With a slightly different form from the second parallel.
27	AS.051: 4	1. Wheel 2. Well-fired 3. Reddish brown 4. Stone and sandy grit with lime particles 5. Coarse.	Whitcomb 1985: Fig. 23: j; Wenke 1975: Fig. 8: 302, 10: 404; Kleiss 1985: Abb. 3: first from top; Keall and Keall 1981: Fig. 10: 4; Trinkaus 1986: Fig. 13: 13, 18: 2.	With a slight profile difference, the parallels are decorated.
28	AS.007: 1	1. Wheel 2. Well-fired 3. Orange 4. Grit with chaff and lime particles 5. Coarse 8. Slip, buff.	Lamberg-Karlovsky 1970: Fig. 5: L; Adams 1970: Fig. 5: p; Wenke 1975: Fig. 11: 503; Lecomte 1987: Pl. 61: 7; Keall and Keall 1981: Fig. 13: 7; Kennet 2004: Fig. 35: type 81.	A slightly different profile from the first parallel.
29	AS.009: 1	1. Wheel 2. High-fired 3. Orange, red, orange 4. Sand and lime particles 5. Coarse 8. Slip, light brown.	Wenke 1975: Fig. 10: 410, 12: 713; Langdon and Harden 1934: Fig. 1: 8.	A larger rim diameter from the Susiana specimen.
30	AS.042: 5	1. Wheel 2. High-fired 3. Greenish buff, orange buff, greenish buff 4. Grit and lime particles 5. Coarse.	Whitcomb 1985: Fig. 47: o; Trinkaus 1986: Fig. 13: 11.	
31	AS.059: 2	1. Wheel 2. High-fired 3. Orange 4. Grit and lime particles 5. Medium.	Alden 1978: Fig. 5: 4; Azarnoush 1994: Fig. 190: e; Wenke 1975: Fig. 10: 400; Eqbal 1976: Fig. 44: m; Puschnigg 2006a: 7.2.	The parallels lack the external grooves of the rims.

Table 5.2 (continued)

No.	Site Identifier	Description (1. Manufacture 2. Firing 3. Fabric Colour (Core Ext. Int.) 4. Inclusion 5. Finish 6. Decoration 7. Exterior Coating. Colour. Treatment 8. Interior Coating. Colour. Treatment)	Reference	Notes
32	AS.007: 10	1. Wheel 2. High-fired 3. Orange 4. Grit and lime particles and chaff 5. Coarse 7. Slip, buff 8. Slip, buff	Whitcomb 1985: Fig. 53: t; Keall and Keall 1981: Fig. 23: 26.	The parallels are decorated externally.
33	AS.018: 65	1. Wheel 2. High-fired 3. Orange 4. Grit and gravel 5. Coarse.	Whitcomb 1985: Fig. 53: u.	The compared specimen is plain.
34	AS.027: 59	1. Wheel 2. High-fired 3. Orange buff 4. Grit and limestone particles 5. Medium.	Boucharlat and Labrousse 1979: Fig. 27: 12.	
35	AS.060: 4	1. Wheel 2. High-fired 3. Orange buff 4. Stone and sandy grit 5. Medium. 7. Slip, buff 8. Slip, buff	Venco Ricciardi 1970: Fig. 90: No. 26; Langdon and Harden 1934: Fig. 1: 18.	The second parallel has ribs on the shoulder.

Table 5.3 Description of Figure 5.3

No.	Site Identifier	Description (1. Manufacture 2. Firing 3. Fabric Colour (Core Ext. Int.) 4. Inclusion 5. Finish 6. Decoration 7. Exterior Coating. Colour. Treatment 8. Interior Coating. Colour. Treatment)	Reference	Notes
1	AS.018: 4	1. Wheel 2. Low-fired 3. Grey, brown 4. Stone and sandy grit with limestone particles 5. Medium.	Azarnoush 1994: Fig. 172: a; Whitcomb 1985: Fig. 23: j, 50: m, 56: a; Wenke 1975: Fig. 8: 302, 11: 511.	Different rim diameter.
2	AS.054: 3	1. Wheel 2. Low-fired 3. Red, orange, red 4. Stone and sandy grit with limestone particles 5. Medium 7. Slip, buff 8. Slip, buff.	Adams 1970: Fig. 6: ce; Wenke 1975: Fig. 8: 302, 10: 402.	With a slight profile difference.
3	AS.053: 12	1. Wheel 2. Low-fired 3. Orange, red, orange 4. Stone and sandy grit with limestone particles 5. Medium 7. Slip, orange 8. Slip, orange.	Adams 1970: Fig. 5: p; Whitcomb 1985: Fig. 23: j; Wenke 1975: Fig. 10: 402, 11: 511; Eqbal 1976: Fig. 46: m.	
4	AS.060: 9	1. Wheel 2. Low-fired 3. Orange 4. Stone and sandy grit with limestone particles 5. Coarse.	Alden 1978: Fig. 5: 2; Azarnoush 1994: Fig. 164: a, 184: c; Phillips 2008: Figs 12: 3, 13: 6; Adams 1970: Fig. 5: p; Simpson 1996: Fig. 3: 8; Kleiss 1985: Abb. 3: fourth from top; Lecomte 1987: Pl. 54: 12 and 14; Trinkaus 1986: Fig. 13: 1.	With a slight profile difference.

Table 5.3 (continued)

No.	Site Identifier	Description (1. Manufacture 2. Firing 3. Fabric Colour (Core Ext. Int.) 4. Inclusion 5. Finish 6. Decoration 7. Exterior Coating. Colour. Treatment 8. Interior Coating. Colour. Treatment)	Reference	Notes
5	AS.018: 24	1. Wheel 2. Low-fired 3. Grey, light grey 4. Stone and sandy grit with limestone particles 5. Coarse.	Venco Ricciardi 1970: Fig. 94: No. 73; Azarnoush 1994: Fig. 174: 1; Langdon and Harden 1934: Fig. 3: 10; Alden 1978: Fig. 5: 2; Wenke 1975: Fig. 13: 712; Whitcomb 1987: Fig. E: b; Mohammadifar and Tahmāsebi 1393 [2014]: S.S.172.	With a slight profile difference.
6	AS.018: 1	1. Wheel 2. Low-fired 3. Grey, reddish brown 4. Stone and sandy grit with limestone particles 5. Medium.	Khosrowzadeh et al. 2020a: Fig. 7: f; Wenke 1975: Fig. 11: 501; Kleiss 1985: Abb. 5: 1; Whitcomb 1987: Fig. F: j.	Apart from Tappe[h] Bardnakōn specimen, parallels lack handle.
7	AS.036: 2	1. Wheel 2. Low-fired 3. Reddish brown 4. Stone and sandy grit with limestone particles 5. Medium.	AS.018: 24; AS.036: 7; Langdon and Harden 1934: Fig. 3: 8; Adams 1970: Fig. 5: p; Kleiss 1985: Abb. 3: second from bottom; Whitcomb 1987: Fig. D: d; Trinkaus 1986: Fig. 18: 6.	With a slightly different form from the Tell Abu Sarifa sample.

No.	Catalogue	Description	References	Notes
8	AS.059: 1	1. Wheel 2. Low-fired 3. Reddish brown 4. Stone and sandy grit with limestone particles 5. Medium.	Wenke 1975: Fig. 11: 501; Eqbal 1976: Fig. 44: k; Keall and Keall 1981: Fig. 10: 22.	With a slight profile difference.
9	AS.017: 3	1. Wheel 2. Low-fired 3. Orange 4. Stone and sandy grit with chaff and limestone particles 5. Coarse 7. Slip, pale orange.	Boucharlat and Labrousse 1979: Fig. 27: 1; Alden 1978: Fig. 5: 12; Adams 1970: Fig. 6: bn; Wenke 1975: Fig. 10: 432, 11: 527.	With a slight profile difference.
10	AS.018: 16	1. Wheel 2. Well-fired 3. Buff, reddish buff 4. Gravel, stone and sandy grit with limestone particles 5. Medium.	AS.018: 8, 11; Azarnoush 1994: Fig. 171: p; Alden 1978: Fig. 5: 7; Whitcomb 1985: Fig. 50: c; Eqbal 1976: Fig. 44: a, 46: b; Wenke 1975: Fig. 13: 728	
11	AS.024: 4	1. Wheel 2. Well-fired 3. Buff, reddish buff 4. Gravel, stone and sandy grit with limestone particles 5. Medium.	AS.020: 1; AS.024: 5; AS.025: 6; Whitcomb 1985: Fig. 51: x.	
12	AS.027: 4	1. Wheel 2. Well-fired 3. Orange 4. Stone and sandy grit with chaff 5. Medium 7. Slip, pale orange 8. Slip, pale orange.	Boucharlat and Labrousse 1979: Fig. 28: 16; Keall and Keall 1981: Fig. 18: 32	Shāōr Palace specimen is glazed and lacks the troughed rim.
13	AS.027: 14	1. Wheel 2. Well-fired 3. Red 4. Stone and sandy grit with limestone particles 5. Coarse 7. Slip, buff 8. Slip, buff.	Lamberg-Karlovsky 1970: Fig. 3: K; Keall and Keall 1981: Fig. 17: 24; Azarnoush, 1994: Fig. 171: e, 180: c; Wenke 1975: Fig. 12: 602.	The parallels lack handle.

Table 5.3 (continued)

No.	Site Identifier	Description (1. Manufacture 2. Firing 3. Fabric Colour (Core Ext. Int.) 4. Inclusion 5. Finish 6. Decoration 7. Exterior Coating. Colour. Treatment 8. Interior Coating. Colour. Treatment)	Reference	Notes
14	AS.018: 11	1. Wheel 2. Low-fired 3. Grey, grey, grey buff 4. Stone and sandy grit with limestone particles and chaff 5. Coarse.	AS.018: 6, 8; Alden 1978: Fig. 5: 7; Eqbal 1976: Fig. 44: a, 46: b; Azarnoush 1994: Fig. 171: Whitcomb 1985: Fig. 50: c; p; Wenke 1975: Fig. 13: 728.	The first two parallels lack the groove on the rim.
15	AS.020: 1	1. Wheel 2. Low-fired 3. Dark grey, orange buff, orange buff 4. Stone and sandy grit with limestone particles 5. Coarse 7. Slip, buff, 8. Slip, buff.	AS.024: 4, 5; Boucharlat and Labrousse 1979: Fig. 27: 17; Azarnoush 1994: Fig. 188: a; Whitcomb 1985: Fig. 50: e; Adams 1970: Fig. 6: ca; Wenke 1975: Fig. 11: 527	With slight profile distinction.
16	AS.027: 3	1. Wheel 2. Low-fired 3. Buff 4. Stone and sandy grit with limestone particles 5. Coarse 6. A rib below the rim 7. Slip, buff, 8. Slip, buff.	Whitcomb 1985: Fig. 52: m; Azarnoush 1994: Fig. 171: p, 188: c; Eqbal 1976: Fig. 46: a; Keall and Keall 1981: Fig. 17: 16.	

17	AS.018: 6	1. Wheel 2. Well-fired 3. Buff, reddish buff 4. Stone and sandy grit with limestone particles 5. Medium.	AS.018: 8, 11; Azarnoush 1994: Fig. 171: p; Whitcomb 1985: Fig. 50: c; Wenke 1975: Fig. 13: 728; Mohammadifar and Tahmāsebi 1393 [2014]: Fig. 7: S.S.98; Alden 1978: Fig. 5: 7; Eqbal 1976: Fig. 44: a, 46: b.	The last two parallels lack the groove on the rim.
18	AS.027: 2	1. Wheel 2. Well-fired 3. Orange 4. Stone and sandy grit with limestone particles 5. Coarse. 7. Slip, buff 8. Slip, buff	Alden 1978: Fig. 5: 7; Azarnoush 1994: Fig. 171: o; Eqbal 1976: Fig. 44: a; Wenke 1975: Fig. 13: 728.	With slight profile difference.
19	AS.055: 3	1. Wheel 2. High-fired 3. Red 4. Grit 5. Medium 6. A rib below the rim 7. Slip, buff 8. Slip, buff	Whitcomb 1987: Fig. D: k; Whitcomb 1985: Fig. 52: r; Eqbal 1976: Fig. 44: b; Trinkaus 1986: Fig. 12: 10.	
20	AS.018: 8	1. Wheel 2. High-fired 3. Orange 4. Stone and sandy grit with lime particles 5. Medium.	AS.018: 6, 1; Azarnoush 1994: Fig. 171: p; Alden 1978: Fig. 5: 7; Whitcomb 1985: Fig. 50: c; Eqbal 1976: Fig. 44: a, 46: b; Wenke 1975: Fig. 13: 728; Mohammadifar and Tahmāsebi 1393 [2014]: Fig. 7: S.S. 98.	

Table 5.3 (continued)

No.	Site Identifier	Description (1. Manufacture 2. Firing 3. Fabric Colour (Core Ext. Int.) 4. Inclusion 5. Finish 6. Decoration 7. Exterior Coating. Colour. Treatment 8. Interior Coating. Colour. Treatment)	Reference	Notes
21	AS.032: 13	1. Wheel 2. High-fired 3. Orange buff 4. Stone and sandy grit with chaff 5. Coarse 7. Olive green glaze.	Keall and Keall 1981: Fig. 18: 33; Alden 1978: Fig. 6: 24; Langdon and Harden 1934: Fig. 1: 3, 2, b: 3; Whitcomb 1985: Fig. 52: p; Wenke 1975: Fig. 10: 431; Eqbal 1976: Fig. 46: c; Kleiss 1987: Abb. 9: 2.	With slight profile difference, the parallels are unglazed.
22	AS.061: 6	1. Wheel 2. High-fired 3. Red, buff, red 4. Stone and sandy grit with lime particles 5. Medium 7. Slip, buff.	Keall and Keall 1981: Fig. 19: 22; Khosrowzadeh et al. 1399 [2020]: Fig. 4: 1; Adams 1970: Fig. 6: bk; Trinkaus 1986: Fig. 15: 5; Mohammadifar and Tahmāsebi 1393 [2014]: Fig. 8: S.S.116.	

23	AS.027: 12	1. Wheel 2. High-fired 3. Buff 4. Stone and sandy grit with lime particles 5. Medium.	AS.017: 17; Alden 1978: Fig. 5: 14, 6: 24; Azarnoush 1994: Fig. 171: k; Langdon and Harden 1934: Fig. 1: 3; Whitcomb 1985: Fig. 52: q; Adams 1970: Fig. 6: aw; Wenke 1975: Fig. 8: 32; Eqbal 1976: Fig. 46: c; Whitcomb 1987: Fig. E: q.	
24	AS.041: 2	1. Wheel 2. High-fired 3. Orange buff 4. Stone and sandy grit with lime particles 5. Medium.	Adams 1970: Fig. 6: bl; Wenke 1975: Fig. 8: 327, 11: 526; Keall and Keall 1981: Fig. 18: 33; Whitcomb 1987: Fig. G: i.	The parallels lack cordon decoration.
25	AS.060: 1	1. Wheel 2. High-fired 3. Orange buff 4. Stone and sandy grit with lime particles and chaff 5. Coarse.	Whitcomb 1987: Fig. F: a; Langdon and Harden 1934: Fig. 1: 3; Adams 1970: Fig. 6: bj; Lecomte 1987: Pl. 46: 7; Wenke 1975: Fig. 10: 435.	With a slight profile difference. The first two parallels lack the external grooves of the rim.
26	AS.042: 1	1. Wheel 2. High-fired 3. Red 4. Stone and sandy grit with lime particles and chaff 5. Coarse 8. Slip, buff.	AS.042: 9; Alden 1978: Fig. 5: 14, 6: 22; Adams 1970: Fig. 6: ca; Wenke 1975: Fig. 8: 326, 10: 435; Whitcomb 1987, Fig. E: s.	With a slight profile difference.
27	AS.067: 1	1. Wheel 2. High-fired 3. Orange 4. Stone and sandy grit 5. Coarse 7. Slip, buff 8. Slip, buff.	Alden 1978: Fig. 6: 22; Whitcomb 1985: Fig. 51: kk.	

Table 5.3 (continued)

No.	Site Identifier	Description (1. Manufacture 2. Firing 3. Fabric Colour (Core Ext. Int.) 4. Inclusion 5. Finish 6. Decoration 7. Exterior Coating. Colour. Treatment 8. Interior Coating. Colour. Treatment)	Reference	Notes
28	AS.006: 3	1. Wheel 2. High-fired 3. Orange 4. Stone and sandy grit 5. Coarse 7. Slip, buff 8. Slip, buff.	Alden 1978: Fig. 6: 22; Azarnoush 1994: Fig. 171: 0; Adams 1970: Fig. 6: ca; Wenke 1975: Fig. 7: 228.	With a slight profile difference.
29	AS.012: 10	1. Wheel 2. Well-fired 3. Buff 4. Sand 5. Medium 7. Glaze, turquoise 8. Glaze, turquoise.	Lecomte 1987: Pl. 61: 4; Wenke 1975: Fig. 10: 429; Kennet 2004: Fig. 5: type 35.	The first parallel is unglazed.
30	AS.054: 11	1. Wheel 2. Well-fired 3. Buff 4. Sand 5. Medium 7. Glaze, green 8. Glaze, green.	Kennet 2004: Fig. 5: type 33.	
31	AS.007: 24	1. Wheel 2. Well-fired 3. Light green 4. Sand 5. Medium 7. Glaze, green 8. Glaze, green.	Boucharlat and Labrousse 1979: Fig. 27: 2; Lecomte 1987: Pl. 61: 5; Wenke 1975: Fig. 10: 429; Kennet 2004: Fig. 5: type 33.	With a slight profile difference. The first two parallels are unglazed.
32	AS.039: 3	1. Wheel 2. Well-fired 3. Orange 4. Sand 5. Medium.	Langdon and Harden 1934: Fig. 1: 1, 3: 1; Simpson 1996: Fig. 3: 3.	With a slight profile difference.
33	AS.039: 3	1. Wheel 2. Well-fired 3. Buff 4. Sand 5. Medium 7. Glaze, blue 8. Glaze, blue.	Langdon and Harden 1934: Fig. 3: 4; Kennet 2004: Fig. 5: type 25.	As AS.039: 3.

No.	Cat. no.	Description	References	Comments
34	AS.055: 10	1. Wheel 2. Well-fired 3. Buff 4. Sand 5. Medium 7. Glaze, blue 8. Glaze, blue.	Kennet 2004: Fig. 5: type 33.	
35	AS.027: 11	1. Wheel 2. High-fired 3. Buff 4. Stone and sandy grit with limestone particles 5. Coarse.	Lamberg-Karlovsky 1970: Fig. 6: N; Lecomte 1987: Pl. 41: 3; Adams 1970: Fig. 6: bc; Wenke 1975: Fig. 8: 333; Simpson 1996: Fig. 3; Whitcomb 1985: Fig. 51: c.	
36	AS.054: 13	1. Wheel 2. High-fired 3. Buff 4. Stone and sandy grit 5. medium.	Wenke 1975: Fig. 8: 333.	With a smaller rim diameter.
37	AS.072: 1	1. Wheel 2. High-fired 3. Orange, red, orange 4. Stone and sandy grit 5. Coarse.	Azarnoush 1994: Fig. 190: a.	The parallel lacks cordon and is internally glazed.
38	AS.053: 2	1. Wheel 2. Well-fired 3. Buff, red, orange 4. Stone and sandy grit 5. Medium 7. Glaze, turquoise 8. Glaze, turquoise.	Kennet 2004: Fig. 5: type 33.	
39	AS.009: 5	1. Wheel 2. High-fired 3. Buff, red, orange 4. Stone and sandy grit with chaff 5. Medium 7. Slip, pale orange 8. Slip, pale orange.	Simpson 1996: Fig. 3: 2.	
40	AS.040: 1	1. Wheel 2. Well-fired 3. Buff 4. Stone and sandy grit 5. Medium 6. Beaded rim 7. Glaze, turquoise 8. Glaze, turquoise.	Langdon and Harden 1934: Fig. 2, b: 1.	With a slight form difference.

Table 5-3 (continued)

No.	Site Identifier	Description (1. Manufacture 2. Firing 3. Fabric Colour (Core Ext. Int.) 4. Inclusion 5. Finish 6. Decoration 7. Exterior Coating. Colour. Treatment 8. Interior Coating. Colour. Treatment)	Reference	Notes
41	AS.053: 4	1. Wheel 2. Well-fired 3. Buff 4. Stone and sandy grit 5. Medium 6. Parallel horizontal grooves below the rim 7. Glaze, blue 8. Glaze, blue.	Boucharlat and Labrousse, 1979: Fig. 27: 3; Khosrowzadeh et al. 1399 [2020]: Fig. 1: 1.	The first parallel is unglazed.
42	AS.027: 20	1. Wheel 2. Well-fired 3. Orange buff 4. Stone and sandy grit 5. Medium.	Boucharlat and Labrousse 1979: Fig. 27: 1; Trinkaus 1986: Fig. 12: 4.	With a slightly different profile.
43	AS.055: 7	1. Wheel 2. Well-fired 3. Buff 4. Sand 5. Medium.	Boucharlat and Labrousse 1979: Fig. 26: 2; Azarnoush 1994: Fig. 174: r, 189: l; Whitcomb 1985: Fig. 19: d; Trinkaus 1986: Fig. 12: 6.	
44	AS.056: 2	1. Wheel 2. Well-fired 3. Buff, green, green 4. Stone and sandy grit 5. Medium 6. Beaded rim 7. Glaze, olive green 8. Glaze, olive green.	Boucharlat and Labrousse 1979: 26: 1, 28: 1; Azarnoush 1994: Fig. 171: e; Wenke 1975: Fig. 11: 532; Lamberg-Karlovsky 1970: Fig. 3: I–K; Venco Ricciardi 1970: Fig. 94: No. 77; Kennet 2004: Fig. 5: type 94.	The first three parallels are unglazed.

Table 5.4 Description of Figure 5.4

No.	Site Identifier	Description (1. Manufacture 2. Firing 3. Fabric Colour (Core Ext. Int.) 4. Inclusion 5. Finish 6. Decoration 7. Exterior Coating. Colour. Treatment 8. Interior Coating. Colour. Treatment)	Reference	Notes
1	AS.069: 5	1. Wheel 2. Well-fired 3. Orange 4. Stone and sandy grit with limestone particles 5. Medium 7. Slip, buff 8. Slip, buff.	Lamberg-Karlovsky 1970: Fig. 5: M; Keall and Keall 1981: Fig. 17: 12; Wenke 1975: Fig. 8: 336; Lecomte 1987: Pl. 51: 12.	
2	AS.012: 1	1. Wheel 2. low-fired 3. Orange, orange buff, light grey 4. Stone and sandy grit with chaff 5. Medium.	Adams 1970: Fig. 6: bc; Whitcomb 1985: Fig. 51: e; Wenke 1975: Fig. 8: 333, 11: 537, 13: 727.	The second parallel is glazed.
3	AS.018: 10	1. Wheel 2. Well-fired 3. Buff 4. Stone and sandy grit 5. Medium.	Wenke 1975: Fig. 13: 728.	
4	AS.018: 19	1. Wheel 2. Well-fired 3. Red 4. Stone and sandy grit 5. Medium 7. Slip, buff 8. Slip, buff.	Whitcomb 1987: Fig. D: j; Whitcomb 1985: Fig. 50: g; Wenke 1975: Fig. 11: 602, 13: 728.	The first parallel has a larger rim diameter and combed decoration.
5	AS.032: 2	1. Wheel 2. Well-fired 3. Light orange 4. Stone and sandy grit with lime particles 5. Medium 7. Glaze, black 8. Glaze, white.	Whitcomb 1987: Fig. E: m; Lamberg-Karlovsky 1970: Fig. 3: I-K.	

Table 5.4 (continued)

No.	Site Identifier	Description (1. Manufacture 2. Firing 3. Fabric Colour (Core Ext. Int.) 4. Inclusion 5. Finish 6. Decoration 7. Exterior Coating. Colour. Treatment 8. Interior Coating. Colour. Treatment)	Reference	Notes
6	AS.032: 10	1. Wheel 2. Well-fired 3. Buff 4. Stone and sandy grit with lime particles 5. Medium 6. Beaded rim 7. Glaze, turquoise 8. Glaze, turquoise.	Boucharlat and Labrousse 1979: Fig. 28: 3; Keall and Keall 1981: Fig. 19: 26.	
7	AS.024: 5	1. Wheel 2. Well-fired 3. Orange 4. Stone and sandy grit with chaff and lime particles 5. Coarse 7. Slip, buff 8. Slip, buff.	AS.024: 4; AS.025: 6; Whitcomb 1985: Fig. 51: x.	With a slightly different profile.
8	AS.025: 6	1. Wheel 2. Well-fired 3. Orange 4. Stone and sandy grit with chaff and lime particles 5. Coarse 7. Slip, buff 8. Slip, buff.	AS.024: 4–5; Whitcomb 1985: Fig. 51: x; Wenke 1975: Fig. 11: 539.	The last parllel lacks the troughed rim.
9	AS.036: 8	1. Wheel 2. High-fired 3. Orange 4. Stone and sandy grit with lime particles and chaff 5. Medium	Boucharlat and Labrousse 1979: Fig. 26: 5.	
10	AS.056: 1	1. Wheel 2. Well-fired 3. Reddish brown 4. Sand with chaff 5. Medium 7. Slip, buff 8. Slip, buff.	Boucharlat and Labrousse 1979: Fig. 26: 5; Lecomte 1987: Pl. 56: 14; Whitcomb 1987: Fig. H: d.	

	ID	Description	References	Notes
11	AS.069: 2	1. Wheel 2. Well-fired 3. Greenish buff 4. Stone and sandy grit with chaff 5. Coarse 6. A broad groove below the rim.	Wenke 1975: Fig. 8: 329, 12: 626; Kleiss 1999: Abb. 5: first from bottom right.	The Susiana example is glazed.
12	AS.002: 2	1. Wheel 2. High-fired 3. Orange 4. Stone and sandy grit with lime particles and chaff 5. Medium	Stronach 1978b: Fig. 123: 3.	With a slight profile difference.
13	AS.055: 4	1. Hand 2. Low-fired 3. Grey buff 4. Grit and gravel 5. Coarse.	Omrani Rekavandi et al. 2008: Fig. 18: 13; Azarnoush 1994, Fig. 171: f; Whitcomb, 1985, Fig. 51: l; Wenke 1975, Fig. 8: 329; Kleiss 1999, Abb. 5: first from bottom right; Puschnigg 2006a: 6.4; Mohammadifar and Tahmāsebi 1393 [2014]: Fig. 23: S.S.179; Barfi et al. 1391 [2012]: Fig. 16: 4.	As AS. 002: 2.
14	AS.069: 14	1. Wheel 2. Low-fired 3. Orange buff 4. Stone and sandy grit with lime particles and chaff 5. Medium 7. Slip, greenish buff 8. Slip, greenish buff.		
15	AS.027: 9	1. Wheel 2. Low-fired 3. Buff 4. Grit with lime particles 5. Medium.		
16	AS.069: 12	1. Wheel 2. Low-fired 3. Green 4. Grit with lime particles and chaff 5. Medium.	Whitcomb 1987: Fig. E: q; Keall and Keall 1981: Fig. 18: 33; Azarnoush 1994: Fig. 171: b; Wenke 1975: Fig. 8: 327, 10: 431, 12: 636; Kleiss 1987: Abb. 5: 15.	

Table 5.4 (continued)

No.	Site Identifier	Description (1. Manufacture 2. Firing 3. Fabric Colour (Core Ext. Int.) 4. Inclusion 5. Finish 6. Decoration 7. Exterior Coating. Colour. Treatment 8. Interior Coating. Colour. Treatment)	Reference	Notes
17	AS.041: 2	1. Wheel 2. Low-fired 3. Orange buff 4. Grit with lime particles 5. Medium.	Adams 1970: Fig. 6: bl; Wenke 1975: Fig. 8: 327, 11: 526; Keall and Keall 1981: Fig. 18: 33; Whitcomb 1987: Fig. G: i	The parallels lack cordon decoration.
18	AS.053: 3	1. Wheel 2. High-fired 3. Reddish orange 4. Stone and sandy grit with lime particles 5. Coarse 7. Slip, buff 8. Slip, buff.	Azarnoush 1994: Fig. 171: b; Wenke 1975: Fig. 12: 636; Keall and Keall 1981: Fig. 18: 14; Trinkaus 1986; Fig. 12: 11.	As AS. 002: 2.
19	AS.018: 26	1. Wheel 2. High-fired 3. Green 4. Sandy 5. Medium 7. Glaze, turquoise 8. Glaze, turquoise.	AS.032: 12; Boucharlat and Labrousse 1979: Fig. 26: 3, 27: 6; Adams 1970: Fig. 6: bu; Langdon and Harden 1934: Fig. 2, b: 3.	
20	AS.070: 4	1. Wheel 2. High-fired 3. Greenish buff 4. Stone and sandy grit 5. Medium.	Langdon and Harden 1934: Fig. 3: 1; Wenke 1975: Fig. 10: 426, 11; 538; Simpson 1996: Fig. 3: 2; Lecomte 1987: Pl. 49: 10.	

21	AS.032: 12	1. Wheel 2. Well-fired 3. Orange buff 4. Stone and sandy grit with lime particles 5. Medium. 7. Glaze, white reminiscence of the glaze 8. Glaze, white reminiscence of the glaze	As.018: 26; Wenke 1975: Fig. 10: 433; Kennet 2004: Fig. 5: type 94.	The Susiana specimen is unglazed. The last parallel has a smaller rim diameter.
22	AS.009: 2	1. Wheel 2. High-fired 3. Red 4. Stone and sandy grit with lime particles and chaff 5. Coarse 6. Cordon decoration below the rim.	Boucharlat and Labrousse 1979: Fig. 27: 15; Adams 1970: Fig. 6: bi; Wenke 1975: Fig. 7: 131, 8: 335, 12: 636; Keall and Keall 1981: Fig. 18: 26; Kleiss 1987: Abb. 5: 4; Whitcomb 1987: Fig. G: i.	The parallels lack the cordon decoration. The Shāōr Palace example is glazed.
23	AS.024: 1	1. Wheel 2. High-fired 3. Red 4. Stone and sandy grit with lime particles 5. Medium.	Wenke 1975: Fig. 8: 337, 10: 435, 11: 636; Keall and Keall 1981: Fig. 17: 14.	
24	AS.012: 3	1. Wheel 2. High-fired 3. Orange, orange buff, light grey 4. Stone and sandy grit with chaff 5. Medium.	Azarnoush 1994: Fig. 171: d; Wenke 1975: Fig. 7: 132, 10: 427; Kleiss 1987: Abb. 5: 1; Keall and Keall 1981: Fig. 19: 10; Whitcomb 1987: Fig. G: i.	With a slight profile difference from Hajiabad sample.
25	AS.070: 1	1. Wheel 2. High-fired 3. Orange 4. Stone and sandy grit with limestone particles 5. Medium 7. Slip, buff 8. Slip, buff	Khosrowzadeh et al. 2020a: Fig. 7: k; Wenke 1975: Fig. 10: 435; Keall and Keall 1981: Fig. 19: 14.	
26	AS.070: 3	1. Wheel 2. High-fired 3. Greenish buff 4. Stone and sandy grit with limestone particles 5. Medium.	Wenke 1975: Fig. 8: 326; Whitcomb 1987: Fig. E: s.	

Table 5.4 (continued)

No.	Site Identifier	Description (1. Manufacture 2. Firing 3. Fabric Colour (Core Ext. Int.) 4. Inclusion 5. Finish 6. Decoration 7. Exterior Coating. Colour. Treatment 8. Interior Coating. Colour. Treatment)	Reference	Notes
27	AS.069: 8	1. Wheel 2. High-fired 3. Orange 4. Stone and sandy grit with limestone particles and chaff 5. Medium 7. Slip, buff 8. Slip, buff.	Khosrowzadeh et al. 1399 [2020]: Fig. 2; Wenke 1975: Fig. 8: 326, 12: 636; Whitcomb 1987: Fig. F: f.	
28	AS.047: 1	1. Wheel 2. High-fired 3. Orange buff 4. Stone and sandy grit 5. Medium 7. Slip, light orange 8. Slip, light orange.	Wenke 1975: Fig. 10: 452; Trinkaus 1986: Fig. 15: 10.	The first parallel is glazed.
29	AS.010: 3	1. Wheel 2. High-fired 3. Orange buff 4. Stone and sandy grit 5. Medium.	Wenke 1975: Fig. 13: 751.	
30	AS.004: 2	1. Wheel 2. High-fired 3. Orange buff 4. Stone and sandy grit 5. Medium.	Wenke 1975: Fig. 11: 552.	With a larger rim diameter.
31	AS.004: 3	1. Wheel 2. High-fired 3. Buff 4. Stone and sandy grit with lime particles 5. Medium.	Wenke 1975: Fig. 7: 252, 8: 352.	
32	AS.048: 3	1. Wheel 2. High-fired 3. Orange buff 4. Stone and sandy grit with lime particles 5. Medium 7. Slip, buff 8. Slip, buff	Wenke 1975: Fig. 12: 657; Whitcomb 1987: Fig. H: w.	

No.	ID	Description	References	Comments
33	AS.053: 11	1. Wheel 2. High-fired 3. Orange buff 4. Stone and sandy grit with lime particles 5. Medium.	Wenke 1975: Fig. 8: 352, 13: 759; Whitcomb 1987: Fig. I: o.	
34	AS.018: 51	1. Wheel 2. High-fired 3. Orange buff 4. Stone and sandy grit with lime particles 5. Medium.	Wenke 1975: Fig. 7: 181, 13: 757; Whitcomb 1987: Fig. H: w.	
35	AS.006: 11	1. Wheel 2. High-fired 3. Buff 4. Stone and sandy grit with chaff 5. Medium 8. Slip, greenish buff.	Wenke 1975: Fig. 8: 351, 11: 557; Trinkaus 1986: Fig. 15: 11.	
36	AS.041: 5	1. Wheel 2. High-fired 3. Orange buff 4. Stone and sandy grit with chaff 5. Medium 8. Slip, greenish buff.	Wenke 1975: Fig. 8: 351, 11: 557, 12: 651; Trinkaus 1986: Fig. 15: 11.	
37	AS.045: 1	1. Wheel 2. High-fired 3. Orange buff 4. Stone and sandy grit with chaff 5. Medium 8. Slip, buff.	Wenke 1975: Fig. 8: 351, 11: 557, 12: 657.	
38	AS.053: 8	1. Wheel 2. High-fired 3. Buff 4. Stone and sandy grit with lime particles 5. Medium.	Wenke 1975: Fig. 12: 652.	
39	AS.024: 7	1. Wheel 2. High-fired 3. Buff 4. Stone and sandy grit with lime particles 5. Medium.	Keall and Keall 1981: Fig. 24: 28; Mohammadifar and Tahmasbi 1393 [2014]: Fig. 24: S.S.242.	
40	AS.060: 7	1. Wheel 2. High-fired 3. Orange 4. Stone and sandy grit with lime particles and chaff 5. Medium 7. Slip, buff 8. Slip, buff.	Keall and Keall 1981: Fig. 27: 18.	With a slightly different profile.

Table 5.4 (continued)

No.	Site Identifier	Description (1. Manufacture 2. Firing 3. Fabric Colour (Core Ext. Int.) 4. Inclusion 5. Finish 6. Decoration 7. Exterior Coating. Colour. Treatment 8. Interior Coating. Colour. Treatment)	Reference	Notes
41	AS.036: 34	1. Wheel 2. High-fired 3. Buff 4. Stone and sandy grit with lime particles 5. Medium 7. Slip, buff 8. Slip, buff.	Wenke 1975: Fig. 11: 556, 12: 652; Trinkaus 1986: Fig. 8: 15.	Susiana samples lack the inner grooves.
42	AS.054: 16	1. Wheel 2. High-fired 3. Orange buff 4. Stone and sandy grit with chaff 5. Medium.	Azarnoush, 1994, Fig. 170: d; Khosrowzadeh et al. 2020a: Fig. 6: 0.	
43	AS.055: 1	1. Wheel 2. High-fired 3. Greenish buff 4. Stone and sandy grit with limestone particles 5. Medium.	Alden 1978: Fig. 6: 19; Azarnoush 1994: Fig. 170: e; Whitcomb 1985: Fig. 52: d; Langdon and Harden 1934: Fig. 3: 2; Boucharlat and Labrousse 1979: Fig. 30: 6.	With a slightly different profile from the first and second parallels.

Table 5.5 Description of Figure 5.5

No.	Site Identifier	Description (1. Manufacture 2. Firing 3. Fabric Colour (Core Ext. Int.) 4. Inclusion 5. Finish 6. Decoration 7. Exterior Coating. Colour. Treatment 8. Interior Coating. Colour. Treatment)	Reference	Notes
1	AS.053: 14	1. Wheel 2. High-fired 3. Orange 4. Stone and sandy grit with limestone particles 5. Coarse 6. Cordon decoration 7. Slip, buff 8. Slip, buff.	Kleiss 1987: Abb. 9: 10; Khosrowzadeh et al. 1399 [2020]: Fig. 11: 6	
2	AS.020: 3	1. Wheel 2. High-fired 3. Orange 4. Stone and sandy grit with limestone particles 5. Medium 6. Cordon decoration.	Trinkaus 1986: Fig. 15: 12.	
3	AS.056: 8	1. Wheel 2. High-fired 3. Reddish brown 4. Grit and gravel with chaff 5. Coarse 6. Incised decoration 7. Slip, buff 8. Slip, buff.	Khosrowzadeh et al. 1399 [2020]: Fig. 11: 8; Mohammadifar and Tahmāsebi 1393 [2014]: Fig. 36.	
4	AS.036: 16	1. Wheel 2. Well-fired 3. Reddish brown 4. Grit with limestone particles 5. Coarse 6. Cordon decoration.		
5	AS.013: 2	1. Wheel 2. High-fired 3. Buff, orange buff 4. Grit with limestone particles 5. Coarse 6. Cordon decoration.	Wenke 1975: Fig. 13: 779; Venco Ricciardi 1970: Fig. 91: No. 42.	

Table 5.5 (continued)

No.	Site Identifier	Description (1. Manufacture 2. Firing 3. Fabric Colour (Core Ext. Int.) 4. Inclusion 5. Finish 6. Decoration 7. Exterior Coating. Colour. Treatment 8. Interior Coating. Colour. Treatment)	Reference	Notes
6	AS.004: 13	1. Wheel 2. High-fired 3. Orange 4. Stone and sandy grit with limestone particles 5. Medium 6. Cordon decoration.	Keall and Keall 1981: Fig. 27: 11; Whitcomb 1987: Fig. I: dd	
7	AS.003: 9	1. Wheel 2. High-fired 3. Orange 4. Gravel and grit 5. Coarse 6. Stamped and pinched decoration 7. Slip, buff.	Azarnoush 1994: Fig. 180: w; Keall and Keall 1981: Fig. 23: 25, 24: 20; Adams 1970: Fig. 9: III; Mohammadifar and Tahmāsebi 1393 [2016]: Fig. 31: S.S.248.	With different decorative motifs from the first two parallels.
8	AS.020: 7	1. Wheel 2. Well-fired 3. Orange 4. Sand and lime particles 5. Medium 6. Stamped and incised decoration 7. Slip, buff 8. Slip, decoration.	Adams, 1970, Fig. 9: III; Mohammadifar and Tahmāsebi 1393 [2016]: Fig. 31: S.S.248.	
9	AS.027: 46	1. Wheel 2. High-fired 3. Red, brownish red, brownish red 4. Sand and grit 5. Coarse 6. Stamped decoration.	Adams, 1970, Fig. 9: III; Mohammadifar and Tahmāsebi 1393 [2016]: Fig. 31: S.S.248.	
10	AS.001: 12	1. Wheel 2. High-fired 3. Red 4. Sand and grit 5. Coarse 6. Incised and pinched decoration.	Keall and Keall 1981: Fig. 25: 23.	

11	AS.073: 1	1. Wheel 2. Well-fired 3. Orange 4. Grit and limestone particles 5. Medium 6. Incised and pinched decoration.	Azarnoush 1994: Fig. 174: f, 176: b, 177: b; Whitcomb 1985: Fig. 52: r; Mohammadifar and Tahmāsebi 1393 [2016]: Fig. 33.
12	AS.018: 41	1. Wheel 2. Well-fired 3. Buff, orange buff 4. Grit and sand 5. Medium 6. Impressed decoration.	Keall and Keall 1981: Fig. 24: 28; Mohammadifar and Tahmāsebi 1393 [2016]: Fig. 30: S.S.321 and 322.
13	AS.003: 11	1. Wheel 2. Well-fired 3. Orange 4. Grit and sand 5. Coarse 6. Impressed decoration 7. Slip, buff.	Mohammadifar and Tahmāsebi 1393 [2016]: Fig. 30: S.S.321 and 322.
14	AS.007: 11	1. Wheel 2. Well-fired 3. Orange 4. Grit and sand 5. Coarse 6. Impressed decoration 7. Slip, buff.	Mohammadifar and Tahmāsebi 1393 [2016]: Fig. 30: S.S.321 and 322.
15	AS.027: 48	1. Wheel 2. Well-fired 3. Orange 4. Grit with limestone particles 5. Medium 6. Incised decoration 7. Slip, buff.	Azarnoush 1994: Fig. 165: a, 185: q; Whitcomb 1985: Fig. 16: f, 43: g-l; Langdon and Harden 1934: Fig. 1: 2; Adams 1970: Fig. 10: s; Wenke 1975: Fig. 10: 478; Keall and Keall 1981: Fig. 24: 12, 28: 25; Whitcomb 1987: Fig. I: cc; Mohammadifar and Tahmāsebi 1393 [2016]: Fig. 33: S.S.328.

Table 5.5 (continued)

No.	Site Identifier	Description (1. Manufacture 2. Firing 3. Fabric Colour (Core Ext. Int.) 4. Inclusion 5. Finish 6. Decoration 7. Exterior Coating. Colour. Treatment 8. Interior Coating. Colour. Treatment)	Reference	Notes
16	AS.002: 2	1. Wheel 2. High-fired 3. Orange 4. Grit with limestone particles and chaff 5. Medium 6. Incised decoration 7. Slip, buff.		
17	AS.009: 11	1. Wheel 2. High-fired 3. Orange 4. Grit and sand with limestone particles 5. Medium 6. Incised decoration.	Venco Ricciardi 1970: Fig. 88: Nos. 7–10; Whitcomb 1985: Fig. 45: a; Adams 1970: Fig. 10: x; Eqbal 1976: Fig. 46: b; Keall and Keall 1981: Fig. 26: 14; Kennet 2004: Fig. 31: LISV class	
18	AS.071: 6	1. Wheel 2. Well-fired 3. Orange buff 4. Sand with limestone particles 5. Medium 6. Incised decoration 7. Slip, buff.	Whitcomb 1985: Fig. 45: a, 50: g, m, n, 56: c; Venco Ricciardi 1970: Fig. 88: No. 7–10; Adams 1970: Fig. 10: x; Eqbal 1976: Fig. 44: b; Keall and Keall 1981: Fig. 26: 14; Kennet 2004: Fig. 31: LISV class	
19	AS.027: 50	1. Wheel 2. High-fired 3. Orange buff 4. Stone and sandy grit 5. Medium 6. Combed decoration 7. Slip, light orange 8. Slip, light orange.	Venco Ricciardi 1970: Fig. 88: No. 7–10; Azarnoush 1994: Fig. 180: t; Eqbal 1976: Fig. 46: b; Adams 1970: Fig. 10: j; Keall and Keall 1981: Fig. 21: 19.	Hajiabad specimen lacks the wavy combed decoration.

20	AS.071: 3	1. Wheel 2. High-fired 3. Buff 4. Sand 5. Fine 6. Combed decoration 7. Glaze, green 8. Glaze, green.	
21	AS.018: 47	1. Wheel 2. High-fired 3. Buff, greenish buff 4. Sand and organic materials 8. Glaze, turquoise.	
22	AS.006: 14	1. Wheel 2. High-fired 3. Orange 4. Stone and sandy grit with lime particles 5. Coarse 8. Slip, buff.	
23	AS.053: 21	1. Wheel 2. High-fired 3. Red 4. Stone and sandy grit with lime particles 5. Medium.	Trinkaus 1986: Fig. 21: 1.
24	AS.003: 6	1. Wheel 2. Well-fired 3. Orange buff 4. Stone and sandy grit with lime particles 5. Medium 7. Slip, buff 8. Slip, buff.	
25	AS.003: 8	1. Wheel 2. High-fired 3. Orange 4. Gravel and grit with lime particles 5. Coarse 7. Slip, buff 8. Slip, buff.	Mohammadifar and Tahmāsebi 1393 [2016]: Fig. 28: S.S.360
26	AS.017: 21	1. Wheel 2. High-fired 3. Orange, buff, orange 4. Gravel and grit with lime particles 5. Coarse 8. Slip, orange buff.	Whitcomb 1985: Fig. 50: j; Mohammadifar and Tahmāsebi 1393 [2016]: Fig. 28: S.S.360
27	AS.020: 4	1. Wheel 2. High-fired 3. Orange 4. Stone and sandy grit with lime particles and chaff 5. Coarse 8. Slip, buff.	Keall and Keall 1981: Fig. 16: 6, 27: 19; Mohammadifar and Tahmāsebi 1393 [2016]: Fig. 28: S.S.360.

Table 5.5 (continued)

No.	Site Identifier	Description (1. Manufacture 2. Firing 3. Fabric Colour (Core Ext. Int.) 4. Inclusion 5. Finish 6. Decoration 7. Exterior Coating. Colour. Treatment 8. Interior Coating. Colour. Treatment)	Reference	Notes
28	AS.027: 22	1. Wheel 2. High-fired 3. Red 4. Stone and sandy grit with lime particles 5. Medium 8. Slip, buff.	AS.027: 35; Mohammadifar and Tahmāsebi 1393 [2016]: Fig. 28: S.S.360	
29	AS.027: 35	1. Wheel 2. High-fired 3. Orange 4. Stone and sandy grit 5. Coarse.	Keall and Keall 1981: Fig. 16: 36; Mohammadifar and Tahmāsebi 1393 [2016]: Fig. 28: S.S.360.	

Table 5.6 Description of Figure 5.6

No.	Site Identifier	Description (1. Manufacture 2. Firing 3. Fabric Colour (Core Ext. Int.) 4. Inclusion 5. Finish 6. Decoration 7. Exterior Coating. Colour. Treatment 8. Interior Coating. Colour. Treatment)	Reference	Notes
1	FS.158: 1	1. Wheel 2. Low-fired 3. Light grey, light brown 4. Stone and sandy grit with occasional fine limestone particles 5. Medium.	Whitcomb 1987: fig. D: x; Trinkaus 1986: Fig. 20: 12; Keall and Keall 1981: Fig. 13: 34.	With a larger rim diameter.
2	FS.181: 7	1. Wheel 2. Well-fired 3. Buff 4. Stone and sandy grit 5. Medium 8. Slip, buff.		
3	FS.042: 7	1. Wheel 2. Well-fired 3. Reddish buff 4. Sand with occasional fine limestone particles 5. Medium 8. Slip, light brown.	Whitcomb 1985: fig. 42: l; Adams 1970: fig. 6: bw; Lecomte 1987: Pl. 55: 11.	
4	FS.117: 10	1. Wheel 2. Well-fired 3. Reddish orange 4. Stone and sandy grit 5. Medium 7. Covered with sediment 8. Covered with sediment.	Khosrowzadeh et al. 2020a: Fig. 6: g; Lamberg-Karlovsky 1970: Figure 5: C; Khosrowzadeh and 'Ali 1383 [2004]: Fig. 17: 4.	With a slightly different form from the last parallel.
5	FS.205: 8	1. Wheel 2. Well-fired 3. Buff 4. Sand with occasional fine limestone particles 5. Medium 7. Slip, greenish cream 8. Slip, greenish cream.		

Table 5.6 (continued)

No.	Site Identifier	Description (1. Manufacture 2. Firing 3. Fabric Colour (Core Ext. Int.) 4. Inclusion 5. Finish 6. Decoration 7. Exterior Coating. Colour. Treatment 8. Interior Coating. Colour. Treatment)	Reference	Notes
6	FS.158: 4	1. Wheel 2. Well-fired 3. Orange buff 4. Sand with occasional fine limestone particles 5. Medium.	Lecomte 1987: Pl. 56: 11; Stronach 1978b: Fig. 123: 8; Khosrowzadeh and 'Ali 1383 [2004]: Fig. 15: 9.	The last parallel has a larger rim diameter and is externally decorated with grooves.
7	FS.160: 12	1. Wheel 2. Well-fired 3. Buff 4. Sand with occasional fine limestone particles 5. Medium.	FS. 158: 4; Whitcomb 1987: fig. D: x.	The Bushehr parallel is glazed.
8	FS.117: 4	1. Wheel 2. Well-fired 3. Beige 4. Sand with occasional fine limestone particles 5. Medium 7. Slip, cream buff 8. Slip, cream buff.	Azarnoush 1994: fig. 164: c.	The parallel has a smaller rim diameter and appliquéd ribs, and lacks slip.
9	FS.117: 6	1. Wheel 2. Well-fired 3. Greenish buff 4. Stone and sandy grit with fine to medium limestone particles 5. Medium.	FS. 170: 10; Alden 1978: fig. 5: 2; Azarnoush 1994: fig. 190: b; Boucharlat and Labrousse, 1979: Fig. 27: 8; Lecomte 1987: Pl. 55: 16.	
10	FS.117: 7	1. Wheel 2. Well-fired 3. Reddish buff 4. Stone and sandy grit 5. Medium.	Azarnoush 1994: fig. 174: r; Lecomte 1987: Pl. 55: 19.	With a slight form difference.

11	FS.119: 7	1. Wheel 2. Well-fired 3. Orange buff 4. Stone and sandy grit 5. Medium.	Adams 1970: fig. 6: bw; Puschnigg 2006a: Figure 7.4; Khosrowzadeh and 'Ali 1383 [2004]: Fig. 14: 11.	The parallels have smaller rim diameters.
12	FS.119: 8	1. Wheel 2. Well-fired 3. Brownish buff 4. Stone and sandy grit 5. Medium.	Adams 1970: fig. 6: bw.	With a slight profile difference, the parallel has a smaller rim diameter.
13	FS.194: 2	1. Wheel 2. Well-fired 3. Orange buff 4. Stone and sandy grit with occasional fine to medium limestone particles 5. Medium 7. Slip, greenish cream 8. Slip, greenish cream.	Whitcomb 1987: fig. G: o; Alden 1978: fig. 6: 10; Venco Ricciardi 1970: fig. 92: No. 53; Lecomte 1987: Pl. 56: 11; Stronach 1978b: Fig. 123: 6.	With a slightly different profile.
14	FS.134: 5	1. Wheel 2. High-fired 3. Light grey, buff 4. Stone and sandy grit with occasional fine to medium limestone particles 5. Medium 7. Slip, buff.	Lecomte 1987: Pl. 57: 2; Simpson 1996: fig. 3: 4; Whitcomb 1987: fig. G: o; Boucharlat and Labrousse 1979: fig. 27: 4.	The first two parallels lack the handle.
15	FS.160: 11	1. Wheel 2. Well-fired 3. Cream buff 4. Sand with occasional fine limestone particles 5. Medium.	Trinkaus 1986: fig. 20: 11.	With a larger rim diameter.
16	FS.170: 10	1. Wheel 2. High-fired 3. brownish buff 4. Sand 5. Medium 7. Slip, greenish cream.	Alden 1978: fig. 5: 2; Whitcomb 1987: fig. E: d; Trinkaus 1986: fig. 12: 4; Keall and Keall 1981: fig. 14: 14; Stronach 1978b: Fig. 123: 11.	
17	FS.170: 8	1. Wheel 2. High-fired 3. Buff, light orange 4. Sand with occasional fine limestone particles 5. Medium.	Lecomte 1987: Pl. 55: 4.	As FS.194: 2.

Table 5.6 (continued)

No.	Site Identifier	Description (1. Manufacture 2. Firing 3. Fabric Colour (Core Ext. Int.) 4. Inclusion 5. Finish 6. Decoration 7. Exterior Coating. Colour. Treatment 8. Interior Coating. Colour. Treatment)	Reference	Notes
18	FS.170: 9	1. Wheel 2. High-fired 3. Beige 4. Sand with occasional fine limestone particles 5. Medium 7. Slip, buff.	Lecomte 1987: Pl. 55: 5.	With a slight profile difference and a larger rim diameter.
19	FS.134: 3	1. Wheel 2. High-fired 3. Light brownish red 4. Sand with occasional fine limestone particles 5. Medium.	Lecomte 1987: Pl. 56: 3.	As FS.194: 2.
20	FS.160: 10	1. Wheel 2. High-fired 3. Reddish buff 4. Stone and sandy grit with occasional fine limestone particles 5. Medium 7. Slip, buff.	FS. 087: 2; FS. 110: 2; Wenke 1975: fig. 10: 408.	As FS.194: 2.
21	FS.110: 2	1. Wheel 2. High-fired 3. Pinkish buff 4. Grit 5. Medium 7. Slip, cream.	FS. 087: 2; FS. 160: 10; Wenke 1975: fig. 10: 408.	The parallel lacks slip.
22	FS. 087: 2	1. Wheel 2. Low-fired 3. Orange buff 4. Sand and fine lime particles 5. Medium 7. Slip, brownish buff.	FS. 110: 2; FS. 117: 9; FS. 160: 10; Lecomte 1987: Pl. 55: 5; Wenke 1975: fig. 10: 408.	The first parallel is polished and lacks the rib.
23	FS.170: 1	1. Wheel 2. High-fired 3. brownish buff 4. Sand and fine lime particles 5. Medium 6. Wavy and straight grooves 7. Slip, greenish cream 8. Slip, greenish cream.	Adams 1970: fig. 5: s.	The parallel lacks the handle and decoration.
24	FS.205: 9	1. Wheel 2. High-fired 3. Reddish orange 4. Stone and sandy grit with fine to large lime particles 5. Medium.	Omrani Rekavandi et al. 2008: Fig. 18: 7; Stronach 1978b: Fig. 123: 6; Khosrowzadeh and 'Ali 1383 [2004]: Fig. 62: 3.	With different decoration.

25	FS.158: 2	1. Wheel 2. High-fired 3. Orange 4. Stone and sandy grit with fine lime particles 5. Medium.	Boucharlat and Labrousse 1979: fig. 27: 11; Azarnoush 1994: fig. 175: k; Puschnigg 2006a: Figure 6.9; Khosrowzadeh and 'Āli 1383 [2004]: Fig. 62: 8.	As FS.194: 2.
26	FS.170: 5	1. Wheel 2. High-fired 3. Brownish buff 4. Sand with occasional fine limestone particles 5. Medium.	FS. 117: 8; Whitcomb 1985: fig. 42: j.	As FS.117: 7.
27	FS.117: 8	1. Wheel 2. High-fired 3. Brownish buff 4. Grit 5. Medium. 7. Slip, light brown 8. Slip, light brown.	FS. 170: 5; Whitcomb 1985: fig. 57: i; Lecomte 1987: Pl. 56: 2.	
28	FS.117: 9	1. Wheel 2. High-fired 3. Orange brown 4. Grit 5. Medium. 7. Slip, light brown 8. Slip, light brown.	FS. 087: 2; Whitcomb 1987: fig. H: f; Boucharlat and Labrousse 1979: fig. 26: 3; Lecomte 1987: Pl. 55: 5.	
29	FS.087: 3	1. Wheel 2. Low-fired 3. Light grey, red 4. Stone and sandy grit with fine to large particles of limestone 5. Medium. 6. Appliquéd decoration 7. Slip, buff 8. Slip, buff.	Keall and Keall 1981: fig. 10: 28.	Comparison only with regard to the decoration.
30	FS.121: 2	1. Wheel 2. High-fired 3. Light orange 4. Stone and sandy grit with fine to large lime particles 5. Medium.	Whitcomb 1987: fig. I: ee; Keall and Keall 1981: fig. 27: 6.	
31	FS.190: 3	1. Wheel 2. High-fired 3. Orange buff 4. Sand with occasional fine limestone particles 5. Medium 8. Slip, orange buff.	Lecomte 1987: Pl. 56: 2; Puschnigg 2006a: Figure 6.6	As FS.194: 2.

Table 5.6 (continued)

No.	Site Identifier	Description (1. Manufacture 2. Firing 3. Fabric Colour (Core Ext. Int.) 4. Inclusion 5. Finish 6. Decoration 7. Exterior Coating. Colour. Treatment 8. Interior Coating. Colour. Treatment)	Reference	Notes
32	FS.119: 12	1. Wheel 2. Well-fired 3. Buff 4. Stone and sandy grit 5. Medium.	Keall and Keall 1981: fig. 14: 14.	As FS.194: 2.
33	FS.205: 6	1. Wheel 2. Low-fired 3. Light orange, reddish orange 4. Stone and sandy grit 5. Medium. 8. Slip, light orange.	Wenke 1975: fig. 12: 626; Keall and Keall 1981: fig. 12: 14; Puschnigg 2006a: Figure 7.10	Difference in technical attributes.
34	FS.042: 9	1. Wheel 2. Low-fired 3. Red 4. Stone and sandy grit with limestone particles 5. Medium 7. Slip, light brown 8. Slip, light brown.	Trinkaus 1986: Fig. 14: 2; Lecomte 1987: Pl. 55: 16; Khosrowzadeh and 'Ali 1383 [2004]: Fig. 17: 7.	
35	FS.160: 1	1. Wheel 2. Well-fired 3. Cream buff 4. Stone and sandy grit with limestone particles 5. Medium.	Azarnoush 1994: fig. 174: l; Lecomte 1987: Pl. 55: 14.	As FS.194: 2.
36	FS.138: 6	1. Wheel 2. High-fired 3. Reddish orange 4. Stone and sandy grit with occasional fine limestone particles 5. Medium.	Azarnoush 1994: fig. 190: b; Lamberg-Karlovsky 1970: Figure 5: C; Keall and Keall 1981: fig. 16: 13; Khosrowzadeh and 'Ali 1383 [2004]: Fig. 15: 9.	The last parallel has a smaller rim diameter and ribs and grooves.
37	FS.181: 9	1. Wheel 2. High-fired 3. Orange 4. Stone and sandy grit with occasional fine limestone particles 5. Medium.	Khosrowzadeh and 'Ali 1383 [2004]: Fig. 16: 7.	The parallel has a larger rim diameter.

38	FS.110: 5	1. Wheel 2. Low-fired 3. Light grey 4. Sand with occasional fine limestone particles 5. Medium 7. Slip, orange.	Whitcomb 1987: fig. H: g.	The parallel, with a slight profile difference, has a smaller rim diameter.
39	FS.120: 8	1. Wheel 2. High-fired 3. Reddish orange 4. Grit 5. Medium 7. Slip, orange 8. Slip, buff.	Azarnoush 1994: fig. 185: l; Khosrowzadeh and ʿAli 1383 [2004]: Fig. 17: 7.	As FS.194: 2.
40	FS.109: 1	1. Hand (?) 2. Low-fired 3. Black, greyish buff 4. Grit 5. Medium 7. Slip, orange.	Whitcomb 1987: fig. H: y; Trinkaus 1986: fig. 18: 8; Keall and Keall 1981: fig. 9: 34; Lamberg-Karlovsky 1970: Figure 5: C	With a slight profile difference, the parallels have smaller rim diameters.
41	FS.120: 5	1. Wheel 2. Low-fired 3. Grey, reddish orange 4. Stone and sandy grit 5. Medium.	Wenke 1975: fig. 10: 404; Trinkaus 1986: fig. 13: 13.	
42	FS.121: 5	1. Wheel 2. Well-fired 3. Light orange 4. Sand with occasional fine limestone particles 5. Medium.	Boucharlat and Labrousse 1979: fig. 27: 2; Puschnigg 2006a: Figure 6: 10; Lecomte; 1987: Pl. 55: 5; Wenke 1975 fig. 11: 535; Khosrowzadeh and ʿAli 1383 [2004]: Fig, 13: 1.	The last parallel, with a slight profile difference, has a larger rim diameter.
43	FS.134: 7	1. Wheel 2. High-fired 3. Reddish orange 4. Sand with occasional fine limestone particles 5. Medium 7. Slip, greenish buff 8. Slip, greenish buff.	Boucharlat and Labrousse 1979: fig. 27: 8; Khosrowzadeh and ʿAli 1383 [2004]: Fig. 63: 2.	

Table 5.6 (continued)

No.	Site Identifier	Description (1. Manufacture 2. Firing 3. Fabric Colour (Core Ext. Int.) 4. Inclusion 5. Finish 6. Decoration 7. Exterior Coating. Colour. Treatment 8. Interior Coating. Colour. Treatment)	Reference	Notes
44	FS.163: 8	1. Wheel 2. High-fired 3. Orange buff 4. Sand with occasional fine limestone particles 5. Medium 7. Slip, greenish buff 8. Slip, greenish buff.	Whitcomb 1987: fig. G: o; Alden 1978: fig. 6: 11; Simpson 1996: fig 3: 3; Lecomte 1987: Pl. 56: 11.	As FS.181: 9.
45	FS.163: 12	1. Wheel 2. Well-fired 3. Buff 4. Sand with occasional fine limestone particles 5. Medium 7. Slip, reddish buff.	Lecomte 1987: Pl. 57: 2.	As FS.194: 2.
46	FS.170: 7	1. Wheel 2. Low-fired 3. Dark grey, orange 4. (?) 5. Fine.	Trinkaus 1986: fig. 20: 1.	As FS.121: 5.
47	FS.190: 5	1. Wheel 2. Well-fired 3. Orange 4. Sand with occasional fine limestone particles 5. Medium 7. Slip, cream.	Whitcomb 1987: fig. H: ff; Lecomte 1987: Pl. 56: 11.	
48	FS.194: 3	1. Wheel 2. High-fired 3. Orange buff 4. Sand with occasional fine limestone particles 5. Medium 7. Slip, buff 8. Slip, buff.	Puschnigg 2006a: Figure 7.9; Khosrowzadeh and 'Ali 1383 [2004]: Fig. 62: 3.	With a slight profile difference.
49	FS.195: 1	1. Wheel 2. Well-fired 3. Buff 4. Stone and sandy grit with occasional fine to large limestone particles 5. Medium 6. Combed and grooved decoration.	Whitcomb, 1985, fig. 57: r.	Comparison in terms of the decorative motifs.

No.	FS	Description	Parallels	Comments
50	FS.163: 7	1. Wheel 2. High-fired 3. Reddish buff 4. Stone and sandy grit with occasional fine particles of limestone 5. Medium 7. Slip, buff.	Whitcomb 1985: fig. 51: g; Boucharlat and Labrousse 1979: fig. 27: 3; Lecomte 1987: Pl. 55: 5; Wenke 1975: fig. 10: 429; 'Ali and Khosrowzadeh 1385 [2006]: Fig. 7: 55.	With smaller rim diameters.
51	FS.190: 4	1. Wheel 2. High-fired 3. Buff 4. Stone and sandy grit with occasional fine particles of limestone 5. Medium.	Lecomte 1987: Pl. 51: 10; Boucharlat and Labrousse 1979: fig. 28: 14; Wenke 1975: fig. 10: 429.	The last parallel is glazed.
52	FS.181: 5	1. Wheel 2. Low-fired 3. Grey, orange 4. Stone and sandy grit with occasional fine to large particles of limestone 5. Medium.	Whitcomb 1985: fig. 52: I; Wenke 1975: fig. 7: 130; Keall and Keall 1981: fig. 19: 20.	As FS.190: 4.
53	FS.191: 4	1. Wheel 2. Low-fired 3. Light grey, light orange 4. Grit with occasional fine to large particles of limestone 5. Medium.	Lamberg-Karlovsky 1970: Fig. 3: I.	The parallel, with slight profile difference, has a turquoise glaze.

Table 5.7 Description of Figure 5.7

No.	Site Identifier	Description (1. Manufacture 2. Firing 3. Fabric Colour (Core Ext. Int.) 4. Inclusion 5. Finish 6. Decoration 7. Exterior Coating. Colour. Treatment 8. Interior Coating. Colour. Treatment)	Reference	Notes
1	FS.117: 3	1. Wheel 2. Well-fired 3. Reddish orange 4. Grit 5. Medium 7. Slip, cream.	Wenke 1975: fig. 11: 526; Khosrowzadeh and 'Ali 1383 [2004]: Fig. 34: 58.	The first parallel, with a slight profile difference, has a smaller rim diameter and lacks slip.
2	FS.190: 2	1. Wheel 2. Low-fired 3. Grey, reddish brown 4. Stone and sandy grit with fine limestone particles 5. Medium.	Kleiss 1987: abb. 9: 2.	The parallel lacks groove.
3	FS.037: 2	1. Wheel 2. Well-fired 3. Orange 4. Stone and sandy grit with fine limestone particles 5. Medium 8. Slip, buff.	Khosrowzadeh et al. 2020a: Fig. 7: I; Alden 1978: fig. 6: 24; Kleiss 1987: Abb. 5: 3; Adams 1970: fig. 6: bj; Wenke 1975: fig. 7: 129; Khosrowzadeh and 'Ali 1383 [2004]: Fig. 58: 34.	The Susiana sample is glazed and has different technical features.
4	FS.194: 1	1. Wheel 2. High-fired 3. Orange buff 4. Stone and sandy grit with chaff and fine limestone particles 5. Medium.	FS. 104: 6; FS. 160: 9; FS. 190: 6; Alden 1978: fig.6: 22; Adams 1970: fig. 6: bj; Keall and Keall 1981: fig. 18: 1; Whitcomb 1987: fig. E: s.	The Bushehr example has a smaller rim diameter and different technical features.

5	FS.138: 4	1. Wheel 2. Well-fired 3. Buff 4. Grit 5. Medium.	Azarnoush 1994: fig. 182: a; Adams 1970: fig. 6: bj; Khosrowzadeh and ʿAli 1383 [2004]: Fig. 14: 5.	The last parallel, with a slightly different form, has smaller rim diameter.
6	FS.117: 2	1. Wheel 2. Well-fired 3. Red 4. Grit 5. Medium.	Whitcomb 1987: fig. D: o; Trinkaus 1986: fig. 17: 8; Stronach 1978b: Fig. 124: 5	With a larger rim diameter than the first two parallels.
7	FS.160: 5	1. Wheel 2. High-fired 3. Orange buff 4. Stone and sandy grit with chaff and fine limestone particles 5. Medium.	Whitcomb 1987: fig. E: k.	With a larger rim diameter.
8	FS.160: 2	1. Wheel 2. Low-fired 3. Grey, brown 4. Stone and sandy grit with occasional fine limestone particles 5. Medium 7. Slip, reddish buff.	Alden 1978: fig. 6: 24; Azarnoush 1994: fig. 171: k; Wenke 1975: fig. 7: 129; ʿAli and Khosrowzadeh 1385 [2006]: Fig. 1: 59.	With a larger rim diameter than the third parallel.
9	FS.160: 9	1. Wheel 2. Low-fired 3. Light grey, orange 4. Stone and sandy grit with occasional fine limestone particles 5. Medium.	FS. 194: 1; Whitcomb 1987: fig. E: s; Wenke 1975: fig. 10: 431; Keall and Keall 1981: fig. 19: 13	
10	FS.042: 2	1. Wheel 2. Well-fired 3. Orange buff 4. Stone and sandy grit with occasional fine limestone particles 5. Medium 8. Slip, buff.	Alden 1978: fig. 6: 24; Whitcomb 1985: fig. 52; Trinkaus 1986: fig. 12: 4; Lecomte 1987: Pl. 56: 12; Wenke 1975: fig. 12: 634; Keall and Keall 1981: fig. 19: 13; ʿAli and Khosrowzadeh 1385 [2006]: Fig. 1: 59.	With a larger rim diameter, except for the Malyan specimen.

Table 5.7 (continued)

No.	Site Identifier	Description (1. Manufacture 2. Firing 3. Fabric Colour (Core Ext. Int.) 4. Inclusion 5. Finish 6. Decoration 7. Exterior Coating. Colour. Treatment 8. Interior Coating. Colour. Treatment)	Reference	Notes
11	FS.158: 3	1. Wheel 2. Well-fired 3. Light buff 4. Stone and sandy grit with occasional fine limestone particles 5. Medium.	Azarnoush 1994: fig. 171: k; Alden 1978: fig. 6: 23; 'Ali and Khosrowzadeh 1385 [2006]: Fig. 59: 1.	
12	FS.117: 1	1. Wheel 2. Well-fired 3. Buff 4. Stone and sandy grit with occasional fine limestone particles 5. Medium.	Wenke 1975: fig. 11: 526; Keall and Keall 1981: 18: 13; 'Ali and Khosrowzadeh 1385 [2006]: Fig. 54: 1; Khosrowzadeh and 'Ali 1383 [2004]: Fig. 13: 6.	The last two parallels lack the groove.
13	FS.163: 4	1. Wheel 2. Low-fired 3. Black, orange 4. Stone and sandy grit with chaff and occasional fine limestone particles 5. Coarse.	Alden 1978: fig. 6: 23; Whitcomb 1985: fig. 52: q; Keall and Keall 1981: fig. 18: 3; 'Ali and Khosrowzadeh 1385 [2006]: Fig.59: 1.	With a slightly different profile from the last two parallels.
14	FS.160: 4	1. Wheel 2. Well-fired 3. Buff 4. Stone and sandy grit with occasional fine limestone particles 5. Medium.	Boucharlat and Labrousse 1979: fig. 26: 15; Adams 1970: fig. 6: bk; Wenke 1975: fig. 12: 626; Keall and Keall 1981: fig. 19: 20; Khosrowzadeh and 'Ali 1383 [2004]: Fig. 13: 4.	

15	FS.120: 1	1. Wheel 2. Low-fired 3. Grey, orange 4. Stone and sandy grit with occasional fine limestone particles 5. Medium.	Wenke 1975: fig. 7: 132; 'Ali and Khosrowzadeh 1385 [2006]: Fig. 61: 10; Keall and Keall 1981: fig. 18: 12.	With a slightly different profile from the last two parallels.
16	FS.190: 1	1. Wheel 2. Low-fired 3. Light grey, orange buff 4. Stone and sandy grit with occasional fine limestone particles 5. Medium.		
17	FS.190: 6	1. Wheel 2. Well-fired 3. Light brown 4. Stone and sandy grit with occasional fine limestone particles 5. Medium.	FS. 104: 6; FS. 181: 3; FS. 194: 1; Alden 1978: fig.6: 22; Keall and Keall 1981: fig. 19: 11.	
18	FS.104: 6	1. Wheel 2. Well-fired 3. Orange 4. Stone and sandy grit with occasional fine limestone particles 5. Medium.	FS. 190: 6; FS. 194: 1; Alden 1978: fig.6: 22; Wenke 1975: fig. 7: 131; 'Ali and Khosrowzadeh 1385 [2006]: Fig. 3: 58.	
19	FS.181: 3	1. Wheel 2. Well-fired 3. Beige 4. Stone and sandy grit with occasional fine limestone particles 5. Medium 7. Slip, brownish buff 8. Slip, brownish buff.	FS. 104; FS. 190: 6; Keall and Keall 1981: fig. 19: 12.	

Table 5.8 Description of Figure 5.8

No.	Site Identifier	Description (1. Manufacture 2. Firing 3. Fabric Colour (Core Ext. Int.) 4. Inclusion 5. Finish 6. Decoration 7. Exterior Coating. Colour. Treatment 8. Interior Coating. Colour. Treatment)	Reference	Notes
1	FS.181: 8	1. Wheel 2. Well-fired 3. Buff 4. Stone and sandy grit with occasional fine limestone particles 5. Medium.	Whitcomb 1985: fig. 52: q.	The parallel lacks the troughed rim and is burnished.
2	FS.160: 8	1. Wheel 2. Well-fired 3. Orange 4. Stone and sandy grit with occasional fine limestone particles 5. Medium.	FS. 042: 10; Trinkas 1986: fig. 17: 7; Wenke 1975: fig. 12: 602; Keall and Keall 1981: fig. 20: 23; Khosrowzadeh and 'Ali 1383 [2004]: Fig. 13: 8.	
3	FS.042: 10	1. Wheel 2. Well-fired 3. Buff 4. Stone and sandy grit with occasional fine limestone particles 5. Medium.	FS. 160: 8; Adams 1970: fig. 6: aw; Wenke 1975: fig. 11: 526; Keall and Keall 1981: fig. 18: 22; Khosrowzadeh and 'Ali 1383 [2004]: Fig. 13: 9.	With a slight profile difference.
4	FS.191: 3	1. Wheel 2. Low-fired 3. Light grey, light orange 4. Stone and sandy grit with occasional fine to large particles of limestone 5. Medium.	Boucharlat and Labrousse 1979: fig. 26: 12; Keall and Keall 1981: fig. 18: 3.	With a slight profile difference, the parallels lack the groove.

	No.	Description	Parallels	Notes
5	FS.087: 1	1. Wheel 2. High-fired 3. Light orange 4. Stone and sandy grit with occasional fine to large particles of limestone 5. Medium 7. Slip, cream.	Lecomte 1987: Pls. 51: 10 and 62: 2; Wenke 1975: fig. 8: 333; 'Ali and Khosrowzadeh 1385 [2006]: Fig. 3: 56.	The parallels lack slip.
6	FS.205: 1	1. Wheel 2. High-fired 3. Light green 4. Stone and sandy grit with occasional fine to large particles of limestone 5. Medium 7. Slip, cream.	Wenke 1975: fig. 10: 433.	With a slight profile difference.
7	FS.170: 2	1. Wheel 2. High-fired 3. Light green 4. Stone and sandy grit with occasional fine to large particles of limestone 5. Medium 7. Slip, cream.	Boucharlat and Labrousse 1979: fig. 26: 13; Wenke 1975: fig. 12: 638.	The first parallel lacks the lid-seated rim and has a rib.
8	FS.205: 5	1. Wheel 2. High-fired 3. Light orange, reddish orange 4. Stone and sandy grit with occasional fine particles of limestone 5. Medium 7. Slip, buff.	Keall and Keall 1981: fig. 18: 30; 'Ali and Khosrowzadeh 1385 [2006]: Fig. 2: 56.	
9	FS.119: 2	1. Wheel 2. Low-fired 3. Grey, reddish brown, grey 4. Stone and sandy grit with occasional fine limestone particles 5. Medium 6. Incised decoration.	Khosrowzadeh et al. 2020a: Fig. 7: d	

Table 5.8 (continued)

No.	Site Identifier	Description (1. Manufacture 2. Firing 3. Fabric Colour (Core Ext. Int.) 4. Inclusion 5. Finish 6. Decoration 7. Exterior Coating. Colour. Treatment 8. Interior Coating. Colour. Treatment)	Reference	Notes
10	FS.134: 4	1. Wheel 2. Low-fired 3. Grey, reddish brown, grey 4. Stone and sandy grit with occasional fine limestone particles 5. Medium 6. Incised decoration.	FS. 160: 3; FS. 163: 2; Khosrowzadeh et al. 2020a: Fig. 7: d; Adams 1970: fig. 10: ah.	The second parallel lacks the groove and incised decoration.
11	FS.160: 3	1. Wheel 2. Low-fired 3. Dark grey, reddish brown, dark grey 4. Stone and sandy grit with occasional fine limestone particles 5. Medium 6. Incised decoration.	FS. 134: 4; FS. 163: 6; Khosrowzadeh et al. 2020a: Fig. 7: d; Trinkaus 1986: fig. 13: 7; Wenke 1975: fig. 11: 503; 'Ali and Khosrowzadeh 1385 [2006]: Fig. 63: 17.	
12	FS.160: 6	1. Wheel 2. Low-fired 3. Dark grey, reddish brown, dark grey 4. Stone and sandy grit with occasional fine limestone particles 5. Medium 6. Incised decoration.	Khosrowzadeh et al. 2020a: Fig. 7: d; Whitcomb 1987: fig. G: j; Wenke 1975: fig. 10: 410.	The last parallel lacks decoration.
13	FS.163: 2	1. Wheel 2. Low-fired 3. Dark grey, reddish brown, dark grey 4. Stone and sandy grit with occasional fine limestone particles 5. Medium 6. Incised decoration.	FS. 134: 4; Khosrowzadeh et al. 2020a: Fig. 7: d; Keall and Keall 1981: fig. 16: 22.	

		1.	2.	
14	FS.163: 6	1. Wheel 2. Low-fired 3. Dark grey, reddish brown, dark grey 4. Stone and sandy grit with occasional fine limestone particles 5. Medium.	FS. 160: 3; Lecomte 1987: Pl. 63: 3.	With a slight profile difference, the parallel is plain.
15	FS.119: 4	1. Wheel 2. Low-fired 3. Dark grey, reddish brown, dark grey 4. Stone and sandy grit with occasional fine limestone particles 5. Medium.	Wenke 1975: fig. 11: 503; Whitcomb 1987: fig. G: j; Adams 1970: fig. 10: ah.	The last two parallels are decorated.
16	FS.119: 5	1. Wheel 2. Low-fired 3. Dark grey, reddish brown, dark grey 4. Stone and sandy grit with occasional fine limestone particles 5. Medium.		
17	FS.120: 3	1. Wheel 2. Low-fired 3. Dark grey, reddish brown, dark grey 4. Stone and sandy grit with occasional fine limestone particles 5. Medium 6. Incised decoration.	FS. 121: 1; Whitcomb 1987: fig G: j; Wenke 1975: fig. 11: 512; Keall and Keall 1981: fig. 16: 22.	
18	FS.121: 1	1. Wheel 2. Low-fired 3. Dark grey, reddish brown, dark grey 4. Stone and sandy grit with occasional fine limestone particles 5. Medium.	FS. 120: 3; Adams 1970: fig. 10: ah; Wenke 1975: fig. 11: 503	
19	FS.134: 6	1. Wheel 2. Well-fired 3. Buff 4. Stone and sandy grit with occasional fine limestone particles 5. Medium.	Eqbal 1976: fig. 46: k; Wenke 1975: fig. 11: 503; Lecomte 1987: Pl. 63: 2.	
20	FS.170: 3	1. Wheel 2. Low-fired 3. Dark grey, light grey 4. Stone and sandy grit with occasional fine limestone particles 5. Medium.	Khosrowzadeh and ʿĀli 1383 [2004]: Fig. 13: 7.	

Table 5.8 (continued)

No.	Site Identifier	Description (1. Manufacture 2. Firing 3. Fabric Colour (Core Ext. Int.) 4. Inclusion 5. Finish 6. Decoration 7. Exterior Coating. Colour. Treatment 8. Interior Coating. Colour. Treatment)	Reference	Notes
21	FS.170: 4	1. Wheel 2. Low-fired 3. Dark grey, reddish brown 4. Stone and sandy grit with occasional fine limestone particles 5. Medium.	Alden 1978: fig. 5: 9; Wenke 1975: fig. 11: 503.	The first parallel has incised decoration and a larger rim diameter.
22	FS.042: 8	1. Wheel 2. Low-fired 3. Dark grey, reddish brown 4. Stone and sandy grit with occasional fine limestone particles 5. Medium.	Adams 1970: fig. 6: bo.	With a slight form difference.
23	FS.042: 1	1. Wheel 2. High-fired 3. Reddish orange 4. Stone and sandy grit with occasional fine limestone particles 5. Medium.		
24	FS.042: 6	1. Wheel 2. Low-fired 3. Grey 4. Stone and sandy grit with occasional fine limestone particles 5. Medium.	Lecomte 1987: Pl. 64: 1; Wenke 1975: fig. 9: 310; ʻAli and Khosrowzadeh 1385 [2006]: Fig. 3: 65.	As FS.042: 8.
25	FS.110: 3	1. Wheel 2. High-fired 3. Brownish orange 4. Stone and sandy grit with occasional fine limestone particles 5. Coarse 7. Slip, cream 8. Slip, cream.	FS. 170: 6; Wenke 1975: fig. 9: 310	

No.	FS code	Description	Parallels	Comments
26	FS.119: 1	1. Wheel 2. Low-fired 3. Grey, brownish red 4. Stone and sandy grit with occasional fine limestone particles 5. Medium 6. Incised decoration.	Azarnoush 1994: fig. 174: n; Wenke 1975: fig. 9: 310; Keall and Keall 1981: fig. 12: 13.	With a slight profile and rim diameter difference.
27	FS.170: 6	1. Wheel 2. Low-fired 3. Grey, brownish red 4. Stone and sandy grit with occasional fine limestone particles 5. Medium.	FS. 110: 3; Lecomte 1987: Pl. 54: 11; Wenke 1975: fig. 10: 401; 'Ali and Khosrowzadeh 1385 [2006]: Fig. 3: 65.	
28	FS.119: 6	1. Wheel 2. Low-fired 3. Grey, brownish red 4. Stone and sandy grit with occasional fine limestone particles 5. Medium.	Azarnoush 1994: fig 164: a; Whitcomb 1987: fig. E: b; Venco Ricciardi 1970: fig. 94: No. 70; Trinkaus 1986: fig. 13: 1; Wenke 1975: fig. 13: 705; 'Ali and Khosrowzadeh 1385 [2006]: Fig. 16: 8.	With a larger rim diameter.
29	FS.120: 4	1. Wheel 2. Low-fired 3. Grey, brownish red 4. Stone and sandy grit with occasional fine limestone particles 5. Medium.	Wenke 1975: fig. 10: 402; Trinkaus 1986: fig. 13: 15; Lecomte 1987: Pl. 54: 11; Keall and Keall 1981: fig. 16: 12; Whitcomb 1987: fig. E: b; 'Ali and Khosrowzadeh 1385 [2006]: Fig. 16: 6.	With a slightly different form from the last two parallels.
30	FS.120: 5	1. Wheel 2. Low-fired 3. Grey, orange red 4. Stone and sandy grit with occasional fine limestone particles 5. Medium.	Trinkaus 1986: fig. 13: 13; Wenke 1975: fig. 10: 404	The first parallel has a smaller rim diameter and troughed rim.

Table 5.9 Description of Figure 5.9

No.	Site Identifier	Description (1. Manufacture 2. Firing 3. Fabric Colour (Core Ext. Int.) 4. Inclusion 5. Finish 6. Decoration 7. Exterior Coating. Colour. Treatment 8. Interior Coating. Colour. Treatment)	Reference	Notes
1	FS.138: 3	1. Wheel 2. Low-fired 3. Grey, orange red 4. Stone and sandy grit with occasional fine to large limestone particles 5. Medium.	Khosrowzadeh et al. 2020a: Fig. 6: d; Azarnoush 1994: fig. 190: e	
2	FS.138: 5	1. Wheel 2. Low-fired 3. Grey, orange red 4. Stone and sandy grit with occasional fine to large limestone particles 5. Medium.	Khosrowzadeh et al. 2020a: Fig. 6: d; Azarnoush 1994: fig. 190: e	The second parallel has a smaller rim diameter and ribs but lacks the groove.
3	FS.120: 2	1. Wheel 2. Low-fired 3. Grey, orange red 4. Stone and sandy grit with occasional fine to large limestone particles 5. Medium.	Khosrowzadeh et al. 2020a: Fig. 6: e; Wenke 1975: fig. 9: 310; 'Ali and Khosrowzadeh 1385 [2006]: Fig. 9: 310.	With a slightly different profile from the second and last parallels.
4	FS.120: 6	1. Wheel 2. High-fired 3. Light orange buff 4. Sand 5. Medium 7. Slip, orange buff 8. Slip, orange buff.	Trinkaus 1986: fig. 18: 4.	With a slight profile difference.
5	FS.119: 11	1. Wheel 2. High-fired 3. Reddish brown 4. Stone and sandy grit with occasional fine limestone particles 5. Medium 7. Slip, orange buff 8. Slip, orange buff.	Wenke 1975: fig. 11: 510; Keall and Keall 1981: fig. 14: 23.	As FS.120: 6.

6	FS.205: 3	1. Wheel 2. High-fired 3. Reddish brown 4. Stone and sandy grit with occasional fine limestone particles 5. Medium.	Wenke 1975: fig 11: 510; Keall and Keall 1981: fig. 12: 6; Whitcomb 1987: fig. H: cc.	As FS.120: 6.
7	FS.160: 7	1. Wheel 2. Well-fired 3. Buff 4. Stone and sandy grit with occasional fine limestone particles 5. Medium.	Khosrowzadeh et al. 2020a: Fig. 7: c; Trinkaus 1986: fig. 13: 6; Wenke 1975: fig. 7: 202; Keall and Keall 1981: fig. 10: 15.	
8	FS.181: 4	1. Wheel 2. Well-fired 3. Brownish buff 4. Stone and sandy grit with occasional fine limestone particles 5. Medium 7. Slip, brownish orange.	Khosrowzadeh et al. 2020a: Fig. 7: b; Trinkaus 1986: fig. 13: 6; Wenke 1975: fig. 11: 505.	
9	FS.104: 1	1. Wheel 2. Well-fired 3. Orange 4. Stone and sandy grit with occasional fine limestone particles 5. Medium 6. Pinched decoration 7. Slip, cream buff.	Whitcomb 1985: fig. 48: o; Trinkaus 1986: fig. 13: 1; Wenke 1975: fig. 10: 401; Keall and Keall 1981: fig. 16: 13.	With a slight profile difference and without the pinched decoration.
10	FS.163: 3	1. Wheel 2. low-fired 3. Dark grey, reddish brown 4. Stone and sandy grit with occasional fine limestone particles 5. Medium 7. Slip, cream buff.	Azarnoush 1994: fig. 171: f; Trinkaus 1986: fig. 18: 5; Lecomte 1987: Pl. 54: 17; Khosrowzadeh and 'Ali 1383 [2004]: Fig. 13: 3.	The Damghan example lacks the handle.
11	FS.191: 2	1. Wheel 2. Well-fired 3. Buff 4. Grit 5. Medium 7. Slip, greenish buff.	Khosrowzadeh et al. 2020a: Fig. 7: f; Trinkaus 1986: fig. 20: 5; Omrani Rekavandi et al. 2008: Fig. 18: 11.	The first parallel has a lug handle.

Table 5.9 (continued)

No.	Site Identifier	Description (1. Manufacture 2. Firing 3. Fabric Colour (Core Ext. Int.) 4. Inclusion 5. Finish 6. Decoration 7. Exterior Coating. Colour. Treatment 8. Interior Coating. Colour. Treatment)	Reference	Notes
12	FS.163: 10	1. Wheel 2. Low-fired 3. Dark grey, brown 4. Stone and sandy grit 5. Medium.	Adams 1970: fig. 6: bl; Keall and Keall 1981: fig. 11: 16.	With a slight profile difference.
13	FS.138: 1	1. Wheel 2. Well-fired 3. Red 4. Stone and sandy grit with occasional fine limestone particles 5. Medium.	Keall and Keall 1981: fig. 11: 3; Stronach 1978b: Fig. 124: 9.	
14	FS.134: 1	1. Wheel 2. Well-fired 3. Red 4. Stone and sandy grit with occasional fine limestone particles 5. Medium 7. Slip, buff.	FS. 104: 2; Keall and Keall 1981: fig. 11: 15.	The parallel has more ribs.
15	FS.104: 2	1. Wheel 2. Well-fired 3. Red 4. Stone and sandy grit with occasional fine limestone particles 5. Medium 7. Slip, buff.	FS. 134: 1; Whitcomb 1985: fig. 42: f; Keall and Keall 1981: fig. 11: 3; Stronach 1978b: Fig. 124: 9; Khosrowzadeh et al. 2020a: Fig. 6: a.	With a slight profile difference.
16	FS.191: 1	1. Wheel 2. Well-fired 3. Grey, orange 4. Stone and sandy grit with occasional fine to large limestone particles 5. Coarse 7. Slip, orange buff.		

17	FS.195: 2	1. Wheel 2. Well-fired 3. Grey, reddish orange 4. Stone and sandy grit with occasional fine to large limestone particles 5. Medium 7. Slip, orange buff 8. Slip, orange buff.	Whitcomb 1985: fig. 43: j; Keall and Keall 1981: fig. 11: 15; Khosrowzadeh et al. 2020a: Fig. 6: a.	The first two parallels are differently decorated.
18	FS.119: 3	1. Wheel 2. Well-fired 3. Grey 4. Stone and sandy grit 5. Coarse.		
19	FS.037: 1	1. Wheel 2. Well-fired 3. Orange 4. Stone and sandy grit with occasional fine to large limestone particles 5. Medium.	Azarnoush 1994: fig. 184: b; Whitcomb 1985: fig. 42: b; Venco Ricciardi 1970: fig. 91: No. 42; Trinkaus 1986: fig. 14: 13; Lecomte 1987: Pl. 66: 5.	With a slightly different profile.
20	FS.042: 3	1. Wheel 2. Well-fired 3. Orange 4. Stone and sandy grit 5. Medium 7. Slip, buff.	Alden 1978: fig. 6: 12; Whitcomb 1985: fig. 42: f.	
21	FS.042: 4	1. Wheel 2. Well-fired 3. Brownish orange 4. Stone and sandy grit with occasional fine to large limestone particles 5. Medium 6. Wavy and straight horizontal grooves 7. Slip, brownish orange.	Kleiss 1987: abb. 12: 8; Keall and Keall 1981: fig. 32: 9; Khosrowzadeh and ʿAli 1383 [2004]: Fig. 17: 5.	With different decoration.
22	FS.042: 5	1. Wheel 2. Well-fired 3. Brownish buff 4. Stone and sandy grit 5. Medium 7. Slip, reddish buff.	Whitcomb 1985: fig. 42: h; Keall and Keall 1981: fig. 11: 3.	The first sample has ribs.

Table 5.9 (continued)

No.	Site Identifier	Description (1. Manufacture 2. Firing 3. Fabric Colour (Core Ext. Int.) 4. Inclusion 5. Finish 6. Decoration 7. Exterior Coating. Colour. Treatment 8. Interior Coating. Colour. Treatment)	Reference	Notes
23	FS.205: 4	1. Wheel 2. High-fired 3. Brownish red 4. Stone and sandy grit 5. Medium 7. Slip, buff.	Khosrowzadeh et al. 2020a: Fig. 6: c; Wenke 1975: fig. 10: 406; Keall and Keall 1981: fig. 14: 32; Whitcomb 1985: fig. 43: l; Stronach 1978b: Fig. 124: 6.	The last three parallels are decorated.
24	FS.163: 1	1. Wheel 2. High-fired 3. Orange buff 4. Stone and sandy grit with occasional fine limestone particles 5. Medium.	Khosrowzadeh and ʿĀli 1383 [2004]: Fig. 13: 1.	With a larger rim diameter.
25	FS.163: 5	1. Wheel 2. High-fired 3. Light grey, orange buff 4. Stone and sandy grit with occasional fine to large limestone particles 5. Medium.	Khosrowzadeh and ʿĀli 1383 [2004]: Fig. 13: 1; Keall and Keall 1981: fig. 11: 15.	The second parallel is plain.
26	FS.181: 2	1. Wheel 2. Low-fired 3. Dark grey, orange buff 4. Stone and sandy grit with occasional fine limestone particles 5. Medium.	Keall and Keall 1981: fig. 11: 15.	The parallel has a troughed rim.
27	FS.181: 6	1. Wheel 2. High-fired 3. Buff, Pinkish buff 4. Stone and sandy grit with occasional fine limestone particles 5. Medium.	Azarnoush 1994: fig. 188: e; Trinkaus 1986: fig. 1; Keall and Keall 1981: fig. 12: 20.	With a slight profile decoration.

Bibliography

ANCIENT SOURCES

Abi-Ya'qub (1977), *Al-baldan, Iran's Section*, transl. A. Azarnoush, Tehran: Boniyād-e farhang-e irān.

Abolghasem Ferdowsi (1384 [2006]), *Shāhnāme-ye ferdowsi, bar asās-e chāpp-e moskow* [Fredowsi's Shāhnāme, based on the Moskow Manuscript], Tehran: Afkār.

Abu Abdallah ibn Battuta (1371 [1993]), *The Travels of Ibn Battuta*, transl. M. A. Movahhed, Tehran: Āgāh.

Abu-Eshāgh Ibrāhim Istakhrī (1340 [1961]), *Masālek va Mamālek. Persian Translation of Masālek al-Mamālek* (Persian Texts Series 9), supervised by I. Afshār, Tehran: Bongāh-e tajome va nashr-e ketāb.

Abu'l-Ḥasan Ḥamza Eṣfahāni (1844–8), *Ketāb ta'riḵ seni moluk al-arż wa'l-anbiā'*, ed. and Latin transl. J. M. E. Gottwaldt, 2 vols, St Petersburg and Leipzig: Vogel.

Abu Yusof Abu Ḥanifa Dinavari (1960), *al-Aḵbār al-ṭewāl*, 'Abd-al-Mon'em 'Āmer and Jamāl-al-Din Šayyāl (eds), Cairo: Dār 'ehiyā' al-kotob al-'arabia.

Al-Balādhori (1866), *Futūḥ al-Buldān*, ed. M. J. de Goeje, Leiden: Brill.

al-Mas'ūdī (1861–77), *Kitāb Murūǧ al-ḍahab* (Les prairies d'or), ed. and French transl. C. B. de Meynard and A. P. de Courteille, 9 volumes, Paris: Société Asiatique.

Ammianus Marcellinus (1939–50), *Rerum gestarum libri qui supersunt* (Loeb Classical Library), ed. and transl. J. C. Rolfe, 3 vols, London: Heinemann.

Anania Širakac'i/ps. Movsēs Xorenac'i (2003), *Ašxarhac'oyc' (Geography)* [Long and Short Recensions] (Matenagirk' Hayoc', Vol. II), pp. 2,123–92, Ant'ilias: Calouste Gulbenkian Foundation.

Arrian (1876), *The Indica of Arrian*, transl. W. McCrindle, Bombay: Education Society's Press, Byculla.

Arrian (1967), *Anabasis Alexandri*, transl. E. I. Robson, 2 vols, vol. 1, London: Heinemann; Cambridge, MA: Harvard University Press.

Arrian (1967), *Anabasis Alexandri*, transl. E. I. Robson, 2 vols, vol. 2, London: Heinemann; Cambridge, MA: Harvard University Press.

Beaulieu, P. A. (1989), *The Reign of Nabonidus, King of Babylon 556–539 B.C.* (Yale Near Eastern Research, 10), New Haven; London: Yale University Press.

Bedjan, P. (ed.) (1891), 'Martyrdom of the Captives', in *acta martyrtum et sanctorum II*, pp. 316–24, Paris: Otto Harrrasowitz.

Bedjan, P. (ed.) (1897), *Martyrdom of Pethion, Adurhormizd, and Anahid*, in P. Bedjan (ed.), *Acta martyrum et sanctorum II*, pp. 559–631, Leipzig and Paris: Otto Harrassowitz.

Cereti, C. (ed. and transl.) (1995), *Zand ī Wahman Yasn, A Zoroastrian Apocalypse*, Rome: Istituto Italiano per il Medio ed Estremo Oriente.

Cereti, C. and G. Terribili (2014), 'The Middle Persian and Parthian Inscriptions on the Paikuli Tower. New Blocks and Preliminary Studies', *Iranica Antiqua*, 49: 347–412.

Chabot, J.-B. (1902), *Synodicon Orientale, ou: Recueil de Synodes Nestoriens* (Notices et extraits des manuscrits de la Bibliothèque nationale et autres bibliothèques 37), Paris: Imprimerie Nationale.

Crawford, V. A. (1954), *Sumerian Economic Texts from the First Dynasty of Isin* (Babylonian Inscriptions in the Collection of James B. Nies), vol. 9, New Haven: Yale University Press.

Daryaee, T. (ed. and transl.) (2002), *Šahrestānīhā ī Ērānšahr. A Middle Persian Text on Late Antique Geography, Epic, and History: with English and Persian Translations and Commentary* (Bibliotheca Iranica, Intellectual traditions series, no. 7), Costa Mesa, CA: Mazda.

de la Fuye, A. (1913), *Documents présargoniques: deuxième partie (DP 266 a DP 467)*, Paris: Ernest Leroux, éditeur.

Dinawarī (1364 [1985]), *Akhbār al-Tiwāl*, transl. M. Mahdavi Damghani, Tehran: Ney.

Diodorus of Sicily (1947), *Diodorus of Sicily, Books XVIII and XIX 1–65* (Loeb Classical Library), ed. and transl. R. M. Geer, 10 vols, vol. 9, London: Heinemann; Cambridge, MA: Harvard University Press.

Diodorus of Sicily (1963), *Diodorus of Sicily, Books XVI 66–95 and XVII* (Loeb Classical Library), ed. and transl. C. B. Welles, 10 vols, vol. 8, London: Heinemann; Cambridge, MA: Harvard University Press.

Doustkhah, J. (ed. and transl.) (1371 [2005]), *Avesta: Kohantarin Soroudhā va Matnhā-ye Irani [Avesta: The Earliest Iranian Songs and Texts]*, 2 vols, Tehran: Morvarid.

Farahvashi, B. (ed. and transl.) (1386 [2009]). *Kārnāme-ye Ardašīr-e Bābakān* [Book of Deeds of Ardashir Pāpakān], Tehran: Tehran University Publication.

Farnbagh Dadagi (1390 [2011]), *Bondaheš*, ed. and transl. M. Bahar, Tehran: Tous.

Farroxmard i Wahrāmān (1391 [2012]), *Madiān ī Hazār Dādestān* [The Book of a Thousand Judgements], ed. and transl. S. Oriān, Tehran: 'Elmi.

Frame, G. (1999), 'The Inscription of Sargon II at Tangi-Var', *Orientalia*, 68: 31–57.

Frame, G. (2020), *The Royal Inscriptions of Sargon II, King of Assyria (721–705 BC)* (The royal Inscriptions of the Neo-Assyrian Period, RINAP 2), University Park, Pennsylvania: Eisenbrauns.

Frayne, D. R. (1990), *Old Babylonian Period (2003–1595 BC)* (The Royal Inscriptions of Mesopotamia, Early Periods, vol. 4), Toronto: University of Toronto Press, Scholarly Publishing Division.

Frayne, D. R. (ed. and transl.) (1992), *The Early Dynastic List of Geographical Names*, American Oriental Series 74, New Haven: American Oriental Society.

Frayne, D. R. (1993), *Sargonic and Gutian Periods (2334–2113 BC)* (The Royal Inscriptions of Mesopotamia, Early Periods, vol. 2), Toronto: University of Toronto Press, Scholarly Publishing Division.

Frayne, D. R. (1997), *Ur III Period (2112–2004 BC)* (The Royal Inscriptions of Mesopotamia, Early Periods, vol. 3/2), Toronto: University of Toronto Press, Scholarly Publishing Division.

Frayne, D. R. (2008), *Presargonic Period (2700–2350 BC)* (The Royal Inscriptions of Mesopotamia, Early Periods, Volume 1), Toronto: University of Toronto Press.

Fuchs, A. and S. Parpola (2001), *The Correspondence of Sargon II, Part III: Letters from Babylonia and the Eastern Provinces* (State archives of Assyria 15), Helsinki: Helsinki University Press.

Gignoux, P. (1971), 'La liste des provinces de l'Ērān dans les inscriptions de Šābuhr et de Kirdīr', *Acta Antiqua Academiae Scientiarum Hungaricae*, 19: 83–94.

Gignoux, P. (1991), *Les quatre inscriptions du Mage Kirdīr. Textes et concordances* (Collection des sources pour l'histoire de l'Asie centrale pré-islamique II/I; Studia Iranica, Cahier 9), Paris: Union Académique Internationale et Association pour l'Avancement des Études iraniennes.

Grayson, A. K. (1975), *Assyrian and Babylonian Chronicles* (Texts from Cuneiform Sources, 5), Locust Valley, NY: Augustin.

Grayson, A. K. (1991), *Assyrian Rulers of the Early First Millennium BC I (1114–859 BC)* (The Royal Inscriptions of Mesopotamia: Assyrian Periods, RIMA 2), Toronto; Buffalo; London: University of Toronto Press.

Grayson, A. K. (1996), *Assyrian Rulers of the Early First Millennium BC, II (858–745 BC)* (Royal Inscriptions of Mesopotamia Assyrian Periods, RIMA 3), Toronto; Buffalo; London: University of Toronto Press.

Grayson, A. K. and J. Novotny (2012), *The Royal Inscription of Sennacherib, King of Assyria (404–681 BC) Part 1* (The Royal Inscriptions of Neo-Assyrian period, Vol. 3/1), Winona Lake, Indiana: Eisenbrauns.

Grenet, F. (2003), *La geste d'Ardashir fils de Pābag (Kārnāmag ī Ardaxšēr ī Pābagān)*, Die: éditions A Die.

Guidi, I. (ed. and transl.) (1903), *Chronicle of Khuzistan* (Chronicon Anonymum CSCO 1–2 Scriptores Syri 1–2), Louvain: Peeters.

Hallock, R. T. (1969), *Persepolis Fortification Tablets* (Oriental Institute Publications 92). Chicago: University of Chicago Press.

Hallock, R. T. (1978), 'Selected Fortification Tablets', *Cahiers de la Délégation Archéologique Française en Iran*, 8: 109–36.

Hedāyat, Ṣ. (1321/1941a), 'Šahrestānhā-ye Irān-šahr', *Mehr*, 7(1): 47–55.

Hedāyat, Ṣ. (1321/1941b), 'Šahrestānhā-ye Irān-šahr', *Mehr*, 7(3): 169–75.

Herodotus (1899), *The Histories of Herodotus*, transl. H. Gary, New York: D. Appleton & Co.

Herodotus (1920), *The Persian Wars* (Loeb Classical Library edition), ed. and transl. A. D. Godley, 4 vols (in Greek and English, originally published 1920–5), *vol. I: Books I and II*, Cambridge, MA: Harvard University Press; London: Heinemann; New York: G. P. Putnam's Sons.

Herodotus (1921), *The Persian Wars* (Loeb Classical Library edition), ed. and transl. A. D. Godley, 4 vols (in Greek and English, originally published 1920–5), *vol. II: Books III and IV*, London: Heinemann; New York: G. P. Putnam's Sons.

Herodotus (1922), *The Persian Wars* (Loeb Classical Library edition), ed. and transl. A. D. Godley, 4 vols (in Greek and English, originally published 1920–5), *vol. III: Books V–VII*, London: Heinemann; New York: G. P. Putnam's Sons.

Hewsen, R. H. (1992), *The Geography of Ananias of Širak (Ašxarhacʿoycʿ): The Long and Short Recensions* (Beihefte zum Tübinger Atlas des Vorderen Orients: Reihe B, Geisteswissenschaften Nr. 77), Wiesbaden: Reichert.

Ibn Balxī (1385/2006), *Fārsnāme*, ed. and transl. G. Lestrenj and R. A. Nicolson, Tehran: Asātīr.

Ibn Khordādbeh (1992), *Masālek va Mamālek*, transl. S. Khakrand, Tehran: Mirās-e melal.

Isidor of Charax (1914), *The Parthian Stations (An Account of the Overland Trade Route between the Levant and India in the First Century B.C.)*, transl. and ed. W. H. Schoff, Philadelphia: The Commercial Museum.

Jacobsen, T. (1939), *The Sumerian King List* (Assyriological Studies 11), Chicago: University of Chricago Press.

Kent, R. G. (1950), *Old Persian: Grammar, Text, Lexicon*, New Haven, CT: American Oriental Society.

Kienast, B. and W. Sommerfeld (1994), *Glossar zu den altakkadischen Königsinschriften* (Freiburger Altorientalische Studien, no. 8), Stuttgart: Franz Steiner Verlag.

Kutscher, R. (1989), *The Brockmon Tablets at the University of Haifa: Royal Inscriptions*, Haifa: Haifa University Press.

Lanfranchi, G. B. and S. Parpola (1990), *The Correspondence of Sargon II, Part II: Letters from the Northern and Northeastern Provinces* (State archives of Assyria 5), Helsinki: Neo-Assyrian Text Corpus Project.

Langdon, S. (1912). *Die neubabylonischen königsinschriften*, German transl. R. Zehnpfund, Leipzig: J. C. Hinrichs.

Lesān-al-saltaneh Sepehr, A. H. (1386 [2007]), *Tārikh-e bakhtiyāri: kholāsat al-a'sār fi tārikh-al-bakhtiyār* [History of the Bakhtiyari: Compendium of Different Eras] (under the supervision of Aliqoli-khān Sardār As'ad), compiled by J. Kiān-far, Tehran: Asātir.

Livy (2018), *History of Rome* (Loeb Classical Library edition), ed. and transl. J. C. Yardley, 14 vols, *vol. X: Books 35–37*, Cambridge, MA: Harvard University Press.

Luckenbill, D. D. (ed. and transl.) (1924), *The Annals of Sennacherib* (OIP, 2), Chicago: Oriental Institute Publication.

Luckenbill, D. D. (1926), *Ancient Records of Assyria and Babylonia*, 2 vols, *vol. I: Historical Records of Assyria from the Earliest Times to Sargon*, Chicago: The University of Chicago Press.

Luckenbill, D. D. (1927) *Ancient Records of Assyria and Babylonia*, 2 vols, *vol. II: Historical Records of Assyria from Sargon to the End*, Chicago: The University of Chicago Press.

MacKenzie, D. N. (1989), 'Kerdir's Inscription (Synoptic Text in Transliteration, Transcription, Translation and Commentary)', in G. Herrmann, D. N. Mackenzie, R. H. Caldecott, *The Sasanian Rock Reliefs at Naqsh-i Rustam: Naqsh-i Rustam 6, the Triumph of Shapur I* (Iranische Denkmäler, Lieferung 13, Reihe II; Iranische Felsreliefs, I), Berlin: Dietrich Reimer.

Markwart, J. (1901), *Ērānšahr nach der Geographie des Ps. Moses Xorenac'i. Mit historisch-kritischem Kommentar und historischen und topographischen Excursen* (Abh. Gessellschaft der Wissenschaften zu Göttingen, N.F. 3/2), Berlin: Weidmann.

Markwart, J. (1931), *A Catalogue of the Provincial Capitals of Ērānshahr (Pahlavi text, version and commentary)* (Analecta orientalia, 3), ed. Giuseppe Messina, Analecta Orientalia 3, Rome: Pontificio istituto biblico.

Mohammed ibn Djarir Ṭabari (1375 [1996]), *Tārikh-e Tabari. Tārikh al-Rrosol wa al-Molouk*, Persian transl. by A. Pāyandeh, 15 vols, vol. 5, Tehran: Asātīr.

Muhammad ibn Jarir al-Tabari (1999), *The History of al-Ṭabarī (Ta'rīkh al-rusul wa'l-mulūk)*, ed. and transl. C. E. Bosworth, *vol. 5. The Sāsānids, the Byzantines, the Lakhmids, and Yemen*, Albany: State University of New York Press.

Nöldeke, T. (Ger. transl. and comm.) (1893), *Die von Guidi herausgegebene syrische Chronik, übersetzt und commentiert* (Sitzungsberichte der kaiserlichen Akademie der Wissenschaften (Philosophisch-Historische, Band 128, 9), Vienna: Tempsky.

'Omar Khayyam (1392/2013), *Nowrōznāme. A Treatise of the Origins, History, and Traditions of Nowrōz*, M. Minovi (ed.), Tehran: Asātir.

Pliny (1961), *Natural History* (Loeb Classical Library edition), 10 vols, *vol. II: Books III–VII*, transl. H. Rackham, Cambridge, MA: Harvard University Press; London: Heinemann.

Plutarch (1919), *Plutarch's Lives* (Loeb Classical Library edition), 11 vols, *vol. VIII: Sertorius, and Eumenes, Phocion and Cato the Younger*, transl. B. Perrin, London: Heinemann; New York: G. P. Putnam's Sons.

Plutarch (1962), *Plutarch's Lives* (Loeb Classical Library edition), 11 vols, *vol. XI: Aratus, Artaxerxes, Galba, Otho*, transl. B. Perrin, Cambridge, MA: Harvard University Press; London: Heinemann.

Polybius (1925), *The Histories* (Loeb Classical Library edition), in 6 vols, *vol. IV: Books 9–15*, transl. W. R. Paton, Cambridge, MA: Harvard University Press; London: Heinemann

Polybius (1968), *The Histories* (Loeb Classical Library edition), in 6 vols, *vol. VI: Books 28–39*, transl. W. R. Paton, Cambridge, MA: Harvard University Press; London: Heinemann.

Polybius (1979), *The Histories* (Loeb Classical Library edition), in 6 vols, *vol. III: Books 5–8*, transl. W. R. Paton, Cambridge, MA: Harvard University Press; London: Heinemann.

Procopius (1914), *History of the Wars* (Loeb Classical Library), ed. and transl. H. B. Dewing, 8 vols, London: Heinemann.

Quintus Curtius Rufus (1854), *Life and Exploits of Alexander the Great*, ed. and transl. W. H. Crosby, New York: D. Appleton & Co.

Rezakhani, K. and S. Bavandpour (Persian transl. and ed.) (1395 [2016]), *The Anonymous Syriac Chronicle Known as the Chronicle of Khuzistan*, Tehran: Sīnā.

Roaf, M. (2021), 'Cyaxares in Assyria', *Nouvelles Assyriologiques Brèves et Utilitaries*, 4: 277–9.

Rougemont, G. (2012), *Inscriptions grecques d'Iran et d'Asie centrale, avec des contributions de Paul Bernard* (Corpus Inscriptionum Iranicarum. Part 2, Inscriptions of the Seleucid and Parthian Periods and of Eastern Iran and Central Asia 1. Inscriptions in Non-Iranian Languages), London: School of Oriental and African Studies.

Schaudig, H. (2001), *Die Inschriften Nabonids von Babylon und Kyros, des Großen samt den in ihrem Umfelt entstandenen Tendenzschriften. Textausgabe und Grammatik* (Alter Orient und Alter Testament 256), Münster: Ugarit-Verlag.

Schmitt, R. (2009), *Die altpersischen Inschriften der Achaimeniden*, Wiesbaden: Reichert Verlag.

Sims-Williams, N. (ed. and transl.) (1985), *The Christian Sogdian Manuscript C2*, pp. 31–68, Berlin: Akademie Verlag.

Skjærvø, P. O. (1983), *The Sassanian Inscription of Paikuli. Part 3.1. Restored text and translation*, Wiesbaden: Reichert.

Skjærvø, P. O. (2006), 'A New Block from the Paikuli Inscription', *Journal of Inner Asian Art and Archaeology*, 1: 119–23.

Starr, I. (1990), *Queries to the Sungod. Divination and Politics in Sargonid Assyria* (State Archives of Assyria 4), Helsinki: Helsinki University Press.

Strabo (1854), *The Geography of Strabo*, ed. and transl. H. C. Hamilton and M. A. Falconer, London: Henry G. Bohn.

Strabo (1930), *The Geography of Strabo* (Loeb Classical Library edition), 8 vols, *vol. VII*, transl. H. L. Jones, London: Heinemann; New York: G. P. Putnam's Sons.

Strabo (1961), *The Geography of Strabo* (Loeb Classical Library edition), 8 vols, *vol. V*, transl. H. L. Jones, London: Heinemann; Cambridge, MA: Harvard University Press.

Strabo (1967), *The Geography of Strabo* (Loeb Classical Library edition), 8 vols, *vol. VIII*, transl. H. L. Jones, Cambridge, MA: Harvard University Press; London: Heinemann.

Tadmor, H. (1994), *The Inscriptions of Tiglath-Pileser III, King of Assyria. Critical Edition, with Introductions, Translations and Commentary*, Jerusalem: The Israel Academy of Sciences and Humanities.

Tadmor, H. and S. Yamada (2011), *The Royal Inscriptions of Tiglath-pileser III (744–727 BC) and Shalmaneser V (726–722 BC), Kings of Assyria* (The royal inscriptions of the Neo-Assyrian period 1), Winona Lake, Indiana: Eisenbrauns.

Tafazzoli, A. (ed. and transl.) (1354/1975), *Mēnō-ye Xerad*, Tehran: Boniyād-e farhang-e iran.

Thureau-Dangin, F. (1903), *Recueil de tablettes chaldéennes*, Paris: Ernest Leroux.

Thureau-Dangin, F. (1910), *Inventaire des tablettes de Tello conservées au Musée Impérial Ottoman 1: Textes de l'époque d'Agadé*, Paris: E. Leroux.

Xenophon (1876), *The Economist of Xenophon* (Bibliotheca Pastorum. Vol. I.), transl. A. D. O. Wedderburn and W. G. Collingwood, London: Ellis & White; Kent: George Allen.

Xenophon (1914), *Xenophon's Cyropaedia*, transl. W. Miller, 2 vols, vol. 2: Books 5–8, London: Heinemann; Cambridge, MA: Harvard University Press.

SECONDARY SOURCES

Abdi, K. (2002), *Pastoralism in the Middle Chalcolithic Period of the West Central Zagros Mountains*, PhD dissertation, University of Michigan.

Abdi, K. (2003), 'The Early Development of Pastoralism in the Zagros Mountains', *Journal of World Prehistory*, 17(4): 395–448.

Abdi, K., A. Azadi, F. Biglari, D. Farmani, S. Heydari, G. Nokandeh and M. Mashkour (2002), 'Tuwah Khoshkeh: A Middle Chalcolithic Pastoralist Campsite in the Islamabad Plain', *Iran*, 40: 43–74.

Abdi, K. and G. Beckman (2007), 'An Early Second-Millennium Cuneiform Archive from Chogha Gavaneh, Western Iran', *Journal of Cuneiform Studies*, 59: 39–92.

Abdollahi, M. and M. Sadeghi-rad (2010), *Report on the Archaeological Survey of Abdanan County, the Sixth Season*, The Organisation of Cultural Heritage, Handicrafts, and Tourism of Ilam Province [unpublished].

Adams, R. McC. (1962), 'Agriculture and Urban Life in Early Southwestern Iran', *Science*, 136(3,511): 109–22.

Adams, R. McC. (1965), *Land Behind Baghdad: A History of Settlement on the Diyala Plain*, Chicago: University of Chicago Press.

Adams, R. McC. (1970), 'Tell Abu Sarifa, A Sasanian-Islamic Ceramic Sequence from South Central Iraq', *Ars Orientalis*, 8: 87–119.

Adams, R. McC. (1981), *Heartland of Cities*, Chicago: University of Chicago Press.

Adams, R. McC. (2006), 'Intensified Large-scale Irrigation as an Aspect of Imperial Policy: Strategies of Statecraft on the Late Sasanian Mesopotamian Plain', in J. Marcus and C. Stanish (eds), *Agricultural Strategies*, pp. 17–37, Los Angeles: Cotsen Institute of Archaeology at UCLA.

Adams, R. McC. and D. P. Hansen (1968), 'Archaeological Reconnaissance and Soundings in Jundi Shapur', *Ars Orientalis*, 7: 53–73.

Adams, R. McC. and H. J. Nissen (1972), *The Uruk Countryside: The Natural Setting of Urban Societies*, Chicago: University of Chicago Press.

Adriansen, H. K. (2005), 'Pastoral Mobility: A Review', *Nomadic Peoples*, 9(1 and 2): 207–14.

Adriansen, H. K. (2008), 'Understanding Pastoral Mobility: The Case of Senegalese Fulani', *Geographical Journal*, 174(3): 207–22.

Agostini, D. and S. Shaked (2013), 'Two Sasanian Seals of Priests', *Bulletin of the Asia Institute* (New Series) 27: 99–105.

Ahanjideh, E. (1378/1999), *Chaharmahal va Bakhtiyari va tamaddon-e dirine-ye Ān* [Chaharmahal va Bakhtiyari and Its Ancient Civilization], Iṣfahan: Mash'al.

Ahmadi, A. A. (2008), *Report of the Archaeological Survey of Abdanan County, the Fourth Season*, The Organisation of Cultural Heritage, Handicrafts, and Tourism of Ilam Province [unpublished].

Ahmed, K. M. (2012), *The Beginnings of Ancient Kurdistan (c. 2500–1500 BC): A Historical and Cultural Synthesis*, PhD dissertation, Leiden University.

Alden, J. R. (1978), 'Excavation at Tal-i Malyan: Part l: A Sasanian Kiln', *Iran*, 26: 79–86.

Alden, J. R. (2013), 'The Kur River Basin in the Proto-Elamite Era. Surface Survey, Settlement Patterns, and the Appearance of Fulltime Transhumant Pastoral Nomadism', in C. A. Petrie (ed.), *Ancient Iran and Its Neighbors: Local Developments and Long-range Interactions in the Fourth Millennium BC* (British Institute of Persian Studies Archaeological Monograph 3), pp. 207–32, Oxford: Oxbow.

Alden J. R. (2015), 'Review of Nomadism in Iran: from Antiquity to the Modern Era by D. T. Potts', *Antiquity*, 89: 996–7. Available at: doi:10.15184/aqy.2015.66 (last accessed 3 July 2019).

Al-Fouadi, A.-H. (1978), 'Inscriptions and Reliefs from Bitwata', *Sumer*, 34: 122–9.

'Āli, A. and A. Khosrowzadeh (1385/2006), 'Sofāl-hā-ye dowrān-e sāsāni ta sadr-e eslām' [Ceramics of Sasanian to Early Islamic Times], in A. Moghaddam (ed.), *Archaeological Surveys of Miānāb of Shushtar*, pp. 249–97, Tehran: Iranian Center Archaeological Research.

Aliakbari, M., M. Gheitasi and E. Anonby (2015), 'On Language Distribution in Ilam Province, Iran', *Iranian Studies*, 48(6): 835–50.

Alibaigi, S. (2017), 'The Location of the Second Stele Commemorating Tiglath-Pileser III's Campaign to the East in 737 BC', in F. M. Fales, S. Ponchia and G.-B. Lanfranchi (eds), *State Archives of Assyria Bulletin 23*, pp. 47–53, Padua: Sargon Editore Padova.

Alibaigi, S., A. Shanbehzadeh and H. Alibaigi (2012), 'The Discovery of a Neo-Assyrian Rock-Relief at Mishkhas, Ilam Province (Iran)', *Iranica Antiqua*, 47: 29–40.

Alibaigi, S., N. Aminikhah and F. Fatahi (2016), 'In Searh for Ḥarḫar (the Neo-Assyrian Kar-Šarrukin) in the Central Zagros Mountains, Western Iran: A New Proposal', *Iran*, 54(2): 25–45.

Alibaigi, S. and J. MacGinnis (2018), 'Bit Ištar and Niššaya/Irnisa: In Search of the Location of Assyrian Zagros Toponyms of the 8th Century BC', in R. Eichmann and M. van Ess (eds), *Zeitschrift für Orient-Archäologie (Band 11)*, pp. 198–211, Berlin: Mann Verlag.

Alijani, B. (2008), 'Effects of the Zagros Mountains on the Spatial Distribution of Precipitation', *Journal of Mountain Science*, 5: 218–31.

Alizadeh, A. (1985), 'Elymaean Occupation of Lower Khuzestan during the Seleucid and Parthian Periods: A Proposal', *Iranica Antiqua*, 20: 175–95.

Alizadeh, A. (1988a), 'Socio-Economic Complexity in Southwestern Iran During the Fifth and Fourth Millennia B.C.: The Evidence from Tall-i Bakun A', *Iran*, 26: 17–34.

Alizadeh, A. (1988b), *Mobile Pastoralism and the Development of Complex Societies in Highland Iran: The Evidence from Tall-e Bakun A*, PhD dissertation, University of Chicago.

Alizadeh, A. (2003), 'Some Observations Based on the Nomadic Character of Fars Prehistoric Cultural Development', in N. F. Miller and K. Abdi (eds), *yeki bud, yeki nabud. Essays on the Archaeology of Iran in Honor of William M. Sumner*, pp. 83–97, Los Angeles: The Costen Institute of Archaeology at UCLA.

Alizadeh, A. (2004a), *The Origins of State Organisations in Prehistoric Highland Fars, South Central Iran*, Chicago: Oriental Institute Publications.

Alizadeh, A. (2004b), 'Mobile Pastoralism and Prehistoric Exchange', in T. Stöllner, R. Slotta and R. Vatandoust (eds), *Persiens Antike Pracht. Bergbau, Handwerk, Archäologie* (Veröffentl. Deutsches Bergbau-Museum 128), pp. 76–91, Bochum: Deutsches Bergbau-Museum.

Alizadeh, A. (2009), 'Prehistoric Mobile Pastoralists in South-Central and Southwesern Iran', in J. Szuchman (ed.), *Nomads, Tribes and the State in the Ancient Near East* (Cross-Disciplinary Perspectives. Oriental

Institute Seminars 5), pp. 129–46, Chicago: The Oriental Institute of the University of Chicago.

Alizadeh, A. (2010), 'The Rise of the Highland Elamite State in Southwestern Iran: "Enclosed" or Enclosing Nomadism?', *Current Anthropology*, 51(3): 353–83.

Alizadeh, A., A. Mahfroozi, A. Ahrar, K. Aqaii, S. Ebrahimi, T. Hartnell, M. Karami, L. Niakan, A. Zalaghi and M. Zare (2005), 'Iranian Prehistoric Project', *2004–2005 Annual Report*, pp. 56–69. Available at: oi.uchicago.edu/oi/AR/04-05/04-05_AR_TOC.html (last accessed 20 June 2008).

Alizadeh, A., L. Ahmadzadeh and M. Omidfar (2015), 'Reflections on the Long-term Socioeconomic and Political Development in the Rām Hormoz Plain, a Highland–Lowland Buffer Zone', *Archäologische Mitteilungen aus Iran und Turan*, 45: 113–48.

Alizadeh, K. (1382/2003), 'An Introduction to the Pottery from the Excavation of the Median Fortress at Bistun Near Kirmanshah', in H. Fahimi (ed.), *Archaeological Reports (2)*, Tehran: Iranian Center for Archaeological Research (in Persian).

Alizadeh, K. (2011), 'Ultan Qalası: A Fortified Site in the Sasanian Borderlands (Mughan Steppe, Iranian Azerbaijan)', *Iran*, 49: 55–77.

Alizadeh, K. (2014), 'Borderland Projects of Sasanian Empire: Intersection of Domestic and Foreign Policies', *Journal of Ancient History*, 2: 93–115.

Alizadeh, K. and J. A. Ur (2006), 'Mughan Steppe Archaeological Project, Ardabil Province', *Archaeological Reports*, 4: 49–56 (in Farsi with English abstract).

Alizadeh, K. and J. A. Ur (2007), 'Formation and Destruction of Pastoral and Irrigation Landscape on the Mughan Steppe, North-Western Iran', *Antiquity*, 81: 148–60.

Alizadeh, K., M. R. Mohammadi, S. Maziar and M. Feizkhah (2021), 'The Islamic Conquest or Flooding? Sasanian Settlements and Irrigation Systems Collapse in Mughan, Iranian Azerbaijan', *Journal of Field Archaeology*, 46(5): 316–32. https://doi.org/10.1080/00934690.2021.1913314 (last accessed 2 January 2022).

al-Jahwari, N. S., D. Kennet, S. Priestman and E. Sauer (2018), 'Fulayj: A Late Sasanian Fort on the Arabian Coast', *Antiquity*, 92(363): 724–41. Available at: 10.15184/aqy.2018.64 (last accessed 29 March 2019).

Altaweel, M., A. Marsh, S. Mühl, O. Nieuwenhuyse, K. Radner, K. Rasheed and S. A. Saber (2012), 'New Investigations in the Environment, History, and Archaeology of the Iraqi Hilly Flanks: Shahrizor Survey Project 2009–2011', *Iraq*, 74: 1–35.

Altaweel, M. and T. Paulette (2013), 'Modeling Nomad-Settlement Interactions', in T. J. Wilkinson, McG. Gibson and M. Widel (eds), *Models of Mesopotamian Landscapes: How Small-Scale Processes Contributed to the Growth of Early Civilizations* (BAR International Series 2552), pp. 204–18, Oxford: Archaeopress.

Altaweel, M., A. Marsh, J. Jotheri, C. Hritz, D. Fleitmann, S. Rost, S. F. Linter, McG. Gibson, M. Bosomworth, M. Jacobson, E. Garzanti, M. Limontana and G. Radeff (2019), 'New Insights on the Role of Environmental Dynamics Shaping Southern Mesopotamia: from the Pre-Ubaid to the Early Islamic Period', *Iraq*, 1–24. Available at: 10.1017/irq.2019.2 (last accessed 17 March 2020).

Álvarez-Mon, J. (2010), *The Arjān Tomb: At the Crossroad of the Elamite and the Persian Empires* (Acta Iranica, 49), Louvain: Peeters.

Álvarez-Mon, J. (2013), 'Braids of Glory. Elamite Sculptural Reliefs from the Highlands: Kūl-e Farah IV', in K. De Graef and J. Tavernier (eds), *Susa and Elam. Archaeological, Philological, Historical and Geographical Perspectives: Proceedings of the International Congress Held at Ghent University*, 14–17 December 2009, pp. 207–48, Leiden; Boston: Brill.

Amanollahi-Baharvand, S. (1367/1989), *Pastoral Nomadism in Iran*, Tehran: Āgāh.

Anschuetz, K. F., R. H. Wilshusen and C. L. Scheick (2001), 'An Archaeology of Landscapes: Perspectives and Directions', *Journal of Archaeological Research*, 9(2): 157–211.

Aro, S. (1998), *Tabal. Zur Geschichte und Materiellen Kultur des zentralanatolischen Hochplateaus von 1200 bis 600 v. Chr.*, Helsinki: Yliopistopaino.

Assar, G. R. F. (2004–5), 'History and Coinage of Elymais during 150/149–122/121 BC', *Nāme-ye Irān-e Bāstān*, 4(2): 27–91.

Aston, M. (2002), *Interpreting the Landscape Archaeology and Local History*, London and New York: Routledge.

Atayi, M. T. (1397/2018), 'Tappeʰ Goštāspi: An Archaeological-Linguistic Approach to a Settlement from the Middle-Elamite Period', in *The Research Week in the Account of the Iranian Center for Archaeological Research (1396/2017–1397/2018)*, Tehran: Research Institute of Cultural Heritage and Tourism (in Persian). https://www.academia.edu/84895967/%D8%B9%D8%B7%D8%A7%D8%A6%DB%8C_%D9%85%D8%AD%D9%85%D8%AF%D8%AA%D9%82%DB%8C_1397_%D8%AA%D9%BE%DB%80_%DA%AF%D8%B4%D8%AA%D8%A7%D8%B3%D9%BE%DB%8C_%D9%86%DA%AF%D8%A7%D9%87%DB%8C_%D8%A8%D8%A7%D8%B3%D8%AA%D8%A7%D9%86_%D8%B4%D9%86%D8%A7%D8%AE%D8%AA%DB%8C_%D8%B2%D8%A8%D8%A7%D9%86_%D8%B4%D9%86%D8%A7%D8%AE%D8%AA%DB%8C_%D8%A8%D9%87_%D8%A7%D8%B3%D8%AA%D9%82%D8%B1%D8%A7%D8%B1%DA%AF%D8%A7%D9%87%DB%8C_%D8%A7%D8%B2_%D8%AF%D9%88%D8%B1%DB%80_%D8%B9%DB%8C%D9%84%D8%A7%D9%85_%D9%85%DB%8C%D8%A7%D9%86%D9%87_%D8%AF%D8%B1_%D9%87%D9%81%D8%AA%DB%80_%D9%BE%DA%98%D9%88%D9%87%D8%B4_%D8%A8%D9%87_%D8%B1%D9%88%D8%A7%DB%8C%D8%AA_%D9%BE%DA%98%D9

%88%D9%87%D8%B4%DA%A9%D8%AF%D9%87_%D8%A8%
D8%A7%D8%B3%D8%AA%D8%A7%D9%86_%D8%B4%D9%8
6%D8%A7%D8%B3%DB%8C_1396_97_%D8%AE%D9%88%D8
%B1%D8%B4%DB%8C%D8%AF%DB%8C_%D8%A7%D9%86%
D8%AA%D8%B4%D8%A7%D8%B1%D8%A7%D8%AA_%D9%
BE%DA%98%D9%88%D9%87%D8%B4%DA%AF%D8%A7%D9
%87_%D9%85%DB%8C%D8%B1%D8%A7%D8%AB_%D9%81
%D8%B1%D9%87%D9%86%DA%AF%DB%8C_%D8%B5_36_31
?email_work_card=title (last accessed 20 August 2022).

Aydin, Z. N. (2004), *The Application of Multi-Sensor Remote Sensing Techniques in Archaeology*, Masters thesis, University of Mississippi.

Azadi, A. (2015), 'A Late Bronze/Early Iron Age Nomadic Site (KR 385) in the Bakhtiari Highlands, South-west Iran', *Antiquity*, 347, Project Gallery.

Azarnoush, M. (1994), *The Sasanian Manor House at Hajiabad, Iran*, Monografie di Mesopotamia lll, Florence: Casa Editorie le lettere.

Azizi, G., H. A. Faraji Sabokbar, R. A. Abaspour and T. Safarrad (2010), 'The Model of the Spatial Variability Precipitation in the Middle Zagros', *Physical Geography Research Quarterly*, 72: 35–51.

Azizi, G., M. Arsalani and E. Moghimi (2013), 'Precipitation Variations in the Central Zagros Mountains (Iran) since AD 1840 Based on Oak Tree Rings', *Palaeogeography*, 386: 96–103. Available at: 10.1016/j. palaeo.2013.05. 009 (last accessed 4 February 2016).

Bahadori, A. (2017), 'Achaemenid Empire, Tribal Confederations of Southwestern Persia and Seven Families', *Iranian Studies*, 50(2): 173–97.

Balatti, S. (2017), *Mountain Peoples in the Ancient Near East: The Case of the Zagros in the First Millennium BCE* (Classica et Orientalia 18.), Wiesbaden: Harrassowitz Verlag.

Balmaki, B. (2013), 'Examination of the Phenomenon of Population Growth in the Central Zagros during the Chalcolithic Period', talk given at the National Conference on Archaeological Studies of Western Iran, Islamic Azad University, Hamadan Branch, 5–6 May 2013.

Banning, E. B. (2002), *Archaeological Survey, Manuals in Archaeological Methods, Theory, and Technique Series*, New York: Kluwer Academic/ Plenum.

Barfi, S., M. Amiri, R. Bidari and M. H. Pak-nezhad (1391/2012), 'Gozāresh-e kōtāh-e se mohavvate-ye now-yāfte az dowre-ye sāsāni dar kāzerōn' [Brief Report of Three Newly-Found Sites from the Sasanian Period in Kazerun], in M. Bahram-zadeh (ed.), *Bastan-shenasi-e Iran* [Archaeology of Iran], 3(3), pp. 111–24, Tehran: International Institute of Tourism Studies and Hasht-mina [in Persian].

Barker, G., P. Daly and P. Newson (2006), 'Impacts of Imperialism: Nabataean, Roman, and Byzantine Landscapes in the Wadi Faynan, Southern Jordan', in E. C. Robertson, J. D. Seibert, D. C. Fernandez and M. U. Zender (eds), *Space and Spatial Analysis in Archaeology*, pp. 269–80, Canada: University of Calgary Press.

Barth, F. (1953), *Principles of Social Organisation in South Kurdistan* (Bulletin No. 7), Oslo: Universitetets Etnografiske Museum.

Barth, F. (1961), *Nomads of South Persia: The Basseri Tribe of the Khamseh Confederacy*, Boston: Little, Brown.

Bashash Kanzagh, R. (1376/1997), 'Four Samples Whispering [?!] of Treasury Objects Attributed to Kalmakara Cave Inscriptions', *Lecture in the First Archaeology Congress in Susa*, Tehran: Cultural Heritage press.

Bashash Kanzagh, R. (1379/2000), *Whispering [?!] of Treasury Objects Attributed to Kalmakara Cave*, Tehran: Deputy for Research Archaeological Research Center.

Baugher, S. and M. S. Spencer-Wood (eds) (2010), *Archaeology and Preservation of Gendered Landscapes*, New York: Springer.

Beck, L. (1980), 'Herd Owners and Hired Shepherds: The Qashqa'i of Iran', *Ethnology*, 19(3): 327–51.

Beckman, G. (2010), 'Temple Building among the Hittites', in M. J. Boda and J. Novotny (eds), *From Foundations to the Crenellations, Essays on Temple Building in the Ancient Near East and Hebrew Bible*, pp. 71–91, Münster: Ugarit-Verlag.

Bendezu-Sarmiento, J. and M. J. Jafari (2018), 'Sassanian Burials in the Tang-i Bulaghi Valley: An Archaeo-Anthropological Approach (Fars, Iran)', in S. Gondet and E. Haerinck (eds), *L'Orient est son jardin. Hommage à Rémy Boucharlat* (Acta Iranica 58), pp. 43–53, Leuven; Paris; Bristol: Peeters.

Bernabeu Auban, J., A. Moreno Martín and C. M. Barton (2012), 'Complex Systems, Social Networks and the Evolution of Social Complexity', in M. Berrocal, L. García Sanjuán and A. Gilman (eds), *The Prehistory of Iberia: Debating Early Social Stratification and the State*, pp. 23–37, New York: Routledge.

Bernard, P. (1980), 'Héraclès, les grottes de Karafto et le sanctuaire du mont Sambulos en Iran', *Studia Iranica*, 9: 301–24.

Bernbeck, R. (1989), *Die neolitische Keramik aus Qale Rostam, Bakhtiyari-Gebiet (Iran): Klassifikation, Produktionsanalyse und Datierungspotential* (Altertumswissenschaften 9 and 10), 2 vols, Rheinfelden; Freiburg [Breisgau]; Berlin: Schäuble.

Bernbeck, R. (1992), 'Migratory Patterns in Early Nomadism: A Reconsideration of Tepe Tula'i', *Paléorient*, 18(1): 77–88.

Bernbeck, R. (2008), 'An Archaeology of Multisited Communities', in W. Wendrich and H. Barnard (eds), *The Archaeology of Mobility. Old World and New World Nomadism* (Cotsen Advanced Seminar), pp. 43–77, Los Angeles: Cotsen Institute of Archaeology Press at UCLA.

Biglari, A., S. Alibaigi and M. Beiranvand (2018), 'The Stele of Sarab-e Sey Khan: A Recent Discovery of a Second-Millennium Stele on the Iranian–Mesopotamian Borderland in the Western Zagros Mountains', *Journal of Cuneiform Studies*, 70: 27–36.

Billerbeck, A. (1898), *Das Sandschak Suleimania: Und Dessen Persische Nachbarlandschaften zur Babylonischen und Assyrischen Zeit*, Leipzig: Pfeiffer.

Binford, L. R. (1982), 'The Archaeology of Place', *Journal of Anthropological Archaeology*, 1: 5–31.

Binford, L. R. (1983), 'Long-term Land Use Patterns: Some Implications for Archaeology', in L. R. Binford (ed.), *Working at Archaeology*, pp. 379–86, New York: Academic.

Binford, L. R. (2001), *Constructing Frames of Reference: An Analytical Method for Archaeological Theory Building Using Hunter-Gatherer and Environmental Sets*, Berkeley and Los Angeles: University of California Press.

Bivar, A. D. H. (1970), 'Trade between China and the Near East in the Sasanian and Early Muslim Periods', in W. Watson (ed.), *Pottery and Metalwork in T'ang China* (Percival David Foundation Colloquies on Art and Archaeology in Asia I), pp. 1–8, London: School of Oriental and African Studies.

Bivar, A. D. and S. Shaked (1964), 'The Inscription at Shimbar', *Bulletin of the School of Oriental and African Studies*, 27: 265–90.

Black-Michaud, J. (1972), 'Tyranny as a Strategy for Survival in an "Egalitarian" Society: Luri Facts Versus an Anthropological Mystique', *Man*, 7: 614–34.

Blaylock, S. (2009), *Tille Höyük 3.1: The Iron Age: Introduction, Stratification and Architecture*, The British Institute at Ankara (Monograph 41), London: The British Institute at Ankara.

Blaylock, S. (2016), *Tille Höyük 3.2: The Iron Age: Pottery, Objects and Conclusions*, The British Institute at Ankara (Monograph 50), London: The British Institute at Ankara.

Boese, J. (1973), 'Zur stilistischen und historischen Einordnung des Felsreliefs von Darband-i-Gaur', *Studia Iranica*, 2: 3–48.

Boese, J. (1982), 'Burnaburiaš II, Melišipak und die mittelbabylonische Chronologie', *Ugarit Forschungen*, 14: 15–26.

Borger, R. (1970), 'Vier Grenzsteinurkunden Merodachbaladans I. von Babylonien. Der Teheran-Kudurru, SB 33, SB 169 und SB 26', *Archiv für Orientforschung*, 23: 1–26.

Börm, H. (2016), 'A Threat or Blessing? The Sasanians and the Roman Empire', in C. Binder, H. Börm, H. and A. Luther (eds), *Diwan: Studies in the History and Culture of the Ancien Near East and Eastern Mediterranean, Festschrift für Josef Wiesehöfer zum 65 Geburtstag*, pp. 615–46, Duisburg: Wellem.

Bosworth, C. E. (1995), 'Dīnavar', in E. Yarshater (ed.), *Encyclopædia Iranica*, vol. 7(4), pp. 416–17, Costa Mesa, CA: Mazda. https://iranicaonline.org/articles/dinavar (last accessed 12 March 2019).

Boucharlat, R. (1989), 'Cairns et pseudo-cairns du Fars', in L. de Meyer and E. Haerinck (eds), *Archaeologia Iranica et Orientalis. Miscellanea in Honorem Louis Vanden Berghe*, vol. 2, pp. 675–712, Gent: Peeters.

Boucharlat, R. (2015), 'Monuments et Sites Arceologiques du "long VI siècle" en Iran', in C. Julien (ed.), *Husraw Ier Reconstructions D'un Regne: Sources et Documents* (Studio Ironic 53), pp. 11–46, Leuven: Peeters.

Boucharlat, R. (2020), 'The Citadel of Ulug Depe and the "Median Forts" in Western Iran', in K. Niknami and A. Hozhabri (eds), *The Archaeology of the Historical Period in Iran* (University of Tehran Science and Humanities Series), pp. 403–18, Cham: Springer.

Boucharlat, R. and A. Labrousse (1979), 'La Plaise d'Artaxerxes ll sur la vive droite du chaur a Suse', *Cahiers de la Délégation Archéologique Française en Iran*, 10: 19–136.

Boucharlat, R. and E. Haerinck (1991), 'Ceramics xii. The Parthian and Sasanian Periods', in E. Yarshater (ed.), *Encyclopaedia Iranica*, 5(3), pp. 304–7, Costa Mesa, CA: Mazda. https://iranicaonline.org/articles/ceramics-xii (last accessed 2 June 2015).

Boucharlat, R. and P. Lombard (2001), 'Le Bâtiment G de Rumeilah (Oasis d'al Ain). Remarques sur les Salles à Poteaux de l'Age du fer en Péninsule d'Oman', *Iranica Antiqua*, 36: 213–38.

Boucharlat, R., H.-F. Francfort and O. Lecomte (2005), 'The Citadel of Ulug Depe and the Iron Age Archaeological Sequence in Southern Central Asia', *Iranica Antiqua*, 60: 479–514.

Boyce, M. (1982), *A History of Zoroastrianism, Vol. II. Under the Achaemenians* (Handbuch der Orientalistik. Erste Abt.: der Nahe und der Mittlere Osten. Achter Bd.: Religion. Erster Abschnitt: Religionsgeschichte des Alten Orients, Lief. 2, Ht. 2A.), Leiden; Cologne: E. J. Brill.

Boyce, M. (1377/1998), *An Extract from the 'A History of Zoroastrianism'*, transl. H. San'atī-zāde, Tehran: Safī'ališāh.

Bradburd, D. (1989), 'Producing Their Fates: Why Poor Basseri Settled but Poor Komachi and Yomut Did Not', *American Ethnologist*, 16(3): 502–17.

Branting, S. (2010), 'Excavations at the "Temple", in G. Summers, F. Summers, S. Branting and N. Yüney (eds), *The Kerkenes Project, A Preliminary Report on the 2010 Season*, pp. 44–54. http://www.kerkenes.metu.edu.tr/kerk2/01reports/pdf/09kerkreportdj.pdf (last accessed 26 May 2018).

Branting, S., S. Baltal Tırpan and J. Lehner (2011), 'New Investigations in an Urban Block', in Y. Hazirlayan, F. Summers and G. Summers (eds), *Kerkenes News* 14, pp. 5–7, Ankara: Metu Press.

Briant, P. (1973), *Antigone le borgne: Les débuts de sa carrière et les problème de l'assemblée macédonienne* (Annales littéraires de l'Université de Besançon, 152), Paris: Les Belles Lettres.

Briant, P. (1976), 'Brigandage: Dissidence et conquête en Asie Achéménide et Hellénistique', *dialogues d'histoire ancienne*, 2/1: 163–258.

Briant, P. (1979), 'Des Achéménides aux rois hellénistiques: continuités et ruptures (Bilan et propositions)', *Annali della Scuola Normale Superiore di Pisa. Classe di Lettere e Filosofia, Serie III* 9(4): 1,375–414 = *Rois, tributs et paysans* (1982): 293–330.

Briant, P. (1982a), *État et pasteurs au Moyen-Orient ancient* (MSH: Collection Production Pastorale et Societe), Cambridge: Cambridge University Press.

Briant, P. (1982b), *Rois, tributs, et paysans: études sur les formations tributaires du Moyen-Orient ancien* (Annales littéraires de l'Université de Besançon), Paris: Les Belles lettres.

Briant, P. (1984), *L'Asie centrale et les royaumes proche-orientaux du premier millénaire (c. VIIIe–IVe siècles avant notre ère)*, Paris: E. R. C.

Briant, P. (1985), 'Les Iraniens d'Asie Mineure après la chute des achéménide. A propos de l'inscription d'Amyzon', *Dialogues d'histoire ancienne*, 11: 166–95.

Briant, P. (2002), *From Cyrus to Alexander. A History of the Persian Empire*, transl. P. T. Daniels, Indiana: Winona Lake.

Briant, P. (2006), 'L'Asie mineure en transition', in P. Briant and F. Joannès (eds), *La transition entre l'empire achéménide et les royaumes hellénistiques (Persika 9)*, pp. 306–51, Paris: Civilisation.

Briant, P. (2009), 'Alexander the Great', transl. A. Kuhrt, in G. Boys-Stones, B. Graziosi and P. Vasunia (eds), *The Oxford Handbook of Hellenistic Studies*, pp. 77–85, Oxford: Oxford University Press.

Briant, P. (2012), 'From the Indus to the Mediterranean: The Administrative Organisation and Logistics of the Great Roads of the Achaemenid Empire', in S. E. Alcock, J. Bodel and J. A. Talbert (eds), *Highways, Byways and Road Systems in the Pre-Modern World*, pp. 185–201, New York: Wiley.

Briant, P., W. F. M. Henkelman and M. W. Stolper (eds) (2008), *L'archive des fortifications de Persepolis: État des questions et perspectives de recherches* (Persika 12), Paris: De Boccard.

Brinkman, J. A. (1968), *A Political History of Post-Kassite Babylonia* (Analecta Orientalia 43), Rome: Pontificium Institutum Biblicum.

Brinkman, J. A. (1976–80), 'Kassiten', *Reallexikon der Assyriologie*, 5: 464–73.

Brixhe, C. (2008), 'The Phrygian Inscriptions', in C. M. Draycott and G. D. Summers (eds), *Kerkenes Special Studies 1, Sculpture and Inscriptions from the Monumental Entrance to the Palatial Complex at Kerkenes Daq, Turkey* (Oriental Institute Publications, Vol. 135), pp. 71–6, Chicago: University of Chicago Press.

Brown, S. C. (1979), *Kingship to Kingship: Archaeological and Historical Studies in the Neo-Assyrian Zagros*, PhD dissertation, University of Toronto.

Brown, S. C. (1986), 'Media and Secondary State Formation in the Neo-Assyrian Zagros: An Anthropological Approach to an Assyriological Problem', *Journal of Cuneiform Studies*, 38: 107–19.

Brown, S. C. (1988), 'The Mêdikos Logos of Herodotus and the Evolution of the Median State', in H. Sancisi-Weerdenburg and A. T. Kuhrt (eds),

Method and Theory. Proceedings of the London 1985 Achaemenid History Workshop (Achaemenid History III), Istanbul, pp. 71–86, Leiden: Nederlands Instituut voor het Nabije Oosten.

Brown, S. C. (1990), 'Media in the Achaemenid Period: The Late Iron Age in Central West Iran', in H. Sancini-Weerdenburgh and A. T. Kuhrt (eds), *Centre and Periphery (Achaemenid History IV, Proceedings of the Groningen 1986 Achaemenid History Workshop)*, pp. 63–76, Leiden: Nederlands Instituut voor het Nabije Oosten.

Brunner, C. (1978), *Sasanian Stamp Seals in the Metropolitan Museum of Art*, New York: Metropolitan Museum of Art.

Brunner, C. (1983), 'Geographical and Administrative Divisions: Settlements and Economy', in E. Yarshater (ed.), *The Cambridge History of Iran (The Seleucid, Parthian and Sasanian Periods)*, Vol. 3(2), pp. 747–77, Cambridge: Cambridge University Press.

Bryce, T. (2009), *The Routledge Handbook of the Peoples and Places of Ancient Western Asia. From the Early Bronze Age to the Fall of the Persian Empire*, London and New York: Routledge.

Burger, O., L. C. Todd and P. Burnett (2008), 'The Behavior of Surface Artifacts: Building a Landscape Taphonomy on the High Plans', in L. L. Scheiber and B. J. Clark (eds), *Archaeological Landscapes on the High Plains*, pp. 203–36, Colorado: The University Press of Colorado.

Callieri, P. and A. Askari Chaverdi (2013), 'Media, Khuzestan, and Fars Between the End of the Achaemenids and the Rise of the Sasanians', in D. T. Potts (ed.), *The Oxford Handbook of Ancient Iran*, pp. 690–717, Oxford: Oxford University Press. Available at: 10.1093/oxfordhb/9780199733309.013.0020 (last accessed 23 November 2016).

Calmeyer, P. (1987), 'Art in Iran ii. Median Art and Architecture', in E. Yarshater (ed.), *Encyclopædia Iranica*, vol. 2(6), pp. 565–9, Costa Mesa, CA: Mazda. http://www.iranicaonline.org/articles/art-in-iran-ii-median (last accessed 16 July 2015).

Calmeyer, P. (1990), 'Medische Kunst', *Reallexikon der Assyriologie*, 7(7/8): 618–19.

Calvet, Y. (1987), 'Le Sondage x 36 de Tell el-Oueili, in huot', in J.-L. (ed.), *La Préhistoire de la Mesopotamie*, pp. 33–93, Paris: Editions du CNRS.

Cameron, G. G. (1969), *History of Early Iran*, Chicago: The University of Chicago Press.

Campopiano, M. (2017), 'Cooperation and Private Enterprise in Water Management in Iraq: Continuity and Change between the Sasanian and Early Islamic Periods (Sixth to Tenth Centuries)', *Environment and History*, 23(3): 385–407.

Canepa, M. P. (2014), 'Seleukid Sacred Architecture, Royal Cult and the Transformation of Iranian Culture in the Middle Iranian Period', *Iranian Studies*, 1–27. http://dx.doi.org/10.1080/00210862.2014.947788 (last accessed 24 October 2014).

Canepa, M. P. (2018), *The Iranian Expanse: Transforming Royal Identity through Architecture, Landscape, and the Built Environment, 550 BCE–642 CE*, Oakland: University of California Press.

Carter, E. (1971), *Elam in the Second Millennium B.C.: The Archaeological Evidence*, PhD dissertation, University of Chicago.

Carter, E. and M. Stolper (1984), *Elam: Survey of Political History and Archaeology*, Near Eastern Studies 25, Berkeley, Los Angeles and London: University of California Press.

Carter, E. and H. T. Wright (2010), 'Ceramic Phase Indicators in Surface Assemblages', in H. T. Wright and J. A. Neely (eds), *Elamite and Achaemenid Settlement in Deh Lurân Plain: Towns and Villages of the Early Empires in the Southwestern Iran*, pp. 11–22, Michigan: Ann Arbor.

Carter, R. A., K. Challis, S. M. N. Priestman and H. Tofighian (2006), 'The Bushehr Hinterland Results of the First Season of the Iranian-British Archaeological Survey of Bushehr Province, November–December 2004', *Iran*, 44: 63–103. https://www.jstor.org/stable/4300704 (last accessed 25 August 2019).

Carvalhoa, M., F. Sagrario, L. Pujiac, C. Rochaa, C. Rodríguezb and F. Zellib (2013), 'Architecture, Archaeology and Landscape, an Interdisciplinary Educational Experience in Archaeological Sites', *Procedia Chemistry*, 8: 292–301.

Cereti, C. (2007), 'Middle Persian Geographic Literature II: Chapters X and XII of the Bundahišn', in R. Gyselen (ed.), *Des Indo-Grecs aux Sassanides: données pour l'histoire et la géographie historique* (Res Orientales, XVII), pp. 55–64, Bures-sur-Yvette: Groupe pour l' Étude de la Civilisation du Moyen-Orient.

Cereti, C. (2020), 'Remarks on *The Cities of Ērānšahr* and its Date in the Light of the *Xwadāy-nāmag* and Sasanian Primary Sources', in M. Ashtiany and M. Maggi (eds), *A Turquoise Coronet Studies in Persian Language and Literature in Honour of Paola Orsatti*, pp. 79–96, Wiesbaden: Reichert. https://reichert-verlag.de/9783954905102_a_tur quoise_coronet-detail (last accessed 30 May 2021).

Cereti, C. and S. Gondet (2015), 'The Funerary Landscape between Naqš-e Rostam and Estaḫr (Persepolis Region). Discovery of a New Group of Rock-cut Niches', *Iranica Antiqua*, 50: 367–403.

Chabot, J. B. (1902), *Synodicon Orientale ou recueil de synods nestoriens* (Notices et extraits des manuscrits de la Bibliothique Nationale 37), Paris: Imprimerie nationale.

Chamaza, G. W. (1994), 'Der VIII. Feldzug Sargons II', *Archäologische Mitteilungen aus Iran*, 27: 91–118.

Charpin, D. (2004), 'Histoire politique du Proche-Orient Amorrite (2002–1595)', in D. Charpin, D. O. Edzard and M. Stol (eds), *Mesopotamien: Die altbabylonische Zeit*, pp. 23–482, Fribourg and Göttingen: Academic Press Fribourg; Vandenhoeck & Ruprecht Göttingen.

Chaumont, M.-L. (1974), 'Étude d'histoire parthe. III. Les villes fondees par les Vologese', *Syria*, 51: 75–89.

Chegini, N. N. and A. V. Nikitin (1996), 'Sasanian Iran – Economy, Society, Arts and Crafts', in B. A. Litvinsky (ed.), *History of Civilizations of Central Asia, vol. 3, The Crossroads of Civilizations: AD 250 to 750*, pp. 35–77, Paris: UNESCO.

Christaller, W. (1966), *Central Places in Southern Germany*, transl. C. W. Baskin, Englewood Cliffs, NJ: Prentice-Hall.

Christensen, A. (1933a), *Kulturgeschichte Des Alten Orients* (Dritter Abschnitt. Erster Lieferung), Munich: Beck.

Christensen, A. (1933b), *L'Iran sous les Sassanides*, Copenhagen: Munksgaard.

Clark, B. J. and L. L. Scheiber (2008), 'A Sloping Land: An Introduction to Archaeological Landscapes on the High Plains', in L. L. Scheiber and B. J. Clark (eds), *Archaeological Landscapes on the High Plains*, pp. 1–16, Colorado: The University Press of Colorado.

Clutton-Brock, J. (1978), 'Domestication and the Ungulate Fauna of the Levant during the Prepottery Neolithic Period', in W. C. Brice (ed.), *The Environmental History of the Near and Middle East Since the Last Ice Age*, pp. 29–40, New York: Academic.

Clutton-Brock, J. (1981), *Domesticated Animals from Early Times*, London: British Museum of Natural History.

Colburn, H. P. (2013), 'Connectivity and Communication in the Achaemenid Empire', *Journal of the Economic and Social History of the Orient*, 56: 29–52.

Collon, D. (1990), 'The Life and Times of Teḫeš-Atal', *Revue d'assyriologie et d archéologie orientale*, 84(2): 129–36.

Compana, S. and S. Piro (2009), *Seeing the Unseen: Geophysics and Landscape Archaeology*, London: CRC Press.

Conolly, J. (2008), 'Geographical Information Systems and Landscape Archaeology', in B. David and J. Thomas (eds), *Handbook of Landscape Archaeology, World Archaeological Congress Research Handbooks in Archaeology*, pp. 583–95, Walnut Creek, CA: Left Coast Press.

Conolly, J. and M. Lake (2006), *Geographic Information Systems in Archaeology* (Manuals in Archaeology), Cambridge: Cambridge University Press.

Cooper, J. S. (1983), *The Curse of Agade*, Baltimore and London: Johns Hopkins University Press.

Crane, K., R. Lal and J. Martini (2008), *Iran's Political, Demographic, and Economic*, Santa Monica, CA – Arlington, VA – Pittsburgh, PA: RAND.

Cribb, R. (1993), *Nomads in Archaeology*, Cambridge: Cambridge University Press.

Cronin, S. (2000), 'Riza Shah and the Disintegration of Bakhtiyari Power in Iran, 1921–1934', *Iranian Studies*, 33(3–4): 349–76. https://doi.org/10.1080/00210860008701986 (last accessed 25 December 2015).

Cronin, S. (2003), 'Riza Shah and the Disintegration of Bakhtiyari Power in Iran, 1921–1934', in S. Cronin (ed.), *The Making of Modem Iran: State and Society under Riza Shah, 1921–1941*, pp. 241–68, London: Routledge.

Cronin, S. (2005), 'Riza Shah, the Fall of Sardar Asad, and the "Bakhtiyari plot"', *Iranian Studies*, 38(2): 211–45. https://doi.org/10.1080/00210860500096311 (last accessed 3 August 2010).

Curtis, J. (1984), *Nush-i Jan III, The Small Finds*, London: The British Institute of Persian Studies.

Curtis, J. (1989), *Excavations at Qasrij Cliff and Khirbet Qasrij* (Saddam Dam Report 10), London: British Museum Press.

Curtis, J. (2005), 'The Achaemenid Period in Northern Iraq', in P. Briant and R. Boucharlat (eds), *L'archéologie de l'empire achéménide: nouvelles recherches* (Persika 6), pp. 175–95, Paris: De Boccard.

Curtis, J. (1389 [2010]), 'Introduction', in J. Curtis (ed.), *Early Mesopotamia and Iran: Contact and Conflict 3500–1600 BC (Proceedings of a Seminar in Memory of Vladimir Lukonin)*, Persian transl. Z. Basti, pp. 13–25, Tehran: SAMT.

Dabrowsky, V., C. Buchaud, M. Tangberg, A. Zazzo and S. Priestman (2021), 'Archaeobotanical Analysis of Food and Fuel Procurement from Fulayj Fort (oman, 5th–8th c. Ce) Including the Earliest Secure Evidence for Sorghum in Eastern Arabia', *Journal of Arid Environments*, 190: 104512.

Daghmechi, M., S. M. N. Priestman, G. Puschnigg, J. Nokandeh, E. E. Intagliata, H. Omrani Rekavandi and E. W. Sauer (2022), 'Comparative Study of the Sasanian Ceramics from Forts on the Great Wall of Gorgan and Fortifications in Its Hinterland', in in E. W. Sauer, J. Nokandeh and H. Omrani Rekavandi (eds), *Ancient Arms Race. Antiquity's Largest Fortresses and Sasanian Military Networks of Northern Iran* (A Joint Fieldwork Project by the Iranian Centre for Archaeological Research, the Reasearch Institute of Cultural Heritaage and Tourism and the University of Edinburgh (2014–16), pp. 475–550, Oxford–Philadelphia: Oxbow.

Dan, R. (2020), 'Tille Höyük Level X: A "Median" or Achaemenid Period Citadel in the Euphrates Valley?', *Iranica Antiqua*, 55: 145–63. Available at: 10.2143/IA.55.0.3289194 (last accessed 28 June 2021).

Dandamaev, M. A. and V. G. Lukonin (1989), *The Culture and Social Institutions of Ancient Iran*, Cambridge: Cambridge University Press.

Dandamaev, M. and I. Medvedskaya (2006), 'Media', in E. Yarshater (ed.), *Encyclopædia Iranica, Online Edition*. http://www.iranicaonline.org/articles/media (last accessed 12 March 2007).

Daryaee, T. (1995), 'National History or Keyanid History?: The Nature of Sasanid Zoroastrian Historiography', *Iranian Studies*, 28(3–4): 129–41.

Daryaee, T. (2003). 'The Ideal King in the Sasanian World Ardaxšīr ī Pābagān or Xusrō Anōšag-ruwān?', *Nâme-ye Irân-e Bâstân*, 3(1): 33–45.

Daryaee, T. (1383/2004), *Shāhanshāhi-e sāsāni* [Sasanian Empire], transl. M. Sāqeb-far, Tehran: Qoqnous.

Daryaee, T. (2009), *Sasanian Persia: The Rise and Fall of an Empire*, London and New York: I. B. Tauris.

Daryaee, T. (2010a), 'Bazaars, Merchants, and Trade in Late Antique Iran', *Comparative Studies of South Asia, Africa, and the Middle East*, 30(3): 401–9. Available at: 10.1215/1089201x-2010-023 (last accessed 8 December 2011).

Daryaee, T. (2010b), 'Review Essays: The Fall of the Sasanian Empire to the Arab Muslims: from Two Centuries of Silence to Decline and Fall of the Sasanian Empire: The Partho-Sasanian Confederacy and Arab Conquest of Iran', *Journal of Persianate Studies*, 3: 239–54.

Darvill, T. (2008), 'Pathways to a Panoramic Past: A Brief History of Landscape Archaeology in Europe', in B. David and J. Thomas (eds), *Handbook of Landscape Archaeology* (World Archaeological Congress Research Handbooks in Archaeology), pp. 60–76, Walnut Creek, CA: Left Coast Press.

David, B. and J. Thomas (2008a), 'Historical Perspective', in B. David and J. Thomas (eds), *Handbook of Landscape Archaeology* (World Archaeological Congress Research Handbooks in Archaeology), pp. 25–6, Walnut Creek, CA: Left Coast Press.

David, B. and J. Thomas (2008b), 'Landscape Archaeology: Introduction', in B. David and J. Thomas (eds), *Handbook of Landscape Archaeology* (World Archaeological Congress Research Handbooks in Archaeology), pp. 27–43, Walnut Creek, CA: Left Coast Press.

Debevoise, N. C. (1938), *Political History of Parthia*, Chicago: The University of Chicago Press.

De Cardi, B. (2008), 'Londo-ware: A Parthian-period Ceramic in Baluchistan', in *Parthian, Sasanian and Early Islamic Pottery: Dating, Definition and Distribution; A Specialist Workshop at The British Museum*, Organised by S. Priestman and St J. Simpson, pp. 33–6.

De Graef, K. (2006), *De la dynastie de Simaški au Sukkalmahat. Les document fin PE IIB – début PE III du chantier B à Suse* (Mémoires de la délégation archéologique en Iran 55). Ghent: University of Ghent.

De Graef, K. (2008), 'Annus Simaškensis: L'usage des noms d'année pendant la periode Simaškéenne (ca. 1930–1880 A V. notre ère) à Suse', *Iranica Antiqua*, 43: 67–87.

De Graef, K. (2012), 'Dual Power in Susa: Chronicle of a Transitional Period from Ur III via Šimaški to the Sukkalmas', *Bulletin of the School of Oriental and African Studies*, 75: 525–46. Available at: doi:10.1017/S0041977X1200136X (last accessed 25 July 2016).

De Graef, K. (2015), 'Susa in the Late 3rd Millennium: from a Mesopotamian Colony to an Independent State (MC 2110–1980)', in W. Sallaberger and I. Schrakamp (eds), *ARCANE (Associated Regional Chronologies for* the Ancient Near East and the Eastern Mediterranean) III: History and Philology*, pp. 289–96, Turnhout: Brepols.

de Gruchy, M. and J. Jotheri (2019), 'Filling in the Gaps of the Khandaq Shapur', in *BANEA 2019: Mind the Gap*, University of Liverpool, 22–4 February 2019, Archaeology, Classics and Egyptology.

Dehpahlavan, M., M. Malekzadeh and Z. A. Chaharrahi (1397/2018), 'Barrasi-e bāstān-shenāsi-e bakhshi az shāhrāh-e khorāsān: gardane-ye pātāq yā darband-e mādi' [Archaeological Survey of Part of the Great Khorasan Road, So-Called Pataq Defile or Median Gate], *Pazhohesh-ha-ye Bastanshenasi Iran*, 8(19): 127–46.

de Menasce, J. (1966), 'Textes pehlevis sur les qanats', *Acta Orientalia*, 30: 167–75.

De Miroschedji, P. (1981), 'Fouilles du Chantier Ville Royale II a Suse (1975–77), I. Les Niveaux Elamite', *Délégation archéologique française en Iran*, 12: 35–88.

de Miroschedji, P. (1986), 'La localisation de Madaktu et l'organisation politique de l'Élam à l'époque néo-élamite', in L. De Meyer, H. Gasche and F. Vallat (eds), *Fragmenta Historiae Elamicae: Mélanges offerts à M. J. Steve*, pp. 209–25, Paris: Éditions Recherche sur les civilisations.

de Miroschedji, P., N. Desse-Berset and M. Kervran (1987), 'Fouilles du Chantier Ville Royale II a Suse (1975–77), II. Niveaux d'Époques Achéménide, Séleucide, Parthe et Islamique', *Cahiers de la Délégation Archéologique Française en Iran*, 15: 11–103.

Denman, D. R. and S. Prodano (1972), *Land Use: An Introduction to Proprietary Land Use Analysis*, London: Allen & Unwin.

Denham, T. (2008), 'Environmental Archaeology: Interpreting Practices-in-the-Landscape through Geoarchaeology', in B. David and J. Thomas (eds), *Handbook of Landscape Archaeology* (World Archaeological Congress Research Handbooks in Archaeology), pp. 468–81, Walnut Creek, CA: Left Coast Press.

de Planhol, X. (2003), 'Hamadān iii Historical Geography', in E. Yarshater (ed.), *Encyclopædia Iranica, Online Edition*, vol. 11(6), pp. 605–7. Costa Mesa, CA: Mazda. http://www.iranicaonline.org/articles/hamadan-iii (last accessed 30 December 2012).

de Smet, W. (1990), '"Kashshû" in Old-Babylonian Documents', *Akkadica*, 68: 1–19.

Diakonoff, I. M. (1985), 'Media', in E. Yarshater (ed.), *Cambridge History. Iran II*, pp. 36–148, Cambridge: Cambridge University Press.

Diakonoff, I. M. (1991), 'The Cities of the Medes', in M. Cogan and I. Eph'al (eds), *Ah, Assyria ...: Studies in Assyrian History and Ancient Near Eastern Historiography Presented to Hayim Tadmor* (Scripta Hierosolymitana, Publications of the Hebrew university of Jerusalem, vol. 33), pp. 13–20, Jerusalem: The Magnes Press.

Digard, J. P. (1981), *Techniques des Nomades Baxtyâri d'Iran*, Cambridge: Cambridge University Press.

Dittmann, R. (1986), *Betrachtungen zur Frühzeit des Südwest-Iran, Regionale Entwicklungen vom 6. Bis zum frühen 3. vorchristlichen Jahrtausend* (Berliner Beiträge zum Vorderen Orient, Band 4), Berlin: Dietrich Reimer.

Dittmann, R. (1994), 'Glyptikgruppen am Übergang von der Akkad- zur Ur III-Zeit', *Baghdader Mitteilungen*, 25: 75–117.

Djamali, M., J.-L.d. Beaulieu, V. Andrieu-Ponel, M. Berberian, N. F. Miller, E. Gandouin, H. Lahijani, M. Shah-Hosseini, P. Ponel, M. Salimian and F. Guiter (2009), 'A Late Holocene Pollen Record from Lake Almalou in NW Iran: Evidence for Changing Land-Use in Relation to Some Historical Events During the Last 3700 Years', *Journal of Archaeological Science*, 36: 1,364–75.

Djamali, M., N. F. Miller, E. Ramezani, V. Andrieu-Ponel, J.-L. de Beaulieu, M. Berberian, F. Guibal, H. Lahijani, R. Lak and P. Ponel (2010), 'Notes on Arboricultural and Agricultural Practices in Ancient Iran based on New Pollen Evidence', *Paléorient* 36(2): 175–88.

Djamali, M., M. D. Jones, J. Migliore, S. Balatti, M. Fader, D. Contreras, S. Gondet, Z. Hosseini, H. Lahijani, A. Naderi, L. S. Shumilovskikh, M. Tengberg and L. Weeks (2016), 'Olive Cultivation in the Heart of the Persian Achaemenid Empire: New Insights into Agricultural Practices and Environmental Changes Reflected in a Late Holocene Pollen Record from Lake Parishan, SW Iran', *Vegetation History and Archaeobotany*, 25: 255–69. https://doi.org/10.1007/s00334-015-0545-8 (last accessed 12 August 2018).

Dobrez, L. (2009), 'New and Old Paradigms: The Question of Space', in G. Dimtriadis (ed.), *Landscape in Mind: Dialogue on Space Between Anthropology and Archaeology* (BAR International Series 2003), pp. 5–8, Oxford: Archaeopress.

Draycott, C. M. (2008), 'Sculpture (Cat. Nos. 1–0)', in C. M. Draycott and G. D. Summers (eds), *Kerkenes Special Studies 1, Sculpture and Inscriptions from the Monumental Entrance to the Palatial Complex at Kerkenes Daq, Turkey, vol. 135*, pp. 8–60, Chicago: Oriental Institute Publications.

Draycott, C. M. and G. D. Summers (2008), *Kerkenes Special Studies 1, Sculpture and Inscriptions from the Monumental Entrance to the Palatial Complex at Kerkenes Daq, Turkey, Vol. 135*, Chicago: Oriental Institute Publications.

Duffy, P. R. (2015), 'Site Size Hierarchy in Middle-range Societies', *Journal of Anthropological Archaeology*, 37: 85–99.

Duke, P. (2008), 'Places in the Heartland: Landscape Archaeology on the Plains', in L. L. Scheiber and B. J. Clark (eds), *Archaeological Landscapes on the High Plains*, pp. 277–85, Colorado: The University Press of Colorado.

Dusinberre, E. R. M. (2002), 'An Excavated Ivory from Kerkenes Dağ, Turkey: Transcultural Fluidities, Significations of Collective Identity, and the Problem of Median Art', *Ars Orientalis (Medes and Persians: Reflections on Elusive Empires)*, 32: 17–54.

Dyke, C. (1999), 'Bourdieuean Dynamics: The American Middle-Class Self-Constructs', in R. Shusterman (ed.), *Bourdieu: A Critical Reading*, pp. 192–213, Oxford, UK; Malden, MA: Wiley-Blackwell.

Dyson, R. H. (1965), 'Problems in the Relative Chronology of Iran, 6000–2000 B.C.', in R. W. Ehrich (ed.), *Chronologies in Old World Archaeology*, Chicago: University of Chicago Press.

Dyson, R. H. (1989), 'Rediscovering Hasanlu', *Expedition*, 31(2–3): 3–11.

Edzard, D. O. (1973), 'Zwei Inschriften am Felsen von Sar-i-Pūl-i- Zohāb: Anubanini 1 und 2', *Archiv für Orientforschung*, 24: 73–7.

Edzard D. O. and G. Farber (1974), *Die Orts- und Gewässernamen der Zeit der 3. Dynastie von Ur* (Répertoire géographique des textes cunéiformes, Bd. 2.; Beihefte zum Tübinger Atlas des Vorderen Orients., Reihe B; Geisteswissenschaften, Nr. 7), Wiesbaden: Reichert.

Edzard, D. O., G. Farber and E. Sollberger (1977), *Die Orts- und Gewässernamen der Präsargonischen und Sargonischen Zeit, Répertoire géographique des textes cuneiforms 1*, Wiesbaden: Dr Ludwig Reichert.

Eidem, J. (1985), 'News from the Eastern Front: The Evidence from Tell Shemshara', *Iraq*, 47: 83–107.

Eidem, J. (1992), *The Shemshāra Archives 2, The Administrative Texts* (Historisk-filosofiske skrifter), Copenhagen: Kongelige Danske Videnskabernes Selskab.

Eidem, E. and J. Læssøe (2001), *The Shemshara Archives 1, The Letters* (Historisk-filosofiske skrifter 23), Copenhagen: Kongelige Danske Videnskabernes Selskab.

Eilers, W. (1954), 'Der Name Demawend', *Archiv Orientalni*, 22: 267–374.

Elling, R. C. (2013), *Minorities in Iran: Nationalism and Ethnicity after Khomeini*, New York: Palgrave Macmillan.

Elman, Y. (2004), '"Up to the Ears" in Horses' Necks (B. M. 108a): On Sasanian Agricultural Policy and Private "Eminent Domain"', *Jewish Studies: An Internet Journal*, 3: 95–149. http://www.biu.ac.il/JS/JSIJ/3-2004/Elman.pdf (last accessed 5 October 2007).

El-Moslimany, A. P. (1987), 'The Late Pleistocene Climates of the Lake Zeribar Region (Kurdistan, Western Iran) Deduced from the Ecology and Pollen Production of Non-Arboreal Vegetation', *Vegetatio*, 72(3): 131–9.

Eppihimer, M. A. (2009), *The Visual Legacy of Akkadian Kingship*, PhD dissertation, Harvard University.

Eqbal, H. (1976), 'The Seleucid, Parthian and Sasanian Periods on the Izeh Plain', in H. T. Wright (ed.), *Archaeological Investigations in the Izeh Plain*, pp. 114–18, Ann Arbor: University of Michigan Museum of Anthropology Technical Report, no 10.

Esmaeali Jelodar, M. (1393 [2014]), 'Preliminary Report on the Salvage Excavations at the Site Kārkhāne 1, Trench D10, in the Area of Kouhrang's

Third Tunnel in Chaharmahal va Bakhtiyari, First Part', *Gamāne*, 2: 13–41 [in Persian].

Esmaeali Jelodar, M. and S. Zolqadr (1393/2014), 'Analysis of the Results of Excavations at the Nomadic Site of Shahriyāri II in the Bīregān Area of Kouhrang', *Pazhouhesh-hā-ye bāstān-shenāsi-e irān*, 6: 85–104 [in Persian with an English abstract].

Evans, J. A. S. (1982), 'Persian Expansion into Europe', in J. A. S. Evans (ed.), *Herodotus – Twayne's World Authors Series 645*: 65–78, Boston, MA: Twayne. http://go.galegroup.com.ezproxy.is.ed.ac.uk/ps/i.do?p=G-Twayne&u=ed_itw&id=GALE|CX1896000013&v=2.1&it=r&sid=G-Twayne&asid=c5a88125 (last accessed 11 April 2019).

Ezzatyar, A. (2016), *The Last Mufti of Iranian Kurdistan: Ethnic and Religious Implications in the Greater Middle East*, New York: Palgrave MacMillan.

Fahimi, H. (2003), 'Iron Age at Sialk: Preliminary Report on the Iron Age Potteruy of Sialk', in S. Malek Shahmirzadi (ed.), *The Silversmiths of Sialk, Sialk Reconsideration Project, Report No. 2*, Tehran: Iranian Center for Archaeological Research [in Persian].

Fahimi, H. (1382 [2004]), 'Shamshirgah: A Settlement Related to the Cemetry of Sarm', *Iranian Journal of Archaeology and History*, 18(1), Serial No. 35: 61–9.

Fahimi, H. (1389 [2010]), 'An Iron Age Fortress in Central Iran: Archaeological Investigations in Shamshirgah, Qom, 2005: Preliminary Report', in P. Matthiae, F. Pinnock, L. Nigro and N. Marhetti (eds), *Proceedings of the 6th International Congress on the Archaeology of the Near East, 2008, Sapienza-Università di Roma*, pp. 165–83, Wiesbaden: Harrassowitz.

Faizi, M., N. Faizi and Y. H. Baba-Kamal (2012), 'The Study of the Effect of the Dominant Cultural Processes on the Early Islamic Pottery Decorations of Seymareh: Non-Glazed Potteries', *Archaeological Research of Iran*, 2(3): 131–52.

Fales, F. M. (1996), 'Evidence for West–East Contacts in the 8th Century BC: The Bukān Stele', in G. B. Lanfranchi, M. Roaf and R. Rollinger (eds), *Continuity of Empire (?) Assyria, Media, Persia*. (History of the Ancient Near East/Monographs – V), pp. 131–47, Padua: S.a.r.g.o.n. editrice e libreria.

Fatahi, M. (1995), *The Study of Zagros' Oak Forests and the Most Important Factors of its Destruction*, Tehran: Forests and Pastures Research Institute.

Fiey, J. M. (1970), 'Médic chrétienne', *Parole de l'Orient*, 1: 357–84.

Fincke, J. (1993), *Répertoire géographique des Textes cunéiformes 10: Die Orts- und Gewässernamen der Nuzi-Texte*, Wiesbaden: Reichert.

Fleming, A. (2006), 'Post-processual Landscape Archaeology: A Critique', *Cambridge Archaeological Journal*, 16: 267–80.

Forbes, T. B. (1983), *Urartian architecture* (BAR international series, 170), Oxford: B.A.R.

Forrer, E. (1920), *Die Provinzeinteilung des Assyrischen Reiches*, Leipzig: J. C. Hinrichs.

Frayne, D. R. (1992), 'The Old Akkadian Royal Inscriptions: Notes on a New Edition', *Journal of the American Oriental Society*, 112: 619–38.

Frayne, D. R. (1999), 'The Zagros Campaigns of Šulgi and Amar-Suena', in D. I. Owen and G. Wilhelm (eds), *Nuzi at Seventy-Five* (Studies on the Civilization and Culture of Nuzi and the Hurrians X), pp. 141–201, Bethesda: CDL Press.

Frayne, D. R. (2011), 'Simurrum', *Reallexikon der Assyriologie*, 12(7–8): 508–11.

Freestone, I. (2008), 'Partho-Sasanian Glass and Glazes', in *Parthian, Sasanian and Early Islamic Pottery: dating, definition and distribution; A specialist workshop at The British Museum*, Organised by S. Priestman and St J. Simpson, pp. 3–5.

French, C. (2003), *Geoarchaeology in Action: Studies in Soil Micromorphology and Landscape Evolution*, London; New York: Routledge.

French, D. H. (1982), 'Tille 1981', *Kazı Sonuçları Toplantısı*, 4: 415–18.

French, D. H. (1983), 'Excavation at Tille Höyük (1982)', *Kazı Sonuçları Toplantısı*, 5: 169–70.

French, D. H. (1984a), 'Tille 1983 (The Year's Work)', *Anatolian Studies*, 34: 4–6.

French, D. H. (1984b), 'Tille Höyük 1983', *Kazı Sonuçları Toplantısı*, 6: 245–58.

French, D. H. (1985a), 'Tille 1984 (The Year's Work)', *Anatolian Studies*, 35: 5–6.

French, D. H. (1985b), 'Tille 1984', *Kazı Sonuçları Toplantısı*, 7: 211–15.

French, D. H. (1986a), 'Tille 1985 (The Year's Work)', *Anatolian Studies*, 36: 5–6.

French, D. H. (1986b), 'Tille', *Kazı Sonuçları Toplantısı*, 8(1): 205–12.

French, D. H. (1988), 'Tille 1987 (The Year's Work)', *Anatolian Studies*, 38: 6–8.

French, D. H. (1991), 'Tille Höyük 1989', *Kazı Sonuçları Toplantısı*, 7(1): 311–23.

French, D. H. (1992), 'Tille 1990', *Kazı Sonuçları Toplantısı*, 8(1): 337–52.

French, D. H., J. Moore and H. F. Russel (1982), 'Excavations at Tille 1979–1982: An Interim Report', *Anatolian Studies*, 32: 161—87.

Fuchs, A. (2011), 'Das Osttigrisgebiet von Agum II. bis zu Darius I', in P. A. Miglus and S. Mühl (eds), *Between the Cultures: The Central Tigris Region from the 3rd to the 1st Millennium B.C.*, Vol 14, pp 229–320, Heidelberg: Heidelberger Studien zum Alten Orient.

Fujii, H. (ed.) (1981), 'Preliminary Report of Excavations at Gubba and Songor', *al-Rafidan*, 2: 131–242.

Gaffeney, V. and M. van Leusen (1995), Postscript – GIS Environmental Determinism and Archaeology: A Parallel Text', in G. Lock and

Z. Stanchich (eds), *Archaeology and Geographical Information Systems: A European Perspective*, pp. 367–82, London; Bristol, PA: Taylor and Francis.

Gariboldi, A. (2015), 'The Great "Restoration" of Husraw I', in C. Jullien (ed.), *Husraw Ier reconstructions d'un règne: sources et documents* (Studia Iranica, Cahier 53), pp. 47–84, Paris: Association pour l'Avancement des Études iraniennes.

Gasche, H., ed. (2005), 'The Persian Gulf Shorelines and the Karkhe, Karun and Jarrahi Rivers: A Geo-Archaeological Approach. First Progress Report Part 2', *Akkadica*, 126(1): 1–43.

Gasche, H., ed. (2007), 'The Persian Gulf Shorelines and the Karkhe, Karun and Jarrahi Rivers: A Geo-Archaeological Approach. First Progress Report Part 3', *Akkadica*, 128(1–2): 1–72.

Gebel, H. G. (1994), 'Die Silexindustrie von Qale Rostam, NE-Zagros, Iran', in H. G. Gebel and S. K. Kozlowski (eds), *Neolithic Chipped Stone Industries of the Fertile Crescent* (Studies in Early Near Eastern Production, Subsistence and Environment 1), pp. 117–42, Berlin: ex oriente.

Gelb, I. J. and B. Kienast (1990), *Die altakkadischen Königsinschriften des Dritten Jahrtausends v. Chr.* (Freiburger altorientalische Studien, Bd. 7), Stuttgart: F. Steiner.

Genito, B. (1986), 'The Medes: A Reassessment of the Archaeological Evidence', *East and West*, 36(1–3): 11–81.

Gentili, P. (2012), 'Chogha Gavaneh: An Outpost of Ešnunna on the Zagros Mountains', *Egitto e Vicino Oriente*, 35: 165–73.

George, A. R. (ed.) (2011), *Cuneiform Royal Inscriptions and Related Texts in the Schøyen Collection* (CUSAS 17), Bethesda: CDL Press.

Ghirshman, R. (1939), *Fouilles de Sialk, près de Kashan, 1933, 1934, 1937, vol. II* (Musée du Louvre; Départment des Antiquités Orientales, Série Archéologique V), Paris: Librairie Orientaliste Geuthner.

Ghirshman, R. (1963), *Perse: Proto-iraniens. Mèdes-Achéménides* (Univers des Formes), Paris: Gallimard.

Ghirshman, R. (1976), *Terrasses sacrées de Bard-e Nechande et de Masjid-i Solaiman. L'Iran du sud-ouest du VIIIe s. av. notre ére au Ve s. de notre ére', vol. 1, Texte* (Mémoires de la Délégation Archéologique en Iran 45), Paris: E. J. Brill.

Ghirshman, R. (1978), *Iran: From the Earliest Times to the Islamic Conquest*, Harmondsworth: Penguin Books.

Ghodrat-Dizaji, M. (2016), 'Remarks on the Location of the Province of Parthia in the Sasanian Period', in V. Sarkhosh Curtis, E. J. Pendleton, M. Alram and T. Daryaee (eds), *The Parthian and Early Sasanian Empires: Adaptation and Expansion* (Proceedings of a Conference Held in Vienna, 14–16 June 2012), pp. 42–76, Oxford and Philadelphia: Oxbow Books.

Gilbert, A. S. (1983), 'On the Origins of Specialized Nomadic Pastoralism in Western Iran', *World Archaeology*, 15(1): 115–19.

Gignoux, P. (1984), 'Der Grossmagier Kirdīr und seine Reise in das Jenseits', in *Orientalia J. Duchesne-Guillemin emerito oblate (Hommages et Opera Minora, 9). Acta Iranica 23*, pp. 191–206, Leiden: Peeters.

Glassner, J.-J. (1986), *La chute d'Akkadé: l'événement et sa memoire* (Berliner Beiträge zum Vorderen Orient), Berlin: D. Reimer.

Glassner, J.-J. (1994), 'La fin d'Akkadé: approche chronologique', *Nouvelles assyriologiques brèves et utilitaires*, 9: 8–9.

Glassner, J.-J. (1996), 'Les dynasties d'Awan et de Shimashki', *Nouvelles assyriologiques brèves et utilitaires*, 34.

Glatz, C. (2018), 'Transitional Landscapes and Borderland Communities in the Zagros-Mesopotamian Interface', *Archaeology Seminars*, University of Edinburgh, Meadows Lecture Theatre, 20 September 2018.

Glatz, C. and J. Casana (2016), Of Highland-Lowland Borderlands: Local Societies and Foreign Power in the Zagros-Mesopotamian Interface', *Journal of Anthropological Archaeology*, 44: 127–47.

Glatzer, B. and M. J. Casimir (1983), 'Herds and Households among Pashtun Pastoral Nomads: Limits of Growth', *Ethnology*, 22(4): 307–25.

Goff, C. (1968), 'Luristan in the First Half of the First Millennium B.C', *Iran*, 6: 105–34.

Goff, C. (1969), 'Excavations at Baba Jan 1967: Second Preliminary Report', *Iran*, 7: 115–30.

Goff, C. (1970), 'Excavations at Baba Jan 1968: Third Preliminary Report', *Iran*, 8: 141–56.

Goff, C. (1977), 'Excavations at Baba Jan: The Architecture of the East Mound, Levels II and III', *Iran*, 15: 103–40.

Goff, C. (1978), Excavations at Baba Jan: The Pottery and Metal from Levels III and II, *Iran* 16: 29–65. http://www.jstor.org/stable/4299647 (last accessed 5 January 2011).

Gol-Mohammadi, Z., R. Naseri and M. Malekzadeh (1393/2014), 'Qolām-tappe[h] of Ja'far-ābād: Re-Evaluation of a Satellite Settlement of Sialk-VI Period in the Kashan Piedmonts', in M. H. Azizi Kharaneghi, R. Naseri and M. Khanipour (eds), *Abstracts International Congress of Young Archaeologist, University of Tehran, Aban 1390*, pp. 337–57, Tehran: OCTH; University of Tehran.

Gopnik, H. (2003), 'The Ceramics from Godin II from the 7th to the 5th Centuries BC', in G. L. Lanfranchi, M. Roaf and R. Rollinger (eds), *Continuity of Empire (?) Assyria, Media, Persia* (History of the Ancient Near East/Monographs V), pp. 249–67, Padua: S.a.r.g.o.n. Editrice e Liberia.

Gopnik, H. (2010), 'Why Columned Halls', in J. Curtis and S. J. Simpson (eds), *The World of Achaemenid Persia: History, Art and Society in Iran and the Ancient Near East*, proceedings of a conference at the British Museum, 29 September–1 October 2005, pp. 195–206, London; New York: I. B. Tauris; New York.

Gopnik, H. (2011), 'The Median Citadel of Godin Period II', in H. Gopnik and M. S. Rothman (eds), *On the High Road: The History of Godin Tepe, Iran*, pp. 285–364, Costa Mesa, CA: Mazda.

Gorris, E. (2014), *Power and Politics in the Neo-Elamite Kingdom*, 2 vols, PhD dissertation, Université catholique de Louvain.

Gorris, E. (2020), *Power and Politics in the Neo-Elamite Kingdom* (Acta Iranica, 60), Louvain: Peeters.

Grayson, A. K. (1975), *Assyrian and Babylonian Chronicles* (Texts from Cuneiform Sources 5), Winona Lake, Indiana: Eisenbrauns.

Grayson, A. K. and L. D. Levine (1975), 'The Assyrian Relief from Shkaft-i Gul Gul', *Iranica Antiqua*, 11: 29–38.

Greco, A. (2003), 'Zagros Pastoralism and Assyrian Imperial Expansion: A Methodological Approach', in G. B. Lanfranchi, M. Roaf and R. Rollinger (eds), *History of the Ancient Near East/Monographs V, Continuity of Empire (?); Assyria, Media, Persia*, pp. 65–78, Padua: S.a.r.g.o.n. Editrice e Lireria.

Greenwood, T. (2011), 'A Reassessment of the Life and Mathematical Problems of Anania Širakacʻi', *Revue des Études Arméniennes*, 33: 131–86.

Greenwood, T. (2018), Ananias of Shirak (Anania Širakacʻi), in E. Yarshater (ed.), *Encyclopædia Iranica, Online Edition*. http://www.iranicaonline. org/articles/ananias-shirak (last accessed 17 December 2019).

Griffiths, H. I., A. Schwalb and L. R. Stevens (2001), 'Environmental Change in Southwestern Iran: the Holocene Ostracod Fauna of Lake Mirabad', *The Holocene*, 11: 757–64.

Gropp, G. and S. Najmabadi (1970), 'Bericht über eine Reise in West- und Südiran', *Archaeologische Mitteilungen aus Iran*, 3: 173–230.

Gurney, O. R. and S. N. Kramer (1976), *Sumerian Literary Texts in the Ashmolean Museum*, Oxford: Clarendon Press.

Gyselen, R. (1979), 'Ateliers monétaires et cachets officiels sasanides', *Studia Iranica*, 8(2): 189–212.

Gyselen, R. (1989), *La géographie administrative de l'Empire sassanide. Les témoignages sigillographiques* (Res Orientales, I), Bures-sur-Yvette: Groupe pour l'Étude de la Civilisation du Moyen-Orient.

Gyselen, R. (1997), 'Economy iv. In the Sasanian Period', in E. Yarshater (ed.), *Encyclopaedia Iranica*, vol. 8(1), pp. 104–7, Costa Mesa: Mazda.

Gyselen, R. (2001a), *The Four Generals of the Sasanian Empire: Some Sigillographic Evidence* (Conferenze, 14), Rome: Istituto Italiano per l'Africa e l'Oriente.

Gyselen, R. (2001b), 'La province sassanide d'Abhar. Nouvelles données dans les collections des Musees Royaux d'Art et d'histoire de Bruxelles', *Studia Iranica*, 30: 31–44.

Gyselen, R. (2001c), 'La désignation territoriale des quatre *spāhbed* de l'empire sassanide d'après les sources primaires sigillographiques', *Studia Iranica*, 30: 137–41.

Gyselen, R. (2008), 'Gay, or the Continuity of a Sasanian Province's Administrative Status', in O. Tabibzadeh and T. Daryaee (eds), *Festschrift fur Erich Kettenhofen. Iranistik: Deutschsprachige Zeitschrift fur Iranistische Studien, 5. Jahrgang, Heft 1 and 2, 2006–2007, Alexander von Humboldt Stiftung*, pp. 31–8.

Gyselen, R. (2011), 'Hamadan and Marw: Two Stations on the Silk Road. New Evidence for Their Administrative and Monetary History (3rd–7th Centuries AD)', *Proceedings, International Symposium on Ancient Coins and the Culture of the Silk Road*, Shangai, 5–12 December 2006, pp. 284–97, Shanghai: Shanghai shuhua chubanshe.

Gyselen, R. (2019), *La géographie administrative de l'empire sassanide. Les témoignages épigraphiques en moyen-perse* (Res Orientales, XXV), Bures-sur-Yvette: Groupe pour l'Étude de la Civilisation du Moyen-Orient.

Habibi, H. (in press), 'Sasanian Royal Spaces and Political Culture', in L. Lavan (ed.), *Late Antique Archaeology: Imperial Archaeologies* (papers of conference held at Birkbeck, University of London, 1 December 2018), Leiden: Brill.

Habibi, H. (1390/2012), *Analysis of the Settlement Pattern of Farsan County in the Sasanian Period*, MA dissertation, University of Tehran.

Habibi, H. (1401/2022), 'Motāle'āt-e goghrāfiā-ye edāri-e shāhanshāhi-e sāsāni. Be bahāne-ye enteshār-e ketāb-e La géographie administrative de l'empire sassanide. Les témoignages épigraphiques en moyen-perse (goghrāfiā-ye shāhanshāhi-e sāsāni. Šavāhed-e katībe-shenākhti-e pārsī-e miāne)' [Field of the Administrative Geography of the Sasanian Empire. On the Auspicious Occasion of the Publication of La géographie administrative de l'empire sassanide. Les témoignages épigraphiques en moyen-perse], *Critical Studies in Texts & Programs of Human Sciences and Council for the Study of Humanities Texts and Books* 22(9): 89–109 [in Persian with an English abstract]. https://criticalstudy.ihcs.ac.ir/article_7751.html?lang=en (last accessed 27 July 2022).

Habibi, H. and A. Khosrowzadeh (2014), 'Analysis of Sasanian Settlement Pattern in the Intermontane Plain and Valleys of Farsan, Iran', in *Proceedings of the Age of Sensing 5th International Conference on Remote Sensing in Archaeology, Duke University*, pp. 16–17, North Carolina: Durham University Press.

Habibi, H. and Y. Heydari (2015), 'Sasanian Pottery of Western Chaharmahal va Bakhyiyari, Based on the Pottery Samples Acquired from Archaeological Survey of Farsan County', *Payām-e bāstān-shenās*, 11(22): 79–102 [in Persian with English abstract].

Habibi, H. and Y. Mohammadifar (2020), 'Landscape Archaeology of the Sasanian Period Abdanan', in K. A. Niknami and A. Hozhabri (eds), *Archaeology of Iran in the Historical Periods* (University of Tehran Science and Humanities Series), pp. 329–55, Cham: Springer. https://doi.org/10.1007/978-3-030-41776-5_26 (last accessed 27 May 2020).

Haerinck, E. (1986), 'The Chronology of Luristan, Pusht-i Kuh in the Late Fourth and First Half of the Third Millennium B.C.', *Préhistoire de la Mésopotamie*: 55–72.

Haerinck, E. (2003), 'Again on Tang-i Sarvak II, NE-Side. Goddesses Do Not Have Moustaches and Do Not Wear Trousers', *Iranica Antiqua*, 38: 221–45.

Haerinck, E. (2008), 'Le Luristan à l'âge du bronze (vers 3100–1300 av. J.-C.)', in A. -J. Esparceil (ed.), *Bronzes du Luristan: Énigmes de l'Iran ancien, IIIe–Ier mill é naire av. J.-C.*, 33–41, Paris: Paris musées.

Haerinck, E. (2011), 'Painted Pottery of the First Half of the Early Bronze Age (Late 4th–First Centuries of the 3rd Millennium BC) in Luristan, W–Iran', *Iranica Antiqua*, 46: 55–106.

Haerinck, E. and B. Overlaet (2002), 'The Chalcolithic and Early Bronze Age in Pusht-i Kuh, Luristan (West-Iran): The Chronology and Mesopotamian Contacts', *Akkadica*, 123: 163–81.

Haerinck, E. and B. Overlaet (2004), 'The Chronology of the Pusht-i Kuh, Luristan: Results of the Belgian Archaeological Expedition in Iran', in K. Folsach, H. Thrane, I. Thuesen and P. Mortensen (eds), *From Handaxe to Khan: Essays Presented to Peder Mortensen on the Occasion of his 70th Birthday*, pp. 118–36, Aarhus: Aarhus University Press.

Haerinck, E. and B. Overlaet (2006a), *Bani Surmah: An Early Bronze Age Graveyard in Pusht-i Kuh, Luristan* (LED 6). Leuven: Peeters.

Haerinck, E. and B. Overlaet (2006b), 'Pošt-e Kuh', in E. Yarshater (ed.), *Encyclopædia Iranica, Online Edition*. https://iranicaonline.org/articles/post-e-kuh (last accessed 5 June 2010).

Haerinck, E. and B. Overlaet (2008a), 'Holy Places in Pusht-i Kuh, Luristan. Rural Islamic Shrines in The Central Zagros, W-Iran', in K. D'Hulster and J. van Steenbergen (eds), *Continuity and Change in the Realms of Islam: Studies in Honour of Professor Urbain Vermeulen* (Orientalia Lovaniensia Analectca 171), pp. 287–310, Leuven: Peeters en Department Oosterse Studies.

Haerinck, E. and B. Overlaet (2008b), *The Kalleh Nisar Bronze Age Graveyard in Pusht-i Kuh, Luristan* (LED 7), Leuven: Peeters.

Haerinck, E. and B. Overlaet (2010a), 'Bronze and Iron Age pottery from the Ilam Graveyard (Pusht-i Kuh, Iran)', *Iranica Antiqua*, 45: 277–304.

Haerinck, E. and B. Overlaet (2010b), *The Early Bronze Age Graveyards to the West of the Kabir Kuh (Pusht-i Kuh, Luristan)* (LED 8), Leuven: Peeters.

Hallo, W. W. (1957–71), 'Gutium', *Reallexikon der Assyriologie*, 3: 708–20.

Hallo, W. W. (2005), 'New Light on the Gutians', in W. van Soldt (ed.), *Ethnicity in Ancient Mesopotamia*, Papers read at the 48th Rencontre Assyriologique Internationale, Leiden, 1–4 July 2002 (PIHANS Volume 102), pp. 147–61, Leiden: Peeters.

Hartnell, T. (2014), 'Agriculture in Sasanian Persis: Ideology and Practice', in R. Payne and M. Soroush (eds), *The Archaeology of Sasanian Politics, Journal of Ancient History* (special issue), 2(2): 182–208.

Hasanpour, A. (2014), 'Examination of the Architecture and Stuccos Discovered at Qala Gouri, Seymare', in M. H. Azizi Kharanaghi, M. Khanipour and R. Naseri (eds), *International Congress of Young Archaeologist*, pp. 447–52, Tehran: Tehran University Publication.

Hasanpour, A. (2015), 'Comparative study of the Plaster Casts Found from the Buildings Excavated at Qala Gouri, Ramavand', *The Proceedings of the Conference Archaeological Research at the Seymareh Dam Basin*, pp. 268–79, Tehran: ICAR.

Hausleiter, A., E. J. Keall and M. Roaf (2000), 'Map 92 Ecbatana-Susa', in R. J. A. Talbert (ed.), *Barrington Atlas of the Greek and Roman World: Map-by-map Directory*, 2 vols, vol. 1, Princeton, NJ: Princeton University Press.

Hasanpour, A., F. Delfan and E. Beyranvand (2016), 'Analysis of the Architecture Unearthed in the First Season of Excavation at Qala Gouri, Ramavand', *Athar*, 37(74): 37–60.

Hecker, K., W. G. Lambert, G. G. W. Müller, W. von Soden and A. Ünal (1994), *Texte aus der Umwelt des Alten Testaments (TUAT)* (Band III-Weisheitstexte), Mythen und Epen, Gütersloh: Gütersloher Verlagshaus.

Heidary, M. and S. B. Hosseini. (1394/2015), 'Survey and Study of bard-e gōri Structures in Chaharmahal va Bakhtiyari, in M. Ashrafi (ed.), *Proceedings of the First Engraved Architecture Conference*, Kerman, 12–14 Ordibehesht 1391, Tehran: Research Institute of Cultural Heritage and Tourism.

Heinz, M. (1995), 'Migration und Assimilation im 2. Jt. v. Chr.: Die Kassiten', in K. Bartl, R. Bernbeck and M. Heinz (eds), *Zwischen Euphrat und Indus. Aktuelle Forschungsprobleme in der vorderasiatischen Archäologie*, pp. 165–74, Hildesheim: Georg Olms.

Helm, P. R. (1981), 'Herodotus' Mêdikos Logos and Median History', *Iran*, 19(1): 85–90.

Henige, D. (2004), "Herodotus' Median Chronology from a Slightly Different Perspective', *Iranica Antiqua*, 39: 239–48.

Henkelman, W. F. M. (2003a), 'Persians, Medes and Elamites: Acculturation in the Neo-Elamite Period', in G. B. Lanfranchi, M. Roaf and R. Rollinger (eds), *Continuity of Empire (?) Assyria, Media, Persia* (History of the Ancient Near East/Monographs V), pp. 181–231, Padua: S.a.r.g.o.n. Editrice e Libreria.

Henkelman, W. F. M. (2003b), 'Defining "Neo-Elamite History", review-article M. Waters, A Survey of Neo-Elamite History (SAAS 12), Helsinki 2000', *Bibliotheca Orientalis*, 60(3–4): 251–64.

Henkelman, W. F. M. (2008a), *The Other Gods Who Are: Studies in Elamite-Iranian Acculturation Based on the Persepolis Fortification Tablets* (Achaemenid History 14), Leiden: Peeters.

Henkelman, W. F. M. (2008b), 'From Gabae to Taoce: The Geography of the Central Administrative Province, in P. Briant, W. F. M. Henkelman and M. W. Stolper (eds), *L'archive des Fortifications de Persépolis. État des questions et perspectives de recherches (Persika 12). Actes du colloque organisé au Collège de France par la « Chaire d'histoire et civilisation du monde achéménide et de l'empire d'Alexandre » et le « Réseau international d'études et de recherches achéménides (GDR 2538 CNRS)*, 3–4 novembre 2006*, pp. 303–16, Paris: De Boccard.

Henkelman, W. F. M. (2011), 'Cyrus the Persian and Darius the Elamite: A Case of Mistaken Identity', in R. Rollinger, B. Truschnegg and R. Bichler (eds), *Herodot und das Persische Weltreich – Herodotus and the Persian Empire (Akten des 3. Internationalen Kolloquiums zum Thema, »Vorderasien im Spannungsfeld klassischer und altorientalischer Überlieferungen«, Innsbruck, 24–28 November 2008)*, pp. 577–634, Wiesbaden: Harrassowitz Verlag.

Henkelman, W. F. M. (2013), 'Administrative Realities: The Persepolis Archives and the Archaeology of the Achaemenid Heartland', in D. T. Potts (ed.), *The Oxford Handbook of Iranian Archaeology*, pp. 528–46, Oxford: Oxford University Press.

Henkelman, W. F. M. (2017), 'Imperial Signature and Imperial Paradigm: Achaemenid Administrative Structure and System Across and Beyond the Iranian Plateau', in B. Jacobs, W. F. M. Henkelman and M. W. Stolper (eds), *Die Verwaltung im Achämenidenreich: Imperiale Muster und Strukturen/Administration in the Achaemenid Empire: Tracing the Imperial Signature, Akten des 6. Internationalen Kolloquiums zum Thema »Vorderasien im Spannungsfeld klassischer und altorientalischer Überlieferungen« aus Anlass der 80-Jahr Feier der Entdeckung des Festungsarchivs von Persepolis, Landgut Castelen bei Basel, 14. 17. Mai 2013*, pp. 45–256, Wiesbaden: Harrassowitz Verlag.

Henkelman, W. F. M. and M. W. Stolper (2009), 'Ethnicity and Ethnic Labelling at Persepolis: The Case of the Skudrians', in P. Briant and M. Chauveau (eds), *Organisation des pouvoirs et contacts culturels dans les pays de l'empire achéménide* (Persika), Paris: De Boccard.

Henkelman, W. F. M., B. Jacobs and M. W. Stolper (2017), 'Einleitung: Imperiale Muster und Strukturen/Introduction: Tracing the Imperial Signature', in B. Jacobs, W. F. M. Henkelman and M. W. Stolper (eds), *Die Verwaltung im Achämenidenreich: Imperiale Muster und Strukturen/Administration in the Achaemenid Empire: Tracing the Imperial Signature, Akten des 6. Internationalen Kolloquiums zum Thema »Vorderasien im Spannungsfeld klassischer und altorientalischer Überlieferungen« aus Anlass der 80-Jahr Feier der Entdeckung des Festungsarchivs von Persepolis, Landgut Castelen bei Basel, 14. 17. Mai 2013*, pp. VIII–XXXIII, Wiesbaden: Harrassowitz Verlag.

Henning, W. B. (1952), 'The Monuments and Inscriptions at Tang-i Sarvak', *Asia Major*, 2: 151–78 [reprinted (1977), *Acta Iranica*, 15: 359–86].

Henning, W. B. (1957), 'Gabae', *Asia Major*, 1951: 144 [reprinted (1977), *Acta Iranica*, 15: 357].

Henning, W. B. (1977), 'The Monuments and Inscriptions at Tang-i Sarvak', *Asia Major*, 2: 151–78 [reprinted (1977), *Acta Iranica*, 15: 359–86].

Henrickson, R. C. (1983), 'A Reconstruction of the Painted Chamber Ceiling at Baba Jan', *Iranica Antiqua*, 18: 81–96.

Henrickson, E. F. (1985), 'The Early Development of Pastoralism in the Central Zagros Highlands (Luristan)', *Iranica Antiqua*, 20: 1–42.

Herzfeld, E. (1924), *Paikuli: Monument and Inscription af the Early History of the Sasanian Empire* (Forschungen zur Islamischen Kunst Herausgegeben von Friedrich Sarre III), 2 Volumes, Berlin: Dietrich Reimer.

Herzfeld, E. (1932), 'Sakastan, Geschichtliche Untersuchungen zu den Ausgrabungen am Kūh i Khwadja', *Archäologische Mitteilungen aus Iran*, 4: 1–116.

Herzfeld, E. (1968), *The Persian Empire. Studies in Geography and Ethnography of the Ancient Near East*, Wiesbaden: Franz Steiner.

Heydari, S. (2007), 'The Impact of Geology and Geomorphology on Cave and Rock Shelter Archaeological Site Formation, Preservation, and Distribution in the Zagros Mountains of Iran', *Geoarchaeology*, 22(6): 653–69.

Heyvaert, V. M. A., J. Walstra, P. Verkinderen, H. J. T. Weerts and B. Ooghe (2012), 'The Role of Human Interference on the Channel Shifting of the Karkheh River in the Lower Khuzestan Plain (Mesopotamia, SW Iran)', *Quaternary International*, 251: 52–63.

Hinz, W. (1970), s.v. 'Persis', *Paulys Realencyclopädie der Classischen Altertumswissenschaft*, Suppl. 12: 1,022–38.

Hinz, W. (1971), 'Persia c. 2400–1800 BC', in I. E. S. Edwards, C. J. Gadd and N. G. L. Hammond (eds), *The Cambridge Ancient History I*, Part 2, pp. 644–80, Cambridge: Cambridge University Press. https://doi.org/10.1017/CHOL9780521077910.014 (last accessed 10 December 2019).

Hoffmann, G. (1880), *Auszüge aus syrischen Akten persischer Märtyrer* (Abhandlungen für die Kunde des Morgenlandes, Bd. 7, Nr. 3.), Leipzig: Brockhaus.

Högemann, P. (1992), *Das alte Vorderasien und die Achämeniden* (Tübinger Atlas des Vorderen Orients/Beihefte/B), Wiesbaden: Reichert.

Hole, F. (1978), 'Pastoral Nomadism in Western Iran', in Richard A. Gould (ed.), *Explorations in Ethnoarchaeology*, pp. 127–67, Albuquerque: University of New Mexico Press.

Hole, F. (1979), 'Rediscovering the Past in the Present: Ethnoarchaeology in Luristan, Iran, in Carol Cramer (ed.), *Ethnoarchaeology; Implications of Ethnography for Archaeology*, pp. 192–218. New York: Colombia University Press.

Hole, F. (1984), 'A Reassessment of the Neolithic Revolution', *Paléorient*, 10(2): 49–60.

Hole, F. (1996), 'The Context of Caprine Domestication in the Zagros Region', in D. R. Harris (ed.), *The Origins and Spread of Agriculture and Pastoralism in Eurasia*, pp. 263–81, London: UCL Press.

Hole, F. (2004), 'Campsites of the Seasonally Mobile in Western Iran', in K. V. Folsach, H. Thrane and I. Thuesen (eds), *From Handaxe to Khan: Essays Presented to Peder Mortensen on the Occasion of his 70th Birthday*, pp. 67–85, Aarhus: Aarhus University Press.

Hopper, K. and T. J. Wilkinson (2013), 'Population and Settlement Trends in South-west Iran and Neighbouring Areas', in C. A. Petrie (ed.), *Ancient Iran and Its Neighbours: Local Developments and Long-range Interactions in the 4th Millennium BC*, pp. 35–49, Oxford: Oxbow Books.

Hourshid, S. and S. R. Mousavi Haji (2015), 'Archeological Excavation at Barzghavaleh, the Seymareh Dam Basin', *Athar*, 36(68): 93–108.

Howard-Johnston, J. D. (2010), 'The Sasanian Strategic Dilemma', in H. Börm and J. Wiesehöfer (eds), *Commutatio et Contentio. Studies in the Late Roman, Sasanian, and Early Islamic Near East*, pp. 37–70, Dusseldorf: Wellem Verlag.

Hozhabri, A. (1380/2001), *Motāle'e-ye tatavvor-e farhangi-e dowre-ye sāsāni bar asās-e sofāl (mowred-e mohavvate-ye bāstāni-e māhōr-siāh)* [Study of the Cultural Evolution in the Sasanian Period according to Pottery (The Case Study of the Archaeological Site of Māhōr-siāh)], MA thesis, University of Tehran [in Persian with an English abstract].

Hrouda, B. (1976), *Iranische Denkmäler: Lieferung 7 enthaltend Reihe II Iranische Felsreliefs C: Sarpol-i Zohab*, Berlin: Dietrich Reimer Verlag.

Huff, D. (1986), 'Archaeology: IV. Sasanian', in E. Yarshater (ed.), *Encyclopedia Iranica*, vol. 2, pp. 302–308, Costa Mesa: Mazda. https://iranicaonline.org/articles/archeology-iv (last accessed 27 August 2014).

Huff, D. (1999), 'Fārs v. Monuments', in E. Yarshater (ed.), *Encyclopaedia Iranica* 9(4), pp. 351–6, Costa Mesa, CA: Mazda.

Huff, D. (2008), 'Formation and Ideology of the Sasanian State in the Context of Archaeological Evidence, in V. S. Curtis and S. Stewart (eds), *The Sasanian Era (The Idea of Iran, vol. III)*, pp. 31–59, London: I. B. Tauris.

Huff, D. (2011), 'Architecture iii, Sasanian Period', in E. Yarshater (ed.), *Encyclopaedia Iranica*, vol. 2(3), pp. 329–34, Costa Mesa: Mazda. http://www.iranicaonline.org/articles/architecture-iii (last accessed 27 June 2014).

Huff, D. (2014), 'Das Plansystem von Ardašīr-xwarrah: Agrarkolonisatorisches Großprojekt und gebautes Staatsmodell eines von Gott gegebenen Königtums', in K. Rezanian (ed.), *Raumkonzeptionen in Antiken Religionen: Beiträge des Internationalen Symposiums in Göttingen, 28 und 29 Juni 2012* (Philippika 69), pp. 153–210, Wiesbaden: Harrassowitz.

Huff, D. and P. Gignoux (1973), 'Ausgrabungen auf Qal'-ye Dukhtar bei Firuzabad 1976', *Archaeologische Mitteilungen aus Iran*, 6: 117–50.

Huyse, P. (1994), [published 1996]. 'Review essay of La géographie administrative de l'Empire sassanide. Les témoignages sigillographiques, by R. Gyselen, 1989', *Bulletin of the Asia Institute*, 8: 327–30.

Huyse, P. (1999), *Die dreisprachige Inschrift Šābuhrs I. an der Ka'ba-i Zardušt (ŠKZ)* (Corpus Inscriptionum Iranicarum, Part III. Pahlavi Inscriptions. Vol. I. Royal Inscriptions, with their Parthian and Greek Versions. Texts I), 2 Volumes, London: School of Oriental and African Studies.

Ii, H. (1988), 'Seals and Seal Impressions from Tell Gubba', *al-Rafidan*, 9: 97–134.

Ii, H. (1989), 'Finds from Tell Gubba: Beads/Pendants/Rings, Glass Objects, Spindle Whorls, Metal and Bone Objects', *al-Rafidan*, 10: 167–243.

Ii, H. (1990), 'Excavations at Tell Gubba: The Third Millennium B.C. Graves', *al-Rafidan*, 11: 143–74.

Ii, H. (1993), 'Catalogue of Pottery from Tell Gubba: Level VII', *al-Rafidan*, 14: 209–65.

Imanpour, M. T. (1382/2003), 'Makān-e goghrāfiyai-e pārsuā, pārsuāsh va pārsumāsh' [The Geographical Location of Pasua, Parsuash and Parsumash], *Historical Studies (Ferdowsi University of Mashhad)*, 1 and 2: 29–50 [in Persian].

Invernizzi, A. (2020), 'On the Post Achaemenid rock reliefs at Bisutun', *Parthica*, 22: 35–82.

Irons, W. (1974), 'Nomadism as a Political Adaptation: The Case of the Yomut Turkmen', *American Ethnologist*, 1(4) Uses of Ethnohistory in Ethnographic Analysis: 635–58.

Irons, W. (1994), 'Why Are the Yomut Not More Stratified?', in C. Chang and H. A. Koster (eds), *Pastoralists at the Periphery: Herders in a Capitalist World*, pp. 175–96, Tucson: University of Arizona Press.

Jackson Bonner, M. R. (2011), *Three Neglected Sources of Sasanian History in the Reign of Khusraw Anushirvan* (Studia Iranica, Cahier 46), Association pour l'avancement des études Iraniennes, Paris, Leuven: Peeters.

Jacobs, B. (2011), 'Achaemenid Satrapies', in E. Yarshater (ed.), *Encyclopædia Iranica, Online Edition*. http://www.iranicaonline.org/articles/achaemenid-satrapies (last accessed 20 September 2016).

Jacobs, B. (2017), 'Kontinuität oder kontinuierlicher Wandel in der achämenidischen Reichsverwaltung? Eine Synopse von PFT, dahyāva-Listen und den Satrapienlisten der Alexanderhistoriographen', in B. Jacobs, W. F. M. Henkelman and M. W. Stolper (eds), *Die Verwaltung im Achämenidenreich: Imperiale Muster und Strukturen/Administration in the Achaemenid Empire: Tracing the Imperial Signature, Akten des 6. Internationalen Kolloquiums zum Thema »Vorderasien im Spannungsfeld klassischer und altorientalischer Überlieferungen« aus Anlass der 80-Jahr*

Feier der Entdeckung des Festungsarchivs von Persepolis, Landgut Castelen bei Basel, 14. 17. Mai 2013, pp. 3–44, Wiesbaden: Harrassowitz Verlag.

Jacobsen, T. (1982), *Salinity and Irrigation Agriculture in Antiquity, Diyala Basin Archaeological Projects: Report on Essential Results, 1957–58* (Bibliotheca Mesopotamica 14), Malibu: Undena.

Javanmardzadeh, A. (2010), *The Report of Archaeological Survey of Abdanan County, the Fifth Season*, The Organisation of Cultural Heritage, Handicrafts, and Tourism of Ilam Province [unpublished].

Johnson, D. (1969), *The Nature of Nomadism*, Chicago: University of Chicago Press.

Johnson, G. (1982), 'Organisational Structure and Scalar Stress', in C. Renfrew, M. J. Rowlands and B. A. Segraves (eds), *Theory and Explanation in Archaeology*, pp. 389–421. New York: Academic Press.

Johnson, M. (2007), *Ideas of Landscape*, Oxford: Blackwell.

Johnston, R. J. (ed.) (1981), *The Dictionary of Human Geography*, Oxford: Blackwell.

Jones, B. (1997), *The Archaeology of Hunter-Gatherers as Complex Adaptive Agents*, Jones' Axed Dissertation Section, University of Connecticut. https://www.academia.edu/1319664/ The Archaeology of Hunter-Gatherers as Complex Adaptive Agents 1998 (last accessed 1 December 2016).

Jones, S. (2005), 'Transhumance Re-Examined', *The Journal of the Royal Anthropological Institute*, 11(2): 357–9.

Jotheri, J. (2018), 'Recognition Criteria for Canals and Rivers in the Mesopotamian Floodplain', in Y. Zhuang and M. Altaweel (eds), *Water Societies and Technologies from the Past and Present*, pp. 111–26, Los Angeles: UCL Press.

Jullien, F. (2004), 'Parcours a travers l'*Histoire d'Išōʿsabran*, martyr sous Khosrau II', in R. Gyselen (ed.), *Contributions a l'histoire et la géographie historique de l'empire sassanide* (Res Orientales, XVI), pp. 171–83, Bures-sur Yvette: Groupe pour l'Étude de la Civilisation du Moyen-Orient.

Jullien, F. (2009), 'La chronique du Ḫūzistān. Une page d'histoire', in P. Gignoux, C. Jullien and F. Jullien (eds), *Trésors d'Orient: Mélanges offerts à Rika Gyselen* (Studia Iranica, Cahier 42), pp. 159–86, Paris: Association pour l'Avancement des Études Iraniennes.

Kahrstedt, U. (1950), *Artabanus III. Und seine Erben* (Dissertationes Bernenses 1, 2.), Bern: A. Francke.

Kamp, K. A. and N. Yoffee (1980), 'Ethnicity in Ancient Western Asia during the Early Second Millennium B. C.: Archaeological Assessments and Ethnoarchaeological Prospective', *Bulletin of the American Schools of Oriental Research*, 237: 85–104.

Karamian, G. (2015), *The Sasanian City of Ramāvand in Lurestan (Archaeological Excavations of Barz-e Ghawāleh)*, Tehran: Abrishami.

Karamian, G. and K. Farrokh (2017), 'Sassanian Stucco Decorations from the Ramavand (Barz Qawaleh) Excavations in the Lorestan Province of Iran', *Historia i Świat*, 6: 69–88.

Kargar, B. (1383/2004), 'Qalaichi: Zirtu, Centre of Manna, Period Ib', in M. Azarnoush (ed.), *Proceedings of the International Symposium on Iranian Archaeology: Northwestern Region, 17th to 20th June 2004, Urmia, Iran*, pp. 229–45, Tehran: I.C.A.R. [in Persian].

Kavosi, A. and S. Sarlak (1398/2019), 'Excavations at Tepe Sarm: New Evidence of Diverse Grave Structures', in Y. Hassanzadeh, A. A. Vahdati and Z. Karimi (eds), *Proceedings of the International Conference on The Iron Age in Western Iran and Neighbouring Regions, Kurdistan University, Sanandaj, 2–3 Nov. 2019, vol. 1*, pp. 359–69, Tehran: Research Institute for Cultural Heritage and Tourism (RICHT); National Museum of Iran; Kurdistan: Kurdistan Province ICHHTO.

Kawami, T. S. (1987), *Monumental Art of the Parthian Period in Iran* (Acta Iranica 26. Textes et Mémoires XIII), Leiden: Peeters.

Keall, E. J. and M. J. Keall (1981), 'The Qal'eh-i Yazdgird Pottery: A Stratistical Approach', *Iran*, 19: 33–80.

Kehl, M. (2009), 'Quaternary Climate Change in Iran – the State of Knowledge', *Erdkunde*, 63(1): 1–17.

Kennet, D. (2002), 'Sasanian Pottery in Southern Iran and Eastern Arabia', *Iran*, 40: 153–62.

Kennet, D. (2004), *Sasanian and Islamic Pottery from Ras al-Khaimah: Classification, Chronology and Analysis of Trade in the Western Indian Ocean*, Oxford: Archaeopress.

Kennet, D. (2007), 'The Decline of Eastern Arabia in the Sasanian Period', *Arabian Archaeology and Epigraphy*, 18: 86–122.

Kent, M. and P. Coker (1992), *Vegetation Description and Analysis: A Practical Approach*, London: Belhaven.

Kessler, K. (1986), 'Zu den Beziehungen zwischen Urartu und Mesoptamien', in V. Hans (ed.), *Das Reich Urartu. Ein altorientalischer Staat im 1. Jahrtausend v. Chr.* (Xenia 17), pp. 59–86, Konstanz: Universitätsverlag Konstanz.

Kessler K. (1998) 'Namar/Namri', *Reallexikon der Assyriologie und vorderasiatischen Archäologie*, 9: 91–2.

Kettenhofen, E. (1993), *Das Sāsānidenreich, Tübinger Atlas des vorderen Orients* (TAVO), B VI 3: 1: 6, Wiesbaden: Reichert.

Khazanov, A. M. (1984), *Nomads and the Outside World*, Cambridge: Cambridge University Press.

Khazanov, A. M. (1994), *Nomads and the Outside World*, 2nd edition, Madison: University of Wisconsin Press.

Khazanov, A. M. (2009), 'Specific Characteristics of Chalcolithic and Bronze Age Pastoralism in the Near East', in J. Szuchman (ed.), *Nomads, Tribes, and the State in the Ancient Near East. Cross-Disciplinary*

Perspectives (Oriental Institute Seminars 5), pp. 119–28, Chicago: The Oriental Institute of University of Michigan.

Khazeni, A. (2006), *Opening the Land: Tribes, State, and Ethnicity in Qajar Iran, 1800–1911*, PhD dissertation, Yale University.

Khosravi, L., S. M. Mousavi Kouhpar, J. Neyestani and A. Hojabri Nobari (2012), 'Unknown Rulers of Neo-Elamite in Loristan during 1st Millennium B.C.', *International Journal of Humanities*, 17(2): 39–54.

Khosravi, S., S. Alibaigi and M. Rahbar (2018), 'The Function of Gypsum Bases in Sasanid Fire-temples: A Different Proposals', *Iranica Antiqua*, 53: 267–98.

Khosrowzadeh, A. (2010), 'Preliminary Results of the 1st Season of Archaeological Survey of Farsan, Bakhtiari Region, Iran', in P. Matthiae, F. Pinnock, L. Nigro and N. Marchetti (eds), *Proceedings of the 6th International Congress on the Archaeology of the Ancient Near East, May, 5th–10th 2008, 'Sapienza' – Università di Roma*, Vol. 2, pp. 317–37, Wiesbaden: Harrassowitz Verlag.

Khosrowzadeh, A. (1391/2012), 'Examination of the Settlement Patterns of Farsan County, Chaharmahal va Bakhtiyari, from Prehistory to Islamic Times', in H. Fahimi and K. Alizadeh (eds), *Nāmvar-nāme: Papers in Honour of Masoud Azarnoush*, pp. 169–88, Tehran: Negār [in Persian with an English abstract].

Khosrowzadeh, A. (1392/2013), 'Mohavvate-hā va esteqrar-hā-ye ashkāni-e qeshm' [The Parthian Camps and Tappe^h-s of Qeshm Island], *Archaeological Research of Iran*, 5(3): 79–100.

Khosrowzadeh, A. (2014), 'The Second Season of the Archaeological Survey of the Qeshm Island, Iran', *Motāle'āt-e bāstān-shenāsi [Iranian Journal of Archaeological Studies]*, 4: 21–39 [in Persian with an English abstract].

Khosrowzadeh, A. (2015), 'The Chalcolithic Period in the Bakhtiari Highlands: Newly Found Sites of Farsan, Chaharmahal va Bakhtiari, Iran', *International Journal of the Society of Iranian Archaeologists*, 2(2): 32–53.

Khosrowzadeh, A. and M. Bahrami-nia (1391/2012), 'Neolithic Period in the West of Chahrmahal va Bakhtiyari, Newly-Founded Sites in the Miān-kouh District of Ardal County', *Nāme-ye bāstān-shenāsi*, 3(2): 61–80 [in Persian with an English abstract].

Khosrowzadeh, A. and A. 'Āli (1383/2014), 'Description, Classification and Typological Analysis of the Parthian and Sasanian Ceramics of Māh-neshān (Zanjan)', in M. Azarnoush (ed.), *Papers of the International Conference of Archaeology of Iran (North-western Zone)*, pp. 45–70, Tehran: Iranian Center Archaeological Research.

Khosrowzadeh, A. and H. Habibi (1394/2015), 'Study of the Sasanian Settlement Pattern in the Intermontane Plain of Farsan in the Chahar-mahal va Bakhtiari', *Pazhuhesh-hā-ye Bāstān-shenāsi-e irān*, 8(5): 99–118 [in Persian with an English abstract].

Khosrowzadeh, A., A. Norouzi and H. Habibi (2020a), 'A Newly-Discovered Administrative Center of the Late Sasanian Empire: Tappeh Bardnakoon, Farsan, Iran', *Near Eastern Archaeology*, 83.4: 222–33.

Khosrowzadeh, A., A. Norouzi, R. Gyselen and H. Habibi (2020b), 'Administrative Seal Impressions on Bullae Discovered on Tappeh Bardnakoon', in R. Gyselen (ed.), *Persia (552 BCE–758 CE): Primary Sources, Old and New* (Res Orientales, XXVIII), pp. 83–112, Bures-sur-Yvette: Groupe pour l'Étude de la Civilisation du Moyen-Orient.

Khosrowzadeh, A., A. Norouzi, R. Gyselen and H. Habibi (2020c), 'Administrative Bullae from Tappeh Bardnakoon. A Newly Found Late Sasanian Administrative Centre', *Iranica Antiqua*, 55: 165–220.

Kim, G. G. (1991), 'Diachronic Analysis of Changes in Settlement Patterns of the Hamrin Region (Iraq)', *Korean Journal of Ancient History*, 5: 207–92.

Kinnier Wilson, J. V. (1962), 'The Kurba'il statue of Shalmaneser III', *Iraq*, 24: 90–115.

Kleiss, W. (1970), 'Zur Topographie des Partherhangs in Bisotun', *Archäologische Mitteilungen aus Iran*, 3: 133–68.

Kleiss, W. (1983) 'Khowrabad und Djamgaran, Zwei vorgeschichtiche Siedlungen am westrand des zentraliranischen Plateaus', *Archäologische Mitteilungen aus Iran*, 16: 69–103.

Kleiss, W. (1985), 'Der Säulenbau von Khurha', *Archäologische Mitteilungen aus Iran*, Neue floge, 18: 173–80.

Kleiss, W. (1987), 'Cal Tarkhan Suudostlich von Rye', *Archäologische Mitteilungen aus Iran*, 20: 309–18.

Kleiss, W. (1996a), 'Vorwort', in W. Kleiss and P. Calmeyer (eds), *Bisutun. Ausgrabungen und Forschungen in den Jahren 1963–1967* (Teheraner Forschungen VII), pp. 7–14, Berlin: Gebr. Mann.

Kleiss, W. (1996b), 'Die medische Festung', in W. Kleiss and P. Calmeyer (eds), *Bisutun. Ausgrabungen und Forschungen in den Jahren 1963–1967* (Teheraner Forschungen VII), pp. 21–3, Berlin: Gebr. Mann.

Kleiss, W. (1999), 'Der Chahartaq von Navis im Bergland von Tafresh', in A. Alizadeh, Y. Majidzadeh and S. M. Shahmirzadi (eds), *The Iranian World: Essays on Iranian Art and Archaeolog Presented to Ezat O. Negahban*, pp. 200–9, Tehran: Iran University Press.

Klengel, H. (1965), 'Lullubum: Ein Beitrag zur Geschichte der altvorderasiatischen Gebirgsvölker', *Mitteilungen des Instituts für Orientforschung*, 11: 349–71.

Klengel, H. (1988), 'Lullu(bum)', *Reallexikon der Assyriologie und Vorderasiatischen Archäologie*, 7(3 and 4): 164–8.

Kluiving, S. J., F. Lehmkuhl and B. Schütt (2012), 'Landscape Archaeology at the LAC2010 Conference', *Quaternary International*, 251: 1–6.

König, F. W. (1938), 'Bikni', *Reallexicon der Assyriologie*, 2: 28–9.

Kowalewski, S. A. (2008), 'Regional Settlement Pattern Studies', *Journal of Archaeological Research*, 16: 225–85.

Küchler, A. W. (1967), *Vegetation Mapping*, New York: Ronald Press.

Kuhrt, A. (2014), 'State Communications in the Persian Empire', in K. Radner (ed.), *State Correspondence in the Ancient World, From New Kingdom Egypt to the Roman Empire* (Oxford Studies in Early Empires), pp. 112–40, Oxford, New York: Oxford University Press.

Krader, L. (1981), 'The Ecology of Nomadic Pastoralism', in J. G. Galaty and P. E. Salzmann (eds), *Change and Development in Nomadic and Pastoral Society*, pp. 499–510, Leiden: Brill.

Kradin, N. N. (2002), 'Nomadism, Evolution and World-Systems: Pastoral Societies in Theories of Historical Development', *Journal of World Systems Research*, 8(3): 368–88.

Kuniholm, P. I. (1990), 'Archaeological Evidence and Non-evidence for Climate Change', in S. J. Runcorn and J.-C. Pecker (eds), *Philosophical Transactions of the Royal Society of London* (Series A, Mathematical and Physical Sciences, The Earth's Climate and Variability of the Sun Over Recent Millennia: Geophysical, Astronomical and Archaeological Aspect) 330(1,615), pp. 645–55, London: Royal Society.

Labbaf Khaniki, M. (1387 [2008]), 'Sofālhā–ye sāsāni-e shomal-sharq-e Irān' (tabaqe-bandi, moqāyese va tahlil bas asās-e vizhegi-hā-ye shekli) [Sasanian Pottery of Northeastern Iran (Classification, Comparison, and Analysis Based on the Form)], *Journal of the Faculty of Literature and the Humanities of University of Tehran*, 186(4): 143–77 [in Persian with an English abstract].

Lafont, B. (1996), 'L'extraction du minerai du cuivre en Iran à la fin du IIIe millenaire', in O. Tunca and D. Deheselle (eds), *Tablettes et images aux pays de Sumer et d'Akkad: Melanges offerts a Monsieur H. Limet* (Association pour la promotion de l'Histoire et de l'Archéologie), pp. 87–93, Leuven: Peeters.

Lakpour, S. (2010), *Archaeological Excavation in Dareshahr, Seymare*, Tehran: Pāzine.

Lamberg-Karlovsky, C. C. (1970), *Excavations at Tepe Yahya, Iran. 1967–1969. Progress Report I*, Cambridge, MA: Harvard University.

Lambert, M. (1972), 'Hutelutush-Inshushinak et le paysd'Anzan', *Revue d'assyriologie n.s.* 66: 61–76.

Lanfranchi, G. B. and R. Rollinger (2021), 'Some General Considerations on Assyria and North-Western Iran from a Historical Perspective', in S. Heinsch, W. Kuntner and R. Rollinger (eds), *Befund und Historisierung: Dokumentation und ihre Interpretationsspielräume* (ARAXES I. Studies in the Archaeology and History of the Caucasus Area and Adjacent Regions), pp. 57–72, Turnhout: Brepols.

Langdon, S. and D. B. Harden (1934), 'Excavation at Kish and Barghutiat', *Iraq*, 1: 113–23.

Lawrence, D. and T. J. Wilknson (2017), 'The Northern and Western Borderlands of the Sasanian Empire: Contextualizing the Roman/Byzantine and Sasanian Frontier', in E. Sauer (ed.), *Sasanian Persia:*

Between Rome and Steppes of Eurasia, pp. 1–27, Edinburgh: Edinburgh Press.

Leach, E. R. (1940), *Social and Economic Organisation of the Rowanduz Kurds*, London: London School of Economics.

Lecomte, O. (1987), 'La ceramique sassanide', in R. Boucharlat and O. Lecomte (eds), *Fouiles de Tureng-tepe I*, Les périodes sassanides et islamiques, sous la direction de Jean Deshayes (Éditions Recherche sur les Civilisations Mémoire No. 74.), pp. 93–113, Paris: Centre National de la Recherche Scientifique.

Lecomte, O. (2013), 'Activités archéologiques françaises au Turkménistan', in J. Bendezu-Sarmiento (ed.), *L'archéologie française en Asie Centrale* (Cahiers d'Asie Centrale 21/22), pp. 165–90, Paris: Éditions de Boccard.

Lees, Susan H. and D. G. Bates. (1974), 'The Origins of Specialized Nomadic Pastoralism: A Systemic Model', *American Antiquity*, 39(2): 187–93.

Le Rider, G. (1965), *Suse sous les Séleucides et les Parthes* (Mémoires de la délégation archéologique en Iran XXXVIII), Paris: Librairie orientaliste Paul Geuthner.

Le Strange, G. (1905), *The Lands of the Eastern Caliphate: Mesopotamia, Persia, and Central Asia from the Moslem Conquest to the Time of Timur*, Cambridge: Cambridge University Press.

Levine, L. D. (1972), *Two Neo-Assyrian Stelae from Iran*, Royal Ontario Museum (Art and Archaeology Occasional paper, 23), Toronto: Royal Ontario Museum.

Levine L. D. (1973), 'Geographical Studies in the Neo-Assyrian Zagros-I', *Iran*, 11: 1–27.

Levine L. D. (1974), 'Geographical Studies in the Neo-Assyrian Zagros-II', *Iran*, 12: 99–124.

Levine, L. D. (1977), 'Sargon's Eighth Campaign', in L. D. Levine and T. C. Young (eds), *Mountains and Lowlands: Essays in the Archaeology of the Greater Mesopotamia* (Biblioteca, Mesopotamia, vol. 7), pp. 135–52, Malibu: Undena.

Levine, L. D. (1989), 'K. 4675+: The Zamua Itinerary', *State Archives of Assyria Bulletin*, 3: 75–92.

Levine, L. (1382 [2003]) [originally published 1987], 'The Iron Age', in F. Hole (ed.), *The Archaeology of Western Iran: Settlement and Society from Prehistory to the Islamic Conquest* (Smithsonian Series in Archaeological Inquiry, Vol. 27), transl. Z. Basti, pp. 448–96, Tehran: Samt [originally Michigan: Smithsonian Institution Press).

Lewy, H. (1971), 'Assyria, *c.* 2600–1816 BC', in I. E. S. Edwards, C. J. Gadd and N. G. L. Hammond (eds), *The Cambridge Ancient History I*, Part 2, pp. 750–2, Cambridge: Cambridge University Press.

Liu, X. (2001), 'Migration and Settlement of the Yuezhi-Kushan: Interaction and Interdependence of Nomadic and Sedentary Societies', *Journal of World History*, 12(2): 261–92.

Liverani, M. (2003), The Rise and Fall of Media, in History of the Ancient Near East/Monographs-V, in G. B. Lanfranchi, M. Roaf and R. Rollinger (eds), *Continuity of Empire (?) Assyria, Media, Persia*, pp. 1–12, Padua: S.a.r.g.o.n. Editrice e Libreria.

Lock, G., M. Kormann Rodrigues and J. Pouncett (2014), 'Visibility and Movement: Towards a GIS-based Integrated Approach', in S. Polla and P. Verhagen (eds), *Computational Approaches to the Study of Movement in Archaeology: Theory, Practice and Interpretation of Factors and Effects of Long Term Landscape Formation and Transformation* (TOPOI, Berlin Studies of the Ancient World 23), pp. 23–42, Berlin; Boston: De Gruyter.

Luschey, H. (1968), 'Studien zu dem Darius-Relief in Bisutun', *Archäologische Mitteilungen aus Iran*, 1: 63–94.

Luschey, H. (1974), 'Bisutun, Geschichte und Forschungsgeschichte', *Archäologischer Anz.*, 89: 114–49.

Luschey, H. (1996), 'Die seleukidische Heraklesfigur', in W. Kleiss and P. Calmeyer (eds), *Bisutun. Ausgrabungen in den Jahren 1963–1967* (Tehraner Forschungen 7), pp. 59–60, Berlin: Gebr. Mann.

Luschey, H. (2013), 'Bisotun ii. Archeology', in E. Yarshater (ed.), *Encyclopaedia Iranica*, vol. 4(3), pp. 291–9, Costa Mesa, CA: Mazda.

MacGinnis, J. (2020), 'Assyrian Exploitation of Iranian Territories', in K. A. Niknami and A. Hozhabri (eds), *Archaeology of Iran in the Historical Period*, Cham: Springer, pp. 37–54. Available at: 10.1007/978-3-030-41776-5_4 (last accessed 22 December 2021).

Magee, P. (2001), 'Excavations at the Iron Age Settlement of Muweilah in 1997–2000', *Proceedings of the Seminar for Arabian Studies, Vol. 31* (Papers from the thirty-fourth meeting of the Seminar for Arabian Studies held in London, 20–2 July 2000), pp. 115–30, Oxford: Archaeopress.

Magnusson Staaff, B. (2000), 'Hannah Arendt and Torsten Häerstand: Converging Tendencies in Contemporary Archaeological Theory?', in C. Holtorf and H. Karlsson (eds), *Philosophy and Archaeological Practice: Perspectives for the First 21st Century*, pp. 135–52, Götenberg: Bricolieur Press.

Mahboubian, H. (1995), *Treasures of the Mountains. The Art of the Medes* (private exhibition catalogue), London: Houshang Mahboubian.

Maidman, M. P. (1987), 'JEN VII 812: An Unusual Personnel Text from Nuzi', in D. I. Owen and M. A. Morrison (eds), *General Studies and Excavations at Nuzi 9/1* (Studies on the Civilization and Culture of Nuzi 2), pp. 157–66, Winona Lake: Eisenbrauns.

Majbouri, M. and S. Fesharaki (2019), 'Iran's Multi-ethnic Mosaic: A 23-year Perspective', *Social Indicators Research* 145: 831–59. https://doi.org/10.1007/s11205-017-1800-4 (last accessed 6 January 2020).

Majidzadeh, Y. (1379 [2000]), 'Excavations at Ozbaki: First Preliminary Report 1998', *Iranian journal of Archaeology and History*, 13(1), Serial No 25: 57–81 (in Persian, English summary p. 3).

Majidzadeh, Y. (1380 [2001]), 'Excavations at Ozbaki: Second Preliminary Report 1998', *Iranian journal of Archaeology and History*, 14(2), Serial No 28: 38–49 (in Persian, English summary p. 4).

Majidzadeh, Y. (1389 [2000a]), *Excavations at Ozbaki*, 2 vols, vol. 1, Tehran: Tehran OCTH (in Persian).

Majidzadeh, Y. (1389 [2000b]), *Excavations at Ozbaki*, 2 vpls, vol. 2, Tehran: Tehran OCTH (in Persian).

Makinson, M. (1999), 'La culture matérielle du moyen Euphrate au premier millennaire avant J.-C.', in G. del Olmo Lete and J. L. Montero Fenellos (eds), *Archaeology of the Upper Syrian Eupharates: The Tshrin Dam Area, Barcelona 1998*, pp. 363–91, Barcelona: Sabadell.

Malek Shahmirzadi, S. (1382 [2003]), *Sialk's Silversmiths: Report of the Second Season of the Sialk Revisionary Project* (ICAR, Archaeological Reports 3), Tehran: Iranian Center for Archaeological Research (ICAR) (in Persian).

Malekzadeh, M. (1382 [2003]), 'A Stone Structure at Zar Bolagh, Qom: A Median Sanctuary (?): Report on a Preliminary Reconnaissance, Fall 2002', *Iranian Journal of Archaeology and History*, 17(2), Serial No. 34: 52–64 (in Persian).

Malekzadeh, M. (1383 [2004]), 'The Stone Structure at Vasoon-e Kahak, A Possible Median Period Construction: Report on the Winter 2003 Survey', *Iranian Journal of Archaeology and History*, 18(2), Serial No. 36: 42–51 (in Persian).

Malekzadeh, M. (1385/2006), 'Painted Bricks of the Late Iron Age in Eastern Media, Sialk, Shamshirgāh, Qoli-Darvish, Some Thoughts on the Comparative Chronology', *The Iranian Quarterly Journal of History of Iran*, 3: 18–45.

Malekzadeh, M. and R. Naseri (1384 [2005]), 'Painted Bricks of the Late Iron Age in Eastern Media, Another Median Blade', *Bāstān-shenasi*, 1(1): 82–4.

Malekzadeh, M. and R. Naseri (2013), 'Shamshirgah and Sialk: Bricks with Impressions', *Antiquity*, 087(335), Project Gallery.

Malekzadeh, M., S. Saeedyan and R. Naseri (2014), 'Zar Bolagh: A Late Iron Age Site in Central Iran', *Iranica Antiqua*, 49: 159–91.

Malko, H. O. (2014), *Investigation into the Impacts of Foreign Ruling Elites in Traditional State Societies: The Case of the Kassite State in Babylonia (Iraq)*, PhD dissertation, Stony Brook University.

Manning, S. W., B. Kromer, P. I. Kuniholm and M. W. Newton (2001), 'Anatolian Tree Rings and a New Chronology for the East Mediterranean Bronze-Iron Ages', *Science*, 294(5,551): 2,532–5. Available at: 10.1126/science.1066112 (last accessed 17 May 2012).

Manoto TV, *Tunel-e Zaman*, Series 14, Episode 2. https://www.manototv.com/episode/%D8%A7%D9%81%D8%AA%D8%AA%D8%A7%D8%AD-%D9%86%D8%AE%D8%B3%D8%AA%D9%8A%D9%86-%D8%A8%D9%86%D8%A7%D9%87%

D8%A7%DB%8C-%D8%A8%D9%84%D9%86%D8%AF-%
D9%85%D8%B3%D9%83%D9%88%D9%86%
DB%8C-%D8%AA%D9%88%D8%B3%D8%B7-
%D8%B4%D8%A7%D9%87/6703 (last accessed 30 November
2019).

Marchesi, G. (2010), 'The Sumerian King List and the Early History of
Early Mesopotamia', in M. G. Biga and M. Liverani (eds), *Ana turri
gimilli: Studi dedicati al Padre Werner R. Mayer, S. J. da amici e allievi*,
pp. 231–48, Rome: Quaderni di Vicino Oriente 5.

Margueron, J.-C. (1999), 'Notes d'archéologie et d'architecture orientales:
10. L'architecture circulaire dans l'univers syro-mésopotamien au début
du IIIe millénaire', *Syria*, 76: 19–55. http://www.jstor.org/stable/4199288
(last accessed 9 January 2011).

Marrieta-Flores, P. (2014), 'Developing Computational Approaches for
the Study of Movement. Assessing the Role of Visibility and Landscape
Markers in Terrestrial Navigation During Iberian Late Prehistory', in
S. Polla and P. Verhagen (eds), *Computational Approaches to the Study
of Movement in Archaeology: Theory, Practice and Interpretation
of Factors and Effects of Long Term Landscape Formation and
Transformation* (TOPOI. Berlin Studies of the Ancient World 23),
pp. 99–132, Berlin; Boston: De Gruyter.

Martin, A. M. (2013), *Archaeology Beyond Postmodernity: A Science of
the Social*, Lanham, MD: AltaMira Press.

Mashkour, M. (2003), 'Biochemistry for Tracking the Ancient "Nomads":
An Isotopic Research on the Origins of vertical Transhumance in the
Zagros Region', *Nomadic People*, 7(2) Special Issue: Nomads and
Nomadism in Post-revolutionary Iran: 36–47.

Mashkour, M. and K. Abdi (2002), 'The Question of Mobile Pastoralists
in Archaeology: The Case of Tuwah Khushkeh', in H. Buitenhuis,
A. Choyke, M. Mashkour and A. H. Al Shayb (eds), *Archaeozoology of
the Near East*, pp. 211–27, Groningen: ARC.

Mashkour, M., H. Boucherens and I. Moussa (2005), 'Long Distance
of Sheep and Goats of Bakhtiari Nomads tracked with Intra-Tooth
Variations of Stable Isotopes (13C and 18O)', in J. Davies, M. Fabiš,
I. Mainland, M. Richards and R. Thomas (eds), *Diet and Health in
Past Animal Populations: Current Research and Future Directions*
(Proceedings of the 9th the International Conference of Archaeozoology,
Durham, 2002), pp. 113–24. Oxford: Oxbow. https://www.jstor.org/
stable/43123698 (last accessed 2 September 2011).

Mathiesen, H. E. (1992), *Sculpture in the Parthian Empire. A Study in
Chronology*, Aarhus: Aarhus University Press.

Maton, K. (2010), 'Habitus', in M. Grenfell (ed.), *Pierre Bourdieu: Key
Concepts*, pp. 49–66, London: Routledge.

Matthews, W., Y. Mohammadifar, A. Motarjem, H. Ilkhani, L.-M. Shillito
and R. Matthews (2013), 'Issues in the Study of Palaeoclimate and

Palaeoenvironment in the Early Holocene of the Central Zagros, Iran', *International Journal of Archaeology*, 1(2): 26–33.

McFadyn, L. (2008), 'Building and Architecture as Landscape Practice', in B. David and J. Thomas (eds), *Handbook of Landscape Archaeology* (World Archaeological Congress Research Handbooks in Archaeology), pp. 307–14, Walnut Creek, CA: Left Coast Press.

McGill, B. (2015), 'Land Use Matters', *Nature*, 520: 38–9.

Medvedskaya, I. (1992), 'The Question of the Identification of 8–7 Century Median Sites and the Formation of the Iranian Architectural Tradition', *Archäologische Mitteilungen aus Iran*, 26: 73–9.

Medvedskaya, I. (1999), 'Media and Its Neighbours: The Localization of Ellipi', *Iranica Antiqua*, 34: 53–70.

Medvedskaya, I. (2000), 'Zamua, Inner Zamua and Mazamua', in R. Dittmann, B. Hrouda, U. Low', P. Matthiae and R. Mayer-Opificius (eds), *Variatio delectat: Iran und der Westen. Gedenkschrift für Peter Calmeyer* (Altes Orient und Altes Testament 272), pp. 426–43, Münster: Ugarit-Verlag.

Medvedskaya, I. (2002), 'Were the Assyrians at Ecbatana?', *Journal of Kurdish Studies*, 16: 45–57.

Mehrafarin, R. and E. Ahmadi Hedayati (1381 [2011]), 'Chahār Qāpi, a Fire-temple in Khurbarān Kust (Sassanid's Western State)', *Bāq-e Nazar*, 8(18): 75–81 [in Persian].

Mehrkiyan, J. (1997), 'The Elymaian Rock-carving at Shavand, Izeh', *Iran*, 35: 67–72.

Mehr Kian, J. and V. Messina (2019), 'Preliminary Report on the Iranian–Italian Joint Expedition into Khuzestan: Kal-e Chendar; Shami (2013–2016)', *Archeology*, 3(4): 49–78. http://archj.richt.ir/article-10-291-en.html (last accessed 23 January 2020).

Melville, C. (1984), 'Meteorigical Hazards and Disasters in Iran: A Preliminary Survey', *Iran*, 22: 113–50.

Messina, V. (2015), 'Hung-e Azhdar. Report on the Research of the Iranian–Italian Joint Expedition in Khuzestan (2008–2011)', *Parthica*, 17: 9–234.

Messina, V. and J. Mehr Kian (2010), 'The Iranian–Italian Joint Expedition in Khuzistan Hung-E Azdhar: 1st Campaign (2008)', *Parthica*, 12: 31–46.

Messina, V. and J. Mehr Kian (2014a), 'Return to Shami. Preliminary Survey of the Iranian–Italian Joint Expedition in Khuzestan at Kal-e Chendar', *Iran*, 52: 65–77.

Messina, V. and J. Mehr Kian (2014b), 'The Religious Complex at Shami. Preliminary Report on the Research of the Iranian–Italian Joint Expedition in Khuzestan at Kal-e Chendar', in R. A. Stucky, O. Kaelin and H.-P. Mathys (eds), *Proceedings of the 9th International Congress on the Archaeology of the Ancient Near East. Basel 3*, pp. 439–48, Wiesbaden: Harrassowitz.

Michalowski, P. (2008), 'Observations on "Elamites" and "Elam" in Ur III Times', in P. Michalowski (ed.), *On the Third Dynasty of Ur: Studies in Honor of Marcel Sigrist* (JCS Suppl. Series 1), pp. 109–24, Boston: American Schools of Oriental Research.

Michalowski, P. and E. Reiner (1993), *Letters from early Mesopotamia*, Atlanta, GA: Scholars Press.

Michalowski, P., P. de Miroschedji and H. T. Wright (2010), 'Textual Documentation of the Deh Lurân Plain: 2550–325 B.C.', in H. T. Wright and J. A. Neely (eds), *Elamite and Achaemenid Settlement on the Deh Lurân Plain: Towns and Villages of the Early Empires in Southwestern Iran*, pp. 105–12, Michigan: Ann Arbor.

Miller, N. F. (2004), 'Long-term Vegetation Changes in the Near East', in C. L. Redman, S. K. James, R. K. Fish and J. D. Rogers (eds), *The Archaeology of the Global Change*, pp. 130–40. Washington: Smithsonian Books.

Miraskandari, S. M. and A. Chaychi Amirkhiz (1398/2019), 'The Analysis of Archaeological Evidence from the Fourth Floor (C) of Karafto Cave in Northwest of Iran', *Athar*, 40(1): 1–16 [in Persian with an English abstract].

Mlekuž, D. (2014), 'Exploring the Topography of Movement', in S. Polla and P. Verhagen (eds), *Computational Approaches to the Study of Movement in Archaeology: Theory, Practice and Interpretation of Factors and Effects of Long Term Landscape Formation and Transformation* (TOPOI. Berlin Studies of the Ancient World 23), pp. 5–22, Berlin; Boston: De Gruyter.

Mofidi Nasrabadi, B. M. (2004), 'Beobachtungen zum Felsrelief Anubaninis', *Zeitschrift für Assyriologie und vorderasiatische Archäologie*, 94: 291–301.

Moghaddam, A. and N. Miri (2007), 'Archaeological Surveys in the "Eastern Corridor", Southwetern Iran', *Iran*, 45: 23–55.

Mohammadifar, Y. (2010), *Archaeological Excavations at the Seyrom-shāh Fort (Rescue Archaeological Projects in the Seymareh Dam's Basin)*, The Organisation of Cultural Heritage, Handicrafts, and Tourism – The Research Institute for Archaeology [unpublished].

Mohammadifar, Y. (2014), 'Rescue Excavations at Two Sassanian Sites of the Seymareh Dam, Luristan', in *9th International Congress on the Archaeology of the Ancient Near East* (ICAANE), Abstracts, Sections, Posters, Workshops, 9–13 June 2014, University of Basel, Switzerland.

Mohammadifar, Y. and A. Motarjem (2001), 'The Report of Archaeological Survey of Abdanan County, the Second Season', The Organisation of Cultural Heritage, Handicrafts, and Tourism of Ilam Province [unpublished].

Mohammadifar, Y. and A. Motarjem (2012), 'Julian: A Newly Discovered Fire-Temple in Ābdānān', transl. G. Watson, *Sasanika*, 6.

Mohammadifar, Y and E. Tahmasebi (2014), 'The Classification of the Ceramics Acquired from Seymare: The Case Study of the Seyrom-shāh Fort', *Archaeological Research of Iran*, 4(7): 133–52.

Mohammadifar, Y. and H. Habibi (2017), 'Kerkenes Daq: A Median Colony or A Phrygian City?', *Journal of Iran's Pre-Islamic Archaeological Essays*, 1(2): 1–15 [in Persian with an English abstract].

Mohammadifar, Y. and H. Habibi (2018), 'The Sophisticated Falsificationism: A Solution for the Critical Situation of the Epistemology of Archaeology', *Archaeological Researches of Iran*, 8(17): 7–26 [in Peresian with an English abstract].

Mollazadeh, K. (1388/2009), 'The Kingdom of Mannea. An Appraisal of the Cultural, Social and Political Structures of Mannea Based on the Evidence from Archaeological and Historical Geography', *Bāstān-pazhuhi*, 4(7): 45–53 [in Persian].

Mollazadeh, K. (1391/2012), 'Parshua, Parsua, Parsuash, Parsumash and Its Relation to the Persians and Their Migration to Iran', *Pazhuhesh-hā-ye 'olum-e tārikhi*, 4(2): 107–23 [in Persian].

Mollazadeh, K. (1393/2014), *Bāstān-shenāsi-e mād* [Archaeology of Media], Tehran: SAMT [in Persian].

Mollazadeh, K. and A. Goudarzi (1395/2016), 'Historical Geography of the Kingdom of Ellipi', *Pazhohesh-hā-ye bāstān-shenāsi-e irān*, 6(10): 83–100.

Monkhouse, F. J. (1970), *A Dictionary for Geography*, 2nd edition, Chicago: Aldine.

Moradi, E. (2005), 'Report on the Third Season of Archaeological Survey of Abdanan County, Mourmouri District', The Organisation of Cultural Heritage, Handicrafts, and Tourism of Ilam Province [unpublished].

Moradi, Y. (2016), 'On the Sasanian Fire-temples: New Evidence from the Čahār-Tāq of Mil-e Milagah', *Parthica*, 18: 31–52.

Moradi, Y. (2019), 'Epigraphical and Iconographical Analysis of a Parthian Bas-relief from Javanroud, Western Iran (with a Note on the Inscription by Seiro Haruta)', *Parthica*, 21: 143–58.

Moradi, Y. and Keall, E. J. (2019): 'The Sasanian Fire-temple of Gach Dawar in Western Iran: New Evidence', *Iran*, 58(1): 27–40. Available at: 10.1080/05786967.2019.1566761 (last accessed 25 February 2021).

Moritz, M., J. Giblin, M. Ciccone, A. Davis, J. Fuhrman, M. Kimiaie, S. Madzsar, K. Olson and M. Senn (2011), 'Social Risk Management Strategies in Pastoral Systems: A Qualitative Comparative Analysis', *Cross-Cultural Research* 45(3): 286–317. https://doi.org/10.1177/10693 97111402464 (last accessed 17 January 2012).

Morkholm, O. (1965), 'A Greek Coin Hoard from Susiana', *Acta Archaeologica*, 36: 127–56.

Morony, M. G. (1994), 'Land Use and Settlement Pattern in Late Sasanian and Early Islamic Iraq', in G. R. D. King and A. Cameron (eds), *The Byzantine and Early Islamic Near East, II Land Use and Settlement Patterns*, pp. 221–30, Princeton, NJ: Darwin Press.

Morony, M. G. (2004), 'Economic Boundaries? Late Antiquity and Early Islam', *Journal of the Economic and Social History of the Orient*, 47(2): 166–94. http://www.jstor.org/stable/25165033 (last accessed 15 December 2011).

Morony, M. G. (2012), 'Iran in the Early Islamic Period', in T. Daryaee (ed.), *The Oxford Handbook of Iranian History*, Oxford: Oxford University Press. Available at: 10.1093/oxfordhb/9780199732159.013.0009 (last accessed 26 August 2019).

Mortazavi, M. and M. Heydari Dastenaei (1398/2019), 'Demographic Studies of the Era between Neolithic and Bronze Age in Lārān District of Chaharmahal va Bakhtiyari', *Jāme'e-shenāsi-e tārikhi*, 11(2): 291–316 [in Persian with an English abstract].

Mortensen, I. D. (1993), *Nomads of Luristan: History, Material Culture, and Pastoralism in Western Iran*, London: Thames & Hudson.

Mortensen, P. (1972), 'Seasonal Camps and Early Villages in the Zagros', in P. Ucko, R. Tringham and G. W. Dimbleby (eds), *Man, Settlement and Urbanism*, pp. 293–7, London: Duckworth.

Mortensen, P. (1974), 'A Survey of Prehistoric Sites in the Holailan Valley in Lorestan', *Proceedings of the Second Annual Symposium on Archaeological Research in Iran, 1973*, pp. 34–52, Tehran: Iranian Centre for Archaeological Research, Muzeh-ye Iran-e Bastan.

Mortensen, P. (1976), 'Chalcolithic Settlements in the Holailan Valley', in F. Bagherzadeh (ed.), *Proceedings of the 4th Symposium on Archaeological Research in Iran*, pp. 42–62, Tehran: Iranian Center for Archaeological Research.

Mo'tamedi, N. (1371 [1992]), 'Mehrābe-ye vīzenhār-e qla'e kohzād/ vīzenhār [mehrābe of Qla'e Kohzād]', *Mirās-e Farhangī*, 3(5): 8–16 [in Persian].

Mo'tamedi, N. (1376 [1997]), 'Ziviye. The Excavations of the Year 1374, Architecture and Description of the Pottery', in M. Malekzadeh (ed.), *Archaeological Reports* 1, pp. 143–70, Tehran: OCTH.

Motarjem, A. and Y. Mohammadifar (2000), 'Report on Archaeological Survey of Abdanan County, the First Season', The Organisation of Cultural Heritage, Handicrafts, and Tourism of Ilam Province [unpublished].

Motarjem, A. and Z. Bakhtiyari (2015), 'The First Season of Salvage Excavations at Barz-e Qala (Lelar) in the Basin Seymareh River Dam', in L. Niakan (ed.), *Archaeological Investigations in the Seymareh Dam Basin*, pp. 200–10, Tehran: ICAR.

Mousavi, A. (2008), 'A Survey of the Archaeology of the Sasanian Period During the Past Three Decades', *Sasanika Archaeological Reports, e-Sasanika* 1. http://www.sasanika.org/e-categories/archeological-reports/ (last accessed 15 September 2010).

Mousavi, A. (2020), 'Sāleh Dāvood', in *The Archaeological Gazetteer of Iran: An Online Encyclopedia of Iranian Archaeological Sites*, UCLA Pourdavoud Center for the Study of the Iranian World. https://irangazetteer.humspace.ucla.edu/catalogue/saleh-davood-%d8%b5%d8%a7%d9%84%d8%ad-%d8%af%d8%a7%d9%88%d9%88%d8%af/# (last accessed 27 April 2021).

Mousavi, A. and T. Daryaee (2012), 'The Sasanian Empire: An Archaeological Survey, c.220–AD 640', in D. Potts (ed.), *A Companion to the Archaeology of the Near East*, vol. 1, pp. 1,076–94, Malden, MA; Oxford; Chichester: Wiley-Blackwell.

Muscarella, O. W. (1986), 'The Location of Ulhu and Uiše in Sargon II's Eighth Campaign', *Journal of Field Archaeology*, 13(4): 465–75.

Muscarella, O. W. (1987), 'Median Art and Medizing Scholarship', *Journal of Near Eastern Studies*, 46(1987): 109–27.

Muscarella, O. W. (1994), 'Miscellaneous Median Matters', in A. Kuhrt, M. C. Root and H. Sancisi-Weerdenburg (eds), *Continuity and Change* (Achaemenid History, 8), pp. 57–64, Leiden: Nederlands Instituut voor het Nabije Oosten.

Muscarella, O. W. (2003), 'The Date of the Destruction of the Early Phrygian Period at Gordion', *Ancient West & East*, 2(2): 225–52.

Muscarella, O. W. (2008), 'The Iranian Iron III Chronology at Muweilah in the Emirate of Sharjah', *Ancient West and East*, 7: 189–202.

Muscarella, O. W. (2013), *Archaeology, Artifacts and Antiquities of the Ancient Near East: Sites, Cultures, and Proveniences* (Culture and History of the Ancient Near East), Leiden and Boston: Brill.

Myres, J. L. (1941), 'Nomadism', *The Journal of Royal Anthropological Institute of Great Britain and Ireland*, 71(1/2): 19–42.

Nashef, K. (1982), *Die Orts- und Gewässernamen der mittelbabylonischen und mittelassyrischen Zeit* (Répertoire géographique des textes cunéiformes 5), Wiesbaden: L. Reichert.

Neely, J. A. (1974), 'Sasanian and Early Islamic Water-Control and Irrigation Systems on the Deh Luran Plain, Iran', in T. E. Downing and McG. Gibson (eds), *Irrigation's Impact on Society*, pp. 21–42, Tucson: The University of Arizona Press.

Neely, J. A. (2011), 'Sasanian Period Drop-Tower Gristmills on the Dehluran Plain, Southwestern Iran', *Journal of Field Archaeology*, 36(3): 232–54.

Neely, J. A. (2016), 'Parthian and Sasanian Settlement Patterns on the Dehluran Plain, Khuzistan Province, Southwestern Iran', *Iranica Antiqua*, 51: 235–300.

Niakan, L. (2015a), 'The Preliminary Report of Salvage Excavations at Lelar in the Seymareh Dam Basin', in L. Niakan (ed.), *Archaeological Investigations in the Seymareh Dam Basin*, pp. 187–99, Tehran: ICAR.

Niakan, L. (ed.) (2015b), *The Proceedings of the Conference Archaeological Research at the Seymareh Dam Basin*, Tehran: Iranian Center for Archaeological Research (ICAR) [in Persian].

Niakan, L. (2019), 'Rouha, Sassanian Building in the Seymareh Coast', *Pazhohesh-ha-ye Bastanshenasi Iran* 9(20): 129–48 [in Persian].

Nissen, H. J. and A. Zagarell (1976), 'Expedition to the Zagros Mountains', in F. Bagherzadeh (ed.), *Proceedings of the 4th Annual Symposium on*

Archaeological Research in Iran, 1975, pp. 159–89, Tehran: Iranian Center for Archaeological Research.

Nöldeke, T. (1874), 'Griechische Namen Susiana's', *Nachrichten von der Königlichen Gesellschaft der Wissenschaften, und der Georg-August Universität zu Göttingen* 8 (Geschäftliche Mitteilungen): 173–97.

Norouzi, A. (1388/2010), 'Archeological Studies on Northern Karūn Basin (Chahārmahāl-o-Bakhtiyārī Province', *Motāle'at-e bāstān-shenāsi [Iranian Journal of Archaeological Studies]*, 1(2): 161–75 [in Persian with an English abstract].

Norouzi, A. and M. Heydari Dastenaei (1397/2018), 'Preliminary Report of Archaeological Surveys in the Lower Basin of the Southern Zāyande-rōd, Lārān District, Chaharmahal va Bakhtiyari', *Motāle'at-e bāstān-shenāsi [Iranian Journal of Archaeological Studies]*, 17(1): 207–26 [in Persian with an English abstract].

Nowrouzzadeh, N. (1381/2002), 'Bricks with Seal Impressions', in S. Malek Shahmirzadi (ed.), *Sialk's Zigurat. Sialk's Revisionary Project, First Season*, pp. 171–5, Tehran: OCHT.

Oates, J. (1987a), 'The Choga Mami Transitional', in J.-L. huot (ed.), *La Préhistoire de la Mesopotamie*, pp. 163–80, Paris: Armand Colin.

Oates, J. (1987b), 'La Choga Mami Transitional et l'Obeid 1, Synthèse de la Séance', in J.-L. huot (ed.), *La Préhistoire de la Mesopotamie*, pp. 199–206, Paris: Editions du CNRS.

Oberlander, T. (1965), *The Zagros Streams: A New Interpretation of Transverse Drainage in an Orogenic Zone* (Syracuse Geographical Series 1), Syracuse, NY: Syracuse University Press.

Oded, B. (1979), *Mass Deportations and Deportees in the Neo-Assyrian Empire*, Wiesbaden: Reichert.

Oguchi, K. and K. Matsumoto (2001), 'Archaeology: Expeditions and Discoveries in West Asia by Japanese Archaeologists', *Orient* 36: 7–23. https://doi.org/10.5356/orient1960.36.7 (last accessed 24 February 2008).

Olbrycht, M. J. (2010), 'Macedonia and Persia', in J. Roisman and I. Worthington (eds), *A Companion to Ancient Macedonia*, pp. 342–70, Malden, MA; Oxford: Wiley-Blakwell.

Olwig, K. R. (1996), 'Recovering the Substantive Nature of Landscape', *Annals of the Association of American Geographers*, 86(4): 630–53.

Omrani Rekavandi, H., E. W. Sauer, T. Wilkinson, G. A. Abbasi, S. Priestman, E. Safari Tamak, R. Ainslie, M. Mahmoudi, N. Galiatsatos, K. Roustai, J. Jansen Van Rensburg, M. Ershadi, E. MacDonald, M. Fattahi, C. Oatley, B. Shabani, J. Ratcliffe and L. Steven Usher-Wilson (2008), 'Sasanian Walls, Hinterland Fortresses and Abandoned Ancient Irrigated Landscapes: The 2007 Season on the Great Wall of Gorgan and The Wall of Tammishe', *Iran*, 46: 151–78. http://www.jstor.org/stable/25651440 (last accessed 26 April 2013).

Orton, C., P. Tyers and A. Vince (2007), *Pottery in Archaeology* (Cambridge Manuals in Archaeology), Cambridge: Cambridge University Press.

Oshima, T. (2012), 'Another Attempt at Two Kassite Royal Inscriptions: The Agum-Kakrime Inscription and the Inscription of Kurigalzu son of Kadashmanharbe', in L. Kogan (ed.), *Babel und Bibel*, 6, pp. 255–65, Winona Lake: Eisenbrauns.

Overlaet, B. (2003), *The Early Iron Age in the Pusht-i Kuh, Luristan (LED IV), Belgian Archaeological Mission in Iran, The Excavations in Iran, Pusht-i Kuh, Luristan (1965–1979), The Ghent University and the Royal Museum of Art and History, Brussels Joint Expedition (Acta Iranica 40), Directed by Louis Vanden Berghe*, Leuven: Peeters,

Overlaet, B. (2005), 'The Chronology of the Iron Age in the Pusht-i Kuh, Luristan', *Iranica Antiqua*, 40: 1–33.

Pace, M., A. Bianco Prevot, P. Mirti and R. Venco Ricciardi (2008), 'The Technology of Production of Sasanian Glazed Pottery from Veh Ardashir (Central Iraq)', *Archaeometry*, 50(4): 591–605.

Packard, N. H. (1988a), *Adaptation Toward the Edge of Chaos*, Technical Report, Center for Complex Systems Research (CCSR), Illinois: University of Illinois at Urbana-Champaign.

Packard, N. H. (1988b), 'Adaptation Toward the Edge of Chaos', in J. A. S. Kelso, A. J. Mandell and M. F. Schlesinger (eds), *Dynamic Patterns in Complex Systems* (Proceedings of the Conference in Honor of Hermann Haken's 60th Birthday), pp. 293–301, Singapore: World Scientific.

Palumbi, G. (2010), 'Pastoral Models and Centralised Animal Husbandry. The Case of Arsalantepe', in M. Frangipane (ed.), *Economic Centralisation in Formative States. The Archaeological Reconstruction of the Economic System in 4th Millennium Arslantepe* (Studi di Preistoria Orientale (SPO) 3), pp. 149–66, Rome: Sapienza Universita di Roma.

Panahipour, M. (2018), 'Patterns of Land-Use and Political Administration Beyond the Core Areas of the Sasanian Empire', *Presented at the 82nd Annual Meeting of the Society for American Archaeology*, Washington, DC.

Panahipour, M. (2019), 'Land Use and Environment in a Zone of Uncertainty: A Case of the Sasanian Expansion in Eastern Iraq – Western Iran', *Iran*, 57(6): 1–19. https://doi.org/10.1080/05786967.2019.16577 81 (last accessed 22 May 2020).

Parpola, S. (1970), *Neo-Assyrian Toponyms (Alter Orient und Altes Testament, 6)*, Kevelaer: Verlag Butzon & Bercker; Neukirchen-Vluyn: Neukirchener Verlag.

Parpola, S. and M. Porter (2001), *The Helsinki Atlas of the Near East in the Neo-Assyrian Period* (The Neo-Assyrian Text Corpus Project), Helsinki: Casco Bay Assyriological Institute.

Paulette, T. (2013), 'Pastoral Systems and Economies of Mobility', in T. J. Wilkinson, McG. Gibson and M. Widel (eds), *Models of Mesopotamian Landscapes: How Small-scale Processes Contributed to the Growth of Early Civilizations* (BAR International Series 2,552), pp. 130–9, Oxford: Archaeopress.

Payne, R. (2010), *Christianity and Iranian Society in Late Antiquity, ca. 500–700 CE*, PhD dissertation, Princeton University.

Payne R. (2014), 'The Archaeology of Sasanian Politics', *Journal of Ancient History*, 2(2): 1–13.

Payne, R. (2015), *A State of Mixture: Christians, Zoroastrians, and Iranian Political Culture in Late Antiquity*, Oakland: University of California Press.

Peterson, M. R. (2008), 'Prehistoric Settlement Patterns on the High Plains of Western Nebraska and the Use of Geographic Information Systems for Landscape Archaeology', in L. L. Scheiber and B. J. Clark (eds), *Archaeological Landscapes on the High Plains*, pp. 237–76, Colorado: The University Press of Colorado.

Petrie, P. (2005), 'Exploring Routes and Plains in Southwest Iran', *ArchAtlas, Version 5.0*. https://www.archatlas.org/journal/cpetrie/routesandplains/ (last accessed 11 May 2021).

Pettinatto, G., H. Waetzoldt and F. Pomponio (1977), *Testi economici de Lagač del Museo di Istanbul: La. 7001–7600* (Materiali per il vocabolario neosumerico 6), Rome: Bonsignori editore.

Phillips, C. (2008), 'Late Finds from Kalba (United Arab Emirates)', in S. Priestman and S. T. Simpson (organisers), *Parthian, Sasanian and Early Islamic Pottery: Dating, Definition and Distribution; a Specialist Workshop at The British Museum*, pp. 17–28.

Pigulevskaya, N. (1387 [2008]), *Shahrhā-ye irān dar ruzegār-e pārtiān va sāsāniān* [Cities of Iran in Parthian and Sasanian Times], transl. E. Reza, Tehran: 'Elmi va farhangi.

Polla, S. and P. Verhagen (2014), 'Introduction', in S. Polla and P. Verhagen (eds), *Computational Approaches to the Study of Movement in Archaeology: Theory, Practice and Interpretation of Factors and Effects of Long Term Landscape Formation and Transformation* (TOPOI. Berlin Studies of the Ancient World 23), pp. 1–4, Berlin; Boston: De Gruyter.

Pomponio, F. (2011), 'Quello che accade (forse) dopo la morte di Šar-kali-šarrī', in G. Barjamovic, J. L. Dahl, U. S. Koch, W. Sommerfeld and J. G. Westenholz (eds), *Akkade is King! A Collection of Papers by Friends and Colleagues Presented to Aage Westenholz on the Occasion of his 70th Birthday 15th of May 2009* (Publications de l'institut historique et archéologique néerlandais de Stamboul, 118), pp. 227–43, Leiden: Nederlands Instituut voor het Nabije Oosten.

Postgate, N. J. (1979), 'The Historical Geography of the Hamrin Basin', *Sumer*, 35: 591–94.

Postgate, N. J. and M. Roaf (1997), 'The Shaikhan Relief', *Al-Rāfidān*, 18: 143–56.

Postgate, N. J. and P. J. Watson (1979), Excavations in Iraq, 1977–78, *Iraq*, 41(2): 141–81. http://www.jstor.org/stable/4200109 (last accessed 24 February 2014).

Potts, D. T. (1998), 'Namord Ware in Southeastern Arabia', in C. S. Philips, D. T. Potts and S. Searight (eds), *Arabia and Its Neighbours, Essays on Prehistorical and Historical Developments Presented in Honour of Beatrice De Cardi* (Abiel II), pp. 207–20, Turnhout: Brepols.

Potts, D. T. (2005), 'Cyrus the Great and the Kingdom of Anshan', in V. S. Curtis and S. Stewart (eds), *Birth of the Persian Empire (The Idea of Iran, Vol. 1)*, pp. 7–28, London: I. B. Tauris.

Potts, D. T. (2010), 'Adamšah, Kimaš and the Miners of Lagaš', in H. D. Baker, E. Robson and G. Zólyomi (eds), *Your Praise is Sweet: A Memorial Volume for Jeremy Black from Students, Colleagues and Friends*, pp. 245–54, London: British Institute for the Study of Iraq.

Potts, D. T. (2013), 'Luristan and The Central Zagros in The Bronze Age', in D. T. Potts (ed.), *The Oxford Handbook of Ancient Iran*, pp. 203–16, Oxford: Oxford University Press.

Potts, D. T. (2014), *Nomadism in Iran: From Antiquity to the Modern Era*, Oxford: Oxford University Press. Available at: 10.1093/acprof: oso/9780199330799.001.0001 (last accessed 2 April 2015).

Potts, D. T. (2016), *The Archaeology of Elam; Formation and Transformation of an Ancient Iranian State*, 2nd edition, New York: Cambridge University Press.

Potts, D. T. (2017), 'Elamite Karintaš and Avestan Kvirinta: Notes on the Early History of Kerend', *Iranian Studies*, 50/3: 345–67. http://dx.doi.org /10.1080/00210862.2017.1301201 (last accessed 1 August 2017).

Potts, D. T. (2018), 'Arboriculture in Ancient Iran: Walnut (Juglans regia), Plane (Platanus Orientalis) and the "Radde dict um"', *Dabir* (Hanns Peter-Schmidt (1930–2017) Gedenkschrift), 6: 101–9.

Potts, D. T. (2020), 'On Cultural Boundaries and Languages in Western Iran: The Case of the Zagros Gates', in K. A. Niknami and A. Hozhabri (eds), *Archaeology of Iran in the Historical Period* (University of Tehran Science and Humanities Series), pp. 55–63, Cham: Springer Nature Switzerland. https://doi.org/10.1007/978-3-030-41776-5_5 (last accessed 3 September 2021).

Potts, D. T. (2021), 'The Sea of Zamua', in A. J. D. Monedero, C. Del Cerro Linares, F. J. Villaba Ruiz Del Toledo and F. L. Borrego Gallardo (eds), *Nomina in aqua scripta: Homenaje a Joaquín María Córdoba Zoilo*, pp. 557–69, Madrid: UAM Ediciones.

Potts, D. T. and K. Roustaei (eds) (2009), *The Mamasani Archeological Project Stage One: A Report on the First Two Seasons of the ICAR – University of Sydney Expedition to the Mamasani District, Fars Province, Iran* (British Archaeological Reports International Series 2044), Oxford: Archaeopress.

Pourshariati P. (2008), *Decline and Fall of the Sasanian Empire; The Sasanian–Parthian Confederacy and the Arab Conquest of Iran* (International Library of Iranian Studies), London: I. B. Tauris.

Priestman, S. M. N. (2013a), 'Regional Ceramic Diversity in the Sasanian World', Talk given at Persia and Rum, A British Institute of Persian Studies conference hosted by The British School at Rome on 14 and 15 November 2013, *The Sasanian Empire and Rome*, 14 November 2013.

Priestman, S. M. N. (2013b), 'Sasanian Ceramics from the Gorgān Wall and Other Sites on the Gorgān Plain', in E. W. Sauer, H. Omrani Rekavandi, T. J. Wilkinson and J. Nokandeh (eds), *Persia's Imperial Power in Late Antiquity: The Great Wall of Gorgan and Frontier Landscapes of Sasanian Iran* (British Institute of Persian Studies Archaeological Monograph Series 2), pp. 447–534, Oxford–Oakville: Oxbow.

Priestman, S. M. N., N. S. Al Jahwari, D. Kennet and E. Sauer (2022), 'Fulayj: A Late Sasanian Fort on the Batinah, Oman and its Transformation in the Early Islamic Period', *55th Seminar for Arabian Studies*, Humboldt Universität, 5 August 2022. https://www.academia.edu/84210737/Priestman_Al_Jahwari_Kennet_et_al_2022_Fulayj_A_Late_Sasanian_Fort_on_the_Batinah_Oman_and_its_Transformation_in_the_Early_Islamic_Period (last accessed 1 August 2022).

Przeworsky, S. (1929), 'Die Lage von Pteria', *Archiv Orientálni*, 1: 312–15.

Puschnigg, G. (2006a), 'Ceramics in Sasanian Archaeology', in P. J. Ucko and G. Puschnigg (eds), *Ceramics of the Merv Oasis*, pp. 3–16, New York: Routledge.

Puschnigg, G. (2006b), *Ceramics of the Merv Oasis: Recycling the City* (University College London Institute of Archaeology Publications), Walnut Creek, CA: Left Coast Press.

Puschnigg, G. (2008), 'Beyond Merv: Sasanian Pottery in Its Regional Context', in *Parthian, Sasanian and Early Islamic Pottery: dating, definition and distribution; A Specialist Workshop at The British Museum*, organised by Seth Priestman and St John Simpson, pp. 37–8.

Radner, K. (2003), 'An Assyrian View on the Medes', in G. B. Lanfranchi, M. Roaf and R. Rollinger (eds), *Continuity of Empire (?): Assyria, Media, Persia*, pp. 37–64, Padua: S.a.r.g.o.n.

Radner, K. (2017), 'Zamua', *Reallexikon der Assyriologie und Vorderasiatischen Archaologie*, 15: 210–13.

Radner, K., M. Masoumian, H. Karimian, E. Azizi and K. Omidi (2020a), 'Neo-Assyrian Royal Monuments from Lake Zeribar in Western Iran: A Stele of Sargon II and a Rock Relief of Shalmaneser III', *Zeitschrift für Assyriologie und Vorderasiatische Archäologie*, 110: 84–93.

Radner, K., S. Amelirad and E. Azizi (2020b), 'A First Radiocarbon Date for the Iron Age Cemetery of Sanandaj: Dating an Elite Burial in the Assyrian Province of Parsua', in S. Hasegawa and K. Radner (eds), *The Reach of the Assyrian and Babylonian Empires: Case studies in Eastern and Western Peripheries* (Studia Chaburensia, 8), pp. 95–109, Wiesbaden: Harrassowitz. Available at: 10.13173/9783347114776_95 (last accessed 7 May 2021).

Rahbar, M. (1979), 'Remarks on Some Seleucid Objects in the Iran Bastan Museum', in *Akten des VII. Internationalen Kongress für Iranische Kunst und Archäologie, München 7–10 September 1976* (*Archäologische Mitteilungen aus Iran* 6), pp. 249–76, Berlin: D. Reimer.

Rahbar, M. (1376 [1998]), 'Archaeological Excavations at Golālak, Shushtar', in S. M. Mousavi (ed.), *Memoir of the Archaeological Congress of Susa, 25–27 Farvardin 1373*, pp. 175–208, Tehran: OCTH.

Rahbar, M. (1391 [2012]), 'Ārāmgāh-e zirzamini-ye elymā'i dar Sāleh Dāvood', in H. Fahimi and K. Alizadeh (eds), *Nāmvarnāmeh. Papers in Honour of Massoud Azarnoush*, pp. 289–314, Tehran: Iran-negār.

Rahbar, M., S. Alibaigi, E. Haerinck and B. Overlaet (2014), 'In Search of the Laodikea Temple at Laodikea Media/Nahavand, Iran', *Iranica Antiqua*, 49: 301–29.

Ranhao, S., Z. Baiping and T. Jing (2008), 'A Multivariate Regression Model for Predicting Precipitation in the Daqing Mountains', *Mountain Research and Development*, 28: 318–25.

Rawlinson, H. C. (1839), 'Notes on a March from Zohab, at the Foot of Zagros, along the Mountains to Khuzistan (Susiana), and from Thence through the Province of Luristan to Kirmanshah, in the Year 1836', *Journal of the Royal Geographical Society of London*, 9: 26–116.

Razmjou, S. (2005), 'In Search of the Lost Median Art, *Iranica Antiqua*, 40: 271–314.

Reade, J. E. (1976), 'Elam and Elamites in Assyrian Sculpture', *Archäologische Mitteilungen aus Iran*, 9: 97–106.

Reade, J. E. (1977), 'Shkaft-i Gul Gul: Its Date and Symbolism', *Iranica Antiqua*, 12: 33–48.

Reade, J. E. (1978), 'Kassites and Assyrians in Iran', *Iran*, 16: 137–43.

Reade, J. E. (1979), 'Hasanlu, Gilzanu, and Related Consideration', *Archäeologische Mitteilungen aus Iran*, 12: 175–81.

Reade, J. E. (1995), 'Iran in Neo-Assyrian Period', in M. Liverani (ed.), *Neo-Assyrian Geography* (Quaderni di geografia storica, 5), pp. 31–42, Rome: Università di Roma, Dipartimento di scienze storiche, archeologiche e antropologiche dell'Antichità.

Reiner, E., R. D. Biggs, R. I. Caplice, M. B. Rowton, P. D. Daniels and J. Robinson (eds) (1984), *The Assyrian Dictionary*, vol. 15, S, Chicago: Oriental Institute.

Reitz, E. J., L. A. Newsom, S. J. Scudder and C. M. Scarry (2013), 'Introduction to Environmental Archaeology', in E. J. Reitz, C. M. Scarry and S. J. Scudder (eds), *Case Studies in Environmental Archaeology*, pp. 3–20, New York: Springer.

Renfrew, C. (2006), 'Becoming Human: The Archaeological Challenge', *Proceedings of the British Academy* 139: 217–38.

Rezaei, S. and A. Bahrami (2019), 'Attitudes toward Kurdish in the City of Ilam in Iran', in S. H. Mirvahedi (ed.), *The Sociolinguistics of Iran's*

Languages at Home and Abroad: The Case of Persian, Azerbaijani, and Kurdish, pp. 77–106, New York: Palgrave Macmillan.

Rezakhani, K. (2021), 'Nobles and Land: The Formation of the South (Nēmrōz) and the Politics of the Elite in the Sasanian Empire', in S. Balatti, H. Klinkott and J. Wiesehöfer (eds), *Paleopersepolis: Environment, Landscape and Society in Ancient Fars. Proceedings of the International Colloquium held in Kiel 4th–6th July 2018*, pp. 241–66, Stuttgart: Franz Steiner Verlag.

Rhind, D. and R. Hudson (1980), *Land Use*, London and New York: Mathuen.

Ricciardi, R. V. (1970), 'Sasanian Pottery from Tell Mahuz (North-West Mesopotamia)', *Mesopotamia* V–Vl: 427–42.

Richards, T. (2008), 'Survey Strategies in Landscape Archaeology', in B. David and J. Thomas (eds), *Handbook of Landscape Archaeology, World Archaeological Congress Research Handbooks in Archaeology*, pp. 551–61, Walnut Creek, CA: Left Coast Press.

Rigg, H. A. (1942), 'Sargon's Eight Military Campaign', *Journal of American Oriental Society*, 62(2): 130–8.

Ritter, N. C. (2009), 'Vom Euphrat zum Mekong. Maritime Kontakte zwischen Vorder und Südostasien in vorislamischer Zeit', *Mitteilungen der Deutschen Orient-Gesellschaft zu Berlin* 141: 143–71.

Ritter, N. C. (2017), 'Gemstones in pre-Islamic Persia: Social and Symbolic Meanings of Sasanian Seals', in A. Hilgner, S. Greiff and D. Quast (eds), *Gemstones in the first Millennium AD: Mines, Trade, Workshops and Symbolism* (international conference, 20–2 October 2015, Römisch-Germanisches Zentralmuseum, Mainz), pp. 277–92, Mainz: Verlag des Römisch-Germanischen Zentralmuseums.

Roaf, M. (1990), *Cultural Atlas of Mesopotamia and Ancient Near East*, Oxford: Facts on File.

Roaf M. (1995), 'Media and Mesopotamia: History and Architecture', in J. Curtis (ed.), *Later Mesopotamia and Iran: Tribes and Empires 1600–539 B.C.*, pp. 54–66, London: British Museum Pubns Ltd.

Roaf, M. (2003), 'The Median Dark Age', in G. B. Lanfranchi, M. Roaf and R. Rollinger (eds), *Continuity of Empire (?) Assyria, Media, Persia*, pp. 13–22, Padua: S.a.r.g.o.n. Editrice e Libreria.

Roaf, M. and D. Stronach (1973), 'Tape Nush-i Jan, 1970: Second Interim Report', *Iran*, 11: 129–40.

Roberts, N. J. and S. G. Evans (2006), 'Seymareh (Saidmarreh) Landslide, Zagros Mountains, Iran', *Geophysical Research Abstracts* 10, EGU2008-A-00764, 2008, SRef-ID: 1607-7962/gra/EGU2008-A-00764, EGU General Assembly 2008.

Rollinger, R. (1999), 'Zur Lokalisation von Parsu(m)a(š) in der Fārs und zu einigen Frage der frühen persischen Geschichte', *Zeitschrift für Assyriologie*, 89: 115–39.

Rollinger, R. (2003a), 'The Western Expansion of the Median "Empire": A Re-Examination', in G. B. Lanfranchi, M. Roaf and R. Rollinger (eds),

Continuity of Empire (?) Assyria, Media, Persia (History of the Ancient Near East/Monographs-V), pp. 289–319, Padua: S.a.r.g.o.n. Editrice e Libreria.

Rollinger, R. (2003b), 'Kerkenes Dağ and the Median 'Empire', in G. B. Lanfranchi, M. Roaf and R. Rollinger (eds), *Continuity of Empire (?) Assyria, Media, Persia (History of the Ancient Near East/Monographs-V)*, pp. 321–6, Padua: S.a.r.g.o.n. Editrice e Libreria.

Rollinger, R. (2010), 'Das medische Königtum und die medische Suprematie im sechsten Jahrhundert v. Chr', in G. B. Lanfranchi and R. Rollinger (eds), *Concepts of Kingship in Antiquity (History of the Ancient Near East/Monographs XI). Proceedings of the European Science Foundation Exploratory Workshop. Padua, November 28th–December 1st, 2007*, pp. 63–86, Padua: S.a.r.g.o.n. Editrice e Libreria.

Rollinger, R. (2016), 'The Relief at Bisitun and its Ancient Near Eastern Setting: Contextualizing the Visual Vocabulary of Darius' Triumph over Gaumata', in C. Binder, H. Borm and A. Luther, *Diwan. Studies in the History and Culture of the Ancient Near East and the Eastern Mediterranean (Untersuchungen zu Geschichte und Kultur des Nahen Ostens und des östlichen Mittelmeerraumes im Altertum. Festschrift für Josef Wiesehofer zum 65. Geburtstag)*, pp. 5–51, Duisburg: Wellem.

Rollinger, R. (2018), 'Between Deportation and Recruitment: Craftsmen and Specialists from the West in Ancient Near Eastern Empires (from Neo-Assyrian Times through Alexander III)', in B. Woytek (ed.), *Infrastructure and Distribution in Ancient Economies (Österreichische Akademie der Wissenschaften Philosophisch-historische Klasse Denkschriften 506. Band)*. Proceedings of a conference held at the Austrian Academy of Sciences, 28–31 October 2014, pp. 425–44, Vienna: Austrian Academy of Science Press.

Rollinger, R. (2021), 'The Median Dilemma', in B. Jacobs and R. Rollinger (eds), *A Companion to the Achaemenid Persian Empire*, Volume I, pp. 337–50, Hoboken, NJ: Wiley Blackwell. https://doi.org/10.1002/9781119071860.ch25 (last accessed 25 July 2022).

Rosen, S. A. (1992), 'Nomads in Archaeology: A Response to Finkelstein and Perevolotsky', *Bulletin of the American Schools of Oriental Research*, 287: 75–85.

Rougemont, G. (2013), 'The Use of Greek in Pre-Sasanian Iran', in D. T. Potts (ed.), *The Oxford Handbook of Ancient Iran*, pp. 795–801, Oxford: Oxford University Press.

Rouse, I. (1960), 'The Classification of Artifacts in Archaeology', *American Antiquity*, 25(3): 313–23.

Roustaei, K. (2010), 'Discovery of Middle Paleolithic Occupation at High Altitude in the Zagros Mountains, Iran', *Antiquity*, 84(325), Project Gallery.

Roustaie, K. (2012), 'Archaeological Survey of the Shahroud Area, Northeast Iran: A Landscape Approach', *Archäologische Mitteilungen aus Iran und Turan*, 44: 191–220.

Roustaei, K. (1394/2015), 'Typology of Archaeological Sites in the Kouhrang-e Bakhtiyari Area', *Pazhohesh-hā-ye Bāstān-shenāsi-e irān*, 9: 27–46 [in Persian with an English abstract].

Rowton, M. B. (1973a), 'Autonomy and Nomadism in Western Asia', *Orientalia*, 42: 247–58.

Rowton, M. B. (1973b), 'Urban Autonomy in a Nomadic Environment', *Journal of Near Eastern Studies*, 32: 201–15.

Rowton, M. B. (1974), 'Enclosed Nomadism', *Journal of the Economics and Social History of the Orient*, 17: 1–30.

Sa'adati, M. and H. Naseri Somei (2019), 'Social Life of the Ancient City of Seymareh from its Formation to Collapse', *Archaeological Research of Iran*, 9(22): 163–80.

Sadeghi-rad, M. and F. Zargoush (1394 [2015]), 'Posht-qal'e-ye abdanan, banāea sāsāni-eslāmi dar dāmane-ye jonoubi-e kabirkooh' [Posh-qal'e of Abdanan. A Sasanian-Islamic Structure on the Southern Flanks of Kabirkooh], in H. Hāshemi Zorj-ābād (ed.), *Abstracts of the Second National Conference of Archaeology of Iran*, p. 191, Birjand: Chahār derakht.

Saeedyan, S. (1397 [2018]), 'Historical Geography of the Central Zagros in the Neo-assyrian Period: Namri, Hamban, Karalla, Parsua and Allabria', *Archaeological Research of Iran*, 19(8): 105–26 [in Persian with an English abstract].

Saeedyan, S. (1398 [2019]), 'Decorative Elements of Iron Age Temples: Painted Bricks, Doors with Dentate Frames, and Recessed Niches', in Y. Hassanzadeh, A. A. Vahdati and Z. Karimi (eds), *Proceedings of the International Conference on The Iron Age in Western Iran and Neighbouring Regions*, Kurdistan University, Sanandaj, 2–3 Nov. 2019, vol. 1, pp. 295–324, Tehran: Research Institute for Cultural Heritage and Tourism (RICHT); National Museum of Iran; Kurdistan: Kurdistan Province ICHHTO (in Persian with an English abstract).

Saeedyan, S. and B. Firouzmandi (1395 [2016]), 'From Mount Silhazu to Mount Bikni: Historical Geography of Media in the Neo-Assyrian Period', *Iranian Journal of Archaeological Studies*, 8(2): 71–90.

Saeedyan, S. and F. Gholizadeh (1398 [2019]), 'Rabat-tappe[h]: Ancient Hubushkia', *Iranian Journal of Archaeological Studies*, 11(1): 111–31 [in Persian with an English abstract].

Saeidabadi, R., M. S. Najafi, G. R. Roshan, J. M. Fitchett and S. Abkharabat (2016), 'Modelling Spatial, Altitudinal and Temporal Variability of Annual Precipitation in Mountainous Regions: The Case of the Middle Zagros, Iran', *Asia-Pac. Journal of Atmospheric Sciences*, 52(5): 437–49.

Safarrad, T, S. H. Faraji, G. Azizi and R. Abbaspour (2013), 'Spatial Analysis of Precipitation Variations in Middle Zagros Using Geo-Statistical Methods (1995–2004)', *Iranian Journal of Geography and Development*, 31: 149–64.

Sahlins, M. (1968), *Tribesmen*, Englewood Cliffs, NJ: Prentice-Hall.

Sa'idyan, A. (1388 [2009]), *Dāyerat al-ma'āref-e sarzamin va mardom-e irān* [Encyclopaedia of the Land and People of Iran], Tehran: Ārām.

Salaris, D. (2017), *The Kingdom of Elymais (ca. 301 BC–224 AD). A Comprehensive Analysis (Archaeological, Artistic, and Textual) of One of the Most Important Minor Reigns in Southern Iran*, PhD dissertation, Macquarie University, Sydney.

Salaris, D. and G. P. Basello (2019), ὀρεινὰ καὶ λῃστρικὰ ἔθνη (Strabo XVI.1.17): Mountain Tribes of Elymais and State Powers, from Neo-Elamite Kingdom(s) to Alexander the Great', in L. Prandi (ed.), *EstOvest: Confini e conflitti fra Vicino Oriente e mondo Greco-Romano* (Monografie/Centro ricerche e documentazione sull'antichità classica, 46), pp. 79–116, Rome: «L'ERMA» di Bretschneider.

Salavarzi-zadeh, M. (1381/2012), *Emkān-sanji-e towse'e-ye shahr-e abdanan be onvān-e yek shahr-e kouchak dar ostān-e ilām* [Examination of the Potentialities of Development for Abdanan as a Town in Ilam Province], MA thesis, University of Tehran [in Persian with an English abstract].

Sallaberger, W. and A. Westenholz (1999), *Mesopotamien: Akkade-Zeit und Ur III-Zeit*, Freiburg; Göttingen: OBO 160/3.

Sallaberger, W. and I. Schrakamp (2015), 'Part I: Philological Data for a Historical Chronology of Mesopotamia in the 3rd Millennium', in W. Sallaberger and I. Schrakamp (eds), *ARCANE (Associated Regional Chronologies for the Ancient Near East and the Eastern Mediterranean) III: History and Philology*, pp. 1–136, Turnhout: Brepols.

Sallaberger, W. and W. F. M. Henkelman (2022), 'A New Elamite Archive from Goshtaspi: Agricultural Administration in the Late Middle-Elamite Kingdom (around 1100 BCE)', A 3-Year-Project of *The Iranian Highlands Programme*. https://iranhighlands.com/a-new-elamite-archive/ (last accessed 18 January 2022).

Salzman, P. C. (1971), 'Movement and Resource Extraction among Pastoral Nomads: The Case of the Shah Nawazi Baluch', *Anthropological Quarterly*, 44(3), Comparative Studies of Nomadism and Pastoralism (Special Issue): 185–97.

Salzman, P. C. (2004), *Pastoralists: Equality, Hierarchy, and the State*, Boulder, CO: Westview.

Sanasarian, E. (2004), *Religious Minorities in Iran*, Cambridge: Cambridge University Press.

Sancisi-Weerdenburg, H. (1988), 'Was There Ever a Median Empire?', *Achaemenid History*, 3: 197–212.

Sarfaraz, A. A. (1347 [1968]), 'The Cuneiform Inscription of Uramanat', *Iranian Journal of Historical Studies*, 3(5): 13–27.

Sarfaraz, A. A. (1348 [1970]), 'The Historical City of Dastuvā, Shushtar', *Archaeology and Art of Iran*, 4: 72–9.

Sarlak, S. (1388 [2009]), 'Analysis of the Function of the Iron Age Architectural Spaces at the Qoli-Darvish Site of Jamkarān', *Athar*, 45: 86–104.

Sarlak, S. (1389 [2010]), *The Seven-Thousands Years Long Culture of Qom (Excavations of the Qoli-Darvish Site of Jamkarān in Qom)*, Qom: Qom's OTCH and Naghsh.

Sarlak, S. (1390 [2011]), *Archaeology and History of Qom: The Results of Archaeological Excavations and Stratigraphy of the Sites of Qoli-Darvish and Shād-Qoli-Khān, Test Trenches and Surveys in the Historical, Cultural, and Religious Zone of Qom*, Qom: Qom's OTCH and Shākhes.

Sarlak, S. and M. Malekzadeh (1384 [2005]), 'Painted Bricks of the Late Iron Age in Eastern Media, Brick Platform of Qoli-Darvish of Jamkarān and the Large Structure of Sialk of Kashan', *Iranian Journal of Archaeology*, 1(1): 52–66.

Sassmannshausen, L. (1999), 'The Adaptation of the Kassites to the Babylonian Civilization', in K. van Lerberghe and G. Voet (eds), *Languages and Cultures in Contact. At the Crossroads of Civilizations in the Syro-Mesopotamian Realm*, Proceedings of the 42th RAI [1995], pp. 409–24, Leuven: Peeters.

Sassmannshausen, L. (2001), *Beiträge zur Verwaltung und Gesellschaft Babyloniens in der Kassitenzeit* (Baghdader Forschungen 21), Mainz: von Zabern.

Sassmannshausen, L. (2004) 'Kassite Nomads: Fact or Fiction', in C. Nicolle (ed.), *Nomades et sédentaires dans le Proche-Orient Ancien*, pp. 287–301, Paris: Compte rendu de la XLVI Rencontre Assyriologique Internationale.

Sauer, E. (ed.) (2017), *Sasanian Persia: Between Rome and the Steppes of Eurasia*. Edinburgh: Edinburgh University Press.

Sauer, E., J. Nokandeh, H. Omrani Rekavadi, T. J. Wilkinson, G. A. Abbasi, J.-L. Schwenninger, M. Mahmoudi, D. Parker, M. Fattahi, L. S. Usher-Wilson, M. Ershadi, J. Ratcliffe and R. Gale (2006), 'Linear Barriers of Northern Iran: The Great Wall of Gorgan and the Wall of Tammishe', *Iran*, 44: 121–73.

Sauer, E., L. S. Usher-Wilson, J. Ratcliffe, B. Shabani, H. Omrani Rekavadi, T. J. Wilkinson, G. A. Abbasi, E. Safari Tamak, R. Ainslie, M. Mahmoudi, N. Galiatsatos, K. Roustai, J. Jansen Van Rensburg, M. Ershadi, E. MacDonald, M. Fattahi, C. Oatley and B. Shabani (2008), 'Sasanian Walls, Hinterland Fortresses and Abandoned Ancient Irrigated Landscapes: the 2007 Season on the Great Wall of Gorgan and the Wall of Tammishe', *Iran*, 46: 151–78.

Sauer, E., H. Omrani Rekavandi, T. J. Wilkinson and J. Nokandeh (2013), *Persia's Imperial Power in Late Antiquity: The Great Wall of Gorgan and Frontier Landscapes of Sasanian Iran* (British Institute of Persian Studies Archaeological Monograph Series 2), Oxford–Oakville: Oxbow.

Sauer, E., H. Omrani Rekavandi, T. J. Wilkinson and J. Nokandeh (2015), 'Innovation at Persia's frontiers: Sasanian Campaign Bases and Defensive Barriers', in L. Vagalinski and N. Sharankov (eds), *Limes XXII. Proceedings of the XXIInd International Congress of Roman Frontier Studies*, Ruse 2012, Bulletin of the National Archaeological Institute, Sofia.

Sauer, E., St J. Simpson, M. Jahed, M. Mansouri Razi, M. Moslehi, M. Nemati, J. Nokandeh, H. Omrani Rekavandi, T. Penn and A. Salari (2022), 'Small Objects and Other Finds', in E. W. Sauer, J. Nokandeh and H. Omrani Rekavandi (eds), *Ancient Arms Race. Antiquity's Largest Fortresses and Sasanian Military Networks of Northern Iran* (Joint Fieldwork Project by the Iranian Centre for Archaeological Research, the Reasearch Institute of Cultural Heritage and Tourism and the University of Edinburgh (2014–16)), pp. 601–40, Oxford–Philadelphia: Oxbow.

Sepehr, M. and J. W. Cosgrove (2004), 'Structural Framework of the Zagros Fold–Thrust Belt, Iran', *Marine and Petroleum Geology*, 21(7): 829–43.

Seyyed Sajjadi, M. (1989), 'A Class of Sasanian Ceramics from Southeastern Iran', *Rivista di Archeologia*, 13: 31–40.

Schacht, R. M. (1987), 'Early Historic Cultures', in F. Hole (ed.), *The Archaeology of Western Iran: Settlement and Society from Prehistory to the Islamic Conquest (Smithsonian Series in Archaeological Inquiry)*, pp. 171–203, Washington, DC: Smithsonian Institution Press.

Scheil, V. (1931), 'Dynasties Élamites d'Awan et de Simaš', *Revue d'Assyriologie et d'archéologie orientale*, 28(1): 1–8, 46.

Schippmann, K. (1971), *Die iranischen Feuerheiligtümer* (Religions-geschichtliche Versuche und Vorarbeiten, 31), Berlin: De Gruyter.

Schippmann, K. (1990), *Grundzüge der Geschichte des sasanidischen Reiches*, Darmstadt: WBG (Wissenschaftliche Buchgesellschaft).

Schippmann, K. (1383 [2004]), *Tārikh-e shāhanshāhi-e sāsāni* [History of the Sasanian Empire], transl. F. Najd-e Sami'ea, Tehran: Iran Cultural Heritage and Tourism Organisation.

Schmidt, E. F. (1929), 'The Excavations in the City on Kerkenes Dagh', *American Journal of Semitic Languages and Literatures*, 45: 83–92.

Schmidt, E. F., M. N. Van Loon and H. H. Curvers (1989), *The Holmes Expedition to Luristan* (Oriental Institute Publications 108), 2 vols, Chicago: University of Chicago.

Schmitt, R. (1993), 'Cossaeans', in E. Yarshater (ed.), *Encyclopaedia Iranica*, vol. 6(3), p. 333, Costa Mesa, CA: Mazda. https://iranicaonline.org/articles/cossaeans-lat (last accessed 13 March 2016).

Schrakamp, I. (2012), 'Lullubi', in R. S. Bagnall, K. Brodersen, C. B. Champion, A. Erskine and S. R. Huebner (eds), *The Encyclopedia of Ancient History*, pp. 4,166–7, Boston/Oxford: Wiley-Blackwell.

Schütze, A. (2017), 'The Idumaean Ostraca as Evidence of Local Imperial Administration', in B. Jacobs, W. F. M. Henkelman and M. W. Stolper (eds), *Die Verwaltung im Achämenidenreich: Imperiale Muster und Strukturen/Administration in the Achaemenid Empire: Tracing the Imperial Signature, Akten des 6. Internationalen Kolloquiums zum Thema » Vorderasien im Spannungsfeld klassischer und altorientalischer Überlieferungen« aus Anlass der 80-Jahr Feier der Entdeckung des Festungsarchivs von Persepolis, Landgut Castelen bei Basel, 14. 17. Mai 2013*, pp. 469–88, Wiesbaden: Harrassowitz Verlag.

Schwarz, P. (1969), *Iran im Mittelalter nach den arabischen Geographen*, Hildesheim; New York: Nachdruck Olms.

Shaffer, A, N. Wasserman and U. Seidl (2003), 'Iddi(n)-Sîn, King of Simurrum. A New Rock-Relief Inscription and a Reverential Seal', in W. Sallaberger, U. Seidl and G. Wilhelm (eds), *Zeitschrift für Assyriologie und Vorderasiatische Archäologie*, pp. 1–5, Sonderdruck: Walter de Gruyter.

Shayegan, M. R. (1999), *Aspects of Early Sasanian and Historiography*, PhD dissertation, Harvard University.

Shayegan, M. R. (2003), 'Approaches to the Study of Sasanian History', in S. Adhami (ed.), *Paitimâna: Essays in Iranian, Indo-European, and Indian Studies in Honor of Hans-Peter Schmidt*, vols. I and II, pp. 363–84, Costa Mesa, CA: Mazda.

Shayegan, M. R. (2007), 'Prospographical Notes: The Iranian Nobility During and After the Macedonian Conquest', *Bulletin of the Asia Institute*, 21: 97–126.

Shayegan, M. R. (2011), *Arsacids and Sasanians: Political Ideology in Post-Hellenistic and Late Antique Persia*, Cambridge: Cambridge University Press.

Shayegan, M. R. (2013), 'Sasanian Political Ideology', in D. T. Potts (ed.), *Oxford Handbook of Ancient Iran*, pp. 805–13, Oxford and New York: Oxford University Press.

Shepard, A. O. (1985), *Ceramics for the Archaeologist* (Publication 609, Carnegie Institution of Washington), Washington, Ann Arbor: Braun-Brumfield.

Sherwin-White, S. M. (1984), 'Shami, the Seleucids and Dynastic Cult: A Note', *Iran*, 22: 160–1.

Sherwin-White, S. and A. Kuhrt (1993), *From Samarkand to Sardis* (Hellenistic Culture and Society), Berkeley; Los Angeles: University of California Press.

Shishegar, A. (2005), *The Excavation of the Sorkh-dom-e Laki in the Koohdasht of Lurestan, Seasons of Second-Sixth*, Tehran: The Organisation of Cultural Heritage, Handicrafts, and Tourism – The Research Centre (in Persian).

Shumilovskikh, L., M. Djamali, V. Andrieu-Ponel, P. Ponel, J.-L. de Beaulieu, A. Naderi-Beni and E. W. Sauer (2017), 'Palaeoecological Insights into Agri-Horti-Cultural and Pastoral Practices Before, During and After the Sasanian Empire', in E. W. Sauer (ed.), *Sasanian Persia: Between Rome and the Steppes of Eurasia*, pp. 51–73. Edinburgh: Edinburgh University Press.

Simpson, S. J. (1996), 'From Tekrit to the Jaghjagh: Sasanian Sites, Settlement Pattern and Material Culture in Northern Mesopotamia', in K. Bartl and S. R. Hauser (eds), *Continuity and Change in Northern Mesopotamia from the Hellenistic to the Islam Period*, pp. 8–126, Berlin: Dietrich Reimer.

Simpson, S. J. (2000), 'Mesopotamia in the Sasanian Period: Settlement Patterns, Arts and Crafts', in J. Curtis (ed.), *Mesopotamia and Iran in the Parthian and Sasanian Periods: Rejection and Revival c. 238 BC – AD 642. Proceedings of a Seminar in Memory of Vladimir G. Lukonin*, pp. 57–66, London: British Museum Press.

Simpson, S. J. (2003), 'From Mesopotamia to Merv: Reconstructing Patterns of Consumption in Sasanian Households', in D. T. Potts, M. Roaf and D. Stein (eds), *Culture through Objects. Ancient Near Eastern Studies in Honor of P. R. S. Moorey*, pp. 347–75, Oxford: Griffith Institute.

Smith, P. E. L. and T. C. Young (1972), 'The Evolution of Agriculture and Culture in Greater Mesopotamia: A Tribal Model', in B. Spooner (ed.), *Population Growth: Anthropological Implications*, pp. 1–59, Cambridge, MA: MIT Press.

Soroush, M. (2019), 'The Lords of Canals and Bridges: Re-examining the Sasanian Hydraulic Landscapes and Their Heritage in the Islamic Period', *Pourdavoud Centre Lecture Series*, UCLA, 306 Royal Hall.

Speiser, E. A. (1928), 'Southern Kurdistan in the Annals of Ashurnasirpal and Today', *The Annual of the American Schools of Oriental Research*, 8 for 1926–7: 1–41.

Speiser, E. A. (1930), *Mesopotamian Origins: The Basic Population of the Near East*, Philadelphia: University of Pennsylvania Press.

Spooner, B. (1971), 'Towards a Generative Model of Nomadism', *Anthropological Quarterly*, 44: 198–210.

Spooner, B. (1973), *The Cultural Ecology of Pastoral Nomads* (Issue 45 of Addison-Wesley module in anthropology), Reading, MA: Addison-Wesley.

Stein, A. (1940), *Old Routes of Western Iran: Narrative of an Archaeological Journey Carried Out and Recorded by Sir Aurel Stein, K.C.I.E.*, London: Macmillan.

Steinkeller, P. (1982), 'The Question of Marḫaši: A Contribution to the Historical Geography of Iran in the Third Millennium B.C.', *Zeitschrift für Assyriologie*, 72: 237–65.

Steinkeller, P. (1988), 'On the Identity of the Toponym LU.SU(.A)', *Journal of the American Oriental Society*, 108: 197–202.

Steinkeller, P. (2007), 'New Light on Šimaški and Its Rulers', *Zeitschrift für Assyriologie*, 97: 215–32.

Steinkeller, P. (2013a), 'Puzur-Inšušinak at Susa: A Pivotal Episode of Early Elamite History Reconsidered', in K. De Graef and J. Tavernier (eds), *Susa and Elam. Archaeological, Philological, Historical and Geographical*

Perspective: Proceedings of the International Congress Held at Ghent University, December 14–17, 2009 (Mémoires de la Délégation en Perse 58), pp. 293–317, Leiden: Brill.

Steinkeller, P. (2013b), 'New Light on Marhaši and its Contacts with Makkan and Babylonia', in J. Giraud and G. Gernez (eds), *Aux marges de l'archéologie. Hommage à Serge Cleuziou*, Travaux de la Maison René Ginouvès 16, pp. 261–74. Paris: ed. De Boccard.

Steinkeller, P. (2014a), 'Marhaši and Beyond: The Jiroft Civilization in a Historical Perspective', in B. Cerasetti, C. C. Lamberg-Karlovsky and B. Genito (eds), *'My Life is Like a Summer Rose'. Marizio Tosi e l'archaeologia come modo di vivere. Papers in Honour of Maurizio Tosi for His 70th Birthday* (BAR International Series 2690), pp. 691–707, Oxford: Archaeopress.

Steinkeller, P. (2014b), 'On the Dynasty of Šimaški: Twenty Years (or so) After', in M. Kozuh, W. F. M. Henkelman, C. E. Jones and C. Woods (eds), *Extraction and Control: Studies in Honor of Matthew W. Stolper* (Studies in Ancient Oriental Civilization 68), pp. 287–96, Chicago: The Oriental Institute of the University of Chicago.

Steinkeller, P. (2015), 'The Gutian Period in Chronological Perspective', in W. Sallaberger and I. Schrakamp (eds), *ARCANE (Associated Regional Chronologies for the Ancient Near East and the Eastern Mediterranean) III: History and Philology*, pp. 281–8, Turnhout: Brepols.

Steinkeller, P. (2018), 'The Birth of Elam in History', in J. Álvarez-Mon, G. P. Basello and Y. Wicks (eds), *The Elamite World* (Routledge Worlds), pp. 177–202, London: Routledge.

Stève, M.-J., F. Vallat and H. Gasche (2002), 'Suse', *Supplément au Dictionnaire de la Bible*, 73 and 74: 359–512.

Stevens, L. R., H. E. Wright, Jr and E. Ito (2001), 'Proposed Changes in Seasonality of Climate during the Late Glacial and Holocene at Lake Zeribar, Iran', *The Holocene*, 11(6): 747–55.

Stiehl, R. (1959), 'Chronologie der Fratadiira', in F. Altheim and R. Stiehl (eds), *Geschichte der Hunnen*, 5 Volumes, *Vol. 1, Von den Anfängen bis zum Einbruch in Europa*, pp. 375–9. Berlin: De Gruyter

Stol, M. (1987), *Studies in Old Babylonian History*, Leiden: Institut historique-archéologique néerlandais de Stamboul.

Stolper, M. W. (1982), 'On the Dynasty of Šimaški and the Early Sukkalmahs', *Zeitschrift für Assyriologie und Vorderasiatische Archäologi*, 72: 42–67.

Stolper, M. W. (1984), 'Political History, Part I, in Ilam: Surveys of Political History and Archaeology', in E. Carter and M. W. Stolper (eds), *Near Eastern Studies* 25, pp. 3–100, Berkeley: University of California Press.

Strang, V. (2008a), 'Uncommon Ground: Landscape as Social Geography', in B. David and J. Thomas (eds), *Handbook of Landscape Archaeology, World Archaeological Congress Research Handbooks in Archaeology*, pp. 123–30, Walnut Creek, CA: Left Coast Press.

Strang, V. (2008b), 'The Social Construction of Water', in B. David and J. Thomas (eds), *Handbook of Landscape Archaeology, World Archaeological Congress Research Handbooks in Archaeology*, pp. 51–9, Walnut Creek, CA: Left Coast Press.

Streck, M. (1900), 'Das Gebiet der heutigen Landschaften Armenien, Kurdistân und Wetpersien nach den Babylonisch-assyrischen Keilinschriften', *Zeitschrift für Assyriologie und verwandte Gebiete: Fachzeitschrift der Deutschen Morgenländischen Gesellschaft (1886)* 15: 103–72.

Strobel, K. (1999), 'Kerkenes Dağı, H. Conick', in H. Schneider and M. Landfester (eds), *Der Neue Pauly. Enzyklopädie der Antike*, 6: 442–3.

Strobel, K. (2001), 'Phryger-Lyder-Meder: Politische, ethnische un kulturelle Größen zentalanatoliens bei Erichtung der achaimenidischen Herrschaft', in T. Bakir (ed.), *Achaemenid Anatolia: Proceedings of the First International Symposium on Anatolia in the Achaemenid Period, Bandirma, 15–18 August 1997 (Pihans)*, pp. 43–55, Leuven: Peeters.

Strommenger, E. (1963), 'Das Relief von Darband-i Gawr', *Baghdader Mitteilungen*, 2: 83–8.

Stronach, D. (1969), 'Excavations at Tepe Nush-I Jan, 1967', *Iran*, 7: 1–20.

Stronach, D. (1978a), 'Excavations at Tepe Nush-i Jan: Part 2, Median Pottery from the Fallen Floor in the Fort', *Iran*, 16: 11–24.

Stronach, D. (1978b), *Pasargadae: A Report on the Excavations Conducted by the British Institute of Persian Studies from 1961 to 1963*, Oxford; London; Glasgow: Oxford University Press.

Stronach, D. (2003), 'Independent Media: Archaeological Notes from Homeland', in G. L. Lanfranchi, M. Roaf and R. Rollinger (eds), *Continuity of Empire (?) Assyria, Media, Persia* (History of the Ancient Near East/ Monographs V), pp. 233–48, Padua: S.a.r.g.o.n. Editrice e Liberia

Stronach, D. and M. Roaf (1978), 'Excavations at Tepe Nush-i Jan: Part I, A Third Interim Report', *Iran*, 16: 1–11.

Stronach, D. and M. Roaf (2007), *Nush-i Jan I: The Major Buildings of the Median Settlement*, London; Leuven: The British Institute of Persian Studies and Peeters.

Strootman, R. (2017), 'Imperial Persiansim: Seleukids, Arsakids and Fratarakā', in R. Strootman and M. J. Versluys (eds), *Persianism in Antiquity* (Oriens et Occidens 25), pp. 177–200, Stuttgart: Franz Steiner Verlag.

Summers, G. D. (1997), 'The Identification of the Iron Age City on Kerkenes Dağ in Central Anatolia', *Journal of Near Eastern Studies*, 56(2): 81–94.

Summers, G. D. (1998), 'Tille Höyük, Control of an [sic] Euphrates Crossing', in H. Erkanal, V. Donbaz and A. Ugoruglu (eds), *The Relations between Anatolia and Mesopotamia (XXXIVième Rencontre Assyriologique Internationale/XXXIV, Istanbul)*, pp. 399–406, Ankara: Türk Tarih Kurumu Basimevi.

Summers, G. D. (2000a), 'The Median Empire Reconsidered: A View from Kerkenes Dağ', *Anatolian Studies*, 50: 55–73.

Summers, G. D. (2000b), 'Media, Medes', in P. Bienkowski and A. Millard (eds), *British Museum Dictionary of the Ancient Near East*, p. 192, London: British Museum.

Summers, G. D. (2008a), 'Architectural Elements', in C. M. Draycott and G. D. Summers (eds), *Kerkenes Special Studies 1, Sculpture and Inscriptions from the Monumental Entrance to the Palatial Complex at Kerkenes Daq, Turkey* (Oriental Institute Publications, Vol. 135), pp. 61–6, Chicago: University of Chicago.

Summers, G. D. (2008b), 'Discovery of Sculpture and Inscriptions', in C. M. Draycott and G. D. Summers (eds), *Kerkenes Special Studies 1, Sculpture and Inscriptions from the Monumental Entrance to the Palatial Complex at Kerkenes Daq, Turkey* (Oriental Institute Publications, Vol. 135), pp. 1–7, Chicago: University of Chicago.

Summers, G. D. and F. Summers (2003), 'The Kerkenes Project', *Anatolian Archaeology*, 9: 22–4.

Summers, G. D. and F. Summers (2009), *The Kerkenes Project, A Preliminary Report on the 2009 Season*, Ankara: Metu Press.

Summers, G. D., F. Summers and S. Branting (2004), 'Megarons and Associated Structures at Kerkenes Dag: An Interim Report', *Anatolia Antiqua*, 12: 7–41.

Summers, G. D., F. Summers, S. Branting and D. Langis-Barsetti (2011), 'The Spring Geophysical Survey', in G. D. Summers, F. Summers, S. Branting and D. Langis-Barsetti (eds), *The Kerkenes Project, A Preliminary Report on the 2011 Season*, pp. 17–32, Ankara: Metu Press.

Sumner, W. M. (1986), 'Achaemenid Settlement in the Persepolis Plain', *American Journal of Archaeology*, 90(1): 3–31. http://www.jstor.org/stable/505980 (last accessed 5 March 2014).

Sumner, W. M. (1994), 'The Evolution of Tribal Society in the Southern Zagros Mountains, Iran', in G. Stein and M. S. Rothman (eds), *Chiefdoms and Early States in the Near East. The Organisational Dynamics of Complexity*, pp. 47–66, Madison: Prehistory Press.

Tafazzoli, A. (1974), 'A List of Trades and Crafts in the Sasanian Period', *Archäologische Mitteilungen aus Iran*, 7: 191–6.

Tafażżolī, A. (1999), 'Fahlavīyāt', in E. Yarshater (ed.), *Encyclopaedia Iranica*, vol. 9(2), pp. 158–62, Costa Mesa, CA: Mazda. http://www.iranicaonline.org/articles/fahlaviyat (last accessed 20 January 2012).

Taj-bakhsh, R. and M. Azarnoush (1392/2013), 'Gounehā-ye sofāli-ye sāsāni-ye be dast āmade az tappe[h] hegmatāne' [Sasanian Pottery Types Found from Tappe[h] Hegmatāne], in A. Hozhabri (ed.), *Papers Presented about Archaeology and History of Hamadan on the Occasion of the 100th year of Excavations at Hamadan*, pp. 219–36, Tehran: Cultural Heritage and Tourism Organisation of Iran [in Persian].

Tarn, W. W. (1951), *The Greeks in Bactria and India*, Cambridge: Cambridge University Press.

Taylor, C. (1998), 'To Follow a Rule ...', in R. Shusterman (ed.), *Bourdieu: A Critical Reading*, pp. 29–44, Oxford and MA: Blackwell.

Taylor, W. G. (1996), 'Statistical Relationships between Topography and Precipitation in Mountainous Area', *Northwest Sciences*, 70: 164–78.

Tilley, C. (2008), 'Phenomenological Approach to Landscape Archaeology', in B. David and J. Thomas (eds), *Handbook of Landscape Archaeology, World Archaeological Congress Research Handbooks in Archaeology*, pp. 271–6, Walnut Creek, CA: Left Coast Press.

Tolini, G. (2011), *La Babylonie et l'Iran: les relations d'une province avec le cœur de l'empire achéménide (539–331 avant notre ère)*, 2 vols, PhD dissertation, Université Paris I.

Trinkaus, K. M. (1986), 'Pottery from the Damghan Plain, Iran: Chronology and Variability from the Parthian to the Early Islamic Periods', *Studia Iranica*, 15: 23–88.

Tuplin, C. (1987), 'The Administration of the Achaemenid Empire', in I. Carradice (ed.), *Coinage and Administration in the Athenian and Persian Empires. The Ninth Oxford Symposium on Coinage and Monetary History* (British Archaeological Reports 343), pp. 109–66, Oxford: B.A.R.

Tuplin, C. (2003), 'Xenophon in Media', in G. B. Lanfranchi, M. Roaf and R. Rollinger (eds), *Continuity of Empire (?) Assyria, Media, Persia*, pp. 351–89, Padua: S.a.r.g.o.n. Editrice e Libreria

Tuplin, C. (2004), 'Medes in Media, Mesopotamia, and Anatolia: Empire, Hegemony, Domination or Illusion?', *Ancient West and East*, 3(2): 223–51.

Tuplin, C. J. (2005), 'Darius' Accession in (the) Media', in P. Bienkowsky, C. Mee and E. Slater (eds), *Writing and Ancient Near Eastern Society. Papers in Honour of Alan R. Millard*, pp. 217–44, New York; London: T. & T. Clark.

Tuplin, C. J. (2009). 'The Seleucids and their Achaemenid Predecessors. A Persian Inheritance', in S. M. R. Darbandi and A. Zournatzi (eds), *Ancient Greece and Ancient Iran: Cross-Cultural Encounters*, pp. 109–36, Athens: National Hellenic Research Foundation.

Tuplin, C. J. (2010), 'Xenophon and Achaemenid Courts', in B. Jacobs and R. Rollinger (eds), *Der Achämenidenhof. The Achaemenid Court. Akten des 2. Internationalen Kolloquiums zum Thema »Vorderasien im Spannungsfeld klassischer und altorientalischer Überlieferungen« Landgut Castelen bei Basel, 23–25 Mai 2007*, pp. 189–230, Wiesbaden: Harrassowitz.

Tuplin, C. J. (2011), 'Managing the World. Herodotus on Achaemenid Imperial Organisation', in R. Rollinger, B. Truschnegg and R. Bichler (eds), *Herodotus and the Persian Empire. Akten des 3. Internationalen Kolloquiums zum Thema »Vorderasien im Spannungsfeld klassischer und altorientalischer Überlieferungen«* Innsbruck, 24–28 November 2008, pp. 39–64, Wiesbaden: Harrassowitz Verlag.

Ulrich, B. (2011), 'Oman and Bahrain in Late Antiquity: The Sasanians' Arabian Periphery', in Proceedings of the Seminar for Arabian Studies 41, pp. 377–86, Oxford: Archaeopress.

Ünal, A. (1988), 'Hittite Architect and a Rope-Climbing Ritual', in Yaşar Yügel (ed.), *Belleten Périodique Paraissant tous Les Quatre Mois*, Vol. 204, pp. 1,469–504, Ankara: Imprimerie De La Societé Turque d'Histoire.

Ur, J. A. and K. Alizadeh (2013), 'The Sasanian Colonization of the Mughan Steppe, Ardebil Province, Northwestern Iran', *Journal of Iranian Archaeology*, 4: 98–110.

Vallat, F. (1992), 'L'inscription du cylinder néo-élamite de Chigha Sabz (Luristan)', *Nouvelles assyriologiques brèves et utilitaires*, 13 (note 14).

Vallat, F. (1993), *Les noms géographiques des sources suso-elamites* (Répertoire géographique des textes cunéiformes 11. Tübinger Atlas des Vorderen Orients Beiheft B7), Wiesbaden: Dr Ludwig Reichert.

Vallat, F. (1996), 'Le royaume élamite de SAMATI', *Nouvelles Assyriologiues brèves et utilitaires*, 37: 21–2.

Valtz, E. (1985), 'La Campagna di Yelkhi', in G. Gullini (ed.), *La Terra tra I Due Fiumi: venti anni di archeologia italiana in Medio Oriente, la Mesopotamia dei tesori*, pp. 69–71, Turin: Quadrante.

Vandaee, M. and M.-J. Jafari (2012), 'Siāh-Kal: A Newly Discovered Chahar Taq in Zarne[h] of the Ilam Province', *Sasanika* (Archaeology) 9.

Van De Mieroop, M. (2002), 'Gutians', in E. Yarshater (ed.), *Encyclopaedia Iranica*, vol. 11(4), pp. 408–10, New York; London; Costa Mesa, CA: Mazda.

Vanden Berghe, L. (1968), 'La nécropole de Bani Surmah: Aurore d'une civilisation du Bronze', *Archeologia*, 24: 52–63.

Vanden Berghe, L. (1970a), 'La nécropole de Kalleh Nisar', *Archeologia*, 32: 64–73.

Vanden Berghe, L. (1970b), 'Prospections archéologiques dans la région de Badr', *Archeologia*, 36: 10–21.

Vanden Berghe, L. (1973a), 'Excavations in Luristan: Kalleh Nisar', *Bulletin of the Asia Institute*, 3: 25–56.

Vanden Berghe, L. (1973b), 'Le Luristan à l'âge du Bronze: Prospections archéologiques dans le Pusht-i Kuh central', *Archeologia*, 63: 24–36.

Vanden Berghe, L. (1977), 'Les chahār tāqs du Pusht-i Kūh, Luristan', *Iranica Antiqua*, 12: 175–90.

Vanden Berghe, L. (1979a), 'La construction des tombes au Pusht-i Kūh, Luristān au 3e millénaire avant J.-C.', *Iranica Antiqua*, 14: 39–50.

Vanden Berghe, L. (1979b), 'La nécropole de Mīr Khair au Pusht-i Kūh, Luristān', *Iranica Antiqua*, 14: 1–37.

Vanden Berghe, L. (1984), 'Le Chahar Taq de Qanat-i Bagh (Fars) et l'inventaire des Chahar Taqs en Iran', *Iranica Antiqua*, 19: 201–25.

Vanden Berghe, L., C. Langeraerts, B. Overlaet and E. Haerinck (1982), *Luristan, een verdwenen bronskunst uit West-Iran* (Centrum voor Kunst en Cultuur, Sint-Pietersabdij, Gent), Gent: Het Centrum.

Vanden Berghe, L. and E. Haerinck (1984), 'Prospections et fouilles au Pušt-i Kūh, Luristān', *Archiv für Orientforschung*, 31: 200–9.

Vanden Berghe, L. and A. Tourovets (1992), 'Prospections archéologiques dans le district de Shīrwān-Chardawal (Pusht-i Kūh, Luristān)', *Iranica Antiqua*, 27: 1–73.

Vanden Berge, L. and K. Schippmann (1386 [2007]), *Les reliefs rupestres d'Elymaide (Iran) de l'epoque parthe*, transl. Y. Mohammadifar and A. Mohabbat-khou, Tehran: SAMT.

Van der Spek, R. J. (1977), 'The Assyrian Royal Rock Inscription from Shkaft-i Gul Gul', *Iranica Antiqua*, 12: 45–7.

Van Dijk, J. (1970), 'Le site de Guti'um et d'Ak-s[a$^?$-a]k^{kii}', *Archiv für Orientforschung*, 23: 71–2.

Van Dijk, J. (1978), 'Ishbierra, Kindattu, l'homme d'Elam, et la chute d'Ur', *Journal of Couneiform Studies*, 30: 189–208.

Van Loon, M. (1957), 'Review of Dark Ages and Nomads c. 100 B.C., Studies in Iranian and Anatolian Archaeology, ed. by M. J. Mellink', *Bibliotheca Orientalis*, 24(1 and 2): 21–6.

Van Zeist, W. (1967), 'Late Quarternary Vegetation History of Western Iran', *Review of Palaeobotany and Palynology*, 2: 301–11.

Van Zeist, W., Wright, H. E. (1963), 'Preliminary Pollen Studies at Lake Zeribar, Zagros Mountains, Southwestern Iran', *Science*, 140: 65–7.

Van Zeist, W., Timmers, R. W. and Bottema, S. (1968), 'Studies of Modern and Holocene Pollen Precipitation in Southeastern Turkey', *Palaeohistoria*, 14: 19–39.

Van Zeist, W. and Bottema, S. (1977), 'Palynological Investigations in Western Iran', *Palaeohistoria*, 19: 19–85.

Van Zeist, W. and Woldring, H. (1978), 'A Postglacial Pollen Diagram from Lake Van in East Anatolia', *Review of Palaeobotany and Palynology*, 26: 249–76.

Venco Ricciardi, R. (1970), 'Sasanian Pottery from Tell Mahuz (Northwest Mesopotamia)', *Mesopotamia*, 5–6: 427–42.

Vergés, J., E. Saura, E. Casciello, M. Fernàndez, A. Villaseñor, I. Jiménez-Munt and D. García-Castellanos (2011), 'Crustal-Scale Cross-Sections across the NW Zagros Belt: Implications for the Arabian Margin Reconstruction', *Geological Magazine*, 148(5–6): 739–61. Available at: doi:10.1017/S0016756811000331 (last accessed 28 August 2016).

Vink, A. P. A. (1983), *Landscape Ecology and Land Use*, London and New York: Longman.

von Gall, H. (1978), 'Die Kulträume in den Felsen von Karaftu bei Takab (West-Azarbaidjan)', *Archäologische Mitteilungen aus Iran*, 11: 91–112.

von Gall, H. (1996), Der grosse Reliefblock am sog. Partherhang, in W. Kleiss and P. Calmeyer (eds), *Bisutun. Ausgrabungen Forschungen in den Jahren 1963–1967* (Teheraner Forschungen), pp. 85–8, Berlin: Gebr. Mann.

von Gall, H. (2010), Karafto Caves, in E. Yarshater (ed.), *Encyclopaedia Iranica*, Vol. XV, Fasc. 5, pp. 533–6, Costa Mesa, CA: Mazda.

Wäfler, M. (1975), *Nicht-Assyrer neuassyrischer Darstellungen* (Alter Orient und Altes Testament 26), Kevelaer: Verlag Butzon and Bercker; Neukirchen-Vluyn: Neukirchener Verlag.

Walker, M. (1985), *The Tigris Frontier: A Philologic and Historical Synthesis*, PhD dissertation, Yale University.

Waters, M. W. (2010), 'Cyrus and the Medes', in J. Curtis and St. John Simpson (eds), *The World of Achaemenid Persia: History, Art and Society in Iran and the Ancient Near East* (British Museum), pp. 63–71, London: I. B. Tauris.

Waters, M. W. (2013), 'Elam, Assyria and Babylonia in the Early First Millennium BC.', in D. T. Potts (ed.), pp. 478–99, *The Oxford Handbook of Ancient Iran*, Oxford; New York: Oxford University Press.

Watson, P. J. (1979), *Archaeological Ethnography in Western Iran* (Viking Fund Publications in Anthropology 57), Tucson, AZ: University of Arizona Press.

Watson, P. J. (1980), 'The Theory and Practice of Ethnoarchaeology with Special Reference to the Near East', *Paléorient*, 6: 55–64.

Weißbach, F. H. (1910a), 'Γαβαι', *Realencyclopädie der classischen Altertumswissenschaft* 7(13): 411.

Weißbach, F. H. (1910b), 'Gabiene', *Realencyclopädie der classischen Altertumswissenschaft* 7(13): 420.

Wenke, R. J. (1975–6), 'Imperial Investments and Agricultural Developments in Parthian and Sassanian Khuzestan: 150 BC to AD 640', *Mesopotamia*, 10–11: 99–137.

Wenke, R. J. (1981), 'Elymaeans, Parthians, and the Evolution of Empires in Southwestern Iran', *Journal of the American Oriental Society*, 101(3): 303–15.

Wenke, R. J. (1987), 'Western Iran in the Partho-Sasanian Period: The Imperial Transformation', in F. Hole (ed.), *The Archaeology of Western Iran*, pp. 251–82. Washington, DC: Smithsonian Institution Press.

Westenholz, J. G. (1997), *Legends of the Kings of Akkade: The Texts* (Mesopotamian Civilizations 7), Winona Lake, IN: Eisenbrauns.

Whitcomb, D. (1985), *Before the Roses and Nightingales, Excavations at Qasr-i Abu Nasr, Old Shiraz*, New York: The Metropolitan Museum of Art.

Whitcomb, D. (1987), 'Bushire and the Angali Canal', *Mesopotamia*, 22: 311–36.

Whitcomb, D. (2014), 'Landscape Signatures in Sasanian Archaeology', *Journal of Ancient History*, 2(2): 209–15.

Whitehouse, D. (1991), 'Epilogue: Roman Trade in Perspective', in V. Begley and R. D. De Puma (eds), *Rome and India: The Ancient Sea Trade*, pp. 216–18. Madison: University of Wisconsin Press.

Whitehouse, D. and A. Williamson (1973), 'Sasanian Maritime Trade', *Iran*, 11: pp. 29–49. http://www.jstor.org/stable/4300483 (last accessed 9 December 2011).

Widgren, M. (2012), 'Landscape Research in a World of Domesticated Landscapes: The Role of Values, Theory, and Concepts', *Quaternary International*, 251: 117–24.

Wiesehöfer, J. (2001), *Ancient Persia: From 550 BC to 650 AD*, transl. A. Azodi, London; New York: I. B. Tauris.

Wiesehöfer, J. (2002), 'Συνοίκησις und ἀπωρία χρημάτων. Antiochos IV. und die Heiligtümer der Elymais', in N. Ehrhardt and M. Günther (eds), *Widerstand – Anpassung Integration. Die griechische Staatenwelt und Rom*, pp. 109–20, Stuttgart: Franz Steiner Verlag.

Wiesehöfer, J. (2009), 'Kawad, Khusro I and the Mazdakites: A New Proposal', in P. Gignoux, C. Jullien and F. Jullien (eds), *Trésors d'orient: Mélanges offerts à Rika Gyselen* (Studia Iranica 42), pp. 391–409, Paris: Association pour l'avancement des études Iraniennes.

Wiesehöfer, J. (2010), 'The Late Sasanian Near East', in C. Robinson (ed.), *The New Cambridge History of Islam*, pp. 98–152, Cambridge: Cambridge University Press. Available at: doi:10.1017/CHOL9780521838238.005 (last accessed 12 September 2014).

Wiesehöfer, J. (2014), 'Parther und Sasaniden: Imperien zwischen Rom und China', in M. Gehler and R. Rollinger (eds), *Imperien und Reiche in der Weltgeschichte, Vol. I: Imperien des Altertums, mittelalterliche und frühneuzeitliche Imperien*, pp. 449–78, Wiesbaden: Harrassowitz.

Wiesehöfer, J. (2015), *Das frühe Persien: Geschichte eines antiken Weltreichs* (Beck'sche Wissen Reihe), 5th edition, Munich: C. H. Beck.

Wiesehöfer, J. (2019), 'Parthians, Romans, and Early Sasanians. Reflections on a Change of Power and Its Antique and Modern Evaluation', a talk given at *Ancient Iran and the Classical World. An International Symposium*, Pourdavoud Center for the Study of the Iranian World, UCLA, 30 May 2019.

Wiesehöfer, J. (2020a), 'Evidence for Arsakid Economic History', in S. von Reden (ed.), *Handbook of Ancient Afro-Eurasian Economies, Vol. 1: Contexts*, pp. 477–96, Berlin; Boston: De Gruyter Oldenbourg. https://doi.org/10.1515/9783110607741-017 (last accessed 5 February 2021).

Wiesehöfer, J. (2020b), 'Review Essay: La géographie administrative de l'empire sassanide. Les témoignages épigraphiques en moyen-perse (Res Orientales, XXV) by R. Gyselen', *Journal of Near Eastern Studies*, 79(1): 146–7.

Wilkinson, T. J. (2000), 'Regional Approaches to Mesopotamian Archaeology: The Contribution of Archaeological Surveys', *Journal of Archaeological Research*, 8(3): 219–67.

Wilknsom, T. J. (2004), 'The Archaeology of Landscape', in J. Bintliff (ed.), *A Companion to Archaeology*, pp. 334–56, Oxford: Blackwell.

Wilkinson, T. J. and L. Rayne (2010), 'Hydraulic Landscapes and Imperial Power in the Near East', *Water History*, 2(2): 115–44.

Wilkinson, T. J., R. Boucharlat, M. W. Ertsen, G. Gillmore, D. Kennet, P. Magee, K. Rezakhani and T. De Schacht (2012), 'From Human Niche Construction to Imperial Power: Long-term Trends in Ancient Iranian Water Systems', *Water History*, 4(2): 155–76.

Wilkinson, T. J., L. Rayne and J. Jotheri (2015), 'Hydraulic Landscapes in Mesopotamia: The Role of Human Niche Construction', *Water History*, 7: 397–418.

Will, É. (1967), *Histoire politique du monde hellénistique (323–30 av. J.-C.), Vol. II: Des avènements d'Antiochos III et de Philippe V à la fin des Lagides* (Annales de l'Est, Mémoire no. 32), Nancy: The Faculty of Letters and Human Sciences of the University of Nancy.

Windfuhr, G. L. (1974), 'Isoglosses: A Sketch on Persians and Parthians, Kurds and Medes', in *Monumentum H. S. Nyberg, Hommages et Opera Minora* (Acta Iranica, 5), pp. 457–72, Tehran; Liège: Bibliothèque Pahlavi.

Winterbottom, S. J. and D. Long (2006), 'From Abstract Digital Models to Rich Virtual Environments: Landscape Contexts in Kilmartin Glen, Scotland', *Journal of Archaeological Science*, 33: 1,356–67.

Wordsworth, P. D. and M. M. Wencel (2018), 'The Dramatic Abandonment of a Late-Antique Settlement in the South Caucasus: The First Archaeological Findings from Qaratəpə, Bərdə Rayon, Azerbaijan', *Journal of Field Archaeology*, 43: 300–15.

Wright, H. E. (1961), 'Pleistocene Glaciation in Kurdistan', *Eiszeitalter Gegenw.*, 12: 131–64.

Wright, H. E., J. H. McAndrews and W. van Zeist (1967), 'Modern Pollen Rain in Western Iran, and Its Relation to Plant Geography and Quaternary Vegetational History', *The Journal of Ecology*, 55(2): 415–43.

Wright, H. T. and Neely, J. A. (2010), 'Introduction to Elamite and Achaemenid Settlement on the Deh lurân Plain', in H. T. Wright and J. A. Neely (eds), *Towns and Villages of the Early Empires in Southwestern Iran*, pp. 1–16, Michigan: Ann Arbor.

Yaghoubian, N. D. (2014), *Ethnicity, Identity, and the Development of Nationalism in Iran*, New York: Syracuse University Press.

Yesiltas, O. (2016), 'Contested Notions of National Identity, Ethnic Movements and Democratisation in Iran', *Studies of Transition States and Societies* 8(1): 53–88.

Zagarell, A. (1975), 'An Archaeological Survey in the Northeast Baxtiari Mountains', in F. Bagherzadeh (ed.), *Proceedings of the 3rd Annual Symposium on Archaeological Research in Iran, 1975*, pp. 145–56, Tehran: Iranian Center for Archaeological Research.

Zagarell, A. (1982a), *The Prehistory of the Northeast Bahtiyari Mountains, Iran: The Rise of a Highland Way of Life* (Tübinger Atlas des Vorderen Orients), Wiesbaden: Dr Ludwig Reichert.

Zagarell, A. (1982b), 'The First Millennium in the Bakhtiyari Mountains', *Archäologische Mitteilungen aus Iran*, 15: 31–52.

Zaitchik B. F., J. P. Evans and R. B. Smith (2007), 'Regional Impact of an Elevated Heat Source: The Zagros Plateau of Iran', *Journal of Climate*, 20(16): 4,133–46.

Zarins, J. (1990), 'Early Pastoral Nomadism and the Settlement of Lower Mesopotamia', *Bulletin of the American Schools of Oriental Research*, 280: 31–65. http://www.jstor.org/stable/1357309 (last accessed 3 February 2009).

Zarrin, A. H. Ghaemi, M. Azadi, A. Mofidi and E. Mirzaei (2011), 'The Effect of the Zagros Mountains on the Formation and Maintenance of the Iran Anticyclone Using RegCM4', *Meteorology and Atmospheric Physics*, 112: 91–100. Available at: 10.1007/s00703-011-0134-z (last accessed 29 October 2015).

Zawadzki, S. (1988), *The Fall of Assyria and Median-Babylonian Relations in Light of the Nabopolassar Chronicle* (Seria Historia), Poznan; Delft: Eburon.

Zedeño, M. N. (2008), 'The Archaeology of Territory and Territoriality', in B. David and J. Thomas (eds), *Handbook of Landscape Archaeology* (World Archaeological Congress Research Handbooks in Archaeology), pp. 210–17, Walnut Creek, CA: Left Coast Press.

Zeder, M. A. (1999), 'Animal Domestication in the Zagros: A Review of Past and Current Research', *Paléorient*, 25: 11–25.

Zeder, M. A. and B. Hesse (2000), 'The Initial Domestication of Goats (capra hircus) in the Zagros Mountains 10.000 Years Ago', *Science*, 287: 2,254–7.

Zendeh-del, H. (1377/1998), *Ostān-e chahārmahāl va bakhtiyāri* [The Province of Chaharmahal va Bakhtiyari], Tehran: Irān-gardān.

Ziegler, N. (2011), 'Die Osttigrisregion im Spiegel der Archive aus Mari', in P. A. Miglus and S. Mühl (eds), *Between the Cultures. The Central Tigris Region from the 3rd to the 1st Millennium BC* (Heidelberger Studien zum Alten Orient 14), pp. 143–55, Heidelberg: Heidelberger Orientverlag.

Zimansky, P. (1990), 'Urartian Geography and Sargon's Eighth Campaign', *Journal of Near Eastern Studies*, 49: 1–21.

Zohary, M. (1973), *Geobotanical Foundations of the Middle East*, vols 1–2, Stuttgart: Fischer.

Zournatzi, A. (2016), 'Karaftō: Greek Apotropaic Inscription', in *Mapping Ancient Cultural Encounters: Greeks in Iran ca. 550 BC – ca. AD 650*, online edition, preliminary draft release. http://iranohellenica.eie.gr/content/catalogue/karafto/documents/1951397892 (last accessed 2 April 2019).

Zurlini, G., I. Petrosillo and M. Cataldi (2008), 'Socioecological Systems', in S. E. Jørgensen and B. D. Fath (eds), *Systems Ecology. Vol. 4 of Encyclopedia of Ecology*, 5 vols., pp. 3,264–9, Oxford: Elsevier.

Index

Note: *n indicates a note.*

EU Authorised Representative: Easy Access System Europe Mustamäe tee 5
0, 10621 Tallinn, Estonia gpsr.requests@easproject.com

Printed and bound by CPI Group (UK) Ltd, Croydon, CR0 4YY

30/04/2025
01857634-0001